ADAPTING TO HIGH-LEVEL WARMING: LAW, GOVERNANCE, AND EQUITY

Katrina F. Kuh & Shannon M. Roesler,
editors

ENVIRONMENTAL LAW INSTITUTE
Washington, D.C.

Thank you to Albany Law School, Pace Haub Environmental Law, and Vermont Law School for sponsoring the fifth workshop of the Environmental Law Collaborative (ELC) at which many of the ideas in this volume were first raised.

ALBANY LAW SCHOOL

PACE | HAUB ENVIRONMENTAL LAW

VL
VERMONT
LAW SCHOOL

Cover art, "Summer," courtsey of Barbara Baum©
and reprinted with permission.

Cover design by Evan Odoms.

1730 M Street NW, Washington, DC 20036

Published October 2024.

Printed in the United States of America
ISBN 978-1-58576-269-9

Table of Contents

About the Authors

Karrigan Börk is an Acting Professor of Law at UC Davis. His publications run the gamut from the definitive text on the history and application of California instream flow law to a hatchery and genetic management plan for spring-run Chinook salmon. He works on the legal and ethical issues in ecological restoration, including local governance issues in ecosystem management. Professor Börk graduated with Distinction and Pro Bono Distinction from Stanford Law School in 2009 and completed his PhD dissertation in Ecology at UC Davis in 2011. He clerked for Tenth Circuit Chief Judge Mary Beck Briscoe, U.S. District Court Judge Julie Robinson, and Judge Janice Karlin on the U.S. Bankruptcy Court for the District of Kansas. In 2022, he received the UC Davis Distinguished Teaching award.

Karen Bradshaw is a Professor of Law at the Sandra Day O'Connor College of Law Arizona State University, a Senior Sustainability Scientist at the Global Institute of Sustainability, a Faculty Fellow at Oxford Centre for Animal Ethics, and a Faculty Affiliate Scholar at the New York University School of Law Classical Liberal Institute.

Cinnamon Carlarne is the 19th President and Dean at Albany Law School, where she is also a Professor. Her research focuses on questions of domestic and international environmental law, centering on climate change law and climate justice. Prior to joining Albany Law School, she was the Associate Dean for Faculty and Intellectual Life and the Robert J. Lynn Chair in Law at Ohio State Law, a Professor at the University of South Carolina School of Law, the Harold Woods Fellow in Environmental Law at Wadham College, Oxford, and an attorney at Akin Gump Strauss Hauer & Feld.

Robin Kundis Craig was, through June 2024, the Robert C. Packard Trustee Chair in Law at the University of Southern California Gould School of Law. In July 2024, she became the Robert A. Schroeder Distinguished Professor at the University of Kansas School of Law. Her research focuses on climate change adaptation, especially as it relates to water law, ocean and coastal law, and the Clean Water Act.

Sarah Fox is an Associate Professor at Northern Illinois University College of Law. Her research focuses on environmental law, land use, and property, particularly the unique environmental issues facing cities and the capacity that local governments may have to solve those problems. Prior to teaching at NIU, Professor Fox was a clinical teaching fellow in the environmental law clinic at Georgetown University Law Center and practiced in the litigation sections of Jones Day and Quinn Emanuel Urquhart & Sullivan.

Joshua Ulan Galperin is an idealist, romantic, and Associate Professor at the Elisabeth Haub School of Law at Pace University. Prior to Pace, Josh was on the faculty at the University of Pittsburgh School of Law and served as the Director of the Environmental Protection Clinic, Lecturer in Law, and a Research Scholar at Yale Law School. Josh was also a lecturer and the Environmental Law and Policy Program Director at the Yale School of the Environment.

Michael B. Gerrard is the Andrew Sabin Professor of Professional Practice and founder and faculty director of the Sabin Center for Climate Change Law at Columbia Law School. He formerly chaired the faculty of Columbia's Earth Institute and the American Bar Association's Section of Environment, Energy and Resources. Before joining the Columbia faculty in 2009 he practiced environmental law full time in New York for 30 years, most recently as partner in charge of the New York office of Arnold & Porter. He is author or editor of 14 books on environmental law.

Keith H. Hirokawa serves as Distinguished Professor of Law at Albany Law School, where he has taught since 2009. His teaching and scholarship involve convergences in environmental and natural resources law, land use planning, climate justice, property law, ecological economics, racial justice, and jurisprudence. Hirokawa studied philosophy and law at the University of Connecticut, where he earned his JD and MA degrees. He earned his LLM in Environmental and Natural Resources Law from Lewis & Clark Law School.

Shi-Ling Hsu is the D'Alemberte Professor at the Florida State University College of Law, where he served as Associate Dean for Environmental Programs from 2015 to 2019. Prior to his current appointment, Professor Hsu was a Professor of Law and Associate Dean for Special Projects at the University of British Columbia Faculty of Law, a Senior Attorney and Economist for the Environmental Law Institute in Washington D.C, and practiced law with the firm of Fenwick & West in Palo Alto, California. He teaches in the areas of environmental and natural resource law, climate change, law and economics, and property, and is the author of Capitalism and the Environment: A Proposal to Save the Planet (2021), The Case for a Carbon Tax: Getting Past Our Hangups to Effective Climate Policy (2011), and is the co-author (with Josh Eagle) of Ocean and Coastal Resources Law (4th ed., 2023).

Katrina Fischer Kuh is the Haub Distinguished Professor of Environmental Law at the Elisabeth Haub School of Law at Pace University. Before entering academia, Professor Kuh worked in the environmental and litigation practice groups in the New York office of Arnold & Porter LLP and served as an advisor on natural resource policy in the United States Senate. She sits on the boards of Green Amendments for the Generations and the Climate Science Legal Defense Fund.

Kevin J. Lynch is an Associate Professor at the University of Denver Sturm College of Law. He is the Ronald V. Yegge Director of Clinical Programs and also teaches the Environmental Law Clinic. Professor Lynch previously worked in the Climate and Energy Program at Environmental Defense Fund, and before law school he worked for several years as a consultant in the energy industry.

Michele Okoh is an Assistant Professor at Lewis & Clark Law School teaching criminal law, criminal procedure, and public health law. Prior to joining the Lewis & Clark Law Faculty, she was a senior lecturing fellow for the Duke Environmental Law & Policy Clinic. Her scholarship is at the intersection of criminal justice, environmental justice, and public health law. She currently serves as the section councilor for the Environment Section of the American Public Health Association (APHA) and represents both the Law Section and Environment Section on the Action Board of APHA. She is also a recipient of the 2021 Rebecca A. Head Award which is presented by the Environment Section of APHA to an outstanding emerging leader working at the intersection of environmental justice, policy, and science.

Jessica Owley is a Professor of Law and Director of the Environmental Law Program at the University of Miami where she is also affiliated with the Abess Center for Ecosystem Science and Policy and has a secondary appointment in the Rosenstiel School of Marine, Atmospheric and Earth Sciences. Her interdisciplinary work focuses on the intersection of property law and environmental social science, with a focus on how the law responds to environmental conditions like climate change. She holds four graduate degrees from the University of California at Berkeley. She briefly practiced land use and environmental law at Morrison & Foerster in San Francisco before entering academia. She is one of the founders of the Environmental Law Collaborative.

Melissa Powers is a Jeffrey Bain Faculty Scholar and Professor of Law at Lewis & Clark Law School. She was a Fulbright-Schuman Scholar in 2014-2015 in Denmark and Spain. Melissa is also the founder and former director of the Green Energy Institute at Lewis & Clark Law School, an organization that designs strategies to transition to a zero-carbon energy system. Melissa's teaching and scholarship focus on U.S. climate change law, electricity regulation, renewable energy law, the energy transition, environmental regulation, and administrative law. Melissa is a member-scholar of the Center for Progressive Reform and a board member of the Environmental Law Collaborative.

Shannon M. Roesler is the Charlotte and Frederick Hubbell Professor of Environmental and Natural Resources Law and the Faculty Director of the Hubbell Environmental Law Initiative at the University of Iowa College of Law. Her scholarship focuses on issues of environmental justice, environmental governance, climate resilience, energy law and policy, and land use.

J.B. Ruhl is the David Daniels Allen Distinguished Chair of Law at Vanderbilt University Law School, and is Co-director of the Energy, Environment, and Land Use Program. His research focuses on environmental law and climate change adaptation, with special attention to endangered species protection, ecosystem services, adaptive management, and complex social-ecological-technological systems. He received his B.A. and J.D. from the University of Virginia, an LL.M. in Environmental Law from George Washington University, and a Ph.D. in Geography from Southern Illinois University.

Jim Salzman is the Donald Bren Distinguished Professor of Environmental Law with joint appointments at the Bren School of Environment and UCLA Law School. In 13 books and more than 100 articles and book chapters, his broad-ranging scholarship has addressed topics spanning drinking water, trade and environment conflicts, ownership engineering, and the legal and institutional issues in creating markets for ecosystem services. Prior to joining the Bren faculty, he held distinguished chairs at Duke's law and environment schools. He has served as a visiting law professor at Columbia, Harvard,

Stanford, and Yale as well as at universities in Australia, China, Israel, Italy, Portugal, and Sweden.

David Takacs teaches environmental, climate change, international, and biodiversity law at UC Law San Francisco. In the past year, he has also taught biodiversity law at Vermont Law School, Leiden Law School, and Melbourne Law School. His research covers biodiversity offsetting, carbon offsetting, the human right to water, the public trust doctrine, and rights of nature.

Clifford J. Villa is the Deputy Assistant Administrator for the U.S. Environmental Protection Agency, Office of Land and Emergency Management, on leave from the University of New Mexico School of Law.

Introduction

Introduction

Robin Kundis Craig, Katrina Fischer Kuh, J.B. Ruhl, and James Salzman

At the Glasgow climate summit in November 2021, governments from around the globe declared their ambition to "hold the increase in the global average temperature to well below [2 degrees Celsius (°C)] above pre-industrial levels."[1] This wordsmithing affirmed the goal set in the Paris Agreement in 2015 by the greatest number of heads of state ever at a negotiation. Fine words, to be sure, and a fine aspiration. The negotiators, however, were politicians and diplomats, not scientists. Robust science increasingly tells a different story. Warming beyond 2°C is likely and warming as high as 3°-4°C, possibly by the end of the 21st century, is a real possibility.

A few short months before the Glasgow climate summit, the authors of this book convened for the fifth workshop of the Environmental Law Collaborative (ELC), a group composed of environmental law professors from law faculties around the United States. Our group was not so sanguine about the prospects of limiting warming to well below 2°C. ELC members Robin Kundis Craig and J.B. Ruhl had recently authored a provocative article simply titled *4°C* that sets out the peer-reviewed science demonstrating that a "beyond 2°C" world is a likely trajectory and that a 4°C world cannot be ruled out. Also using peer-reviewed science, they described the vast disruptions this future could cause for both biophysical and social systems.[2] Subsequent modeling reflects growing acknowledgement that warming beyond 2°C is very likely. It also provides some reason to be hopeful that 3°C is a probable upper bound, although this optimism is tempered by uncertainty about implementation of announced mitigation policies, the potential to cross tipping points, and the dire impacts of even existing levels of warming.

1. Paris Agreement to the United Nations Framework Convention on Climate Change, Dec. 13, 2015, *in* Report of the Conference of the Parties on the Twenty-First Session, U.N. Doc. FCCC/CP/2015/10/Add.1, annex , art. 2, ¶1 (2016).
2. J.B. Ruhl & Robin Kundis Craig, *4°C*, 106 Minn. L. Rev. 191 (2021).
3. U.N. Nationally Determined Contributions Under the Paris Agreement Synthesis Report (Oct. 2022).

Today's newspapers make clear some of the consequences of just the 1.2°C warming experienced to date. It has become normal to witness "unprecedented" impacts in natural systems—record droughts or temperatures now occurring yearly in areas as far apart as the Arctic and the Antarctic—occurring much faster than previously expected.[4] Climate change disruptions extend not only to ecological systems, of course, but to social systems as well. Democratic systems of governance may be particularly unstable in the face of the relentless disruptions caused by climate change, including shocks to the economy, food systems, and internal migration, to name just a few. It would be naive to believe that governance in the United States will be immune to these instabilities.

Yet most legal scholarship to date has embraced the temperature goals enshrined in the Paris Agreement not only for mitigation, but for adaptation as well, by assuming 2°C warming as the upper bound and assessing adaptation policy on that basis.[5] The ELC sought to address the legal and governance challenges of higher level warming head-on, discussing and debating how law professors can meaningfully address the prospect of much greater climate change. Our chapters take seriously what science now tells us. If we are moving toward high-level warming significantly above 2°C, perhaps even a 4°C world, what will be the general and specific challenges to law and policy? How can governance systems and institutions adapt, today, in readiness for these future shocks?

This Introduction provides a short summary of the article, *4°C*, describes the different authors' contributions in this volume, and poses a Rawlsian thought experiment about how to approach the law and policy challenges of this new world.

In their article, *4°C*, Craig and Ruhl take as their starting point the recent "unprecedented" natural disasters around the globe of record temperatures, devastating fires, and floods—all events predicted by scientists a decade ago, but not yet supposed to be happening. Relying on scientific findings reported in leading peer-reviewed journals, the article starts by demonstrating why the

4. Intergovernmental Panel on Climate Change (IPCC), Special Report on the Ocean and Cryosphere in a Changing Climate 6-7, 9 (2019) [hereinafter 2019 IPCC Ocean & Ice Report] ("Each of the last three decades has been successively warmer at the Earth's surface than any preceding decade since 1850."); IPCC, Climate Change 2014: Synthesis Report 6-7 (2014) [hereinafter 2014 IPCC Synthesis Report] (noting that the global land temperature is rising twice as quickly as it should naturally).

5. Researchers are, however, starting to call for preparation for higher level warming. *See* Daniel Steel et al., Opinion, *Climate Change and the Threat to Civilization*, 119 Proc. Nat'l Acad. Sci., no. 42, Oct. 2022, https://www.pnas.org/doi/epdf/10.1073/pnas.2210525119 and Luke Kemp et al., Perspective, *Climate Endgame: Exploring Catastrophic Climate Change Scenarios*, 119 Proc. Nat'l Acad. Sci., no. 34, Aug. 1, 2022, https://doi.org/10.1073/pnas.2108146119.

commonly accepted target of 2°C requires societal transformations now that seem very unlikely. Even with these changes, carbon budgets indicate that temperatures will continue to rise.

To paint a more vivid picture of how a rising global mean temperature will challenge governance institutions, they summarize the scientific evidence of nonlinear change to the planet and the limits of human adaptive capacity, envisioning conditions in the United States under a 4°C scenario. This includes pervasive shifts in forest vegetation (particularly tropical forests), poleward range extensions, changes in abundance and distribution of terrestrial and marine species, and the potential collapse of large vulnerable ecosystems, such as the Amazon rainforest and Caribbean coral reefs.

Although the direct impacts of sea-level rise, drought, heat, and other threat factors may be uneven across the nation and across economic sectors, disruptions will occur in every region. Increasingly unliveable temperatures in some regions, lack of potable water in other regions, and the invasion of the sea in coastal regions are likely to drive significant internal migrations within U.S. borders. The country will feel effects from around the globe as well, where in all cases social-ecological conditions worsen as temperatures increase. Put simply, at 4°C, U.S. comparable wealth will not be enough to stop the "suitable zone" from exiting northward.

So what does this possible future mean for policy? Until fairly recently, the focus was on mitigation while adaptation took a back seat. The inevitability of rising sea levels, hotter climates, bigger storms, and other conditions has eventually forced adaptation into the policy discussion, and it is now seen as an essential partner of mitigation policy for both human communities and conservation resources. Adaptation rests on three modes: (1) resistance (also known as protect, fortify, or defend); (2) resilience (also known as adjust, accommodate, manage, or transform); and (3) retreat (also known as move, resettle, relocate, or avoid). Adaptation policies that have been developed, however, have largely centered around the 1.5°-2°C scenario.

The problem is that the 2°C world is likely the threshold at which, if crossed, climate change takes on new and highly unmanageable properties. Adaptation policy as currently modeled and integrated into "future proofing" policies does not consider runaway interacting positive feedback loops, cascade effects in the climate system, and the impacts they will have on social-ecological systems. As a result, there is growing concern that climate change beyond 2°C will swamp the capacities of planned adaptation and that transformational adaptation policies will need to operate at much larger scales, introduce novel strategies, and contemplate major changes and relocations.

Concluding that the current model is not nearly up to the challenge, Craig and Ruhl propose that a new framing is needed to prepare for adaptation beyond 2°C—a framing they call "redesign." This means letting go of intact, in situ, and close-to-normal as the unyielding goal of adaptation. Even within the United States, we can expect massive human migrations and massive species migrations, relocation of agricultural crop and livestock land, expensive infrastructure projects to supply housing, water, transportation, and other needs for new and expanding human communities, as well as deep disruptions to insurance, finance, welfare, and other social and economic systems. Redesign is thus about designing and facilitating—perhaps even requiring—the relocations and reconfigurations necessary for these adaptations to succeed.

The remainder of their article, and indeed each of the chapters that follow in this book, focuses on governance in a world with high-level warming beyond 2°C. Craig and Ruhl argue that the United States, with strong leadership and funding from the federal government, needs to initiate anticipatory governance practices now to facilitate redesign adaptation in the future, beginning with a new national foresight research program.

In the chapters that follow, other authors offer different strategies, some even more ambitious. To set a broad context for each of these chapters, we first offer a thought experiment that illustrates the complexity and stakes of preparing for high-level warming.

The "veil of ignorance" thought experiment devised by the philosopher John Rawls has long haunted law school seminar rooms and lecture halls—and for good reason. In his ambitious 1971 book, *A Theory of Justice*, Rawls offered a way to determine just principles of law from a purely selfish perspective.[6] What would he have to say to us as we face the prospect of a 4°C world?

Imagine, he says, that you are the lawgiver operating today. If acting purely from self-interest, one would expect you to establish laws that favor you and your friends/family/colleagues. There's no surprise that we see this behavior around us every day. Rawls' thought experiment, though, changes the game. You are still the lawgiver, but you are now operating behind a veil of ignorance—you don't know who you will be when the laws apply. Once you have established the laws and removed the veil, you will then learn whether you are rich or poor, white or black, young or old, a citizen of the United States or Bangladesh.

Rawls argues that operating in ignorance of your identity, you will choose principles that ensure the fair and equitable allocation of rights, duties, and

6. John Rawls, A Theory of Justice 136 (1971).

opportunities among everyone in the society. Because you don't know who you will be, it's best to provide for every possibility and favor people equally.

Prof. Edith Brown Weiss took Rawls' veil of ignorance one step further, asking what it means for sustainable development.[7] In her version, you not only do not know who you are, you also do not know *when* in the future you will live. It could be in the present, or three or six generations hence. If you were negotiating under this veil of ignorance, what types of rules would you want to impose?

In this framing, our obligations to future generations become immediate. Professor Weiss proposes a principle of "intergenerational equity" that would seek to ensure future people will "inherit the earth in as good condition as did their ancestors and with at least comparable access to its resources."[8] Because you don't know who you will be, it's best to provide for every possibility and favor people equally, now and in the future.

Let's play this mind game a little further. Imagine, if you will, that you are still the ruler operating behind a veil of ignorance—you do not know who you will be or when in the future you will be. But, and here's the twist, you *do* know that the world is unavoidably on a path to 4°C over the next century. You could live anywhere on that path—2°C, 3°C, 4°C—you don't know. With this knowledge, what laws would you establish today to best ensure a fair and equitable society over the next 100 years of climate change? And how would these be different than Professor Weiss' framing for sustainable development?

The climate change veil of ignorance alters the game in two important respects. First, although scientists can develop rough scenarios of what the world experiences along the climate change path, significant uncertainty remains, especially at local scales. You'll have to design rules for the future now without a firm grasp of what the future looks like for many people. Second, it is more likely than not that climate conditions for many people will deteriorate, making it nearly impossible to set up rules in the present that will ensure future generations inherit an earth in as good a shape as prior generations experienced. You can't stop sea-level rise or increasing temperatures, so you can't satisfy the goal of Professor Weiss' thought experiment.

These constraints change the kind of thinking that Rawls and Weiss expected of their rulemaker in three ways. First, given the century of vastly changing conditions that lies ahead, the rules you design today must be rap-

7. Edith Brown Weiss, *In Fairness to Future Generations and Sustainable Development*, 8 Am. U. Int'l L. Rev. 19 (1992).
8. *Id.* at 21.

idly adaptable as predicted changes evolve and unforeseen changes arise. If you wind up living in the 3°C world, you likely would not want to be bound by rules that applied in the 1.5°C world. As a result, you must design an *adaptive governance* regime, not a fixed set of rules with the hope of locking in socially just conditions in the present and going forward.

Second, you'll need to anticipate tipping points and nonlinear change trajectories without knowing when they will be triggered or what the other side looks like. When will massive domestic migration start, and where do the migrants go? What if you are one of those migrants? Your adaptive governance regime will need to include a substantial planning and monitoring component using updated scenario projections—what social scientists refer to as *anticipatory governance*.

Finally, in addition to the resource consumption trade-off dilemmas that sit at the heart of Weiss' exercise, your rules will also require an ongoing process for determining how much to invest at any given time in protective adaptation measures for future generations. What if you live in the future as a resident of a city that did not build adequate flood control infrastructure or heat wave relief opportunities? But how much should a previous generation have invested? You can't possibly make all those decisions in the present—there's too much uncertainty. The adaptive-anticipatory governance regime you design today thus must focus not only on sustainable resource conservation but also on sustainable adaptation capacity, ensuring continuous decision making for provision of physical and social adaptation infrastructure.

In summary, the climate change veil of ignorance demands a much more fluid governance process, one that continually anticipates unforeseeable change, nimbly adapts the rules, and manages over long time frames for adaptation measures that equitably protect future generations. The fairness question is not how to ensure future generations enjoy the same quality of life, but how to protect those (including possibly you) who will be much worse off.

The contributors to this book have taken up the challenge of thinking about law, governance, equity, and justice under high-level warming from multiple perspectives. The first chapters identify and offer solutions to address the mismatch between today's legal and regulatory systems—specifically, western water law, chemical and waste management, laws aimed at protecting biodiversity, and historic preservation laws—and the conditions and demands of high-level warming.

In the chapter, "Western Water Rights in a 4°C Future," Karrigan Börk, Shi-Ling Hsu, and Kevin Lynch consider the hydrologic impacts of climate change at three scales (across the West, within the Colorado River Basin, and in the San Juan Basin), explain the pathologies of continuing to rely on use-based appropriative water rights under high-level warming, and recommend four steps to adapt western water law: (1) better enforcement of existing laws to ensure the reasonableness and public benefit of existing and future water rights; (2) greater flexibility in existing allocations of water; (3) explicit focus on adjusting water law in an equitable way, including changes that address the racist history of western water rights; and (4) preparation for future short- and long-term water shortages.

Michael B. Gerrard applies a similar lens to the legal regimes governing the management of chemicals and waste in his chapter, "Waste and Chemical Management Beyond 2°C." With at least 60% of Superfund sites not on federal property and 3,200 stationary source facilities covered by the Clean Air Act program for the prevention of accidental releases of hazardous chemicals in locations that may be at risk from the effects of climate change, high-level warming poses a critical threat to the safe storage of chemicals and waste. Gerrard surveys the patchwork of laws governing chemical and waste management, highlighting ways in which existing laws do not adequately contemplate climate-related threats, as well as some recent legal reforms motivated by a recognition of the threats posed by climate change. Concluding that no existing laws envision a world beyond two degrees, he then offers ideas for legal reform to prepare for high-level warming.

David Takacs explains the futility of trying to protect biodiversity using approaches that silo biodiversity from climate change mitigation and adaptation. His chapter, "In a 4°C World, the Inexorable Climate Change-Biodiversity Nexus," provides examples of a new approach, climate-biodviersity mitadaptation, that intertwines climate change and biodiversity goals, reflecting a legal and cultural paradigm shift that embraces interconnection with the natural world.

Michele Okoh closes out the book's first section with her chapter, "America Erased," an unsettling examination of how ill-equipped U.S. law, in particular historical preservation law, is to preserve history, culture, and community after the inevitable geographic loss and internal displacement occasioned by high-level warming.

The next set of chapters imagine more broadly the challenges of effective governance—across a range of laws, through democratic processes—under high-level warming. These chapters identify the strains that high-level warming will place on existing modes of governance and suggest reformed or new governance approaches and strategies.

In her chapter, "Climate-Changed Communities," Sarah Fox confronts the distinct challenges to local governance in communities that will shrink, perhaps even disappear, and communities that will grow in response to high-level warming. She proposes constructing a new set of governance possibilities to redefine existing local boundaries, strengthen inter-local cooperation, and provide local governments with greater fiscal freedom to respond to climate-induced changes in property value and population. For shrinking communities experiencing significant population out-migration, this redefinition of boundaries may include disincorporation, potentially followed by annexation into a neighboring jurisdiction.

Kevin J. Lynch likewise considers governance under high-level warming through a federalism lens, exploring in his chapter, "Preemption: Opportunities and Obstacles for Climate Adaptation," how state-level preemption doctrine can be reimagined and applied to support climate adaptation. This requires threading a needle, as high-level warming will make it important both for state legislatures to be able to preempt local policies that would inhibit climate adaptation and for local governments to exercise greater autonomy—consitent with Fox's recommendations—to craft locally relevant adaptation solutions. Using examples of how pathologies in preemption doctrine derailed mitigation in some contexts as a precautionary tale, Lynch suggests how to prevent preemption pathologies from inhibiting climate adaptation, including recommending: (1) clear guidance from state legislatures to prevent broad and unjustified judicial findings of implied or field preemption; (2) support for greater and more specific rights-based approaches to addressing climate change, such as environmental rights amendments in state constitutions or rights of nature; and (3) judicial adoption of a clear statement rule requiring a clear declaration of legislative intent to preempt to override local adaptation policy.

In the chapter that follows, "Reframing Winter Storm Uri," Melissa Powers likewise tells a precautionary tale. The chapter focuses on how public discourse can drive policy development and governance, considering specifically intersections between narratives around climate dislocation and crisis and the emergency of specific climate policies. Her chapter explains how the energy crisis during Winter Storm Uri was (counterintuitively) used to double down on fossil fuel policies and undercut renewable energy policies. She uses Texas' response to Winter Storm Uri to illustrate how storytelling and discourse powerfully shape the societal response to climate crises through policy framing. Powers exhorts clean energy and climate advocates to actively frame policy responses to climate dislocation, and specifically energy crises, to better support mitigation going forward.

Powers' emphasis on the importance of communication and discourse is underscored in the chapters that follow. Jessica Owley, Karen Bradshaw, Keith Hirokawa, and Robin Kundis Craig use high-level warming to illustrate the limitations of a core feature of existing environmental governance—a reliance on environmental baselines to anchor law and policy, define its aims, and evaluate its success. In their chapter, "The Tyranny of Baselines," the authors explain how environmental baselines can create a bias in favor of a (sometimes deeply unsatisfactory) status quo; perpetuate existing inequality; invite resource-draining debates about where to set the baseline; and become so deeply embedded in law and policy as to defy needed reexamination. The authors identify promising new governance alternatives to baselines better suited to navigating climate change, including goal-oriented collaboration, collaborative analysis, collaborative governance, and improved communication that enables co-created policy.

Joshua Ulan Galperin closes out this section of the book with a chapter, "4Cs at 4°C: Counting, Contestation, Communication, and Consideration for Collectively Constructing Concepts of Climate Change," which observes that the balance of nature—similar to the concept of baselines—has long served as an anchoring principle for environmental governance despite the fact that it is scientifically inaccurate. He believes shared stories, even if they are inaccurate myths, can help ground environmental governance and, like the authors of the *Tyranny* chapter, he focuses on collaboration as an alternative shared story to support environmental governance under high-level warming. Galperin centers process over outcome, exhorting that a belief in a robust and healthy democratic process and the collective decisionmaking it enables can undergird an effective societal response to high-level warming.

The book's concluding chapters focus on equity and justice under high-level warming. In "Environmental Justice Beyond 2°C," Clifford J. Villa deploys a nuanced history of the development and meaning of environmental justice to explore what environmental justice could or should mean under high-level warming. Does the concept of environmental justice continue to have salience when everyone is harmed by climate change? Villa answers yes and uses a close account of the 2022 fires in the Sangre de Cristo Mountains in northern New Mexico and their impact on local residents to illustrate the salience of environmental justice, even when climate harms are widespread. By describing the harms to local residents with an eye to their unique life-ways and culture, he illustrates the value of a justice lens to inform improved governmental responses to climate change.

Villa's chaper endorses a continued commitment to justice, even under the stress and demands of high-level warming. Katrina Fischer Kuh's chapter, "Avoiding Performative Climate Justice," interrogates how best to actualize that commitment. Envisioning how high-level warming will strain institutions and train political will on immediate needs, Kuh argues that policymakers today should make precommitments to justice in mitigation and adaptation law that are enduring, automatic, and early (before the onset of emergency climate conditions). She then surveys select state climate laws, identifying measures that constitute effective precommitments to justice and others that do not and therefore risk dissolving in the face of high-level warming.

Robin Kundis Craig's chapter, "Survival Equity and Climate Change Triage: How to Decide Who Lives and Who Dies," confronts the uncomfortable truth that decisions about climate policy are, and will increasingly become, decisions about who lives and who dies. Her chapter considers pathways to advance survival equity that would equalize every human's chances of surviving despite climate change, including through the use of principles developed in the context of medical triage. After concluding that medical triage principles will not be applied in an equitable fashion across national borders in the context of high-level warming, Craig endorses policies that reduce consumerism and equitably discourage the human population's continued growth as the best means to achieve survival equity.

In "Supplying Life Necessities in a Climate-Changed Future," Shi-Ling Hsu advances another strategy to avoid the inequitable distribution of food, water, and energy during climate-driven shortages. He proposes a new governance tool for high-level warming: the creation of a governmental "Resources Trust" that would inject a supplemental supply of life necessities into the market to relieve immediate crises of supply.

In the book's final chapter, "Decentering Dominance for Climate Adaptation in a Worst-Case Climate World," Cinnamon P. Carlarne and Keith H. Hirokawa echo Craig's pessimism that triage conducted against the backdrop of prevailing social and political inequities would produce even more inequitable outcomes. Their remedy is to work to surface and dismantle those inequities most relevant to climate change—what they term "climate dominance." In applying a climate dominance perspective to climate migration, climate gentrification, and ecosystem management, they show how identifying and decentering climate dominance now can allow for more equitable and effective adaptation planning going forward.

The authors of this volume agreed to seriously consider the possibility of a future shaped by high levels of warming. We decided to take on this project because the possibility of high-level warming is significant and largely ignored in existing law and policy. We peered into that bleak future and thought deeply about how law, governance, and equity could help to keep the plumb line in a world heated out of control. Many of the ideas proposed in this book sound wildly ambitious today, but will ultimately appear modest when weighed against the on-the-ground conditions of extreme climate change.

Laws and Regulatory Systems in a Warming World

Western Water Rights in a Warming Future

Karrigan Börk, Shi-Ling Hsu, and Kevin Lynch

Western water rights evolved during a short and stable climate history, but that period of stability is ending. High-level climate change will produce not only higher temperatures, but also decreased snowpack, shifts in runoff patterns,[1] and the dramatic shrinkage of giant reservoirs.[2] Climatic changes that have already traumatized the West will only intensify and cross even more dangerous thresholds,[3] necessitating the deliberate adaptation of water rights systems. In this chapter, we first discuss the historical development of water law and what that history means for the future of water law in a drastically different climate. We then consider the ongoing hydrological changes from climate change within the context of existing water governance. Finally, we conclude with some prognostication about water law in a warming future.

Water Law Historically Adapted to Hydrology

The changes in the West's hydrology will produce changes in water law. Water law has always evolved in response to changing climatic conditions.[4] Early U.S. water law decisions drew heavily on English water law,[5] establishing a system of riparian water rights that were based on ownership of land abutting a watercourse. Riparian rights are suited for a wet climate that is not dependent on irrigation for successful agriculture. For example, riparian rights are

1. A.C. Lute et al., *Projected Changes in Snowfall Extremes and Interannual Variability of Snowfall in the Western United States*, 51 Water Resources Res. 960, 969-70 (2015).
2. Jaweed Kaleem & Thomas Curwen, *"Unrecognizable." Lake Mead, a Lifeline for Water in Los Angeles and the West, Tips Toward Crisis*, L.A. Times, July 11, 2021, https://www.latimes.com/world-nation/story/2021-07-11/lake-mead-hoover-dam-drought-nevada-arizona-california.
3. Hervé Douville et al., *Water Cycle Changes, in* Climate Change 2021: The Physical Science Basis 8-1, 8-96, 8-119 to -121 (Valérie Masson-Delmotte et al. eds., Cambridge Univ. Press 2021).
4. Joseph W. Dellapenna, *United States: The Allocation of Surface Waters, in* The Evolution of the Law and Politics of Water 189, 189 (Joseph W. Dellapenna & Joyeeta Gupta eds., Springer 2009).
5. *See, e.g.*, Tyler v. Wilkinson, 24 F. Cas. 472 (C.C.D.R.I. 1827) (No. 14,312).

generally limited to reasonable use of the water on the riparian land,[6] so any lands that are not riparian do not have a right to water for irrigation or other uses. Riparian rights have other limits that reflect their wet climatic origins: they do not allow storage or long-distance transportation of water, and they are not absolute, leading to some uncertainty about the quantity and reliability of water.[7] Although riparian rights continue to dominate in the eastern United States, historically these limitations meant that riparian rights were poorly suited to western hydrologic regimes where seasonal (and total) water availability patterns require storage and transportation of water to maximize the benefits of available water.

During the early days of its statehood, California developed a system of appropriative rights based on the use of water, not on land ownership.[8] These appropriative rights allow water storage and transportation, key advantages in arid places where there are fewer surface water bodies and therefore less land with access to water. Appropriative rights systems were far better suited to the arid West and spread quickly across the states west of the Mississippi River. Coastal states like California and Washington and midwestern states like Kansas and Nebraska have blended riparian and appropriative doctrines,[9] while drier western states such as Colorado have adopted a pure appropriative rights approach that does not recognize riparian rights at all.[10]

The appropriative water rights systems developed in the West were quite different from riparian systems. Appropriative systems give priority to the first user of the water, an approach often styled "first in time, first in right," so that later users may not get their full allocation of water in dry years. Maintaining appropriative water rights requires constant vigilance; these rights can be lost through disuse or to other users who take the water.[11] Water rights are tied to the land and to its use; transferring the right to someone else or changing the place or use of the water generally requires permission of a state-level water agency. In sum, patterns of surface water law have changed to reflect the hydrological reality confronting whichever society is making the law.[12] This is

6. *See* Anthony Dan Tarlock & Jason Anthony Robinson, *in* Law of Water Rights and Resources §3:7 (2022) [hereinafter Law of Water Rights and Resources 2022].
7. *See* Water Educ. Found., Riparian Rights, https://www.watereducation.org/aquapedia/riparian-rights (last visited Mar. 2, 2023).
8. Irwin v. Phillips, 5 Cal. 140 (1855).
9. *See* Law of Water Rights and Resources 2022, *supra* note 6, §5:11; *see also* Eric T. Freyfogle, *Lux v. Haggin and the Common Law Burdens of Modern Water Law*, 57 U. Colo. L. Rev. 485 (1986) (describing the tensions between riparian and appropriative systems in California).
10. *See* Coffin v. Left Hand Ditch Co., 6 Colo. 443, 447 (1882).
11. *See, e.g.*, Twin Creeks Farm & Ranch Ltd. Liab. Corp. v. Petrolia Irrig. Dist., 461 P.3d 91 (Mont. 2020) (discussing abandonment of appropriated water rights through nonuse).
12. Karrigan Bork & Sonya Ziaja, *Amoral Water Markets* (forthcoming 2023) [hereinafter *Amoral Water Markets*].

not to say that the present water rights systems are perfect, or that they reflect existing social values, or that they serve the principles of justice and social responsibility. But they do reflect the values and hydrological systems that were in play at the time they were designed. What can this tell us about future water law under the hydrology of a climate-changed future?

The hydrology of a climate-changed future is inherently uncertain, but the general consensus predicts a dire future for water supply in the arid West. Precipitation patterns are the biggest source of uncertainty due to the potential increase in extreme weather events.[13] This could both increase and decrease water supplies as larger snowstorms could dump more precipitation in some years, while other impacts on the snowpack would lead to declines. Nevertheless, temperatures in the summer and fall are expected to offset potential increases in snowpack in most years, leading to an overall trend of less water supply in a warming future.[14] Warmer temperatures and less frequent precipitation also mean that even normal snowpacks do not necessarily bring relief from droughts. For example, Colorado's 2021 snowpack was almost normal, but because soils were unusually dry, most of the water was absorbed by the soils instead of flowing into streams, rivers, and reservoirs for human uses.[15] Another driver of drought in a warming world is the increase in evapotranspiration caused by higher temperatures as plants need more water and evaporation from rivers and reservoirs increases.[16] Although changes in hydrology will vary extensively by watershed, the overall trend suggests less water and more variability, with significantly less water in major watersheds covering large areas, like the Colorado River.

The appropriative rights and the blended appropriative/riparian rights approaches are both based on historic hydrology and patterns of land use and ownership, so, predictably, several aspects of these rights make them particularly ill-suited to this climate future. For example, both approaches give priority to the earliest water users, not to the use best-suited to a changing climate or to the most valuable uses based on changing societal needs. His-

13. Linda O. Mearns et al., *The North American Regional Climate Change Assessment Program: Overview of Phase I Results*, 98 Bull. Am. Meteorological Soc'y 1337, 1358-59 (2012).

14. Bradley Udall & Jonathan Overpeck, *The Twenty-First Century Colorado River Hot Drought and Implications for the Future*, 53 Water Resources Res. 2404, 2414-15 (2017).

15. Miguel Otárola, *Colorado's Snowpack Was Almost Normal This Winter, But It May Not Be Enough Water for the Year*, CPR News, Apr. 2, 2021, https://www.cpr.org/2021/04/02/colorados-snowpack-was-almost-normal-this-winter-but-it-may-not-be-enough-water-for-the-year/.

16. M.F. Wehner et al., *Droughts, Floods, and Wildfires*, *in* 1 Climate Science Special Report: Fourth National Climate Assessment 231, 232, 236-39, 247 (Donald J. Wuebbles et al. eds., U.S. Global Change Res. Prog. 2017) [hereinafter Climate Science Special Report: Fourth National Climate Assessment], https://science2017.globalchange.gov/downloads/CSSR_Ch8_Drought_Floods_and_Wildfires.pdf.

torical aspects of water rights thus sometimes allow lower value agricultural uses to take priority over domestic and industrial uses. Western states have statutory authority that might allow for reallocation of water, such as the broadly applicable requirement that water use be reasonable and beneficial, however, courts and water boards rarely invoke these to rein in inefficiency.[17]

Recent droughts have shown many existing uses of water to be even more anachronistic. Because most water in the West is already appropriated, in a drier, climate-changed future, a modernized rethinking of priorities seems necessary. Simply allowing the continued use of the water by the first person who happened to put it to use seems a poor way to prepare for a drastically different climate future.

California's agricultural sector provides a concrete example of the interplay between hydrology, water rights, social goals, and the future. Early European arrivals to California were able to gain ownership of much of California's Central Valley under state and federal land policies that encouraged the transfer of productive lands into private ownership.[18] This ownership gave the early Californians significant riparian rights to the great rivers of the Central Valley. Those Californians whose land did not abut a water source found other ways to divert water, often in the Sierra foothills, creating appropriative rights for themselves under the newly recognized appropriative rights system.[19] The existing water laws, which were based on values that prioritized maximizing productive use of water, resulted in the creation of significant water rights in California's agricultural sector before much of the state had even begun to develop.

These historic rights are tremendously important and shape current water allocation. Under California law, riparian rights are paramount and are filled before appropriative rights, but within appropriative rights, older rights are filled first. As a result, California's agricultural users have some of the strongest and largest water rights in the state, and this history made California's agricultural sector a significant political and social force in the state. Although productive and valuable, California's agricultural sector constitutes about 80% of the state's human water use,[20] while accounting for less than

17. Janet C. Neuman, *Beneficial Use, Waste, and Forfeiture: The Inefficient Search for Efficiency in Western Water Use*, 28 Envtl. L. 919, 922 (1998) [hereinafter Neuman].
18. Gabriel J. Chin, *A Nation of White Immigrants: State and Federal Racial Preferences for White Noncitizens*, 100 B.U. L. Rev. 1271 (2020); Kate Poole, Water, Rights and Wrongs, in California, https://www.nrdc.org/experts/kate-poole/water-rights-and-wrongs-california (Apr. 28, 2022).
19. *See* Charles F. Wilkinson, *Prior Appropriation 1848-1991*, 21 Envtl. L. xxix (1991) (humorously discussing the origins of prior appropriation in California).
20. Cal. Dep't of Water Resources, *Agricultural Water Use Efficiency*, https://water.ca.gov/Programs/Water-Use-And-Efficiency/Agricultural-Water-Use-Efficiency (last visited Jan. 6, 2022).

3% of the state's gross domestic product (GDP).[21] The agricultural sector, however, has become significantly more efficient in the past 30 years, using less total water to produce more agricultural value.[22]

Nevertheless, in a climate-changed future, it will no longer be prudent to use 80% of California's developed water for agriculture, and thus, significant shifts in California agriculture practices will be necessary. For example, growing less rice (which requires flooding the fields in the summer) or alfalfa or almonds will be necessary, as will producing less beef, milk, and cheese. In some cases and in some years, California water currently used in agriculture will be more valuable as drinking water or as water to support ecosystems. California is not unique in this regard, and similar situations are playing out in states across the West.

Finally, although existing water rights systems in California and other western states have succeeded in spurring economic development, they have done so at great environmental and social cost. Use-based appropriative rights inherently value use over conservation or other "passive" uses, such as recreation or fish and wildlife habitat. The extensive, massive water diversions that have made California the most productive agricultural state in the United States[23] also completely transformed the entire Central Valley and altered the ecology of much of the state, driving many native species to extinction and pushing others to the brink of extinction.[24]

Water rights systems must adapt by encouraging and accommodating changes that make more efficient and higher valued uses of water. Existing water rights systems are very slow to induce changes in agricultural practices that reduce waste, particularly because users pay the state nothing for the

---

21. Division of Agric., Econ. Impact of Agric., Univ. of Ark., *California*, https://economic-impact-of-ag.uada.edu/california (last visited Jan. 6, 2022).
22. Jeffrey Mount & Ellen Hanak, PPIC Water Pol'y Cent., Water Use in California (2019), https://www.ppic.org/wp-content/uploads/jtf-water-use.pdf.
23. Economic Res. Serv., U.S. Dep't of Agric., *Cash Receipts by State*, https://data.ers.usda.gov/reports.aspx?ID=17843#P9c68c7a5c4354e2998c56e99e444d414_5_17iT0R0x5 (last updated Dec. 1, 2021).
24. Water Educ. Found., *California Water 101*, https://www.watereducation.org/photo-gallery/california-water-101 ("Fish populations have been depleted. . . . Invasive plants and species are changing ecosystems and altering native habitat. Species of many native plants and wildlife have declined or become extinct."); California Dep't of Water Res., *The California Water System*, https://water.ca.gov/water-basics/the-california-water-system ("California's heavily engineered water system is blamed by many for declining fish populations, yet simultaneously praised by others for timely releases of cool water to sustain salmon, steelhead and other species.") (last visited Feb. 11, 2022); Peter B. Moyle et al., *Delta Smelt and Water Politics in California*, 43 Fisheries 42 (2018).

public value of the water they use.[25] Use-it-or-lose-it rules in water law[26] disincentivize water conservation or land use changes that could free up water for other users. Riparian rights give strong rights to riparian landowners—a system that tends to perpetuate existing land uses and distributive inequalities. Thus, use-based appropriative rights have locked in wasteful, anachronistic uses.

Markets seem to offer a way out, by allowing water rights holders to sell water to users who would put it to a higher value use. Obviously, water transfers will be an important part of shifting water to new uses, however, markets cannot account for many of the social values of water. Water markets are also built on "prevailing property arrangements, technical conditions, and the wealth positions of buyers and sellers."[27] Markets can reallocate water, but they cannot update systems of water rights to better reflect altered values and new climatic conditions. That requires water governance.[28]

This first section has demonstrated how water laws have historically adapted to hydrology in service of prevailing social values, and the California example has demonstrated how this history can make future adaption of water law both essential and challenging. In the next section, we discuss the hydrologic impacts of climate change at three scales: (1) across the West; (2) within the enormous Colorado River Basin; and (3) in the San Juan Basin, one smaller tributary basin in the Colorado system—and couple these analyses with some discussion of existing water governance.

Impacts Across the West

Much of the western United States will face more frequent water shortages under future high-level warming. From the Great Plains to the Southwest, increasing water scarcity will become a normal condition, not a singular feature of periodic droughts.[29] As an example, consider current impacts on snowpack in California; this is important because snowpack is the single biggest freshwater storage system for many areas across the West. The snowpack in the Sierra Nevada Mountains recently reached its lowest point in at least

25. W. M. Hanemann, *The Economic Conception of Water*, in Water Crisis: Myth or Reality 61, 76-77 (Peter P. Rogers et al. eds., CRC Press 2006). Users may pay infrastructure or administrative costs associated with water delivery, but the public water is free to the initial water right holder.
26. *See, e.g.*, Henry E. Smith, *Governing Water: The Semicommons of Fluid Property Rights*, 50 Ariz. L. Rev. 445, 469 (2008).
27. Daniel W. Bromley, *Land and Water Problems: An Institutional Perspective*, 62 Am. J. Agric. Econ. 834, 837 (1982).
28. *See Amoral Water Markets*, *supra* note 12.
29. U.S. Global Change Res. Prog., Climate Change Impacts in the United States: The Third National Climate Assessment 11 (2014).

the past 500 years.[30] More broadly, a large increase in global mean temperature will lead to larger declines in snowpack in the western United States, perhaps in the range of a 40% decrease due to generally less precipitation and shifts from snow to rain.[31] Decreasing snowpack reduces water availability throughout hot, dry summers, resulting in significant seasonal water shortages. One recent study projects that critical mountain ranges in the western United States may lose their snowpacks for years at a time by mid-century.[32] How will the West cope with such a significant reduction in their natural water storage capacity? And what does this mean in the context of hotter and drier weather that further stresses water systems by increasing water needs for irrigation and other human use while simultaneously reducing water availability due to increase evaporation and evapotranspiration?

The southwestern United States is expected to be particularly affected by climate change, especially in the Colorado River Basin (see map).[33] Across the Southwest, water use outpaces water supply, and demand is expected to increase while climate change reduces the overall supply.[34] Models suggest an overall decrease in water availability, with maximum stream flow decreased in the range of "36-80% in all water resource regions for all periods . . . relative to historical stream flow, and maximum stream flow decreases of up to 20-45% in the 2080s at sites along the Colorado River used for measuring compliance with interstate and international water agreements."[35] Other modeling suggests a possible increase of 3% down to a decrease of 24-40%, driven in large part by higher temperatures.[36] Data from the actual Colorado River flow shows a decrease of roughly 16-20% over the past century, with increased temperatures due to climate change accounting for just over one-half of that change.[37] The system's annual mean discharge appears to be decreasing by 9.3% per °C of warming; under the high-level warming sce-

30. Soumaya Belmecheri et al., *Multi-Century Evaluation of Sierra Nevada Snowpack*, 6 Nature Climate Change 2, 2 (2016), https://www.nature.com/articles/nclimate2809.pdf.

31. David R. Easterling et al., *Precipitation Change in the United States*, *in* Climate Science Special Report: Fourth National Climate Assessment, *supra* note 16, at 218.

32. Erica R. Siirila-Woodburn et al., *A Low-to-No Snow Future and Its Impacts on Water Resources in the Western United States*, 2 Nature Revs. Earth & Env't 800 (2021), https://www.nature.com/articles/s43017-021-00219-y.epdf.

33. *See, e.g.*, A. Park Williams et al., *Rapid Intensification of the Emerging Southwestern North American Megadrought in 2020-2021*, 12 Nature Climate Change 232 (2022).

34. Olivia L. Miller et al., *Changing Climate Drives Future Streamflow Declines and Challenges in Meeting Water Demand Across the Southwestern United States*, 11 J. Hydrology X 1, 1 (2021).

35. *Id.*

36. P.C.D. Milly & Krista A. Dunne, *Colorado River Flow Dwindles as Warming-Driven Loss of Reflective Snow Energizes Evaporation*, 367 Science 1252 (2020) [hereinafter Milly & Dunne].

37. Mu Xiao et al., *On the Causes of Declining Colorado River Streamflows*, 54 Water Resources Res. 6739 (2018); Milly & Dunne, *supra* note 36.

nario contemplated here, even ignoring feedback loops and other problems, the basin could be facing a nearly 40% decrease in annual flows.[38] That kind of decrease is not only incompatible with existing water law systems, it is incompatible with existing patterns of human life in the Southwest.

Impacts Across the Colorado River Basin

Consider these looming changes in hydrology within the context of the existing Colorado River governance regime. The Colorado River Compact (Compact) governs the use of the Colorado River and its tributaries by the seven states that depend on the river. It divides the river's flow between the upper basin states, Colorado, New Mexico, Utah, and Wyoming, and the lower basin states, Arizona, California, and Nevada, with a later treaty reserving 1.5 million acre-feet (MAF) for Mexico.[39] The Compact divides the seven states into an upper and lower basin and allocates each basin 7.5 MAF of consumptive use per year. Thus, the existing arrangement assumes a flow of roughly 16.5 MAF per year in perpetuity. The Compact further provides that "[t]he States of the Upper Division will not cause the flow of the river at Lee Ferry to be depleted below an aggregate of 75 [MAF] for any period of [10] consecutive years,"[40] although there is some disagreement about what obligations, exactly, this puts on the upper river states.[41]

At the time the Compact was negotiated, the Colorado River flow was estimated to be 18 MAF, so the Compact actually left 1.5 MAF unallocated, above the treaty amount.[42] The 20th-century average has been lower, at 14.8 MAF, due in part to climate change.[43] The result? Both Lake Powell and Lake Mead are at historic lows, and federal managers at the U.S. Bureau of Reclamation (Bureau) are cutting water supplies to the seven states that depend on the river, due to both the long-term structural deficit and an ongoing drought aggravated by climate change.[44] And the climate predictions

38. Milly & Dunne, *supra* note 36.
39. Some watersheds in New Mexico and Utah drain into the river below the dividing point, and watersheds are considered part of the lower basin, but both New Mexico and Utah are categorized as upper basin states. Colorado River Compact of 1922, Ariz.-Cal.-Colo.-Nev.-N.M.-Utah-Wyo., Aug. 19, 1921.
40. *Id.* The 10-year compliance period allows flexibility to make up for years of low flow.
41. Jennifer Yachnin, *Could the Colorado River Compact Adapt to Go With the Flow?*, PoliticoPro (June 1, 2022, 1:18 PM), https://subscriber.politicopro.com/article/eenews/2022/06/01/could-the-colorado-river-compact-adapt-to-go-with-the-flow-00034719.
42. Daniel Craig McCool, *A Better Way to Share Water From the Shrinking Colorado River*, Source N.M. (Dec. 14, 2021, 5:22 AM), https://sourcenm.com/2021/12/14/a-better-way-to-share-water-from-the-shrinking-colorado-river/.
43. *Id.*
44. Williams et al., *supra* note 33, at 232.

Colorado River Basin

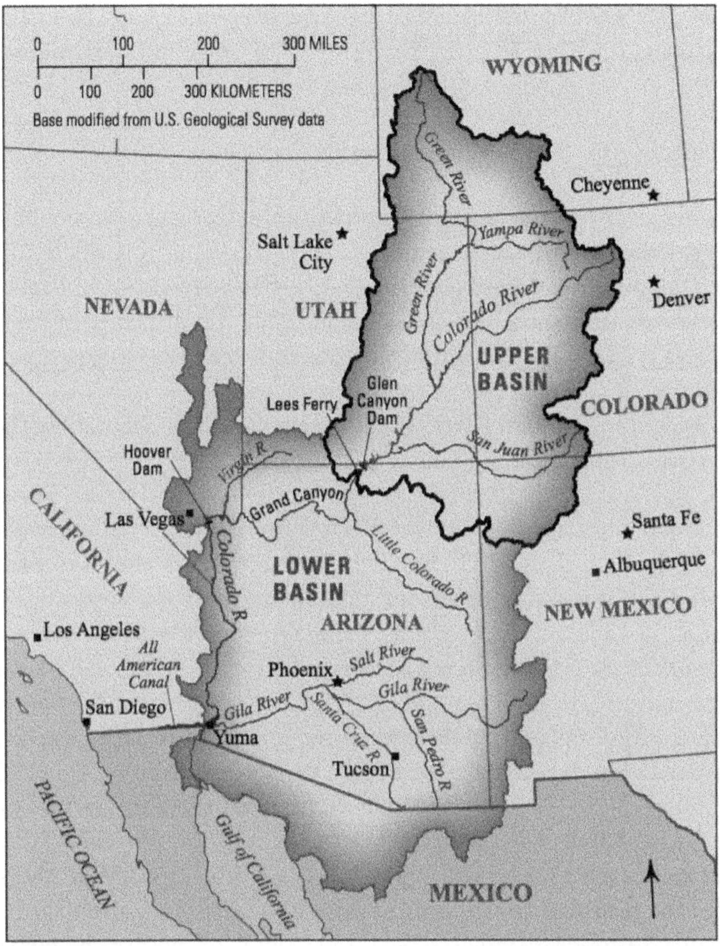

Source: USGS, Colorado River Basin Map, https://www.usgs.gov/media/images/colorado-river-basin-map

above suggest that less water, not more, is in the future: the newer estimates that account for climate change put expected future flows closer to 11 MAF per year. The Compact, based on a climate and hydrology that no longer exists, seems unlikely to survive in its present form. Either a dramatic renegotiation or a reinterpretation will be necessary.

Changes in the Compact, the restrictions already imposed by the Bureau, and the changing climate itself will inevitably affect water rights at the state level as well. Division of waters at the state level will clearly be affected by decreasing availability. Existing distributions of water and water rights at the state level no longer reflect climate reality.

Zooming In: The San Juan River Basin

The concrete challenges facing the parties to the Compact can be illustrated by considering impacts on a smaller scale. Zooming in to a single tributary to the Colorado River illustrates the highly place-dependent impacts of climate change. This place dependence highlights the difficulty of managing ecological systems and navigating the political interests surrounding water allocations.

Consider the San Juan River. The San Juan is a major tributary of the Colorado River, flowing through the four corners region with its own tributaries in four different states. Its headwaters lie mostly in the San Juan Mountains of Colorado, although it draws some water from Arizona and New Mexico. As a part of the Colorado River system, the San Juan is subject to the Compact, and the water that each state takes from the river counts against its allocation of Colorado River waters. Colorado and New Mexico have rights to the bulk of the San Juan River under the Compact, with some water going to Utah and only a small amount going to Arizona. Part of the San Juan is also diverted to supplement the Rio Grande, outside of the Colorado River Basin.[45] This is a dry part of the country, and cities like Durango, Colorado, and Gallup, New Mexico, must pull water from the San Juan to survive. Other users include farms scattered across the region.

The four corners region is also home to many tribes, including the Navajo Nation, the Jicarilla Apache, and the Ute Mountain Utes, and their reservations carry historic federally reserved water rights to most of the flow of the river. The Navajo Nation is the largest water user on the San Juan, diverting significant amounts of water for agricultural and other uses. Despite their strong water rights, a history of underinvestment means that most of their

45. Transbasin diversions occur in other places as well, such as diversions from the Colorado River to the South Platte River in Colorado. Amazingly, new infrastructure to support these diversions is currently being constructed right now at the same time as dire water shortages threaten the entire Colorado River systems. *See, e.g.*, Northern Water Org., *Windy Gap Project*, https://www.northernwater.org/what-we-do/deliver-water/windy-gap-project (last visited July 13, 2022). One of the authors of this chapter has worked in opposition to this project.

Radical Realignment on the Colorado?

The dire situation along the Colorado River has led to calls by environmental and conservation organizations for big changes to be made to the Colorado River Compact and the entire system for managing water in the desert Southwest. Those calls include: (1) stopping new dams and diversions that would further tax the Colorado River system; (2) decommissioning Glen Canyon Dam and draining what little water is in Lake Powell into Lake Mead; (3) enacting policies such as drought plans, water allocation plans, and draining of existing reservoirs to try to save Lake Mead; (4) ensuring that water flows through the Colorado River Delta and into the Sea of Cortez; (5) protecting Native American water rights by subtracting tribal water rights from currently diverted uses; and (6) equitably dividing whatever water is left in the Colorado River among current users of the water. These kinds of large-scale discussions, though painful, will be increasingly necessary in a 4°C world.

tribal rights are underdeveloped; 40% of Navajo households are not connected to water supplies and instead rely on water hauled via trucks to survive.[46]

The San Juan flows directly into Lake Powell, where its waters comingle with the Colorado River, before flowing through the Grand Canyon and into Lake Mead. The San Juan supplies about 15% of the Colorado River's flow below Lake Powell.[47] Both Lake Powell and Lake Mead were, at the time this chapter was being written, operating at the edge of disaster. If the water levels continue to drop, the reservoirs will be unable to produce much-needed hydropower. Eventually, they may fall so much that they will be unable to supply essential water for life in the Southwest. Current patterns of human settlement and water use cannot survive without a viable Lake Powell and Lake Mead, so the situation in these reservoirs directly impacts what happens with San Juan water.

Further complicating matters, both the San Juan itself and the Colorado River downstream are critical habitat for a number of threatened or endangered native fishes: the humpback chub; bonytail chub; razorback sucker; and the Colorado pikeminnow.[48] Most of the water infrastructure in the San Juan watershed is federal, built and operated by the Bureau, and most of

46. U.S. Bureau of Reclamation, *Navajo-Gallup Water Supply Project Planning Report and Final Environmental Impact Statement*, https://www.usbr.gov/uc/envdocs/eis/navgallup/FEIS/index.html (last updated Aug. 12, 2019).
47. Katrina E. Bennett et al., *Threats to a Colorado River Provisioning Basin Under Coupled Future Climate and Societal Scenarios*, 1 Env't Res. Commc'ns 1, 2 (2019).
48. Robert W. Adler, *Restoring the Environment and Restoring Democracy: Lessons From the Colorado River*, 25 Va. Envtl. L.J. 55, 58-59 (2007).

the newer non-tribal rights are held by the Bureau.[49] Because of the federal agency connection, this infrastructure must be operated within the strict confines of the Endangered Species Act (ESA), as implemented by the San Juan River Recovery Plan, which requires minimum flows in the San Juan year-round, coupled with occasional flood flows during the spring months. River managers have consistently struggled to meet the spring flood flow objectives, generally failing to provide flows that meet the highest targets.[50]

In summary, the San Juan River is subject to claims from four states, three tribal governments, many smaller irrigators, federal ESA requirements, and, at the broader scale, four more downstream states and Mexico. In all, this makes for a contentious stew.

Since the 1940s, New Mexico has been trying to work out water rights' claims and priorities within just the New Mexico portion of the San Juan watershed through a complex judicial proceeding known as the San Juan River Basin Adjudication.[51] Pre-1938, private rights were adjudicated in the Echo Ditch Decree in 1948, but that decree left out tribal rights, other federal reserved rights, and later private rights. The broader adjudication is still ongoing, but the dominant tribal water claims have been settled within the last 25 years. The Jicarilla Apache claims were settled in 1999 via court order, and the Navajo Nation agreed to a settlement with New Mexico in 2005. The Navajo Nation's settlement agreement required congressional approval, coupled with significant federal investment in a new water project called the Navajo-Gallup Water Supply Project, which is designed to deliver water to the Navajo Nation, the Jicarilla Apache, and the city of Gallup, New Mexico. It is a carefully calibrated agreement, designed to achieve support from all parties and allow for water development in the region.

Turning away from the legal setting for a moment, expected climate-related changes in the basin include earlier and warmer springs, drier and hotter summers, shifting precipitation periods toward winter months, earlier and higher peak runoff, decreased summer flows, and increased irriga-

---

49. L. Randy Kirkpatrick, *The San Juan River—The Current Controversy*, *in* Water, Growth, and Sustainability: Planning for the 21st Century 41, 47 (2000), https://nmwrri.nmsu.edu/wp-content/uploads/2015/watcon/proc45/TheSanJuanRiver-TheCurrentControversy-Kirkpatrick.pdf ("In the 1955-1968 period, State Engineer Steve Reynolds issued permits to the Department of Interior for all the then-unappropriated water in the San Juan, and the intended use for the water was the Federal projects then planned . . . .").
50. The San Juan River Basin Recovery Implementation Program, Revised Navajo Dam Operating Procedures for the 1999 San Juan River Flow Recommendations (2018), https://coloradoriverrecovery.org/sj/wp-content/uploads/sites/3/2022/03/Flow_Recommendations_Revised_Navajo_Dam_Operating_Procedures_2018.pdf.
51. Jim Dunlap, Bringing Water Rights Adjudications into the 21st Century (2018), https://nmwaterconference.nmwrri.nmsu.edu/2018/speakers/slides/Jim_Dunlap.pdf.

tion demand.[52] Quantitative projections vary extensively due to differences in modeling and emissions assumptions. One study predicted a range of changes in water availability from -38% to +8% by 2099.[53] A second study, based on the current state of greenhouse gas emission growth, predicted a decrease of 14%, again with a great deal of variability around that figure based on modeling assumptions.[54] The second study, by Katrina Bennett and colleagues, also modeled water management, based on the San Juan's legal and physical infrastructure, and future demand, based on full utilization of all existing water rights on the system, which provides a more detailed view of the river's future.

The Bennett study is relatively good news for the San Juan because its modeling suggests that most users will be able to continue their *present* level of use, while still meeting minimum instream flows based on predicted future hydrology. Although the pattern of stream flow will likely change considerably, flows on the San Juan are controlled by the large Navajo Reservoir, and the reservoir has sufficient capacity to buffer the changes and provide for the current levels of water use.[55] Key to maintaining these uses is the flexibility that is incorporated into the agreement, which is necessary for effective management.

The one exception is the diversion to the Rio Grande Basin. The physical infrastructure for that diversion is above the Navajo Reservoir, so the reservoir cannot mitigate the shifting hydrology, and the river will simply be too low for the necessary physical diversions to take place.[56] This is particularly significant because that diversion provides water to Albuquerque and Santa Fe, New Mexico, as well as, tribal users, agricultural users, and some of the Rio Grande's endangered species.[57] The overall exports from the San Juan to the Colorado River downstream would also be reduced.

The Bennett study also includes models that couple future climate projections with future demand growth based on full development of the Navajo Reservoir and other water rights, and those models are grim. Under a full-use-of-all-water-rights scenario, the future hydrology of the basin would fall short

52. Navajo Nation et al., Navajo-Gallup Water Supply Project, at V-144 to -145 (2009), https://www.usbr.gov/uc/envdocs/eis/navgallup/FEIS/vol1/Volume1.pdf.

53. *Id.*

54. Bennett et al., *supra* note 47, at 2.

55. *Id.*

56. Sara Henchey Brosnan, A Case Study of Water Sharing in the San Juan Basin (Apr. 26, 2009) (a professional project submitted in partial fulfillment of the requirements for the degree of Master of Water Resources, Water Resources Program, University of New Mexico), https://digitalrepository.unm.edu/cgi/viewcontent.cgi?referer=&httpsredir=1&article=1024&context=wr_sp.

57. Bennett et al., *supra* note 47, at 2.

of the necessary supply for all uses in many years. On the endangered species side, minimum instream flows would be difficult to achieve in many years.

Ten major water users on the San Juan have negotiated a water sharing agreement to address priority and distribution of water during drought years, [58] and Bennett and colleagues suggest that this agreement is likely to provide the flexibility the basin needs to deal with future shortages as well.[59] The agreement allows the parties involved to make water allocation decisions every year to address changing patterns of runoff. It also allows transfers and payments among the parties to avoid significant impacts to all users. But the agreement has only been tested in small ways thus far, and it remains unclear how well it will work under a very different hydrological regime in the future.[60]

The San Juan example teaches several lessons about future hydrology in a changing climate. First, the local context matters a great deal. Scaling climate projects down to the individual basin necessarily includes a great deal of uncertainty, but robust analysis like that in the Bennett study provide a great deal of useful information for water users at a very local level. The local context here, including the large upstream dam and the shortage sharing agreement, means that many of the water users may be buffered from significant climate impacts. The modeling also reveals the fragile nature of the diversions to the Rio Grande system and provides some notice to water users in that system that they are likely to face future shortages. The local context is also significant in terms of future demand. Modeling here shows that users in the basin are unlikely to be able to fully utilize their existing (albeit underutilized) water rights in the future, particularly a high-level warming future. Current levels of use may be sustainable on the San Juan, at least under some of the more optimistic models. But other localities, like the snowmelt-dependent watersheds in California, face a looming crisis that will render current use patterns impossible and will likely require major social reorganization. Water use is local, and impacts of a high-level warming future will be local too.

Second, regional context matters a great deal and can influence what happens at a local level. The changes in the San Juan hydrology will have

58. Brosnan, *supra* note 56.

59. Bennett et al., *supra* note 47, at 2.

60. Brosnan, *supra* note 56, at 35:

> [T]he shortage sharing provisions have not been tested beyond [a] limited extent . . . . These provisions of the agreement have not been fully utilized due to hydrological circumstances having been generally fairly wet. It will be interesting to see how the agreement(s) fair under more stressful environmental conditions. For now, however, the parties to the agreement appear to be happy with how it is working.

impacts beyond the local basin, and impacts outside of the basin may affect water use on the San Juan. Current water use in the San Juan Basin supports power production and irrigation of crops, and the Rio Grande transfers support municipal and agricultural use in that basin. Moreover, the outflow from the San Juan Basin is critical to maintaining reservoir levels downstream. Changes in water use and availability that affect power production and food production will have some effects in the San Juan Basin but much larger effects for the urban areas that depend on the food and power exports. Demand for water may decrease in some areas as coal-fired power plants are taken off-line, but demand for hydropower may increase downstream. Shortages in the Rio Grande transfer will have significant effects in Albuquerque and Santa Fe and along the mainstem Rio Grande. And decreased total outflow from the San Juan will further impact the already perilously low reservoir levels on Lake Powell and Lake Mead, with significant regional and national power, water, and food impacts. The Colorado River Compact and its follow-on agreements, in turn, may curtail use of available water on the San Juan if the reservoir situation and total water availability in the Colorado River Basin continues to decrease. If that were to happen, the San Juan's ability to withstand local climate change impacts would be swamped by the need for more downstream water at a regional level. Water rights used by the Navajo for relatively low-value irrigation would be much more valuable to other users, and economic and social pressures could force major social and water use changes in the San Juan Basin. Even local areas that have some buffer will see transformations forced by regional change in a warming world.

Third, flexibility in water rights will be essential to mitigate some climate impacts. In a high-level warming scenario, many impacts simply cannot be adequately mitigated, and overall water use will have to decrease. But flexibility to move water to higher value uses and to essential ecological protection can soften the blow somewhat. On the San Juan, the shortage sharing agreement has the potential to reduce the overall impacts of climate change on water users in the region by ensuring that higher value uses and uses that *must* have consistent water availability get their water in most years. This allows a deviation from the typical "first-in-time, first-in-right" approach to water distribution in the West and results in a much more rational distribution of the water.

The San Juan example provides some hope in a grim future. Lest it paint too rosy a picture, though, we note that it is an exception to the general rule: a future so much hotter and drier than the existing social order, including existing water law, must change.

How Can Water Law Adapt to a Warmer Future?

How is the western United States to cope with a world that is warmer and chronically short of water? We suggest four steps, emphasizing that these represent just a few out of many constructive actions that might be taken to prepare for a much warmer, much drier American West. First, existing laws must be better enforced to ensure the reasonableness and public benefit of existing and future water rights in light of climate change. Second, existing allocations of water must be more flexible. Third, water policymakers must explicitly focus on adjusting water law in an equitable way and should use this opportunity to address the racist history of western water rights. Fourth, states should prepare for future short- and long-term shortages. These steps will not prevent future water-related challenges due to high-level warming, but they would provide some much-needed flexibility.

First, existing laws must be better enforced to ensure the reasonableness and public benefit of existing and future water rights in light of climate change. States must ensure that both existing water rights and new diversions comply with existing state laws. Water is a unique common pool resource, essential for life and the public welfare, and so states have extensive power to regulate water use as "the guardian of the public welfare,"[61] a role that allows states to regulate water rights in ways that might offend constitutional protections in other contexts.[62] Using these powers, westerns states have held valid only those water rights put to reasonable[63] or beneficial uses.[64] Although the exact doctrine varies from state to state, water rights have almost always been, at least formally if not in practice, predicated on some consideration of public interest,[65] and no western states protect water rights that are used wastefully.[66] These terms have been ill-defined and poorly enforced. Moreover, they are often defined in a way that gives short shrift to considerations of recreation, conservation, and wildlife.[67] Climate change will require that state agencies and courts take more seriously public interests in water. For exam-

61. Hudson Cty. Water Co. v. McCarter, 209 US. 349, 356 (1908).
62. *See, e.g.*, Dave Owen, *Taking Groundwater*, 91 Wash. U. L. Rev. 253, 286 (2013); John Leshy, *Notes on a Progressive National Water Policy*, 3 Harv. L. & Pol'y Rev. 133, 158-59 (2009); Joseph W. Dellapenna, *Special Challenges to Water Markets in Riparian States*, 21 Ga. St. U. L. Rev. 305, 337 (2004); Joseph L. Sax, *The Constitution, Property Rights, and the Future of Water Law*, 61 U. Colo. L. Rev. 257, 260 n.4 (1990) (collecting cases).
63. *See, e.g.*, Cal. Const. art. X, §2.
64. Thornton v. Fort Collins, 830 P.2d 915 (Colo. 1992).
65. Mark Squillace, *Restoring the Public Interest in Western Water Law*, 2020 Utah L. Rev. 627, 652-54.
66. United States v. Alpine Land & Reservoir Co., 697 F.2d 851, 854 (9th Cir. 1983), *cert. denied*, 464 U.S. 863 (1983) (a water right "cannot include any element of 'waste' [and] cannot be 'unreasonable' considering alternative uses of the water").
67. *See* Sax, *supra* note 62, at 277-79. *See generally* Neuman, *supra* note 17.

ple, the phrase "public interest" has been infrequently deployed to protect passive or instream uses and has in some cases simply been ignored in water permit applications.[68] Passive uses and conservation purposes take on greater importance in a climate-changed future, as water shortage and extreme heat take a toll on ecosystems and their biota, pushing more species toward and possibly over the brink of extinction.

More broadly, determinations of beneficial use or waste or reasonableness, which inherently consider competing uses, water shortages, and the changing times, have not considered a world of high-level temperature increases. Certainly, consideration of new rights must anticipate changed climate conditions when weighing whether the proposed diversions are truly beneficial, non-wasteful uses of an increasingly scarce resource. But because the beneficial use standard is inherently contextual, it changes over time and moves with shifting hydrology.[69] Thus, existing water rights once deemed to be beneficial, non-wasteful uses of water, must also be reconsidered in a warming world.[70] This is particularly true because, in many places in the West, all available water is already allocated, so merely applying the reasonableness and associated requirements to existing rights is insufficient. For example, domestic and industrial uses, generally less elastic than agricultural uses, may require some special protection of their priority should water shortages prove too persistent and severe. Agricultural users continue to hold an inordinately large fraction of water rights, and while some agricultural users have transitioned to higher value crops,[71] many uses remain in low-value goods.[72] Using San Juan water to grow crops in the desert may not be reasonable if that use inordinately decreases water available for hydropower or drinking water. Existing water uses must be reexamined and subjected to a reasonableness test that accounts for the drier, hotter realities of a climate-changed future.[73]

Second, existing allocations of water must be more flexible. As the negotiated water sharing agreement among the major San Juan water users shows, water transfers can mitigate drought impacts by reallocating water to the

---

68. Squillace, *supra* note 65, at 659, 661.
69. *Alpine Land & Reservoir Co.*, 697 F.2d at 855.
70. Brian E. Gray, *Global Climate Change: Water Supply Risks and Water Management Opportunities*, 14 Hastings W.-Nw. J. Envtl. L. & Pol'y 1453, 1459-61 (2008).
71. Mount & Hanak, *supra*, note 22.
72. Peter W. Culp et al., Shopping for Water: How the Market Can Mitigate Water Shortages in the American West 11 (2014):

    In 2013, Southern California farmers used more than 100 billion gallons of Colorado River water to grow alfalfa (a very water-intensive crop) that was shipped abroad to support rapidly growing dairy industries, even as the rest of the state struggled through the worst drought in recorded history.

73. *Id.* at 1455-58.

places where it is needed most. Transfers can take place through a variety of means; research in California has shown that water markets, where water rights holders lease or sell either water or the right itself, can mitigate drought impacts.[74] Water markets in the West tend to be fairly small scale,[75] however, and slow to develop.[76] Water markets are also built on existing power structures and water rights' distributions, which follow strong racial lines, as discussed below. Using markets alone to reallocate water rights would likely continue or even intensify existing disparities in access to water and water rights. Markets may also make state regulation of water rights more difficult.

States also have the power to reallocate water through mechanisms like enforcement of the beneficial use requirements, through existing laws making water rights subject to a host of instream uses,[77] and through modern environmental laws. For example, the California Water Board has used its powers under the public trust doctrine and other California law to require water rights holders to leave water in stream for endangered fish during drought periods.[78] Enforcing these existing laws often allows the state to effect transfers without transgressing constitutional takings protections.[79] As water managers adapt to a high-level warming world, rapid and significant changes in hydrology will require the adjustment of water rights through a variety of mechanisms, and managers should be prepared to use all tools at their disposal.

Third, water policymakers must explicitly focus on adjusting water law in an equitable way and should use this opportunity to address the racist history of western water rights. Because western water rights are built on the foundation of first use (for appropriative rights) and land ownership (for riparian rights), they reflect the West's long history of racially exclusive law and policies. These laws and policies affected many groups. Many immigrants to the West were claiming lands and water rights while Indigenous peoples were still subject to active genocide,[80] while Black people were still subject to ownership, and while Asian and other non-white people were effectively barred

74. Ellen Hanak, *Water Markets in California Can Reduce the Costs of Drought*, Cal. Matters (Feb. 1, 2021), https://calmatters.org/commentary/my-turn/2021/02/water-markets-in-california-can-reduce-the-costs-of-drought/.
75. *Id.*
76. Culp et al., *supra* note 72, at 11 ("[A] myriad of physical, legal, and regulatory restrictions operate to inhibit the movement of water from one user to another and from one type of use to another.").
77. *See* Paul Kibel, Riverflow: The Right to Keep Water Instream (Cambridge Univ. Press 2021).
78. *See* Stanford Vina Ranch Irrig. Co. v. State, 50 Cal. App. 5th 976, *reh'g denied* (July 6, 2020), *as modified* (July 8, 2020), *review denied* (Sept. 23, 2020), *cert. denied*, 141 S. Ct. 1387, 209 L. Ed. 2d 128 (2021).
79. *Id.* at 993 ("[N]or did the emergency regulations and curtailment orders amount to a taking of property, because Stanford Vina did not have a vested right to the unreasonable use of water.").
80. State Water Resources Control Bd. Res. No. 2021-0050 (Cal. 2021).

from participation in state and federal land sales.[81] In the western lands that joined the Union under the Treaty of Guadalupe Hidalgo,[82] many of the existing property rights of former Mexican citizens were extinguished, eliminating their water claims. These laws and policies mean that water rights were simply less available to non-whites, forming an inequitable foundation for modern water rights.[83]

Later policies continued these practices, from federal irrigation policies that disfavored indigenous water developments,[84] as on the San Juan, to farm policies that meant minority farmers were more likely to lose their lands.[85] As the California Water Board noted: "[The] Water Boards' programs were established over a structural framework that perpetuated inequities based on race. These inequities persist."[86] The board also "explicitly acknowledged the role racism has played in creating inequities in affordability and access to clean and safe water and in the allocation and protection of water resources."[87] From drinking water to water rights, past and continuing racist laws and policies affect who gets water. Absent constant vigilance and active anti-racist policymaking, these patterns will continue and perhaps worsen in a warming world.

Fourth, states must actively prepare for future short- and long-term shortages. Even in areas that are not expected to receive less water on average, short-term water shortages will likely be more common.[88] And in many areas, severe and prolonged water shortages will be part of a new normal. States must actively prepare for these shortages, rather than reactively trying to manage them while in an ongoing state of crisis. Having concrete drought plans in place allows water users a measure of certainty and can help states be better positioned to weather changes in hydrology.[89] Preparations can range from clear guidance on when various water rights will be cut off due to short-

81. Gabriel J. Chin, *A Nation of White Immigrants: State and Federal Racial Preferences for White Noncitizens*, 100 B.U. L. Rev. 1271 (2020).
82. John Schelhas, *Race, Ethnicity, and Natural Resources in the United States: A Review*, 42 Nat. Resources J. 723, 723-63 (2002).
83. *See* Katie A. Berry & Sue Jackson, *The Making of White Water Citizens in Australia and the Western United States*, 108 Annals Am. Ass'n Geographers 1354 (2018), https://www.tandfonline.com/doi/pdf/10.1080/24694452.2017.1420463?needAccess=true.
84. Kaylee Ann Newell, *Federal Water Projects, Native Americans, and Environmental Justice: The Bureau of Reclamation's History of Discrimination*, 20 Environs: Envtl. L. & Pol'y J. 40 (1997).
85. Dania V. Francis et al., *Black Land Loss: 1920-1997*, 112 AEA Papers and Proceedings 38 (2022).
86. State Water Resources Control Bd. Res. No. 2021-0050.
87. *Id.*
88. *See* Tiffany Means, *Climate Change and Droughts: What's the Connection?*, Yale Climate Connections (Aug. 18, 2021), https://yaleclimateconnections.org/2021/08/climate-change-and-droughts-whats-the-connection/.
89. Public Pol'y Inst. of Cal., Water Pol'y Ctr., Managing Droughts (2018), https://www.ppic.org/wp-content/uploads/californias-water-managing-droughts-november-2018.pdf.

ages, to firm laws that set enforceable expectations for how much water must be left instream, to new ideas like state-chartered trusts, such as a "resources trust,"[90] that would be charged with gathering up water and water rights to hold in reserve as a source of emergency supply in the future. As discussed further in Shi-Ling Hsu's chapter, "Supplying Life Necessities in a Climate-Changed Future," a resources trust could be created as a governmental entity that could act as a water supplier of last resort should severe shortage arise in a climate-changed future. In hedging against severe and prolonged water shortages, a resources trust might employ a range of legal instruments, such as options, to secure future supply. Importantly, such an entity must acquire water rights through purchase or other mechanisms so as to remove them from priorities of traditional water law. Adequate preparation will not eliminate the impacts from drought, but it may make them more manageable.

Conclusion

Climate change will dramatically change the supply and uses of water in the West. Even in the short time since this chapter was drafted, the crisis on the Colorado River deepened, with Lake Powell reaching its lowest level since it was filled in the 1960s and Lake Mead in similarly bad shape. Resistance to change seems endemic among the seven basin states, especially California, which has insisted on strict application of the "first-in-time, first-in-right" principle of prior appropriation rights for the allocation of Colorado River water. Time will tell how long resistance to change can persist. Perhaps only catastrophe can change anachronistic habits and expectations.

This chapter provides a road map for changes that can help to mitigate the dire situation regarding water in the West. Those changes include renewed commitment to ensuring diversions of water are in the public interest, supporting greater flexilbity allocations of water through water transfers and enforcing the beneficial use doctrine, adjusting water law with an explicit focus on equity, and active preparation for short- and long-term water shortages. Even with these changes, some of the hydrological changes in the West under a high-level temperature increase future will be insurmountable and will alter the fabric of society. Patterns of agriculture and settlement will shift, even with rapid adaptation of water law. We do not yet know how fundamental these shifts will be, but water law will play a vital role as society learns to live in a warming world.

90. Shi-Ling Hsu, *Climate Triage: A Resources Trust to Address Inequality in a Climate-Changed World*, 50 Envtl. L. 97, 99-100 (2020), https://myweb.fsu.edu/shsu/publications/50EnvtlL97.pdf.

Waste and Chemical Management Beyond 2°C

Michael B. Gerrard

Many chemicals and other hazardous substances are kept in places that can withstand ordinary rain but not severe storms or floods. If these events occur and the chemicals are released, people and the environment may be endangered. The law has a long way to go—using existing tools and developing new ones—in protecting against these hazards and coping with the damage when they do occur.

U.S sea levels today are about nine inches higher than a century ago.[1] By the end of the century they could be another six feet or even higher (or lower).[2] Just how high depends mostly on how much greenhouse gas (GHG) we are still emitting and on the rate of melting in Antarctica and Greenland. Moreover, flood risks are hardly limited to the coasts. Over the last century, annual precipitation and also extreme precipitation events have increased across most of the northern and eastern United States (and decreased across much of the southern and western states) due mostly to GHG emissions.[3] Each 1 degree Fahrenheit (1°F) increase in temperature leads to more evaporation and 4% more water vapor in the atmosphere, meaning more rain.[4] This affects inland areas as well as the coasts; flooding across the Midwest and South during 2019 affected nearly 14 million people.[5]

---

1. 2 U.S. Glob. Change Rsch. Program, Impacts, Risks, and Adaptation in the United States: Fourth National Climate Assessment 39 (D.R. Reidmiller et al. eds., 2018) [hereinafter Fourth National Climate Assessment].
2. Jonathan L. Bamber et al., *Ice Sheet Contributions to Future Sea-Level Rise From Structured Expert Judgment,* 116 Proc. Nat'l Acad. Sci. 11195-200 (2019), https://doi.org/10.1073/pnas.1817205116.
3. Fourth National Climate Assessment, *supra* note 1, at 74; Megan C. Kirchmeier-Young & Xuebin Zhang, *Human Influence Has Intensified Extreme Precipitation in North America,* 117 Proc. Nat'l Acad. Sci. 13308 (2020), https://www.pnas.org/content/117/24/13308.
4. *Warmer Air Means More Evaporation and Precipitation,* Climate Cent. (Sept. 6, 2017), https://www.climatecentral.org/climate-matters/hurricanes-climate-change-2017; Andreas F. Prein et al., *The Future Intensification of Hourly Precipitation Extremes,* 7 Nature Climate Change 48 (2017)*; see also* Jiabo Yin et al., *Large Increase in Global Storm Runoff Extremes Driven by Climate and Anthropogenic Changes,* 9 Nature Comm. 4389 (2018).
5. Sarah Almukhtar et al., *The Great Flood of 2019: A Complete Picture of a Slow-Motion Disaster,* N.Y. Times, Sept. 11, 2019, https://www.nytimes.com/interactive/2019/09/11/us/midwest-flooding.html.

Hurricanes have been getting more frequent and more intense since at least the 1970s, and that will continue.[6] While climate change is making hurricanes stronger, it can also slow their lateral movement along the coast and even make them almost stand still, continuously drawing water from the ocean like a massive pump and, as it rotates, dumping torrents of rain on a location for days on end.[7] That is what happened with Hurricane Harvey over the Houston area in 2017, Hurricane Dorian over the Bahamas in 2019, and Hurricane Ian over Florida in 2022.[8]

This chapter discusses the hazards posed to chemical and waste disposal facilities by extreme weather events that would be worsened as a result of climate change and how U.S. laws do (or do not) deal with these hazards. It then considers how the law would need to change to cope with what would happen to these facilities in a world beyond 2 degrees Celsius (2°C).

Current Law

Threats Realized

According to the U.S. Government Accountability Office (GAO): "Over 11,000 facilities across the nation make, use, or store extremely hazardous chemicals in amounts that could harm people, the environment or property if accidentally released."[9] Large concentrations of these facilities are in the areas of New Orleans (hit by Hurricanes Katrina and Rita in 2005, Laura in 2020, and Ida in 2021) and Houston (hit by Hurricane Harvey in 2017). The high winds and rushing waters from these storms caused multiple releases of chemicals into the air or water. Storage tanks buckled, toppled over, or were washed away; the floating roofs atop several tanks sank or were dislodged; pipelines burst.[10] A 14-inch pipeline owned by Williams Companies spewed anhydrous hydrogen chloride for several hours at La Porte, Texas, mixing

---

6. James P. Kossin et al., *Global Increase in Major Tropical Cyclone Exceedance Probability Over the Past Four Decades*, 117 Proc. Nat'l Acad. Sci. 11975-80 (2020), https://www.pnas.org/content/117/22/11975.
7. James P. Kossin, *A Global Slowdown of Tropical-cyclone Translation Speed*, 558 Nature 104 (2018).
8. Elena Shao et al., *How Hurricane Ian Became so Powerful*, N.Y. Times, Sept. 30, 2022, https://www.nytimes.com/interactive/2022/09/29/climate/hurricane-ian-florida-intensity.html; *Warmer Air Means More Evaporation and Precipitation*, Climate Cent. (Sept. 6, 2017), https://www.climatecentral.org/climate-matters/hurricanes-climate-change-2017.
9. U.S. Gov't Acct. Off., Chemical Accident Prevention: EPA Should Ensure Regulated Facilities Consider Risks From Climate Change 1 (2022) [hereinafter GAO Report].
10. Luis Augusto Godoy, *Performance of Storage Tanks in Oil Facilities Following Hurricanes Katrina and Rita*, 21 J. Performance Constructed Facilities 441 (Dec. 2007), https://ascelibrary.org/doi/10.1061/%28ASCE%290887-3828%282007%2921%3A6%28441%29; Tarika Powell, *Hurricane Harvey Highlights Fossil Fuel and Petrochemical Loopholes*, Sightline Inst. (Oct. 18, 2017), https://www.sightline.org/2017/10/18/hurricane-harvey-highlights-fossil-fuel-and-petrochemical-loopholes.

with moisture in the air to form hydrochloric acid and requiring neighboring residents to shelter in place.[11] At ExxonMobil's Olefins Plant in Baytown, Texas, some 457 million gallons of stormwater mixed with untreated wastewater, including oil and grease, and surged into an adjacent creek.[12] Hurricane Ida led to 55 reported oil spills, many of them from abandoned pipelines and offshore oil platforms near the Texas and Louisiana coastlines.[13] During Hurricane Harvey, chemical spills contributed to unhealthy levels of air pollution,[14] and a chemical plant owned by Arkema Inc. exploded after the failure of an essential cooling system. More than a dozen emergency responders were injured and carcinogens were released into the air. The company and two executives were indicted on criminal charges for reckless release of toxic chemicals, but the court found prosecutorial misconduct and incompetence and dismissed the charges; several civil lawsuits continue.[15] Bio-Lab, a plant near New Orleans, burned to the ground during Hurricane Laura and released chlorine that it was producing for swimming pools, leading to another shelter-in-place order.[16] Other hurricanes have caused severe dam-

11. Jordan Blum & Andrew Kragie, *Williams Cos. Says Its Pipeline Was Source of Chemical Leak During Harvey*, Hous. Chron., Aug. 29, 2017, https://www.chron.com/business/energy/article/Williams-Cos-claims-pipeline-that-caused-12123985.php; Frank Bajak & Lise Olsen, *Hurricane Harvey's Toxic Impact Deeper Than Public Told*, Associated Press, Mar. 23, 2018, https://apnews.com/article/environment-hurricanes-storms-tx-state-wire-north-america-e0ceae76d5894734b0041210a902218d.
12. Robin Kundis Craig, *Cleaning Up Our Toxic Coasts: A Precautionary and Human Health-Based Approach to Coastal Adaptation*, 36 Pace Envtl. L. Rev. 1, 12 (2018).
13. Blacki Migliozzi & Hiroko Tabuchi, *After Hurricane Ida, Offshore Platforms Sprout Dozens of Leaks*, N.Y. Times, Oct. 1, 2021, https://www.nytimes.com/interactive/2021/09/26/climate/ida-oil-spills.html; Ari Natter, *Ida Leaves Toxic Chemicals, Sewage Swirling in Its Wake*, Bloomberg, Sept. 2, 2021, https://www.bloomberg.com/news/articles/2021-09-02/ida-s-wake-leaves-toxic-chemicals-sewage-swirling-in-louisiana.
14. Hiroko Tabuchi et al., *Mixing Water and Poison*, WRAL News (Feb. 6, 2018), https://www.wral.com/mixing-water-and-poison/17318447; Ari Phillips, *Preparing for the Next Storm: Learning From the Man-Made Environmental Disasters That Followed Hurricane Harvey*, Envtl. Integrity Proj. 4 (2018).
15. Michelle Homer & Stephanie Whitfield, *Arkema Trial Ends When Judge Dismisses Last Two Criminal Charges, Ending Long Legal Drama*, KHOU-11 (Oct. 1, 2020), https://www.khou.com/article/news/local/arkema-executives-cleared-after-judge-dismisses-charges/285-aa7e62aa-6774-4c41-89f8-5ac78cbed561; Charles P. Pierce, *The Chemical Plant Explosion in Texas Is Not an Accident. It's the Result of Specific Choices*, Common Dreams (Aug. 31, 2017), https://www.commondreams.org/views/2017/08/31/chemical-plant-explosion-texas-not-accident-its-result-specific-choices; Lauren Mulhern, *The Arkema Chemical Facility Incident: How Regulation of Reactive Chemicals and Incorporation of Climate Change Risks in Emergency Response Planning Could Mitigate and Prevent Future Accidental Chemical Releases*, 30 Colo. Nat. Resources, Energy & Envtl. L. Rev. 143, 150 (2019); Prantil v. Arkema Inc., 986 F.3d 570 (5th Cir. 2021).
16. Kristen Mosbrucker, *Burned to the Ground After Hurricane Laura, a Chemical Plant Wants Millions in Tax Breaks to Rebuild*, Advocate, Apr. 26, 2021, https://www.theadvocate.com/baton_rouge/news/business/burned-to-the-ground-after-hurricane-laura-a-chemical-plant-wants-millions-in-tax-breaks/article_69cfc020-a6c5-11eb-926f-d7af9c910e5b.html#:~:text=A%20chemical%20fire%20at%20BioLab,tax%20breaks%20for%20the%20project.; Tristan Baurick, *Fire Fight at Hurricane Laura-Damaged Chemical Plant Near Lake Charles Continues Into 2nd Day*, NOLA.com (Aug. 28, 2020),

age to refineries and other petrochemical plants.[17] One 2022 headline was especially vivid: "Florida county sees spike in deadly infections caused by 'flesh-eating' bacteria after Hurricane Ian."[18] The bacteria in spilled sewage seems to worsen this problem.[19]

Clean Air Act

As part of a comprehensive amendment to the Clean Air Act (CAA) in 1990, Congress adopted a new program on prevention of accidental releases of hazardous chemicals from stationary sources, called the Section 112(r) program.[20] It provided that owners and operators of these sources "have a general duty . . . to identify hazards which may result from such releases using appropriate hazard assessment techniques, to design and maintain a safe facility taking such steps as are necessary to prevent releases, and to minimize the consequences of accidental releases which do occur."[21] Congress told the U.S. Environmental Protection Agency (EPA) to adopt regulations and to require facility owners and operators to prepare and implement "risk management plans."[22] These plans came to include "off-site consequences analyses,"[23] but in 1999, Congress, two years before the 9/11 attacks but already concerned that terrorists might use this information to find targets, amended the law to make it much more difficult for the public to obtain these analyses.[24] Then in 2013, the explosion of a fertilizer plant in the town of West, Texas, killed 15 people, and then-President Barack Obama directed EPA to strengthen the chemical safety rules. EPA issued stronger regulations in January 2017, one week before President Obama left office. The Trump Administration

---

https://www.nola.com/news/environment/fire-fight-at-hurricane-laura-damaged-chemical-plant-near-lake-charles-continues-into-2nd-day/article_6cca4e36-e969-11ea-b1ba-53ec47f5a71b.html.

17. Majid Ebad Sichani et al., *Hurricane Risk Assessment of Petroleum Infrastructure in a Changing Climate*, 6 Frontiers Built Env't 1 (2020), https://www.frontiersin.org/articles/10.3389/fbuil.2020.00104/full; Ana Maria Cruz et al., *Identifying Hurricane-Induced Hazardous Material Release Scenarios in a Petroleum Refinery*, 2 Nat. Hazards Rev. 203 (2001).
18. Emily Mae Czachor, *Florida County Sees Spike in Deadly Infections Caused by "Flesh-Eating" Bacteria After Hurricane Ian*, CBS News (Oct. 17, 2022), https://www.cbsnews.com/news/hurricane-ian-florida-flesh-eating-bacteria-infections-flooding-lee-county.
19. James W. Conrad & Valerie J. Harwood, *Sewage Promotes* Vibrio Vulnificus *Growth and Alters Gene Transcription in* Vibrio Vulnificus *CMCP6*, 10 Microbiol. Spectr. (2022), https://journals.asm.org/doi/epub/10.1128/spectrum.01913-21.
20. 42 U.S.C. §7412(r).
21. *Id.* §7412(r)(1).
22. *Id.* §7412(r)(7)(B)(ii).
23. *Id.* §7412(r)(7)(H).
24. Chemical Safety Information, Site Security, and Fuels Regulatory Relief Act, Pub. L. No. 106-40 (1999).

rescinded the stronger rules.[25] In February 2022, GAO found that about 3,200 facilities covered by the program are in locations that may be at risk from the effects of climate change—flooding, storm surge, wildfire and sea-level rise.[26] In August 2022, EPA proposed a new rule that followed the GAO's recommendation to explicitly require consideration of climate change in preparing their risk management plans.[27] Under existing regulations, the risk management plans must be updated every five years.[28]

Similar to the risk management plans required by EPA, which are designed to protect the environment and the community, the U.S. Occupational Safety and Health Administration (OSHA) requires "process safety management plans" to protect workers.[29] The plans required by EPA must consider the effects of a chemical release on the nearby community; the plans required by OSHA generally look only at the effects in the workplace, and there is no explicit requirement to consider climate change. Both EPA and OSHA require companies, in carrying out these plans, to follow recognized and generally accepted good engineering practices (RAGAGEP). The RAGAGEP are established by such nonprofit organizations as the American Society of Mechanical Engineers (ASME), the American National Standards Institute (ANSI), and the National Fire Protection Association.[30] Some of these practices implicitly consider various effects of climate change (such as flooding and wildfires), but few if any explicitly discuss climate change or the conditions it will cause in the future.[31] Changes to these practices could have a significant impact on industrial practices, as several consulting firms have gone into the business of auditing companies for their compliance with the RAGAGEP.[32]

---

25. Juliet Eilperin, *Trump Administration Scales Back Safety Rules Adopted After Deadly Chemical Explosion*, Wash. Post., Nov. 21, 2019, https://www.washingtonpost.com/climate-environment/2019/11/21/trump-reverses-safety-rules-adopted-after-deadly-chemical-explosion.
26. GAO Report, *supra* note 9, at 19; *see also* David Flores et al., Preventing "Double Disasters": How the U.S. Environmental Protection Agency Can Protect the Public From Hazardous Chemical Releases Worsened by Natural Disasters 6 (2021), https://www.ucsusa.org/sites/default/files/2021-07/preventing-double-disasters%20FINAL.pdf.
27. 87 Fed. Reg. 53556 (proposed Aug. 31, 2022) (codified at 40 C.F.R. §68).
28. 40 C.F.R. §68.36.
29. 29 C.F.R. §1910.119.
30. Thomas M. Galassi, *RAGAGEP, in Process Safety Management Enforcement*, OSHA (May 11, 2016), https://www.osha.gov/laws-regs/standardinterpretations/2016-05-11; *Complying with Process Safety Information (PSI) Resulting From New and Updated Recognized and Generally Accepted Good Engineering Practices (RAGAGEP)*, U.S. EPA (July 12, 2022), https://www.epa.gov/rmp/complying-process-safety-information-psi-resulting-new-and-updated-recognized-and-generally.
31. GAO Report, *supra* note 9, at 33.
32. *E.g.*, *What Is RAGAGEP and Why Does It Matter*, Saftey Consultants & Solutions Provider, https://scspng.com/blog/what-is-ragagep-and-why-does-it-matter; Ron Nichols & Dave Grattan, *Understanding Overpressure Scenarios and RAGAGEP*, AE Solutions (Jan. 26, 2016), https://www.aesolutions.com/post/understanding-overpressure-scenarios-and-ragagep.

As part of the same 1990 Amendments to the CAA, Congress created the Chemical Safety and Hazard Investigation Board (Board), modeled after the National Transportation Safety Board, to investigate accidents at chemical plants and recommend corrective measures.[33] It did not begin operations, however, until Congress finally funded it in 1998, and the Trump Administration tried without success to dismantle it. It has conducted useful investigations but with a very limited staff it has never been able to look into more than a small fraction of chemical plant incidents.[34] In 2020, the Board issued a short guidance document for how chemical plants should deal with extreme weather events, acknowledging an increase in flooding in recent years, but falling short of mentioning climate change.[35] An October 2022 report from EPA's Office of Inspector General found that the Board is still severely understaffed and has only two of five authorized members.[36]

Resource Conservation and Recovery Act

EPA has issued detailed regulations under the Resource Conservation and Recovery Act (RCRA) for the storage of certain chemicals,[37] but they apply only to hazardous *wastes*, not to useful products or to materials that will be used. Moreover, RCRA regulates the units that are most vulnerable to storms—above-ground storage tanks—only if they are holding oil or its products like gasoline.[38] A law enacted after the chemical disaster in Bhopal, India, in 1984, the Emergency Planning and Community Right-To-Know Act (EPCRA) of 1986, requires companies storing large quantities of certain hazardous substances (not only wastes) to report their inventories and make some other disclosures, but it does not impose substantive requirements that would help make sure the tanks do not leak or burst.[39] Many types of chemical storage facilities are unregulated, despite their safety hazards. This regulatory gap was on display in January 2014 in Charleston, West Virginia, when a large leak developed at a tank holding a chemical used as a cleansing agent in the coal mining industry. The liquid poured into the Elk River and rendered the water supply for 300,000 people undrinkable for weeks. The

33. 42 U.S.C. §7412(r)(6).
34. Ian Bennett, *Mitigating the Next Disaster: Strengthening the U.S. Chemical Safety and Hazard Investigation Board*, 34 Envtl. Claims J. 222 (2021).
35. U.S. Chem. Safety & Hazard Investigation Bd., 2020 Hurricane Season: Guidance for Chemical Plants During Extreme Weather Events (2020).
36. U.S. EPA, Fiscal Year 2023 U.S. Chemical Safety and Hazard Investigation Board Management Challenges (2022).
37. 40 C.F.R. pt. 264.
38. *Id.* pt. 112.
39. 42 U.S.C. §11022.

spill occurred during a spell of record low temperatures caused by a "polar vortex" (a phenomenon that some link to climate change),[40] causing "frost heaving" that deformed the ground surface on which the tank was sitting. Though the tank was corroded, it was not subject to EPA's tank regulations because it contained a useful product, not waste or oil. The company and some of its managers were prosecuted criminally and fined, not because the tank was substandard, but because the company did not have a permit under the Clean Water Act (CWA) to discharge into the river and had not taken adequate precautions to prevent a spill.[41] After this incident, West Virginia adopted legislation regulating above-ground storage tanks.

EPA has promulgated very detailed regulations under RCRA for hazardous waste disposal facilities. These include special precautions for facilities sited in a 100-year floodplain.[42] Since rising seas and more intense storms mean that many more areas will have that level of flood risk, those areas will encompass many more facilities. Based on past experience, it is not clear that their operators will be taking the necessary precautions.[43]

Clean Water Act

As enacted in 1972, the CWA requires EPA to "establish procedures, methods, and equipment and other requirements for equipment to prevent discharges of oil and hazardous substances."[44] In 1973, EPA issued standards for the storage of oil.[45] The current regulations require oil storage facilities to have Spill Prevention Control and Countermeasure (SPCC) plans.[46] These plans are very elaborate and no doubt have greatly reduced the amount of oil that gets into the environment, but they are required only for oil. In 2015, several environmental groups sued EPA to compel it to issue similar regulations for hazardous substances, as the CWA requires. EPA agreed in a 2016 consent decree to begin a rulemaking to correct this gap, but the Trump

40. Judah Cohen et al., *Linking Arctic Variability and Change with Extreme Winter Weather in the United States*, 373 SCIENCE 1116 (2021).
41. CHEM. SAFETY AND HAZARD INVESTIGATION BD., INVESTIGATION REPORT: CHEMICAL SPILL CONTAMINATES PUBLIC WATER SUPPLY IN CHARLESTON, WEST VIRGINIA (2017); *Freedom Industries and Former Freedom Industries Plant Manager Sentenced for Roles in Chemical Spill*, U.S. DEP'T OF JUSTICE (Feb. 1, 2016), https://www.justice.gov/usao-sdwv/pr/freedom-industries-and-former-freedom-industries-plant-manager-sentenced-roles-chemical.
42. 40 C.F.R. §264.18(b).
43. Timothy J. Flynn et al., *Implications of Sea Level Rise for Hazardous Waste Sites in Coastal Floodplains*, *in* GREENHOUSE EFFECTS AND SEA-LEVEL RISE: A CHALLENGE FOR THIS GENERATION 206 (M.C. Barth & J.G. Titus eds., 1984).
44. 33 U.S.C. §1321(j)(1)(C).
45. 38 Fed. Reg. 34165 (Dec. 11, 1973).
46. 33 C.F.R. §112.3.

Administration then concluded that new rules were not necessary.[47] The Biden Administration has not indicated if it will take a different position.

In 2019, the Natural Resources Defense Council and others sued EPA under a related provision of the CWA (added by the Oil Pollution Act (OPA) of 1990) that required the president to issue regulations requiring owners or operators of certain onshore facilities to prepare plans "for responding, to the maximum extent practicable, to a worst case discharge, and to a substantial threat of such a discharge, of oil or a hazardous substance."[48] The parties entered into a consent decree in March 2020 requiring EPA to propose regulations complying with this requirement within two years, and in March 2024, EPA issued its final rule on "Clean Water Act Hazardous Substance Worst Case Discharge Planning."[49] EPA indicated that climate change could cause or worsen these worst-case events and should be considered in the plans.

Even when SPCC plans are required, they often ignore the perils that climate change poses to tanks that hold large amounts of oil. In 2016, the Conservation Law Foundation sued ExxonMobil alleging that its oil tank farm on the Mystic River near Boston is not prepared for storm surge or other possible impacts of climate change, in violation of the CWA and RCRA. The same group followed up with similar suits against Gulf Oil and Shell Oil concerning different tank farms. These cases are in active litigation.[50]

Another kind of litigation—that under tort law—does little to induce greater care in protecting chemical facilities from climate risks. A damaging hurricane like Katrina or Harvey can cause multiple spills, leading to the intermingling of chemicals in a toxic soup and making it impossible to prove what facility caused what injury.[51] Unless stronger standards are imposed, in many cases plaintiffs will also have difficulty proving that the companies were negligent, which would be necessary for most of these suits to succeed.[52]

---

47. *Final Action on Clean Water Act Hazardous Substance Spill Prevention*, U.S. EPA (2022), https://www.epa.gov/rulemaking-preventing-hazardous-substance-spills/final-action-clean-water-act-hazardous-substances; Clean Water Act Hazardous Substances Spill Prevention, 84 Fed. Reg. 46100 (Sept. 3, 2019) (codified at 40 C.F.R. §151); Noah M. Sachs, *Toxic Floodwaters: Strengthening the Chemical Safety Regime for the Climate Change Era*, 46 Colum. J. Envtl. L. 73, 109-112 (2020).
48. 33 U.S.C. §1321(j)(5)(A)(i).
49. Clean Water Act Hazardous Substance Worst-Case Discharge Planning, 89 Fed. Reg. 21924 (Mar. 28, 2024) (codified at 40 C.F.R. pts. 188, 300).
50. *See* Conservation Law Found. v. Exxon Mobil Corp., 3 F.4th 61 (1st Cir. 2021); Conservation Law Found. v. Shell Oil Co., 2022 U.S. Dist. LEXIS 167377 (D. Conn. Sept. 16, 2022).
51. Mary Fox et al., *Potential for Chemical Mixture Exposures and Health Risks in New Orleans Post-Hurricane Katrina*, 15 Hum. & Ecological Risk Assessment 831 (2009), https://www.tandfonline.com/doi/abs/10.1080/10807030903051309?journalCode=bher20.
52. *See generally* Sachs, *supra* note 47.

Comprehensive Environmental Response, Compensation, and Liability Act

The best-known program for contaminated sites that are no longer active (as opposed to operating factories) is under the Comprehensive Environmental Response, Compensation, and Liability Act (CERCLA). EPA places the worst sites on its national priorities list (NPL); these are commonly called Superfund sites. These sites are disproportionately located in or near communities of color.[53] After listing, each site undergoes an elaborate process called the remedial investigation and feasibility study, leading to EPA's selection of a way to address the contamination, called a "remedy." Some common remedies include digging up the material and hauling it to a licensed disposal site; leaving it in place and placing an impervious cover over it; or pumping out contaminated groundwater, treating it, and putting it back in the ground. Of the Superfund sites not on federal property, at least 60% (945 of 1,571) are in locations that under current conditions are vulnerable to flooding, storm surge, wildfires, or sea-level rise.[54] Even more sites will be at risk as climate conditions worsen.

Extreme storms do not necessarily release contaminants from Superfund sites. An EPA study of three 2017 hurricanes (Harvey, Irma, and Maria) found that 252 Superfund or similar sites were exposed to tropical force winds or higher and 63 experienced flooding, but only 16 reported minor damage.[55] One that was affected was the San Jacinto Waste Pits, where Hurricane Harvey damaged a temporary protective cap on a pit of toxic sludge, exposing waste with high levels of dioxins and washing some of it down-

53. David E. Kramar, *A Spatially Informed Analysis of Environmental Justice: Analyzing the Effects of Gerrymandering and the Proximity of Minority Populations to U.S. Superfund Sites*, 11 Envtl. Just. 29 (2018); Jacob Carter & Casey Kalman, A Toxic Relationship: Extreme Coastal Flooding and Superfund Sites 6-7 (2020); U.S. EPA, Population Surrounding 1,857 Superfund Remedial Sites (2020), https://www.epa.gov/sites/default/files/2015-09/documents/webpopulationrsuperfundsites9.28.15.pdf.

54. U.S. Government Accounting Off. (GAO), Superfund: EPA Should Take Additional Actions to Manage Risks From Climate Change 18 (2019).

55. U.S. EPA, Evaluation of Remedy Resilience at Superfund NPL and SAA Sites (2018), https://www.epa.gov/sites/default/files/2019-02/documents/evaluation-of-remedy-resilience-at-superfund-npl-and-saa-sites.pdf.

river.[56] Hurricane Maria stirred up already high levels of polychlorinated biphenyls (PCBs) in Guanica Bay, Puerto Rico.[57]

EPA has identified many ways that a changing climate can worsen the already toxic conditions at contaminated sites. For example, it can transport pollution off-site; mobilize formerly stable contaminants, especially those in sediments at the bottom of bodies of water; damage the often thin caps that cover contaminants that are left in place; and make contaminants more volatile with higher temperatures.[58] Climate change can also increase erosion, raise or lower groundwater levels, flood drainage systems beyond their design conditions, and force soil vapor to migrate, further complicating Superfund remedies.[59]

In 2021, EPA suggested that its officials implementing CERCLA "should assess the vulnerability of a remedial action's components, including its associated site infrastructure and evaluate whether the long-term integrity of a selected remedy may be impaired by adverse effects of climate change," and that "intensities and frequencies of extreme weather events over a time frame corresponding to a remedy's anticipated duration" should be considered.[60] The remedies recently chosen for some sites do include protections against extreme flooding.[61]

EPA has legal options if it finds that climate change has rendered a site remedy inadequate. CERCLA provides that if any contaminants remain at

56. Kiah Collier, *EPA: Hurricane Harvey Compromised Cap on Toxic Waste Site*, Tex. Trib., Sept. 29, 2017, https://www.texastribune.org/2017/09/29/epa-hurricane-harvey-compromised-caps-toxic-waste-site/#:~:text=The%20Environmental%20Protection%20Agency%20confirmed,exposing%20%E2%80%9Cunderlying%20waste%20material.%E2%80%9D.; David Hasemyer & Lise Olsen, *Battered, Flooded and Submerged: Many Superfund Sites Are Dangerously Threatened by Climate Change*, Inside Climate News (Sept. 24, 2020), https://insideclimatenews.org/news/24092020/climate-change-epa-superfund-sites-hurricanes-floods-fires-sea-level-rise.
57. Christopher Flavelle, *"Toxic Stew" Stirred Up by Disasters Poses Long-Term Danger, New Findings Show*, N.Y. Times, July 15, 2019, https://www.nytimes.com/2019/07/15/climate/flooding-chemicals-health-research.html.
58. U.S. EPA, Climate Adaptation Action Plan 5-6 (2021); U.S. EPA, Climate Change Adaptation Implementation Plan 6 (2014); U.S. EPA, Climate Change Adaptation Technical Fact Sheet: Contaminated Sediment Remedies (2015).
59. ASTSWMO Investigation & Remedy Selection Focus Grp., Planning for Resiliency and Sustainability in a Changing Climate 12-13, 18, 24-25 (2022), https://astswmo.org/files/Policies_and_Publications/CERCLA_and_Brownfields/2022-04-Planning-for-Resiliency-and-Sustainability-in-a-Changing-Climate.pdf; U.S. EPA, Climate Change Adaptation Technical Fact Sheet: Groundwater Remediation Systems (2013).
60. Memorandum from Larry Douchand, Dir., Office of Superfund Remediation & Tech. Innovation on Consideration of Climate Resilience in the Superfund Cleanup Process for Non-Federal National Priorities List Sites (June 30, 2021), https://semspub.epa.gov/work/HQ/100002993.pdf; *see also Superfund Climate Resilience*, U.S. EPA, https://www.epa.gov/superfund/superfund-climate-resilience (Feb. 20, 2023); Emily Russell, *Superfund and Climate Change: Lessons From Hurricane Sandy*, 28 Nat. Resources & Env't 3 (2014).
61. *American Cyanamid Superfund Site Reduces Climate Disclosure*, U.S. EPA (May 12, 2022), https://www.epa.gov/arc-x/american-cyanamid-superfund-site-reduces-climate-exposure.

the site, EPA must review the remedial action at least every five years "to assure that human health and the environment are being protected," and if they are not, EPA must take action.[62] Most cleanups of Superfund sites are carried out through consent decrees with the potentially responsible parties, and EPA's model consent decree allows EPA to compel further action at closed sites if required by the circumstances.[63] Therefore, if EPA concludes that the remedy at a Superfund site is vulnerable to climate change, it has considerable authority to require a change, though in practice it has seldom done so.[64] EPA could also go further and amend the regulation that governs the CERCLA cleanup process, called the national contingency plan (NCP), to require more systematic consideration of climate change when identifying sites to be listed as Superfund sites, selecting the remedy, and monitoring its effectiveness.[65]

EPA has designated certain per- and polyfluorinated substances chemicals (PFAS) as hazardous substances under CERCLA and is considering listing more.[66] This could require a new look at the selected remedies at many Superfund sites, and could provide a good occasion for also looking at the storm vulnerability of those sites.

States could secure more stringent cleanups of CERCLA sites by amending their coastal management plans under the federal Coastal Zone Management Act to mandate more climate-resilient cleanups, making these requirements applicable or relevant and appropriate requirements (ARARs) that must be met in CERCLA cleanups.[67]

Related Threats and Applicable Laws

Many hazardous liquid gases are carried by pipelines. In 2022, the Pipeline and Hazardous Materials Safety Administration (PHMSA), part of the U.S.

---

62. 42 U.S.C. §9621(c).
63. Katrina Fischer Kuh, *Climate Change and CERCLA Remedies: Adaptation Strategies for Contaminated Sediment Sites*, 2 Seattle J. Envtl. L. 61, 75-76 (2012); Gregory E. Wannier, *Infrastructure*, *in* The Law of Adaptation to Climate Change 198 (Michael B. Gerrard & Katrina Fischer Kuh eds., 2012).
64. Ozzy Rodriguez, *Adapting Superfund Remedial Plans for Climate Change*, Env't & Energy L. Prog. (May 12, 2021), https://eelp.law.harvard.edu/2021/03/adapting-superfund-remedial-plans-for-climate-change/#_ftnref24.
65. *See* Lindsey Dundas, *CERCLA: It's Time to Prioritize Climate Threats*, 91 U. Colo. L. Rev. 283 (2020).
66. U.S. EPA, *Designation of PFOA and PFOS as hazardous substances under CERLCA Release Reporting Requirements Factsheet*, https://www.epa.gov/epcra/designation-pfoa-and-pfos-hazardous-substances-under-cercla-release-reporting-requirements (last updated May 13, 2024).
67. Grace Pezzeminti, *Keeping Superfund Sites Above Water: Using State Coastal Management Plans to Prevent Storm Event Hazardous Waste Releases*, 13 Geo. Wash. J. Energy & Envtl. L. 142 (2022).

Department of Transportation (DOT), issued an advisory bulletin warning that

> changing weather patterns due to climate change, including increased rainfall and higher temperatures, may impact soil stability [posing] a threat to the integrity of pipeline facilities if those threats are not identified and mitigated. Owners and operators should consider monitoring geological and environmental conditions, including changing weather patterns, in proximity to their facilities.[68]

PHMSA documented numerous instances where earth movement had ruptured pipelines and caused the release of their often hazardous contents.[69]

One seldom-recognized risk arises if a site is downstream of a dam that is holding back a large volume of water. One investigation identified 81 dams in 24 states that if they failed, could flood a major toxic waste site and potentially spread its contamination.[70] The design of remedies at Superfund sites does not tend to consider this risk. Moreover, many dams are themselves holding back not only water, but also piles of contaminated sediment that have accumulated over the years; failure or removal of the dam would also release this contamination downstream.[71] For example, in 1973, a dam on the Hudson River was intentionally removed by its owner; a large quantity of sediment, heavily contaminated with PCBs from General Electric (GE) factories upstream, was washed downstream, the Hudson River became a Superfund site, and GE has spent about $1.6 billion cleaning it up.[72] Around 1,700 dams have been identified in 44 states and Puerto Rico that are rated in poor or unsatisfactory condition and that could cause loss of life if they

---

68. *Pipeline Safety: Potential for Damage to Pipeline Facilities Caused by Earth Movement and Other Geological Hazards*, 87 Fed. Reg. 33576 (June 2, 2022).
69. *Id.* at 33577.
70. James Dinneen & Alexander Kennedy, *Below Aging U.S. Dams, a Potential Toxic Calamity*, SALON (June 12, 2021), https://www.salon.com/2021/06/12/below-aging-us-dams-a-potential-toxic-calamity_partner/#:~:text=In%202019%2C%20roughly%2017%20percent,due%20to%20new%20downstream%20development.
71. Michael Scott, *Gorge Dam's Toxic Stew Is Cuyahoga River's Biggest Barrier to Continued Improvement*, CLEVELAND.COM (June 16, 2019), https://www.cleveland.com/news/2019/06/gorge-dams-toxic-stew-is-cuyahoga-rivers-biggest-barrier-to-continued-improvement.html#:~:text=AKRON%2C%20Ohio%20%E2%80%93%20The%20biggest%20barrier,heavy%20metals%2C%20oil%20and%20grease; Jeff Hull, *At Toxic Montana Dam, a River Now Runs Through It*, REUTERS (Mar. 28, 2008), https://www.reuters.com/article/us-dam/at-toxic-montana-dam-a-river-now-runs-through-it-idUSN2834669620080329; *State Warns Northern California Dam Holding Back Arsenic-Contaminated Tailings May Collapse This Winter*, ASSOCIATED PRESS (Aug. 15, 2016).
72. *This Is Today's Hudson: How We Got Here*, GEN. ELEC., https://hudsondredging.com/about#:~:text=In%201973%2C%20the%20owner%20of,a%20Superfund%20site%20in%201984; Jesse McKinley, *G.E. Spent Years Cleanup Up the Hudson. Was It Enough?*, N.Y. TIMES, Sept. 8, 2016, https://www.nytimes.com/2016/09/09/nyregion/general-electric-pcbs-hudson-river.html.

failed.[73] As a further matter, these figures tend to reflect only the larger dams; there are around 2.5 million smaller "nonjurisdictional" dams, many of them may also be vulnerable to extreme weather events, and of those, an unknown number are holding back contaminated sediment.[74]

Many dams and impoundments hold the ash that is generated in huge quantities by coal-fired power plants. About 185 pounds of coal ash are generated for each megawatt hour of electricity from a coal plant.[75] This ash, which often contains arsenic, mercury, chromium, and other contaminants,[76] is almost always kept in the open air without any cover. Many severe storms have washed over coal ash impoundments and swept the ash into nearby land or streams.[77] In December 2008, the dike holding up an impoundment of ash in Kingston, Tennessee, from Tennessee Valley Authority coal plants failed (not due to severe weather), releasing 5.4 million cubic yards of coal ash sludge. This disaster went from a massive cleanup operation to multiple lawsuits, involving among others, nearby property owners and workers who became sick performing the cleanup.[78] Partly in reaction to this incident, in 2015, the Obama Administration issued regulations strengthening rules on the disposal of coal ash, but did not list it as a hazardous waste under RCRA, which might have required the impoundments to be lined at the bottom and covered on top.[79] The Trump Administration attempted to weaken those rules, but those efforts were struck down in court.[80] In August 2022,

73. David A. Lieb et al., *At Least 1,680 Dams Across the U.S. Pose Potential Risk*, Associated Press (Nov. 11, 2019), https://apnews.com/article/ne-state-wire-us-news-ap-top-news-sc-state-wire-dams-f5f09a300d394900a1a88362238dbf77#:~:text=An%20Associated%20Press%20investigation%20has,result%20in%20people%20being%20killed.

74. Peter K. Brewitt & Chelsea L.M. Colwyn, *Little Dams, Big Problems: The Legal and Policy Issues of Nonjurisdictional Dams*, 7 WIREs Water 1 (2019), https://doi.org/10.1002/wat2.1393.

75. Bill Nussey, *Straight Facts on the Environmental Impact of Coal*, Freeing Energy (June 5, 2020), https://www.freeingenergy.com/environmental-impact-coal-water-co2-so2-mercury-pollution.

76. Amrika Deonarine et al., Trace Elements in Coal Ash (2015).

77. Gavin Bade, *Hurricane Florence Triggers Coal Ash Spill, Cuts Power to Millions*, Utility Dive (Sept. 17, 2018), utilitydive.com/news/hurricane-florence-triggers-coal-ash-spill-cuts-power-to-millions/532491; James Bruggers, *In Hurricane Florence's Path: Giant Toxic Coal Ash Piles*, Inside Climate News (Sept. 12, 2018), https://insideclimatenews.org/news/12092018/toxic-coal-ash-ponds-hurricane-florence-flood-collapse-risk-north-carolina-virginia/#:~:text=Dozens%20of%20toxic%20coal%20ash,risk%20of%20spills%20or%20collapsing; Zack Colman, *The Toxic Waste Threat that Climate Change Is Making Worse*, Politico (Aug. 26, 2019), https://www.politico.com/story/2019/08/26/toxic-waste-climate-change-worse-1672998#:~:text=More%20than%20100%20storage%20sites,of%20government%20and%20industry%20data.

78. *See* Adkisson v. Jacobs Eng'g Grp., 35 F.4th 421 (6th Cir. 2022); Mays v. Tenn. Valley Auth., 699 F. Supp. 2d 991 (E.D. Tenn. 2010).

79. *See* Environmental Integrity Proj. & Earthjustice, Poisonous Coverup: The Widespread Failure of the Power Industry to Clean Up Coal Ash Dumps (2022), https://environmentalintegrity.org/wp-content/uploads/2022/10/Poisonous-Coverup-11.03.22.pdf.

80. Utility Solid Waste Activities Grp. v. EPA, 901 F.3d 414 (D.C. Cir. 2018); Katherine Clements, *The Coal Ash Rule Trilogy Spanning Obama, Trump, and the D.C. Circuit*, Env't & Energy L. Prog.

Earthjustice brought a lawsuit against EPA seeking stronger rules on coal ash.[81] According to Earthjustice, 172 coal ash impoundments fall within the Federal Emergency Management Agency's 100-year floodplains.[82]

Flooding also afflicts another subject of outdoor disposal—hog waste. This occurs especially in Iowa and North Carolina, each of which has several million hogs. The waste from concentrated animal feeding operations (CAFOs) is flushed into uncovered and unlined lagoons (as they're called) where bacteria partially break it down. Then it is sprayed onto cropland, causing horrific odors and serious health problems for those living nearby,[83] who in North Carolina are disproportionately African American.[84] Hurricanes and other severe storms have flooded these lagoons, spreading the foul mix over large areas and drowning thousands or tens of thousands of hogs and millions of chickens, which are then landfilled or incinerated![85] These lagoons are regulated at the state rather than the federal level, and North Carolina, at least, has been notoriously lax. In 2000, Smithfield Foods, the world's leading pork producer, entered into an agreement with the North Carolina attorney general to fund a research program to find more environmentally sound methods of handling hog waste, but the results were modest.[86] In 2018, Smithfield

(Jan. 28, 2020), https://eelp.law.harvard.edu/2020/01/the-coal-ash-rule-trilogy-spanning-obama-trump-and-the-d-c-circuit/#_ftn20.

81. Complaint for Declaratory and Injunctive Relief, Statewide Org. for Cmty. Empowerment v. EPA, No. 1:22-cv-02562 (D.D.C. Aug. 25, 2022), https://earthjustice.org/wp-content/uploads/2022-08-25_complaint.pdf; *see also* Env't Integrity Proj. & Earthjustice, *supra* note 79.

82. Joshua Irvine, *Rising Waters, Sinking Feeling: From the Great Lakes to the Ohio River, Climate Change Puts Coal Ash Impoundments at Risk*, Great Lakes Now (Aug. 26, 2022), https://www.greatlakesnow.org/2022/08/climate-change-puts-coal-ash-impoundments-at-risk.

83. The Story of Hog Manure, Sierra Club Iowa Chapter, https://www.sierraclub.org/sites/default/files/sce/iowa-chapter/Ag-CAFOs/ManureStory.pdf.

84. Julia Kravchenko et al., *Mortality and Health Outcomes in North Carolina Communities Located in Close Proximity to Hog Concentrated Animal Feeding Operation*, 79 N.C. Med. J. 278 (2018); *see also* Sacoby M. Wilson et al., *Environmental Injustice and the Mississippi Hog Industry*, 110 Env't Health Persp. 195 (2002), https://www.jstor.org/stable/3455053.

85. Kendra Pierre-Louis, *Lagoons of Pig Waste Are Overflowing After Florence. Yes, That's as Nasty as It Sounds*, N.Y. Times, Sept. 19, 2018, https://www.nytimes.com/2018/09/19/climate/florence-hog-farms.html; *Hurricane Florence: Carolina Pig Waste Lagoons Overflow*, BBC (Sept. 19, 2018), https://www.bbc.com/news/world-us-canada-45578485; Jennifer Lu, *During a Hurricane, Where Does All the Pig Poop Go? Into Your Water*, Guardian, Sept. 25, 2018; Michael Graff, *Millions of Dead Chickens and Pigs Found in Hurricane Floods*, Guardian (Sept. 22, 2018), https://www.theguardian.com/environment/2018/sep/21/hurricane-florence-flooding-north-carolina; Kelli Bender, *3.4 Million Chickens, Thousands of Pigs Dead in North Carolina Following Hurricane Florence*, People (Sept. 19, 2018), https://people.com/pets/3-million-chickens-thousands-of-pigs-dead-hurricane-florence; Jedediah Purdy, *The Unequal Distribution of Catastrophe in North Carolina*, New Yorker (Sept. 18, 2018), https://www.newyorker.com/news/our-columnists/the-unequal-distribution-of-catastrophe-in-north-carolina; Associated Press, *Iowa Farms, Cities Battling Water, Stench*, L.A. Daily News, Aug. 29, 2017, https://www.dailynews.com/2008/06/17/iowa-farms-cities-battling-water-stench.

86. D. Lee Miller & Ryke Longest, *Reconciling Environmental Justice With Climate Change Mitigation: A Case Study of NC Swine CAFOs*, 21 Vt. J. Envtl. L. 523 (2020); Talia Buford, *A Hog Waste Agreement Lacked Teeth, and Some North Carolinians Say They're Left to Suffer*, Politico (Nov. 23, 2018).

announced plans to cover most of its hog lagoons to protect them from rain and to capture the methane gas the waste generates for sale to generate energy (though that creates its own environmental problems).[87] Smithfield is owned by a Chinese company, and a considerable amount of pork is exported from North Carolina to China, where some of the environmental regulations of this industry are (surprisingly) tighter.[88] After years of complaints, in 2022, EPA launched a civil rights investigation into whether North Carolina's regulation of aspects of these operations involve environmental racism.[89]

Another important kind of waste is municipal solid waste (MSW)—household garbage. In the United States, about one-half of it—146 million tons a year—goes to landfills.[90] There are now about 1,900 MSW landfills operating in the continental U.S. and many more that are no longer operating (usually because they are full).[91] A significant portion of these are located near a shoreline or river, or in a floodplain. One study found that in Florida, about 1,099 landfills (active or inactive) are within the present 100-year coastal flood zone, and this number will rise considerably as that zone expands.[92]

Unlike hazardous waste landfills, MSW landfills are subject to few federal rules and are mostly under state or local control. Until the enactment of RCRA in 1976 and EPA's adoption of its implementing regulations in 1980, there was little legal distinction between hazardous waste and MSW, and much of what we now think of as hazardous waste went to MSW landfills. That was lawful unless local public health laws provided otherwise. These

---

87. Greg Barnes, *Smithfield Announces Plans to Cover Hog Lagoons, Produce Renewable Energy*, N.C. Health News (Oct. 29, 2018), https://www.northcarolinahealthnews.org/2018/10/29/plans-to-cover-hog-lagoons; Michael Sainato & Chelsea Skojec, *The North Carolina Hog Industry's Answer to Pollution: A $500m Pipeline Project*, Guardian, Dec. 11, 2020, https://www.theguardian.com/us-news/2020/dec/11/north-carolina-hog-industry-lagoons-pipeline#:~:text=The%20product%2C%20called%20biogas%2C%20is,project%20will%20worsen%20the%20problem.

88. Doug Block Clark, *Why Is China Treating North Carolina Like the Developing World?* Rolling Stone (Mar. 19, 2018), https://www.rollingstone.com/politics/politics-news/why-is-china-treating-north-carolina-like-the-developing-world-122892; Corban Addison, Wastelands: The True Story of Farm Country on Trial 64-67 (2022).

89. Aman Azhar, *EPA to Probe Whether North Carolina's Permitting of Biogas From Swine Feeding Operations Violates Civil Rights of Nearby Neighborhoods*, Inside Climate News (Jan. 25, 2022), https://insideclimatenews.org/news/25012022/epa-north-carolina-cafo-biogas-permit/#:~:text=The%20EPA%20has%20decided%20to,and%20Latinos%20who%20live%20nearby.

90. *National Overview: Facts and Figures on Materials, Wastes and Recycling*, U.S. EPA (Dec. 3, 2022), https://www.epa.gov/facts-and-figures-about-materials-waste-and-recycling/national-overview-facts-and-figures-materials#13-14Trends.

91. *Municipal Solid Waste Landfills*, U.S. EPA, https://www.epa.gov/landfills/municipal-solid-waste-landfills#:~:text=A%20municipal%20solid%20waste%20landfill%20(MSWLF)%20is%20a%20discrete%20area,and%20industrial%20nonhazardous%20solid%20waste (Apr. 25, 2022).

92. Robert J. Nicholls, *Coastal Landfills and Rising Sea Levels: A Challenge for the 21st Century*, 8 Frontiers Marine Sci. 1, 14 (2021).

landfills were often sited in low-lying areas, and most of them lacked such modern systems as leachate collection, methane capture, and impervious liners at the bottom and caps on top. When it rained, the water seeped through, picked up contaminants from the waste, and leaked nasty liquid into the groundwater below or the nearby streams. After the enactment of CERCLA in 1980, many of them became Superfund sites. Today more than 250 of the landfills that received both hazardous waste and MSW are on the NPL—about 23% of all sites on that list.[93]

These landfills were not sited or designed with sea-level rise or extreme flooding in mind, and their often primitive engineering means they are vulnerable to extreme weather. They are typically covered with soil and vegetation, and unless they are well maintained, the soil can erode or be washed away, exposing the waste. Rising groundwater—especially if salty—can eat away at whatever liners are in place.[94] If near the shore, some long-buried waste is uncovered and carried away by the waves; this "zombie garbage," as it has been called, adds to the plastics in the ocean.[95] Some landfills are so buoyant that if the groundwater below them rises and is not continually pumped out (into perpetuity, one presumes), they can creep upward, breaking their covers, liners, and piping.[96]

So far, the discussion has concerned how climate change affects waste that exists anyway. But the storms and wildfires that are worsened by climate change can themselves create very large volumes of waste: the debris left behind. The destroyed buildings, toppled trees, and everything else will block roads and cause health and safety hazards that need to be quickly removed. Hurricane Harvey created about 25 million cubic yards of debris, which is two-thirds of the total amount of MSW that Houston would ordinarily generate in a year.[97] The usual systems could not handle that surge of

93. *Municipal Superfund Liability*, FindLaw (Mar. 26, 2008), https://corporate.findlaw.com/law-library/municipal-superfund-liability.html.

94. Flynn et al., *supra* note 43; Xunchang Fei et al., *Climate Change Affects Land-disposed Waste*, 11 Nature Climate Change 1004 (2021); Stephen Stock et al., *Toxins Long Buried May Surface as Groundwater Rises*, NBC Bay Area (Nov. 5, 2021), https://www.nbcbayarea.com/investigations/toxins-long-buried-may-surface-as-groundwater-rises/2718842.

95. Michael Allen, *The Future Is Full of Zombie Garbage*, Hakai Mag. (Dec. 15, 2021), https://hakaimagazine.com/news/the-future-is-full-of-zombie-garbage; Tarek Bazley, *Climate Change Erosion Feeding Deep Ocean Trash Dump*, Aljazeera (Apr. 15, 2019), https://www.aljazeera.com/news/2019/4/15/climate-change-erosion-feeding-deep-ocean-trash-dump.

96. Ozge Kaplan et al., Vulnerability of Waste Infrastructure to Climate Induced Impacts in Coastal Communities 30 (2019).

97. Testimony of Texas Commission on Environmental Quality Chairman Bryan W. Shaw, Ph.D., P.E. to the U.S. Senate Comm. on Env't & Public Works, Subcomm. on Superfund, Waste Management, & Regulatory Oversight 2 (Dec. 6, 2017) [hereinafter Testimony of Shaw] (available at https://www.epw.senate.gov/public/_cache/files/5/a/5ab74817-e4b0-4faa-bf51-918ff4d522d0/9AF7983F9000B93EB511829185A16E74.shaw-testimony-12.06.2017.pdf).

waste. The state suspended many of its rules for waste handling and disposal, set up 228 temporary debris management sites, allowed 25 landfills to exceed their permit limits, burned vegetative debris in special incinerators, and used employees and contractors to haul tens of thousands of loads in trucks.[98] Hurricane Katrina generated about four times that much debris, and its removal and disposal cost $3.7 billion.[99] Wildfires create similar mounds of debris (though, of course, they have been pre-incinerated)[100] and, depending on what they burn, can spew dangerous levels of toxins into the air.[101]

The orderly and lawful demolition of a building involves the careful removal of asbestos-containing material, the draining of ozone-depleting substances from refrigerators, and the special handling and disposal of other hazardous materials. After a disaster, these niceties may not be possible; EPA and other agencies grant emergency exemptions or look the other way, and the landfills where the debris is taken may become laden with yet more toxic material.[102] The debris often goes to old, unlined landfills that had been closed but are reactivated for this purpose. In many places these landfills are disproportionately located in disadvantaged communities.[103]

One cubic yard of uncompacted MSW weighs about 225 pounds. *See* N.H. Dep't of Env't Servs., Volume-to-Weight Conversion Factors, https://www.des.nh.gov/sites/g/files/ehbemt341/files/documents/vol-to-weight-conversion.pdf. Houston generates about 4.3 million tons of MSW per year. *See* David S. Yanke, A Municipal Solid Waste Generation and Diversion Forecast for the City of Houston 9 (2019), https://houstontx.gov/solidwaste/longrange/pdf/2019_4_25.pdf. That works out to 38.27 million cubic yards.

98. Testimony of Shaw, *supra* note 97, at 3; John Sharp, Eye of the Storm: Report of the Governor's Commission to Rebuild Texas 72-73 (2018).

99. U.S. EPA, Planning for Natural Disaster Debris 1 (2019).

100. Emily C. Dooley, *Hauling Away California Fire Rubble to Take a Year, Cost Billions*, Bloomberg Law (Dec. 7, 2018), https://news.bloomberglaw.com/environment-and-energy/hauling-away-california-fire-rubble-to-take-a-year-cost-billions; Sarah Maslin Nir, *In California, Houses Burned, So Did the Toxic Substances They Contained*, N.Y. Times, Nov. 29, 2018, https://www.nytimes.com/2018/11/29/us/california-fire-chemicals.html; Dale Kasler, *"Toxic-Laden Stuff." Will Anyone Take the Camp Fire Debris From Paradise?* Sacramento Bee, Dec. 31, 2018.

101. Matt Vasilogambros, *Proliferating Wildfires Poison Public Health Across the Country*, Pew (Oct. 17, 2022), https://www.pewtrusts.org/en/research-and-analysis/blogs/stateline/2022/10/17/proliferating-wildfires-poison-public-health-across-the-country; *New Analysis Shows Spikes of Metal Contaminants, Including Lead, in 2018 Camp Fire Wildfire Smoke*, Cal. Air Res. Bd. (July 12, 2021), https://ww2.arb.ca.gov/news/new-analysis-shows-spikes-metal-contaminants-including-lead-2018-camp-fire-wildfire-smoke; Rosana Aguilera et al., *Wildfire Smoke Impacts Respiratory Health More Than Fine Particles From Other Sources: Observational Evidence From Southern California*, 12 Nature Commc'ns 1493 (2021), https://www.nature.com/articles/s41467-021-21708-0.

102. U.S. EPA, Planning for Natural Disaster Debris (2019); Michael B. Gerrard, *Emergency Exemptions From Environmental Laws After Disasters*, 20 Nat. Resources & Env't 10 (2006).

103. Robert R.M. Verchick, Facing Catastrophe: Environmental Action for a Post-Katrina World 134-35 (2010).

How Should the Law Change to Cope With a World Beyond Two Degrees?

The environment does not care whether a chemical that has gotten into the air, water, or land is a waste or a product, or whether it was released while in storage or in transport, or accidentally, or deliberately. But the law cares. The environmental statutes and regulations were written at different times and in response to different concerns or incidents, and they reflect interest group lobbying. The result is an often bewildering patchwork of requirements where the care with which a substance is handled depends on arcane regulatory distinctions that bear little relation to the actual environmental or health risk involved. Because RCRA covers only "waste," the U.S. Court of Appeals for the District of Columbia (D.C.) Circuit famously spoke of its "mind-numbing journey through RCRA" in determining whether a certain kind of slag was a waste.[104]

Because RCRA's jurisdiction is limited to waste and to oil, its regulations' extremely detailed command-and-control rules only apply narrowly. EPCRA covers products as well as wastes, but it only requires planning and disclosure; it does not have substantive regulatory requirements. The Hazardous Materials Transportation Act covers a broad array of substances and does have substantive requirements, but it only applies to transport-related activities. CERCLA also applies to many materials (but excludes petroleum) and imposes substantive rules, but only for the cleanup process. The Toxic Substances Control Act (TSCA), despite its broad-sounding name, applies mainly to chemicals that are newly introduced into commerce, with a limited look back at old ones.[105]

The regulations in place have great complexity. EPA's regulations under RCRA, CERCLA, EPCRA, and TSCA take up five volumes of fine print in the Code of Federal Regulations; the DOT's regulations under the HMTA are another two volumes. Nevertheless, the regulations were all written during a 1°C-degree world. Some of them attempt to prepare for the sorts of extreme events that occur during a one-degree world—such as flash floods that quickly subside. But none envisions a world beyond 2°C, whose day-to-day existence may resemble today's extremes; and it is challenging to find even rough depictions of an extreme day in such a world (at least outside of the growing genre of "Cli-Fi"—climate fiction—and its postapocalyptic visions). The most sophisticated of today's engineered landfill designs will not

104. American Mining Cong. v. EPA, 824 F.2d 1177, 1189 (D.C. Cir. 1987).
105. 15 U.S.C. §2603.

work if the landfill is entirely under water or is engulfed in flames. Systems that depend on a continuous flow of water have problems if the rivers have run dry.

As discussed above, EPA could do more with its existing statutory authorities to reduce the spread of hazardous materials caused by extreme weather events. It could revise the NCP under CERCLA, strengthen the regulation of coal ash under RCRA, expand the requirements for spill prevention and countermeasure plans under the CWA and the OPA, and make greater use of §112(r) of the CAA, all to explicitly require greater precautions against floods, storms, and wildfires. But this would only take us so far.

The current system with idiosyncratically different legal requirements applying to very similar activities is dysfunctional if we are heading toward a world beyond 2°C. If the objective is to keep harmful chemicals out of the environment, it should not matter whether they are wastes or products. For example, a barrel of sulfuric acid on its way to disposal is stringently regulated under RCRA; but if that same barrel of that same acid is going to be used in the manufacture of fertilizer or dyes, it is not considered a waste and therefore is not regulated under RCRA. They should be subject to the same kinds of command-and-control rules based on their physical properties. (For some kinds of installations, technology standards may be best; for others, performance standards are used.) The facilities handling these chemicals should be able to withstand the conditions reasonably likely to occur (flooding, heat, etc.) at the end of their useful lives. Flood maps that reflect the latest projections of future flooding should be utilized when siting and designing new facilities. Such maps should be used in the reviews of proposed projects that are subject to the National Environmental Policy Act or its state equivalents. EPA's risk management program rule and OSHA's process safety management standard both require that facility siting be considered,[106] and EPA's 2022 proposed revisions called for more care in siting facilities, though the focus was on proximity to residential communities rather than site vulnerability to extreme weather events.[107]

The situation for *existing* facilities is considerably different. It's one thing to site, design, and build a new facility to withstand future conditions; it's another thing entirely to retrofit a facility that's already in operation (or maybe closed long ago, but has left waste behind). Sometimes sensitive equipment can be raised or protective walls can be built, but often it is not physically

106. 29 C.F.R. §1910.119(e)(3)(v); 40 C.F.R. §68.67(c)(5).

107. *Accidental Release Prevention Requirements: Risk Management Programs Under the Clean Air Act; Safter Communities by Chemical Accident Prevention*, 87 Fed. Reg. 53556, 53571-74 (Aug. 31, 2022) (codified at 40 C.F.R. §68).

possible or economically feasible to protect these places fully. For facilities subject, however, to CAA §112(r), the plans prepared in accordance with EPA's August 2022 proposal would go a long way toward at least requiring companies to consider climate risks in their facility operations. A particularly important measure to protect facilities that handle dangerous chemicals is enhancing the resilience of electric supply, coupled with emergency generators that can withstand extreme weather and have ample fuel supplies, since loss of power has become a common cause of chemical releases, and extreme weather is leading to more power outages.[108]

As noted above, CAA §112(r) gives facilities a "general duty" to minimize hazards. EPA has interpreted this "to generally require owners and operators to adhere to recognized industry practices and standards in addition to any applicable government regulations."[109] If the organizations that set industry standards, such as the American Institute of Chemical Engineers and the ASME, were to establish standards that required consideration of future sea-level rise and other climate-related events in facility siting and operations, that would have important legal and practical effects.

One important step would be to create a nationwide inventory of the existing chemical and waste facilities and contaminated sites that are vulnerable to flooding under likely future climate conditions. (Ideally the inventory would also reflect future wildfire conditions, but for these the mapping is far less advanced.) Then decisions need to be made about priorities. Different facilities will have different probabilities of flooding, and different health and environmental consequences if they do flood. They also have different capacities to pay for improvements ranging from considerable (for some currently operating facilities) to zero (for many and probably most closed facilities).

Difficult choices will be needed in setting priorities, beyond just the calculation of risks, hazards, and costs (complex as those may be). That is particularly the case with CERCLA, the law that imposes the most stringent cleanup requirements. A common rationale in choosing CERCLA remedies is to avoid even a small health risk to people who, someday in the future, may drink water from under the site or to children who someday may play in the dirt there.[110] But it makes little sense to spend large sums of money (especially public money) cleaning up sites for future residents of places that will become

---

108. *Id.* at 53570.
109. In re Hazlehurst Wood Pellets Ltd. Liab. Co., 86 F.R. 13716 (2022); *see also* Order Denying a Petition for Objection to Permit, In re Hazlehurst Wood Pellets Ltd. Liab. Co., Petition No. IV-2020-5 at 13, https://www.epa.gov/sites/default/files/2021-01/documents/hazlehurstorder2020.pdf.
110. Michael B. Gerrard, *Demons and Angels in Hazardous Waste Regulation: Are Justice, Efficiency and Democracy Reconcilable?* 92 Nw. U. L. Rev. 706 (1998).

uninhabitable as a result of climate change. It is true that contaminants from these sites may leak out and cause some environmental damage, but in a world beyond 2°C, the chemicals carried in the water from the globe's flooded waste and industrial sites could make those from many U.S. Superfund sites seem trivial. (To be fair, I have seen no study about this.) Scarce resources should be directed to actions that may have the greatest benefit.

Some have suggested that the waste in landfills that will be flooded should be moved to other locations.[111] Nevertheless, digging up buried waste poses dangers to the construction workers; it can cause some of the waste to become airborne and enter nearby communities; and hauling it by trucks to new disposal locations will, statistically, cause a certain number of fatal accidents. Several studies have found that these risks can exceed, perhaps by orders of magnitude, the risks to the site's neighbors of the contamination staying in place.[112] Moreover, finding a new place for the material is likely to be extraordinarily difficult. It's hard enough to find disposal locations for waste that was generated nearby; persuading a community to accept someone else's trash (or ramming it down their throats) is even harder.

The massive containment areas for coal ash are typically owned or controlled by the electric utilities that used them, and these utilities should be responsible for covering them in a way that protects them from flooding. Likewise, the lagoons with hog waste should be protected from flooding, and the large pork companies that sold the meat from these operations should pay for all of this. Unlike sites covered by CERCLA, where the wastes are often underground, the coal ash and hog waste are very vulnerable to flooding that could cause considerable harm.

It would be wonderful if society stopped generating the wastes that require disposal. The phase out of coal as a source of electricity—an essential part of any decarbonization strategy—will stop the generation of coal ash. Though recycling and composting will moderate the amount of MSW, trends do not indicate major progress in eliminating it.[113] Generation of RCRA hazardous

111. *See* Dave Lindorff, *Coastal Landfills Are No Match for Rising Seas*, Nature (July 26, 2021); White House News Media LLC, *Landfills Are an Important and Ignored Danger for Coastal Waters*, Newswires (Aug. 4, 2021), https://www.einnews.com/pr_news/548069824/landfills-are-an-impending-and-ignored-danger-for-coastal-waters.

112. *See* Michael B. Gerrard, *Safety Hazards in Hazardous Waste Remediation*, N.Y.L.J. (July 25, 2002).

113. *See* National Overview: Facts and Figures on Materials, Wastes, and Recycling, U.S. EPA, fig. 2 (Municipal Solid Waste Management: 1960-2018) (Dec. 3, 2022), https://www.epa.gov/facts-and-figures-about-materials-waste-and-recycling/national-overview-facts-and-figures-materials#:~:text=The%20total%20generation%20of%20municipal,25%20million%20tons%20were%20composted.

waste has been about flat for the past two decades.[114] Nor is there a marked downward trend in pork consumption.[115]

Under any scenario, large amounts of hazardous and noxious substances will continue to be created every day. Dealing with them, and with those that already exist, will be a great challenge as we go into a world beyond 2°C; we are not even doing it adequately in our current 1.2°C world.

114. Deeba Yavrom, *An Overview of Hazardous Waste Generation*, U.S. EPA (Apr. 28, 2021), https://rcrapublic.epa.gov/rcra-public-web/action/posts/2.

115. Caroline Christen, *Meat Consumption in the U.S. Is Growing at an Alarming Rate*, Sentient Media (Mar. 17, 2021), https://sentientmedia.org/meat-consumption-in-the-us.

In a 4°C World, the Inexorable Climate Change-Biodiversity Nexus

David Takacs

The latest report from the Intergovernmental Panel on Climate Change (IPCC),[1] other chapters in this book, and Robin Kundis Craig's and J.B. Ruhl's prescient article[2] lay out various consequences of a 4 degree Celsius (°C) rise in global annual average temperature. The latest report by the Intergovernmental Science-Policy Platform on Biodiversity and Ecosystem Services (IPBES) (the IPCC's regrettably more obscure cousin) predicts that more than one million species are imminently threatened with extinction.[3] This is 1,000 times the background rate (without humans in the picture) and is predicted to increase to 10,000 times the background rate with current population growth and climate change.[4] The International Union for Conservation of Nature (IUCN) grimly lists 41% of amphibian, 27% of mammal, 21% of reptile, and 13% of bird species as threatened with extinction.[5] Climate change exacerbates already dire human threats to biodiversity by raising temperatures, altering precipitation regimes, mistiming synchrony between pollinators and plants, and acidifying oceans, thus rendering protected biodiversity redoubts no longer habitable while leaving few places to which flora and fauna can migrate.[6]

Meanwhile, the human population and associated pressures on natural resources will grow. The United Nations projects that the human population

---

Author's note: Thank you to Donato Catrina, UC Law San Francisco Class of 2023, for research assistance.

1. IPCC, Climate Change 2021: The Pyhysical Science Basis (2021), https://www.ipcc.ch/report/ar6/wg1.
2. J.B. Ruhl & Robin Kundis Craig, *4°C*, 106 Minn. L. Rev. 191 (2021).
3. Press Release, IPBES, Nature's Dangerous Decline "Unprecedented"; Species Extinction Rates "Accelerating," (May 6, 2019), https://ipbes.net/news/Media-Release-Global-Assessment.
4. Jurriaan M. De Vos et al., *Estimating the Background Rate of Species Extinction*, 29 Conservation Biology 452 (2014), https://doi.org/10.1111/cobi.12380.
5. *More Than 42,100 Species Are Threatened With Extinction*, IUCN Red List, https://www.iucnredlist.org.
6. H.O. Potner et al., Biodiversity and Climate Change Workshop Report 15, 30 (2021), https://ipbes.net/sites/default/files/2021-06/20210609_workshop_report_embargo_3pm_CEST_10_june_0.pdf.

will grow from 7.7 today to 9.7 billion in 2050 and 11.2 billion in 2100.[7] Color me skeptical that this many humans can survive if we don't start thinking about and attending to the interplay between climate change mitigation, climate change adaptation, and biodiversity depletion and conservation.

On Thinking About These as Intertwined

Climate change and biodiversity present intertwined, grave threats. Nevertheless, we think of these crises (when we think of them at all) in separate buckets: you over there, think about and tackle greenhouse gas (GHG) buildup and response; and over here, we'll think about biodiversity loss.

But, as George Monbiot puts it: "As Earth systems are assaulted by everything at once, each source of stress compounds the others."[8] It is time to multitask, to simultaneously envision how conserving biodiversity helps us mitigate and adapt to GHG buildup, and how mitigating and adapting to climate change can and must protect and promote biodiversity. First, these grave threats are braided and can and should be addressed symbiotically. Overconsumption and its unheeded externalities, or simply the daily needs of more than eight billion people, put unsustainable pressure on the atmosphere, the land, and the ocean. As each of these problems worsen, they synergistically aggravate the others. And thinking practically and strategically, we only have so much time and money to invest to arrest these cataclysms and sustain a livable planet: we should be merging our approaches to climate change mitigation and adaptation, and biodiversity depletion. Think of it as biodiversity mitadaptation, an amalgam of efforts to reduce GHG pollution, adapt to the GHG pollution we cannot prevent, and secure novel (and bolster traditional) means to protect biodiversity.

As I will describe in this chapter, robust biodiversity helps us mitigate GHG pollution. Healthy biodiversity helps human communities adapt to chaotically changing ecological regimes. Efforts to mitigate GHG accumulation can harm, but could and should sustain biodiversity. And efforts to adapt to climate change can harm, but could and should help biodiversity. In a 4°C future, we must pay more attention to the inexorably linked climate-biodiversity mitadaptation nexus.

---

7. *Population*, U.N., https://www.un.org/en/global-issues/population.
8. *See* with many examples, George Monbiot, *"Green Growth" Doesn't Exist—Less of Everything Is the Only Way to Avert Catastrophe*, GUARDIAN, Sept. 29, 2021, https://www.theguardian.com/commentisfree/2021/sep/29/green-growth-economic-activity-environment.

Synergies

Climate change will deplete and reshape the biodiversity landscape. Functioning ecosystems and the biodiversity that comprise them can, to the extent we choose, help us mitigate and adapt to climate change's impacts.[9] This means considering all options to ensure that biodiversity is sustained in a chaotically, rapidly changing environment.

In a previous book chapter, Jessica Owley and I described the needs and means of "Flexible Conservation in Uncertain Times."[10] Indeed, the prospect of a 4°C (or even a 3°C) world requires not just flexibility to adapt to chaotically changing conditions, but also urgency, creativity, and the need to understand how the climate change and biodiversity emergencies are intertwined and to act accordingly.

The evolutionary genius of photosynthesis endows plants with the ability to suck up carbon dioxide (CO_2) and water to produce food for themselves and, as a happy byproduct, to produce dioxygen (O2) for the rest of the living world. CO_2-hungry plants in terrestrial ecosystems take in around one-quarter of human CO_2 emissions. We should express our gratitude by leaving the floral world to go about its evolutionary business. Instead, deforestation accounts for somewhere between 11% and 28% of GHG emissions.[11] Tropical forest loss is accelerating, particularly due to expanding commodity-driven, corporate agriculture (beef, cereals, oilseeds) in Latin America (especially Brazil) and small-scale agriculture in Africa and Asia. Despite our expanding knowledge of the role that plants play in modulating climate change, one study estimates a doubling of forest carbon emissions from 2015-2019 compared to 2001-2015.[12] Apropos for this chapter, the study does not mention a reasonable hypothesis that with the doubling of carbon loss likely comes a cascade of biodiversity loss. A recent study suggests that 2% of land-based endemic species will go extinct if global temperature increases are held to 1.5°C, while a tenfold increase—20% of land-based endemic species—face

9. *See* various charts in POTNER ET AL., *supra* note 6.

10. Jessica Owley & David Takacs, *Flexible Conservation in Uncertain Times*, *in* CONTEMPORARY ISSUES IN CLIMATE CHANGE LAW AND POLICY: ESSAYS INSPIRED BY THE IPCC (Robin Kundis Craig & Stephen R. Miller eds., 2016).

11. U.N. DEV. PROG. (UNDP), HUMAN DEVELOPMENT REPORT 2007/2008: FIGHTING CLIMATE CHANGE: HUMAN SOLIDARITY IN A DIVIDED WORLD 2007, at 1, 40-41 (2007), http://hdr.undp.org/sites/default/files/reports/268/hdr_20072008_en_complete.pdf; American Clean Energy and Security Act, H.R. 2454, 111th Cong. §752(2) (2009); Gleb Raygorodetsky, *Can REDD Ever Become Green?*, OUR WORLD (Aug. 1, 2012), http://ourworld.unu.edu/en/can-redd-ever-become-green; IPCC, CLIMATE CHANGE 2014: SYNTHESIS REPORT 46 (2014) [hereinafter 2014 IPCC SYNTHESIS REPORT].

12. Yu Feng et al., *Doubling of Annual Carbon Loss Over the Tropics During the Early Twenty-First Century*, 5 NATURE SUSTAINABILITY 444, 445-46 (2022).

extinction if the temperature increases by 3°C.[13] Apparently, the authors did not dare contemplate 4°C.

When we restore or rewild land that has been damaged, or prevent damage from occurring to land, we *mitigate* climate change when biomass retains carbon that would otherwise be released. So, as climate change and human needs degrade natural ecosystems—as plants are felled, burned, or eaten, as tundra melts, as peat bogs desiccate—climate change worsens, further imperiling species and ecosystems. As in other examples that lead to "mitadaptation," functioning ecosystems also simultaneously help human and nonhuman communities *adapt* to climate change by providing resilience against current and future climate change. Healthy ecosystems ward against drought, buffer against floods, purify drinking water, prevent erosion, and sustain crop pollinators and other species that humans require to survive.[14] We take these free ecosystem services for granted, and we abuse them—until the ecosystem no longer provides them for free. Humans increasingly depend more urgently on functioning ecosystems as our population and our needs (and desires) grow. A 4°C world will increasingly undermine these functioning ecosystems.

Climate Change Mitigation as Biodiversity Conservation

Jurisdictions' pledges to achieve the Convention on Biological Diversity's ambitious goal of 30% of land protected by 2030 (30 x 30)[15] could produce synergies if planners thought: How do our plans to reach 30 x 30 produce co-benefits if we think of biodiversity as helping mitigate climate change and helping communities adapt to climate change, that is, if we thought of this global effort to preserve wild spaces as mitadaptation? How could

13. Stella Manes et al., *Endemism Increases Species' Climate Change Risk in Areas of Global Biodiversity Importance*, Biological Conservation, May 12, 2021.
14. Fisheries & Env't, U.S. Dep't of Forestry, SIP 19: Ecological Infastructure for Water Security 14 (2014), https://www.dffe.gov.za/sites/default/files/docs/sip19_ecologicalinfrastructure_watersecurity.pdf [hereinafter SIP 19]; U.N. Env't Prog. (UNEP), Green Infrastructure: Guide for Water Management 5, 14-16 (2014), http://www.unepdhi.org/-/media/microsite_unepdhi/publications/documents/unep/web-unep-dhigroup-green-infrastructure-guide-en-20140814.pdf [hereinafter UNEP, Green Infrastructure]; Barton H. Thompson Jr., *Markets for Nature*, 25 Wm. & Mary Envtl. L. & Pol'y Rev. 261, 295 (2000); *Reducing Emissions From Deforestation: A Key Opportunity for Attaining Multiple Benefits*, UNEP, World Conservation Monitoring Ctr. 9-10 (2007), http://www.unep-wcmc.org/ medialibrary/2010/09/27/fa100d32/REDD_Multiple_benefits.pdf; *see* Johannes Ebeling, *Risks and Criticisms of Forestry-Based Climate Change Mitigation and Carbon Trading, in* Climate Change and Forests: Emerging Policy and Market Opportunities 43, 53 (Charlotte Streck et al. eds., 2008).
15. Convention on Biological Diversity, Zero Draft of the Post-2020 Global Diversity Framework (2020), https://www.cbd.int/doc/c/efb0/1f84/a892b98d2982a829962b6371/wg2020-02-03-en.pdf.

our nascent plans for nature-based solutions to mitadaptation improve outcomes for biodiversity by specifically incorporating and putting biodiversity's needs at the center? Because many biodiversity mitadaptation decisions are project- based, we need not wait for slow-moving, international or national agreements to think holistically, synergistically, and rapidly. Consider the following suggestions.

Our transition to a sustainable future relies on reducing human demand for energy and other resources and then finding zero carbon sources of energy to fuel human needs that remain. As we have been developing low-carbon or zero-carbon energy, we have been slow to think about how to integrate biodiversity conservation into our planning. Extraction and combustion of fossil fuels has significant impacts on biodiversity; even now, the Center for Biological Diversity and WildEarth Guardians recently filed a lawsuit against the U.S. Department of the Interior for approving over 3,500 "applications to drill" on public lands while failing to account for the cumulative impacts the resulting GHGs will have on "150 animals and plants for which climate change is a primary driver of their decline."[16] But the production of renewable energy can also harm species. Distributed, corporate solar energy gobbles up lots of land; wind turbines annihilate migrating birds; geothermal or ocean wave energy carry their own species risks.[17]

Drawing on the notion of "pollution havens"—where the global North's worst consumption and pollution excesses are offshored to the global South—I have written on "mandate havens," where mandates to mitigate one problem (say, GHG pollution from energy generation) end up exacerbating and concentrating ancillary negative environmental consequences downstream.[18] Experts predict that solar energy will supply nearly one-half the U.S. energy supply by 2050.[19] In response to mandates to reduce GHGs, large-scale solar energy developers produce unintended consequences[20] by scarfing down water, destroying or fragmenting habitat, altering local microclimates, and

16. Complaint for Declaratory Judgment and Injunctive Relief at 1, 7, Center for Biol. Diversity v. Department of the the Interior, No. 1:22-cv-1716 ¶1, 7 (D.D.C. June 15, 2022).
17. *E.g.* Press Release, Center for Biological Diversity, Lawsuit Filed to Stop Geothermal Project From Destroying Nevada Springs (Dec. 16, 2021), https://biologicaldiversity.org/w/news/press-releases/lawsuit-filed-to-stop-geothermal-project-from-destroying-nevada-springs-2021-12-16; Johan Lammerant et al., Potential Impacts of Solar, Geothermal, and Ocean Energy on Habitats and Species Protected Under the Birds and Habitats Directives 24, 31 (2020).
18. David Takacs, *Protecting Your Environment, Exacerbating Injustice: Avoiding "Mandate Havens,"* 24 Duke Envtl. L. & Pol'y F. 315 (2014).
19. Ivan Penn, *From 4% to 45%: Energy Department Lays Out Ambitious Blueprint for Solar Power*, N.Y. Times, Sept. 8, 2021, https://www.nytimes.com/2021/09/08/business/energy-etenvironment/biden-solar-energy-climate-change.html.
20. *See* Takacs, *Protecting Your Environment*, *supra* note 18.

singeing or causing collisions of protected species.[21] In the deserts of southern California, utility-scale solar developers are building in undisturbed sections of the Mojave Desert (which comprise as much plant diversity as redwood forests) rather than in previously degraded lands.[22]

In his chapter, "Waste and Chemical Management Beyond 2°C," Michael Gerrard reminds us that to build the kind of low-carbon or zero-carbon energy we need will require triage trade offs: he suggests that we can't set aside land to protect all our imperiled species and develop the low-carbon energy we need. And if we fail to do the latter, a lot more species will go extinct due to climate change than will go extinct due wind, solar, and other deep decarbonization strategies.[23] Nonetheless, we can attempt to mitigate the biodiversity externalities of decarbonizing our energy systems. By carefully planning where and how to develop solar, and by mitigating the ecological degradation solar development causes, developers may minimize damage to biodiversity. Rebecca Hernandez and colleagues describe "techno-ecological synergies" when devising solar energy systems.[24] Exclusion zones can be mapped for very rare species or protected habitats. Developers can create artificial or, preferably, green fences as barriers, and sheep and goats (rather than biocides) can keep vegetation down "naturally." Conversely, planning solar parks as close to existing infrastructure can prevent sprawl into biodiversity hot spots,[25] provided planners avoid burdening already burdened communities with more unaesthetic or polluting infrastructure. Agrophotovoltaics (or agrivoltaics) systems intersperse solar energy with crops.[26]

For example, to account for demand for ecosystem services to support a solar energy development, the community-owned Westmill Solar Park in the United Kingdom[27] managed and achieved biodiversity benefits. They planted native grasses and created pollinator habitat, which simultaneously increases transpiration under the panels, thus cooling them and generating

21. Katherine Harmon Courage, *Solar Farms Are Often Bad for Biodiversity—But They Don't Have to Be*, VOX, Aug. 18, 2021, https://www.vox.com/2021/8/18/22556193/solar-energy-biodiversity-birds-pollinator-land; Kiera Butler, *Big Solar's Death Panels*, Mother Jones (Mar./Apr. 2011), https://www.motherjones.com/environment/2011/02/solar-panels-desert-tortoise-mojave; Lammerant et al., *supra* note 17, at 12.
22. Bobby Magill, *Solar Energy Expansion Could Pose Ecological Risks*, Sci. Am., Oct. 20, 2015, https://www.scientificamerican.com/article/solar-power-expansion-could-pose-ecological-risks.
23. Michael Gerrard, *A Time for Triage*, Env't F. 40, 42 (2022).
24. Rebecca R. Hernandez et al., *Techno-Ecological Synergies of Solar Energy for Global Sustainability*, 2 Nature Sustainability 560 (2019).
25. Lammerant et al., *supra* note 17, at 17, 19.
26. *Id.*
27. *Wider Work*, Westmill Solar Coop., http://westmillsolar.coop/wider-work.

energy more efficiently.[28] When designed properly, such panels can actually reduce extreme temperatures for crops (while the crops' transpiration cools the modules) and conserve water, thus mitigating GHG buildup while helping farmers adapt to the effects of climate change.[29] Photovoltaic (PV) panels sometimes provide nesting sites for birds.[30] Floating PV parks can provide habitat or hiding places for fish and can provide mini-marine protected areas as they block trawlers from accessing the PV sites.[31]

Recently a U.S. wind company was charged $8 million after pleading guilty for killing at least 150 golden and bald eagles at its wind farms.[32] In a dramatic statistic on how two environmental goals sometimes fail to mesh, according to the U.S. Fish and Wildlife Service's 2018 estimates, wind turbines killed between 140,000-500,000 birds each year, with numbers on the rise since then as wind energy has grown.[33] While this is only a small fraction of the 500 million to a billion birds killed each year in the United States due to anthropogenic (or feline) activity,[34] every bit counts (especially for imperiled species), and some of these deaths can be avoided. To mitigate the climate emergency, it is a good thing that 3,000 turbines per year have been constructed each year since 2005, aiming for 20% of U.S. energy production by 2030[35]; it is a bad thing that birds have suffered enormous collateral damage. Scientists believe that wind turbines are now the leading cause of bat mortality.[36] A German study estimates that turbines kill over a trillion flying insects each year, a sobering statistic given the dramatic collapse of insect

28. Alona Armstrong et al., *Solar Park Management and Vegetation Management Effects on Grassland Carbon Cycling*, 11 Envtl. Res. Letters 074106 (2016), https://iopscience.iop.org/article/10.1088/1748-9326/11/7/074016/pdf.
29. Ellen Rosen, *Can Dual-Use Solar Panels Provide Power and Share Space With Crops?*, N.Y. Times, June 28, 2022, https://www.nytimes.com/2022/06/28/business/dual-use-solar-panels-agrivoltaics-blue-wave-power.html.
30. Lammerant et al., *supra* note 17, at 19.
31. Aquatera Ltd., Promoting Aquatic Renewable Energy to Increase Energy Efficiency in Peru 24 (2017), https://assets.publishing.service.gov.uk/government/uploads/system/uploads/attachment_data/file/673493/Executive_Summary_P747_Promoting_aquatic_renewable_energy_to_increase_energy_diversity_in_Peru.pdf.
32. Maya Yang, *Wind Energy Company Pleads Guilty to Killing at Least 150 Eagles*, Guardian, Apr. 11, 2022, https://www.theguardian.com/environment/2022/apr/07/wind-energy-company-guilty-killing-eagles.
33. *Wind Turbines*, U.S. Fish & Wildlife Serv., https://www.fws.gov/birds/bird-enthusiasts/threats-to-birds/collisions/wind-turbines.php, *quoted in* Elinor Colbourn et al., *Renewable Energy: The Intersection of Wildlife Protection and Climate Change Action*, 69 DOJ J. Fed. L. & Prac. 51, 52 (2021).
34. Wallace P. Erickson et al., A Summary of Bird Mortality From Anthropogenic Causes With an Emphasis on Collisions 1029, 1029 (2005) (USDA Forest Service General Technical Report No. PSW-GTR-191), https://www.fs.usda.gov/psw/publications/documents/psw_gtr191/psw_gtr191_1029-1042_erickson.pdf; Scott R. Loss et al., *Direct Mortality of Birds From Anthropogenic Causes*, 46 Ann. Rev. Ecology, Evolution, & Systematics 99 (2015).
35. *See* Colbourn et al., *supra* note 33, at 53.
36. Amy Matthews Amos, *Bat Killings by Wind Turbines Continue*, Sci. Am., June 7, 2016, https://www.scientificamerican.com/article/bat-killings-by-wind-energy-turbines-continue.

populations, the so-called insect apocalypse.[37] Furthermore, as with solar energy, turbines' construction and physical plant disrupts habitat.[38]

Some easy (and difficult) solutions exist, such as cutting turbine speed, slowing or stopping turbines, or changing the configuration of turbine blades during migrations; some solutions—for example, painting turbine blades black to reduce collisions—don't require reducing the amount of low-carbon energy generated.[39] In an experiment in Spain, to reduce impacts on the lesser kestrel (a legally protected species), managers tilled the soil around the base of turbines, decreasing prey that fatally attracts the birds, and thus nearly entirely eliminated kestrel collisions and deaths.[40] In the United States, developers and government officials could employ more rigorous adherence to the Endangered Species Act (ESA) §9 "take" requirements by requiring wind developers to obtain incidental take permits for protected species' deaths their turbines will entail.[41] Highly sensitive habitats or rare species can be mapped in "no go" zones; the Asian Development Bank and BirdLife International are employing a mapping tool to alert developers to where such projects should be avoided.[42] Obviously, all international financial institutions could and should be paying attention to maximizing biodiversity and climate synergies when they invest and avoiding harming one goal while promoting another.

The environmental impact assessment for a Scottish wind farm revealed a golden eagle nesting site, which led developers to relocate the development and to restore wetlands to offset any ancillary damage. Subsequent studies over a long period have shown no impact of the development on eagle survival.[43] After a dispute over windfarm siting in Greece near a Ramsar-designated wetland and Natura 2000 site protecting 20% of the remaining Dalmatian pelican population, the energy company relocated the proposed site and installed a monitoring and collision avoidance system. Of course, no

---

37. Brooke Jarvis, *The Insect Apocalypse Is Here*, N.Y. Times, Nov. 27, 2018, https://www.nytimes.com/2018/11/27/magazine/insect-apocalypse.html.
38. Colbourn et al., *supra* note 33, at 51, 58.
39. Amos, *supra* note 36; Roel May et al., *Paint It Black: Efficacy of Increased Wind Turbine Rotor Blade Visibility to Reduce Avian Fatalities*, 10 Ecology & Evolution 8927 (July 26, 2020).
40. Moisés Pescador et al., *Effectiveness of a Mitigation Measure for the Lesser Kestrel (Falco naumanni) in Wind Farms in Spain*, 231 J. Envtl. Mgmt. 919 (2019).
41. Colbourn et al., *supra* note 33.
42. Beatrice Yulo Gomez & Tris Allinson, *Avoiding Renewable Energy's Unintended Impacts on Birds*, Dev. Asia (May 22, 2022), https://development.asia/insight/avoiding-renewable-energys-unintended-impacts-birds.
43. Wind Europe, Mainstreaming Energy and Climate Policies Into Nature Conservation 12 (2017), https://windeurope.org/wp-content/uploads/files/policy/topics/sustainability/WindEurope-Paper-on-the-role-of-wind-energy-in-wildlife-conservation.pdf [hereinafter Mainstreaming Energy].

avoidance system is perfect, and individuals of protected species still are occasionally killed when dense fog obscures their ability to avoid the turbines.[44]

Each bit of extra green tape and expense added to a renewable energy project disincentivizes or slows low-carbon energy development. Tax incentives, nongovernmental organization support and involvement, and perhaps slightly higher energy costs in the short run would pay big, synergistic benefits for biodiversity in the long run. Careful planning and monitoring can move closer to "the ultimate environmental sweet spot"[45] where GHG mitigation through low-carbon energy meets biodiversity enhancement.

Adaptation as Biodiversity Conservation

Biodiversity helps human communities adapt to the vicissitudes of climate change. For example, coral reefs protect low-lying coastal areas from storms and flooding. Building artificial, biodiversity-enhancing reefs helps human communities adapt and can foster flourishing biodiversity.[46] Naturally occurring coral reefs are rapidly dying due in large part to global heating.[47] For example, the 2022 Australian government survey of the Great Barrier Reef revealed massive coral die-off, the sixth major bleaching event since 1998.[48] Cross-breeding hybrid corals in the laboratory can reveal which are likely to survive warmer waters; these lab hybrids can then be transplanted into the ocean, simultaneously buffering human communities from storm damage and sustaining the complex web of organisms that depend upon coral.[49] Making sure the top predator trophic level is healthy provides cascading carbon effects; for example, reef predators not only consume more herbivores but also result in herbivores hiding—therefore consuming less carbon-storing and carbon-producing reef algae—thus resulting in greater amounts of carbon being stored short term and long term in reef sediment.[50]

---

44. *Greek Enviro Orgs Warn of Poorly Sited Wind Farms After Pelican Deaths*, Renewables Now (Aug. 14, 2020), https://renewablesnow.com/news/greek-enviro-orgs-warn-of-poorly-sited-wind-farms-after-pelican-deaths-709983; Mainstreaming Energy, *supra* note 43, at 14-15.
45. Amos, *supra* note 36.
46. *Artificial Reefs*, U.N. Climate Tech. Centre & Network, https://www.ctc-n.org/technologies/artificial-reefs.
47. *E.g., Reef Snapshot*, Australian Gov't, Great Barrier Reef Marine Park Auth., https://www.gbrmpa.gov.au/the-reef/reef-health/reef-snapshot (Aug. 23, 2022).
48. *E.g., id.*; Adam Morton & Lisa Cox, *"Devastating": 91% of Reefs Surveyed on Great Barrier Reef Affected by Coral Bleaching*, Guardian, May 10, 2022, https://www.theguardian.com/environment/2022/may/10/devastating-90-of-reefs-surveyed-on-great-barrier-reef-affected-by-coral-bleaching-in-2022.
49. Wing Yan Chen et al., *Interspecific Hybridization May Provide Novel Opportunities for Coral Reef Restoration*, 4 Frontiers Marine Sci. 1 (2018).
50. Trisha B. Atwood et al., *Predators Shape Sedimentary Organic Carbon Storage in a Coral Reef Ecosystem*, 6 Frontiers Ecology Evolution 1 (2018).

Moving to cooler climates, much of the Netherlands is famously at or below sea level. That area has long battled threatening seas and is now leading the world in learning to live with rising seas by using a "build with nature" philosophy.[51] The "sand motor" or "sand engine" off the coast of Den Haag proposes a model of techno-ecological adaptation to climate change that simultaneously and explicitly attends to biodiversity. In this project, the Dutch harvested sand offshore (perhaps itself not a sustainable practice) to build its buffer island. The goals of the project explicitly include creation of new habitat for flora and fauna. At the sand motor's 10-year anniversary, researchers found a rich diversity of shellfish and snails, providing food for shorebirds while helping to protect human communities from rising seas and stronger storms.[52]

Initiatives elsewhere[53] also aim to protect areas from climate change-enhanced storms and sea-level rise flooding while explicitly creating more wildlife habitat in the process. In the United States, various organizations seek to construct living seawalls that simultaneously protect communities from sea-level rise and storm surges and encourage biodiversity. The Living Breakwaters project in New York City not only will protect coastal communities, but also is conceived as a "Billion Oyster Project" that aims to improve ecological resiliency and foster a biodiverse local ecosystem.[54]

Biodiversity Conservation as Mitadaptation

Net-zero or carbon-neutral targets often depend on "offsetting" the carbon externalities of development through carbon sequestration in forests. Our remaining forests hold as much carbon (44% in soil, 42% in living biomass, 5% in leaf litter, and 8% in dead wood) as a century's worth of GHG emissions (emitted at our current rate).[55]

Forests comprise a large segment of nature-based solutions (NbS), or "project solutions that are motivated and supported by nature and that may

51. *Sand Motor—Build With Nature Solution to Improve Coastal Protection Along Delfland Coast (the Netherlands)*, ClimateAdapt, https://climate-adapt.eea.europa.eu/metadata/case-studies/sand-motor-2013-building-with-nature-solution-to-improve-coastal-protection-along-delfland-coast-the-netherlands.
52. *Id.*
53. *See, e.g.*, *Medmerry Managed Realignment Scheme*, Mackley, https://mackley.co.uk/capabilities/coastal-protection/medmerry-managed-realignment-scheme.
54. *Living Breakwaters Project Background and Design*, N.Y. State Governor's Off. Storm Recovery, https://stormrecovery.ny.gov/living-breakwaters-project-background-and-design; *Living Breakwaters*, SCAPE, https://www.scapestudio.com/projects/living-breakwaters.
55. *Forest Carbon Stocks*, World Res. Inst.: Global Forest Rev., https://research.wri.org/gfr/biodiversity-ecological-services-indicators/forest-carbon-stocks.

also offer environmental, economic, and social benefits, while increasing resiliency."[56] NbS is an umbrella term uniting various strategies to root our long-term sustainability in natural rather than technological fixes. In other words, when you're thinking about mitadaptation, think about nature first. NbS may provide cost-efficient means to mitigate GHG pollution and adapt to climate change while also protecting the ecosystem services on which human and nonhuman communities depend. The Paris Agreement asks that all signatories explain how they are going to meet their GHG reduction commitments, which they report in their nationally determined contributions (NDCs). Most nations' NDCs include NbS.[57] Experts believe that NbS can provide at least one-third of the GHG reductions needed to keep global temperatures below 2°C.[58]

Of course, as I note elsewhere, NbS also help communities adapt to climate change. Wetlands, barrier islands, coral reefs, and other ecogeo entities help protect communities from flooding and storm damage, while harboring biodiversity that can further sequester carbon, and can have ancillary benefits for agriculture, forestry, tourism, and aesthetic and recreational enjoyment.[59] The 2022 Inflation Reduction Act includes $5 billion for forest conservation, thus, as a Nature Conservancy officer notes, "addressing climate solutions that also address the nature crisis."[60]

But nature-based solutions, paradoxically, don't always prioritize biodiversity or find the synergies between mitadaptation and biodiversity sustenance.

The most frequently deployed NbS is the forest carbon offset. In the carbon-offsetting world, trees are repurposed as carbon sequestration devices. Often packaged under the acronym REDD+ (reducing emissions from deforestation and forest degradation), a government jurisdiction, a private landowner, an individual, or a community landowner preserves trees that would otherwise be cut down or plants trees on degraded land. They can

56. *Strategies for Operationalizing Nature-Based Solutions in the Private Sector*, Nature Conservancy, https://www.nature.org/content/dam/tnc/nature/en/documents/NBSWhitePaper.pdf; Nadja Kabisch et al., *Nature-Based Solutions to Climate Change Mitigation in Urban Areas: Perspectives on Indicators, Knowledge Gaps, Barriers, and Opportunities for Action*, 21 Ecology & Soc'y (2016), https://www.ecologyandsociety.org/vol21/iss2/art39.

57. *Nature-Based Policy Platform*, Univ. Oxford, https://www.nbspolicyplatform.org/adaptation-planning/adaptation-action-types/nature-based-actions.

58. Bronson W. Griscom et al., *Nature Climate Solutions*, 114 Proc. Nat'l Acad. Sci. 11645 (2017), https://doi.org/10.1073/pnas.1710465114.

59. For more in-depth global standards on nature-based solutions, see *IUCN Global Standard for Nature-Based Solutions*, IUCN (2020), https://portals.iucn.org/library/sites/library/files/documents/2020-020-En.pdf.

60. Brady Dennis, *As Congress Funds High-Tech Climate Solutions, It Also Bets on a Low-Tech One: Nature*, Wash. Post, Aug. 14, 2022, https://www.washingtonpost.com/climate-solutions/2022/08/14/nature-climate-solutions-inflation-reduction-act.

then sell stored carbon in that land for a contracted period to anyone who wants to offset their GHG emissions. REDD+ may happen via individual projects or may operate at a broader scale where a jurisdiction reduces deforestation or reforests and is rewarded by carbon-offset money, as long as their efforts result in more sequestered carbon than would have occurred without the funding.[61]

While not the place to debate the (de)merits of REDD+,[62] many billions of dollars have been invested in REDD+ projects and in preparing nations to participate in REDD+ schemes. At the 2021 UNFCCC Conference of Parties, in addition to the billions of dollars already spent on REDD+ readiness or on carbon sequestration results already delivered,[63] developed countries pledged an additional $19 billion to halt and reverse deforestation; much of that will likely go into forest carbon-offsetting programs. The U.N. Food and Agriculture Organization estimates that halting deforestation could immediately achieve 14% of the GHG reductions needed to keep global temperatures under 1.5°C by 2030.[64] If jurisdictions and private entities are to reach their carbon neutrality goals, REDD+ will continue to expand, and that expansion ought to pay focused attention on maximizing not just verifiable carbon but verifiable biodiversity benefits as well.

REDD+ has tremendous potential to sustain and enhance imperiled biodiversity. Humans have driven at least 142 tree species to extinction, and 30% of tree species face future extinction.[65] According to the World Resource Institute, in 2021, forests that are highly (disproportionately) important to biodiversity lost 2.2 million hectares (ha.), losing one-half a percent of their area in that one year alone. Wildfires cause much of this loss, a threat which, of course, will exacerbate with global heating. Felled forests release carbon;

61. *See generally* David Takacs, *Forest Carbon (REDD+), Repairing International Trust, and Reciprocal Contractual Sovereignty*, 37 Vt. L. Rev. 653 (2013); David Takacs, *Forest Carbon: Law and Property Rights*, Conservation Int'l (2009); David Takacs, *Environmental Democracy and Forest Carbon (REDD+)*, 44 Envtl. L. 71 (2014) [hereinafter Takacs, *Environmental Democracy*].

62. *See* my work, e.g., Jessica Owley & David Takacs, *Flexible Conservation in Uncertain Times, in* Contemporary Issues in Climate Change Law and Policy: Essays Inspired by the IPCC (Robin Kundis Craig & Stephen R. Miller eds., 2016) [hereinafter Owley & Takacs, *Flexible Conservation*]; Takacs, *Environmental Democracy*, *supra* note 61; David Takacs, *Measuring, Monitoring, Reporting, and Verifying (MMRV): Negotiating Trust in Transnational Contracts for REDD+*, 106 Am. Soc'y Int'l L. Proc. 518 (2012). For a continuous doom and gloom drumbeat of criticism on REDD+, there is no better source than REDD Monitor Home Page, REDD-Monitor, https://redd-monitor.org.

63. Ecosystems Marketplace, A Green Growth Spurt: State of Forest Carbon Finance 2022, at 39-42 (2021) [hereinafter Ecosystems Marketplace].

64. FAO, State of the World's Forests vi, 27 (2022), https://www.fao.org/3/cb9360en/cb9360en.pdf.

65. *Global Tree Assessment*, Botanic Gardens Conservation Int'l, https://www.bgci.org/our-work/projects-and-case-studies/global-tree-assessment.

the earth heats; more and more destructive forest fires fell more forests.[66] Currently, programs under the aegis of REDD+ do not pay sufficient or any attention to biodiversity co-benefits, and sometimes award credits to single-species tree plantations; they may suck up carbon, but don't do much to abet diverse ecosystems.[67] Ninety-two percent of plantation expansion in the tropics between 2000-2012 occurred in biodiversity hotspots,[68] sometimes fueled by carbon-offset funds, but seldom with biodiversity/climate change mitadaptation in mind.

While the IPCC recommends adding forest land to absorb CO_2 and keep global temperature increases to 1.5°C, this would require adding 24 million ha. (the size of the United Kingdom or West Virginia) each year to 2030. Countries that have submitted plans to help achieve forest conservation and expansion include almost one-half the area as monoculture forest plantations, as monocultures allow "speed and ease."[69] A slower, but even cheaper and easier, approach: let nature heal itself through naturally occurring, biodiverse regeneration. Of course, if one is looking for trees as carbon-uptake devices that also provide income to local people, as well as havens for biodiversity, one can intersperse rapid growing, harvestable, and reforestable species like eucalyptus with natural regeneration.[70] Imagine if these areas were also biodiversity hotspots that prioritized habitat corridor protection and regeneration to allow biodiversity to migrate in response to ecosystem changes wrought by climate change.[71]

To try to remedy this, the climate, community, and biodiversity (CCB) standards, a widely used methodology for certifying REDD+ projects, explicitly mirror the theme of this chapter, linking together mitigation benefits for the climate, adaptation benefits for human communities, and ecosystem benefits for nonhuman communities.[72] Unlike some other REDD+ standards,

66. *Indicators of Biodiversity and Ecological Services: Biodiversity* Conservation, World Res. Inst.: Global Forest R., https://research.wri.org/gfr/biodiversity-ecological-services-indicators/biodiversity-conservation.

67. *See* Jessica Owley & David Takacs, *Flexible Conservation*, *supra* note 62; David Takacs, *Forest Carbon Project and International Law: A Deep Equity Legal Analysis*, 22 Geo. Int'l L. Rev. 521 (2010); Takacs, *Environmental Democracy*, *supra* note 62.

68. Matthew E. Fagan et al., *The Expansion of Tree Plantations Across Tropical Biomes*, 5 Nature Sustainability 681-88 (Mar. 24, 2022), http://dx.doi.org/10.1038/s41893-022-00904-w (retrieved from https://escholarship.org/uc/item/82v2n0j0).

69. Gianluca Cerullo, *Should Tree Plantations Count Toward Reforestation Goals? It's Complicated*, Mongabay, Sept. 10, 2021, https://news.mongabay.com/2021/09/should-tree-plantations-count-toward-reforestation-goals-its-complicated.

70. *Id.*

71. Simon L. Lewis et al., *Restoring Natural Forests Is the Best Way to Remove Atmospheric Carbon*, Nature (Apr. 2, 2019), https://www.nature.com/articles/d41586-019-01026-8.

72. VERRA, Climate, Community & Biodiversity Standards, version 3.1, at 33 (3d ed. 2017), https://verra.org/wp-content/uploads/2017/12/CCB-Standards-v3.1_ENG.pdf.

the CCB standards prioritize native species and ban invasive or genetically modified organisms (GMO). They require that the project developers not allow or mitigate any negative "leakage," that is, any negative biodiversity impacts outside the project.[73] Developers can get extra points (and thus earn more money per credit) by guaranteeing "exceptional biodiversity benefits," that is, those that help a nation meet national pledges to fulfill international agreements.[74] Nonetheless, the Verified Carbon Standard (VERRA), the most widely used market standard,[75] does not require that developers use the CCB standard and thus does not require biodiversity co-benefits. They note that "[m]any AFOLU [Agriculture, Forestry, and Other Land Use] projects achieve benefits beyond reducing GHG emissions by protecting biodiversity," but those projects certainly need not attend to those co-benefits.[76]

All in all, when entities go for carbon neutrality via tree-planting offsets, it often makes short-term sense to plant harvestable timber species that not only gain lucrative offset credits, but can also be chopped down and sold after the contracted carbon sequestration period. Terramatch.org matches funders to local citizens who know how to grow trees for local conditions because "[p]eople and the climate only benefit if the right trees thrive in the right places."[77] So massive global tree campaigns, like the Trillion Trees Initiative,[78] should be recalibrated to place more ecological and economic value on biodiversity benefits.[79]

Peatlands comprise 3% of the earth's land, but store one-quarter of the earth's soil carbon and hold twice as much carbon as do the world's forests. The *Washington Post* labels peatlands "the superhero of the natural world" because they are the most carbon dense habitat on the planet.[80] Drained peatlands emit about 5% of annual global carbon emissions.[81] A *New York Times* article in 2022 highlighted the booming, controversial market in

73. *Id.* at 43, 45.
74. *Id.* at 46-47.
75. Ecosystems Marketplace, *supra* note 63, at 29.
76. VERRA, VCS AFOLU Requirements (2013), https://verra.org/wp-content/uploads/2016/05/FactSheet-AFOLU-2013-UPDATED.pdf.
77. Terra Match, https://www.terramatch.org; Aaron Minnick & Will Anderson, *Connecting People Growing a Trillion Trees the Right Way*, World Res. Inst. (June 18, 2020), https://www.wri.org/insights/connecting-people-growing-trillion-trees-right-way.
78. T1.org, https://www.1t.org.
79. Caitrin Einhorn, *Tree Planting Is Blooming. Here's How That Could Help, or Harm, the Planet*, N.Y. Times, Mar. 14, 2022, https://www.nytimes.com/2022/03/14/climate/tree-planting-reforestation-climate.html.
80. William Booth, *Serious About Climate Change? Get Serious About Peat*, Wash. Post, Nov. 10, 2021, https://www.washingtonpost.com/world/2021/11/10/cop26-peat-carbon.
81. Virginia Gewin, *How Peat Could Protect the Planet*, Nature (Feb. 12, 2020), https://www.nature.com/articles/d41586-020-00355-3#ref-CR1.

peat-bog-offset credits in Scotland.[82] Neither of these high-profile pieces discussed the peat bogs' high endemic biodiversity,[83] which bog enthusiasts label "exceptional."[84] By carefully restoring the peat—which includes, controversially, killing many destructive (and currently predatorless) deer and banning sheep—a few wealthy men are offsetting their own excesses (one is a corporate manufacturer of cheap clothing) and, perhaps, getting wealthier. As the article notes, unfortunately, economic fairness and social justice are not baked into these efforts.

When foresters restore land degraded by industrial logging or destroyed by fires, they usually emphasize rapidly growing monocultures and employ biocides to battle "weeds." That is, they prioritize short-term economic value rather than short-term and long-term ecological value. To paraphrase one article, foresters can't see the forest for the plantations.[85] The U.S. Department of Agriculture (USDA) considers it progressive evolution to consider climate change when reforesting and thus to plant trees uphill 500 feet from where a species has traditionally grown—a few steps uphill in the right direction, but not one that creatively imagines what a biodiversity rich forest will comprise in a 4°C world.[86] Onene British Columbia reforesting project, Seed the North[87] is "[f]ighting climate change, one sprout at a time." They harvest seeds from land-neighboring disturbed areas and employ indigenous people (and not just their knowledge) to harvest and cultivate the seeds. They then use drones to drop diverse, biochar-encased seeds of native species over remote areas. They aim to create vast carbon sinks composed of native species that sustain greater biodiversity and are better able to adapt to changing climate conditions.[88]

Across the African Sahel, the Great Green Wall project has been working to plant millions of trees that simultaneously help mitigate GHG buildup (the goal is to take in 250 million tons of GHGs), help communities adapt to climate change by cooling local environments, increase local rainfall, fertilize soil to feed a burgeoning population at the forefront of droughts and other

82. David Segal, *Who Will Profit From Saving Scotland's Bogs?*, N.Y. Times, May 5, 2022, https://www.nytimes.com/interactive/2022/05/05/headway/scotland-peatlands-climate-change.html.
83. *Biodiversity*, IUCN, https://www.iucn-uk-peatlandprogramme.org/about-peatlands/peatland-benefits/biodiversity.
84. *Peatlands and Biodiversity*, IPS, https://peatlands.org/peatlands/peatlands-and-biodiversity.
85. Cerullo, *supra* note 69.
86. USDA, Creating More Resilient Forests Through Active Management (2018), https://northlab.faculty.ucdavis.edu/wp-content/uploads/sites/195/2020/12/Creating-more-resilient-forests-through-active-management-USDA-pamphlet.pdf.
87. Seed the North, https://seedthenorth.ca/approach.
88. Amanda Follett Hosgood, *Seed the North: Fighting Climate Change One Sprout at a Time*, Grist.Org., May 22, 2021, https://grist.org/science/seed-the-north-fighting-climate-change-one-sprout-at-a-time.

climate change threats, keep the Sahara sands at bay, and provide income, while providing renewed habitat for biodiversity. Citizens plant trees (unfortunately, in this harsh environment, many of the trees do not survive) and nurture others that regenerated naturally.[89]

Cities are increasingly turning to green roofs as a mitadaptation strategy. By adding layers of vegetation, green roofs mitigate GHG emissions by reducing the need for heating and air conditioning. Green roofs help cities adapt more broadly to global heating by lowering roof temperatures as much as 30-40 degrees Fahreheit (°F) and reducing ambient temperatures by up to 5°F, thus helping urban residents cope with global heating.[90] Law can abet green-roof development by offering tax incentives or GHG offset credits for developers, as cities in the Netherlands have done.[91] And if we are going to use green roofs as urban mitadaptation strategy, we ought to focus on native plants to enhance biodiversity, provide a home for endangered plants, and encourage pollinators. The California Academy of Sciences claims "the densest concentration of native wildflowers in San Francisco," which attract native birds, bees, and butterflies, while interspersed with solar panels that provide 10% of the building's electricity, and reduce internal temperatures by about 10°F..[92]

In New York City, environmental managers explicitly tie biodiversity conservation and functioning ecosystems to climate change adaptation and protecting the city from worsening storm damage and flooding. They note that the city has lost nearly all its native salt marshes, streams, and freshwater wetlands; they are working hard to conserve what remains and to recreate the lost adaptation potential via biodiversity where they can, trying to keep up and exceed climate-driven sea-level rise. They refer to the "post-industrial habitats" they are creating to invite biodiversity to return, and mink, bobcats, bald eagles, whales, and rare butterflies are accepting the invitation. As one manager says: It's as if wildlife has said, "You've taken away our habitat. OK, we'll live in yours." If, as one official proclaims, New York City is now

89. The Great Green Wall, https://www.greatgreenwall.org/about-great-green-wall; *How to Make Africa's "Great Green Wall" a Success*, Nature (May 4, 2022), https://www.nature.com/articles/d41586-022-01201-4; Jim Morrison, *The "Great Green Wall" Didn't Stop Desertification, But It Evolved Into Something That Might*, Smithsonian Mag., Aug. 23, 2016, https://www.smithsonianmag.com/science-nature/great-green-wall-stop-desertification-not-so-much-180960171.

90. *Using Green Roofs to Reduce Heat Islands*, U.S. EPA, https://www.epa.gov/heatislands/using-green-roofs-reduce-heat-islands.

91. Elissaveta M. Brandon, *Inside Rotterdam's Quest to Green 10 Million Square Feet of Rooftops.*, Fast Co. (May 27, 2022), https://www.fastcompany.com/90755913/inside-rotterdams-quest-to-green-10-million-square-feet-of-rooftops.

92. The Academy lists nearly 100 native plant species on their roof: *Living Roof*, Cal. Acad. Sci., https://www.calacademy.org/exhibits/living-roof; *California Academy of Sciences (CAS) Living Roof*, Green Roofs, https://www.greenroofs.com/projects/california-academy-of-sciences-cas-living-roof.

"the greenest big city on [e]arth," it is one where the explicit biodiversity-mitadaptation nexus drives conservation planning.[93]

We have scarcely begun to think about "destination cities," places like Buffalo and Detroit where citizens will be fleeing from unlivable conditions in Miami and Phoenix. In her chapter, "Climate-Changed Communities," Sarah Fox encourages destination cities to think creatively and prepare for climate migration. We could be planning for urban expansion now by creating climate-adapted destination cities, following examples like these.

Biodiversity as Mitigation

As if a plethora of wonderful reasons preserving life's gorgeous biodiversity didn't already exist, biodiversity itself may mitigate GHG accumulation. Oswald Schmitz and colleagues show that animals regulate carbon exchange between the atmosphere and ecosystems in important, not always well-understood, ways.[94] Predator/herbivore-prey/carbon relationships are complicated. Trophic cascades[95]—where disappearing apex predators no longer control herbivore populations, resulting in collapse of carbon-storing plants—can be reversed, simultaneously providing an additional rationale for prioritizing carnivore conservation, helping multispecies ecosystems to rebound, and helping to mitigate climate change by allowing more plants to sequester more carbon.

Sea otters prey on sea urchins, thus allowing kelp forests, which have a high rate of carbon retention (and support a diverse array of species), to flourish. Biologists who studied the 5,400 kilometer extent of sea otters' range estimate a 4.4 to 8.7 tetragram increase in carbon in kelp ecosystems with sea otters as opposed to forests without and a more robust fish population—with the added benefit that fish bodies also sequester carbon. It is not merely that the otters eat the urchins, but also that the urchins are more likely to hide, a scenario delightfully described as a "landscape of fear"[96] or "seascape of fear."[97] The urchins then feed on kelp debris, as opposed to feeding on living kelp when otters are not present. This phenomenon has been observed

93. Lisa M. Collins, *Eagles, Beavers, Sea Turtles: Why New York City Is Humming With Wildlife*, N.Y. Times, Oct. 28, 2021, https://www.nytimes.com/2021/10/28/nyregion/nyc-wildlife-habitats-animals.html.
94. Oswald J. Schmitz et al., *Animals and the Zoochemistry of the Carbon Cycle*, 362 Science 1127 (2018), https://www.science.org/doi/10.1126/science.aar3213.
95. R.T. Paine, *Food Webs: Linkage, Interaction Strength, and Community Infrastructure*, 49 J. Animal Ecology 667 (1980).
96. Joel S. Brown & Burt P. Kotler, *Hazardous Duty Pay and the Foraging Cost of Predation*, 7 Ecology Letters 999 (2004).
97. Atwood, *supra* note 50.

elsewhere as well. Just the presence of the apex predator inhibits herbivory and stimulates plant growth.[98] The authors also note that otters thus provide hundreds of millions of dollars of carbon-retention ecosystem services and could certainly provide more if their populations (and thus their associated kelp forests) were able to regenerate.[99]

Scientists note that living whales store tons of carbon, and their excrement nourishes carbon-sucking phytoplankton. When whales die and sink to the bottom of the ocean, they take their stored carbon with them as one big, bloated carbon sink and provide a food source for a vast, poorly understood, biodiverse benthic ecosystem.[100] Whale poo was (and still is, albeit to a lesser extent) the base of complex, bountiful food webs. Unfortunately, only 5% of the whale population from 400 years ago remains; in a single century, whalers killed over 2 million baleen whales, whose weight exceeded that of all of earth's wild mammals today.[101]

It may rub you the wrong way to think of whales as colossal bags of carbon, but if thinking about whales as part of our bridge to a zero-carbon future helps inspire conservation, then so be it. Scientists are experimenting with replacing missing whale poo with rice husks or iron to stimulate carbon-sucking phytoplankton, as well as providing food for carbon-sequestering fish.[102] Of course these efforts are controversial: Should we be messing with ecosystems like this? That objection overlooks the fact that we have dramatically altered the atmosphere and the biosphere already, and careful experiments that aid both climate and biodiversity could repair parts of our damaged planet.

The practice and science of "rewilding" seeks to restore ecosystem function by allowing entire trophic levels to thrive, either by leaving areas alone to regenerate or through intervening and relocating species. Where herbivores or carnivores have disappeared, rewilding envisions restoring the prior

98. Michael S. Strickland et al., *Trophic Cascade Alters Ecosystem Carbon Exchange*, 110 Proc. Nat'l Acad. Sci. 11035 (Dec. 8, 2013), https://doi.org/10.1073/pnas.1305191110.

99. Christopher C. Wilmers et al., *Do Trophic Cascades Affect the Storage and Flux of Atmospheric Carbon? An Analysis of Sea Otters and Kelp Forests*, 10 Frontiers Ecology & Env't 409 (2012), https://doi.org/10.1890/110176.

100. Michelle Carrere, *To Fight Climate Change, Save the Whales, Some Scientists Say*, Mongabay, Mar. 1, 2021, https://news.mongabay.com/2021/03/to-fight-climate-change-save-the-whales-some-scientists-say; Sophie Yeo, *How Whales Help Cool the Earth*, BBC (Jan. 19, 2021), https://www.bbc.com/future/article/20210119-why-saving-whales-can-help-fight-climate-change.

101. Robin McKie, *The Squit and the Whale: Can Artificial Faeces Revive the Ocean Ecosystem?* Guardian, Mar. 6, 2022, https://www.theguardian.com/environment/2022/mar/06/the-squit-and-the-whale-can-artificial-faeces-revive-the-ocean-ecosystem; Ed Yong, *The Enormous Hole That Whaling Left Behind*, Atlantic, Nov. 3, 2021, https://www.theatlantic.com/science/archive/2021/11/whaling-whales-food-krill-iron/620604.

102. McKie, *supra* note 101; Yong, *supra* note 101.

trophic level so that ecosystems may return to some degree of functioning ecology without continued human intervention; humans get the ecosystem balls rerolling, and nature takes it from there.

While it is clear that rewilding (whether passive or active) influences carbon retention or release, it is not always clear which direction a particular rewilding will head.[103] Wolves in boreal ecosystems control moose populations, which, through altered grazing intensity, increases carbon retention in plants.[104] On the other hand, wolves that prey on elk in prairie ecosystems end up releasing more carbon to the atmosphere. In a smash hit 2014 YouTube video (43 million views and counting—how's *your* TED Talk doing?), George Monbiot narrates a story of "How Wolves Change Rivers."[105] According to the narrative, when managers reintroduced wolves to Yellowstone, the carnivores culled the populations of out-of-control elk and other herbivores, which meant more tree seedlings grew to maturity, sequestering more carbon and stabilizing river banks, creating thriving, biodiverse ecosystems. Now some have challenged the original thesis, alleging that other predators (mountain lions, bears) combined with certain climate effects have had more of an effect on tree regeneration.[106]

Loss of entire guilds of herbivores may mean fewer mutualistic plant-insect interactions, slowed or ceased reforestation of plant species that require passage through herbivores' guts to germinate, reduced plant pollination and dispersal, slower and reduced ecosystem nutrient cycling, and, as a result, diminished biodiversity.[107] Forest elephants in central Africa browse smaller trees, alleviating competition and allowing surviving trees to grow larger; researchers estimate that loss of elephants has decreased carbon stocks by 7% in their forest ecosystems.[108] Due to differences in how they digest plant material, replacement of wild carnivores with domestic carnivores globally

103. Christopher J. Sandom et al., *Trophic Rewilding Presents Regionally Specific Opportunities for Mitigating Climate Change*, 375 Phil. Transactions Royal Soc'y (2020); Oswald J. Schmitz et al., *Animals and the Zoochemistry of the Carbon Cycle*, 362 Science 7 (Dec. 7, 2018), https://www.science.org/doi/10.1126/science.aar3213.

104. Chrisopher C. Wilmers & Oswald J. Schmitz, *Effects of Gray Wolf-Induced Trophic Cascades on Ecosystem Carbon Cycling*, 7 Ecosphere (2016).

105. Sustainable Human, *How Wolves Change Rivers*, YouTube (Feb. 13, 2014), https://www.youtube.com/watch?v=ysa5OBhXz-Q.

106. Phoebe Weston, *The Return of the Wolf: How Much Do They Help Rebuilt Ecosystems?* Guardian, June 23, 2022, https://www.theguardian.com/environment/2022/jun/23/rebalancing-act-bringing-back-wolf-fix-broken-ecosystem-aoe?CMP=Share_iOSApp_Other.

107. Elizabeth A. Hunter et al., *Equivalency of Gálapagos Giant Tortoises Used as Ecological Replacement Species to Restore Ecosystem Function*, 27 Conservation Biology 701, 702 (2013); Joris P.G.M. Cromsigt et al., *Trophic Rewilding as a Climate Mitigation Strategy?*, 373 Phil. Transactions Royal Soc'y 3 (2018), https://royalsocietypublishing.org/doi/10.1098/rstb.2017.0440.

108. Fabio Berzaghi et al., *Carbon Stocks in Central African Forests Enhanced by Elephant Disturbance*, 12 Nature Geoscience 725 (2019), https://www.nature.com/articles/s41561-019-0395-6.

has meant a strong increase in methane (a powerful GHG) emissions.[109] Joris Cromsigt and colleagues suggest that rewilding efforts to restore large, non-ruminant herbivores (for example, elephants, rhinos, as well as large migratory herds of wildebeest and others), especially were these to replace livestock, could revitalize ecosystem functions and yield major carbon-sequestration benefits as well. They suggest that such efforts can increase ecotourism, which raises funds to support the rewilding, and potentially obtain REDD+ funding, if the program was expanded to allow biodiversity carbon mitadaptation efforts to qualify for enhanced offset dollars.[110]

Species introductions are controversial, particularly when managers bring in non-native species as part of rewilding efforts. On the other hand, as one group of conservation biologists expresses it, "judging species on the basis of native/non-native is archaic; species should be assessed on the effect they have on the environment, not on their origin."[111] Perhaps revitalizing ecosystem functions and enhancing carbon sequestration provides ample rationale for the radical approach of "ecological replacement," that is, introducing species to where they have never been but could now thrive. When humans arrived on islands in Mauritius, and they were hungry, they quickly wiped out the Mauritian giant tortoise and thus severely impaired the entire ecosystem. Mauritius has lost over 95% of its native ecosystem, and the nation has the second highest proportion of native trees threatened with extinction (57%), second only to Madagascar.[112] The tortoises were ecosystem architects, shaping the ecosystem through grazing, and germinating tree seeds that passed through their guts. Biologists have relocated related (but hitherto not seen on these islands) Aldabran giant tortoises to fill the ecological niche left vacant by extinction. Biologists found the replacements successfully grazed non-native plant species that were outcompeting the endemic species, and the ecosystem shows promising signs of regeneration; of course, more robust plant growth means more carbon retention.[113]

Of course, such replacements must be done carefully, perhaps with field trials and close monitoring. Remaining with tortoises for a moment, in the Gálapagos, Pinta Island's giant tortoises' extinction fundamentally disrupted

109. Cromsigt et al., *supra* note 107.
110. *Id.*
111. Christine J. Griffiths et al., *Assessing the Potential to Restore Historic Grazing Ecosystems With Tortoise Ecological Replacements*, 27 Conservation Biology 690 (2013).
112. Vincent Florens, *The Macaque Monkeys of Mauritius: An Invasive Alien Species, and a Major Export for Research*, Conversation (Feb. 22, 2022), https://theconversation.com/the-macaque-monkeys-of-mauritius-an-invasive-alien-species-and-a-major-export-for-research-176569; *BGCI Launches the State of the World's Trees Report*, Botanic Gardens Conservation Int'l, https://www.bgci.org/news-events/bgci-launches-the-state-of-the-worlds-trees-report.
113. Griffiths et al., *supra* note 111.

the ecosystem, in particular the dispersal of a giant prickly pear cactus whose seed germination is prompted by passage through the tortoises' guts. Managers released (and carefully monitored) two different species of tortoise that had survived on nearby islands. One species chose the cactus habitat and began eating cactus fruit and germinating cactus seeds, and the other did not.[114] But the experiment again reveals that carefully conducted ecological-replacement experiments can lead to species reintroductions or ecological replacements that simultaneously nourish ecosystems and the carbon that those ecosystems create and sequester.

A 4°C world means environmental law must evolve and adapt. What seems fantastical today might be business as usual a few years hence. How far will we engineer the planet in the name of simultaneously promoting ecosystem function and trapping large amounts of carbon or preventing such amounts of carbon from being emitted? Revive & Restore's goal is to "enhance biodiversity through the genetic rescue of endangered and extinct species."[115] That goal includes bringing back the Woolly Mammoth of the boreal tundra of Asia and North America, a goal not as far-fetched as it seems.[116] The organization labels their effort as "An Ecosystem Approach to Confronting Climate Change."[117] In addition to reintroducing grazers (horses, musk ox) to this Siberian ecosystem, more fantastically, mammoth DNA has been unearthed and is similar enough to extant Asian elephants that the genes that code for extreme cold tolerance could be edited into the Asian elephant genome, creating an Asian elephant-mammoth hybrid that could conceivably thrive in the harsh tundra. Elsewhere, reindeer prevent tundra melting by preventing woody shrubs from encroaching and leading to tundra melting, revealing the herbivores/climate nexus in arctic ecosystems.[118] Mammoths and other steppe grazers used to clear away snow in search of food, thus allowing the bitter cold to seep into the tundra, maintaining its permafrost. Now, without such grazers, the cold does not penetrate, and exacerbated by rising global temperatures, the permafrost is melting. As it melts, the GHGs it has been sequestering for millennia are being released. The goal of the "Pleistocene Park" project is to resuscitate this ancient ecosystem and thus slow or reverse the melting of the tundra. Similarly, in various studies in different climes, grasslands have been shown to be highly reliable carbon storage ecosys-

114. Hunter et al., *supra* note 107, at 707.
115. Revive & Restore, https://reviverestore.org.
116. For an explanation of how this all works, and for a defense of the practice, see Ben Jacob Novak, *De-Extinction*, 9 Genes 548 (2018).
117. *Woolly Mammoth Revival*, Revive & Restore, https://reviverestore.org/projects/woolly-mammoth.
118. Cromsigt et al., *supra* note 107.

tems.[119] The reconversion to a grassland ecosystem both enables deeper winter freezing and retards summer melting and therefore release of the carbon sequestered in the ground.[120]

We have no time not to think about biodiversity as we mitadapt, and no time not to think about mitadaptation when we effect biodiversity conservation. Nature-based solutions are predicated on the notion that attending to functioning ecological communities makes human communities function better, as well. It makes practical and economic sense to promote biodiversity when implementing climate change mitigation and adaptation goals and vice versa. If we are to survive this period of rapid ecological transition, we require a cultural paradigm shift[121] where we see ourselves as fundamentally interconnected with the natural world. The mitadaptation examples above sample ways that our actions, policies, and laws could evolve to reflect and reinforce synergistic, holistic, systems-thinking approaches.

Conclusion

One should cite George Monbiot as much as possible, so here he is, again, on the climate change/biodiversity synergy: "The various impacts have a common cause: the sheer volume of economic activity. We are doing too much of almost everything, and the world's living systems cannot bear it. But our failure to see the whole ensures that we fail to address this crisis systematically and effectively."[122]

In many governing bodies, from international treaty regimes to the most local of governments, when people actually pay attention to these issues, responsibility for climate change usually happens in one place, and responsibility for biodiversity happens in some other office, building, city, or country.[123] In the United States, the U.S. Environmental Protection Agency regulates GHGs (to the shrinking extent it's still allowed),[124] and responsibility to implement the Endangered Species Act, Marine Mammal Protection

119. Novak, *supra* note 116; Pawlok Doss et al., *Grasslands May Be More Reliable Carbon Sinks Than Forests in California*, 13 Env't Res. Letters 074027 (2018).

120. *Woolly Mammoth Revival*, Revive & Restore, https://reviverestore.org/projects/woolly-mammoth. Or see the humorously titled, *"Pleistocene Park: Born to Rewild,"* Sci. Mag. YouTube (Dec. 15, 2015), https://www.youtube.com/watch?v=IWnlPYu3ovQ&t=10s.

121. David Takacs, *We Are the River*, 2021 U. Ill. L. Rev. 545.

122. George Monbiot, *"Green Growth" Doesn't Exist—Less of Everything Is the Only Way to Avert Catastrophe*, Guardian, Sept. 29, 2021, https://www.theguardian.com/commentisfree/2021/sep/29/green-growth-economic-activity-environment.

123. Nadja Kabisch et al., *Nature-Based Solutions to Climate Change Mitigation and Adaptation in Urban Areas: Perspectives on Indicators, Knowledge Gaps, Barriers, and Opportunities for Action*, 21 Ecology & Soc'y 39 (2016).

124. West Virginia v. EPA, 142 S. Ct. 2587 (2022).

Act, and the National Forest Management Act is spread among three agencies (further divided among subagencies), none of which is the agency designated to protect the environment. Yes, there can be cross-sectoral cooperation,[125] but there need not be and often is not. The international treaty regimes have long remained separated between the U.N. Framework Convention on Climate Change and the Convention on Biological Diversity, although they occasionally wave at each other from a distance.

Particularly in this "U.N. Decade of Ecosystem Restoration,"[126] efforts to synergize mitadaptation and biodiversity rejuvenation are growing. In 2021 (at last), the IPCC and IPBES held a joint workshop to think about how to synergize their efforts. They play the themes that I sound here: these crises are inexorably intertwined, and "[i]n the worst case it may lead to taking actions that may inadvertently prevent the solution of one or the other, or both issues . . . while avoiding costly and effort-sapping errors."[127] We should break down jurisdictional silos that allow or even compel us to manage these crises separately.

As noted above, the world has created a direct pay-for-performance financial system where trees are repurposed as carbon storage devices to absorb the industrial excesses of the (mostly) global North. To the bureaucrat economists' joy, you can measure a ton of GHGs and slap a price on it. While it's possible to quantify GHGs, it's harder to quantify biodiversity: what is your unit?[128] And if you can't quantify the unit, it's difficult to quantify the price.

We need financial mechanisms that go beyond simplistic REDD+ trees as carbon storage devices, specifically, a system that puts economic value on the complex dynamic between functioning ecosystems and the carbon storage and biodiversity enhancements they provide. International Financial Institutions need a fundamental revamp of finance and loan systems to consider the full value of ecosystem services and their intertwined climate and biodiversity goals, which especially means putting more of a value on the latter. While we've found ways to put a value on the former (social cost of carbon, cap and trade, offsets), we are nowhere on putting a value on the latter beyond saying, as the U.S. Supreme Court noted in *Tennessee Valley Authority v. Hill*, that the value of biodiversity is "incalculable."[129] If you

125. *E.g.*, USDA, Greenhouse Gas Accounting and Mitigation, https://www.usda.gov/oce/energy-and-environment/climate/mitigation.

126. UNEP, U.N. Decade on Ecosystem Restoration, *Preventing, Halting, and Reversing Loss of Nature* https://www.decadeonrestoration.org.

127. Potner et al., *supra* note 6, at 4, 5.

128. David Takacs, *An Aye-Aye for an Aye-Aye: Making Biodiversity Offsets Sustainable*, 45 Colum. J. Envtl. L. 519, 547-57 (2020).

129. 437 U.S. 153, 187 (1978).

can't calculate it, its economic value is meaningless and that means we don't calculate it, i.e., the value is zero. Ecological economists like Robert Costanza may guesstimate the global economic value of ecosystem services at $125-145 trillion/year in U.S. dollars, but try reducing that down to a meaningful, tradable unit.[130] Compounding these difficulties is the myopia of politicians with short reelection schedules and reluctant taxpayers and consumers who value short-term economic savings no matter what the long-term costs; synergistic mitadaptation investments now will save their children big bucks (and maybe just save them, period), but these long-term benefits are more difficult to quantify, understand, or effect.

Many times in this chapter, I've been tempted to start a sentence, *it goes without saying.* As in, *it goes without saying that fossil fuel extraction extracts fossil fuels that will eventually be burned, leading to global heating, which will in turn further destroy biodiversity, which will further exacerbate the climate emergency, which imperils current and future human generations* . . . but if it went without saying, and anyone paid attention to it being said, we wouldn't be doing it. In a lovely article, David Orr visits the ecological and social destruction wrought at the coal fields of West Virginia and by the-more-powerful-than-it-would-otherwise-have-been-were-it-not-for-global-heating Hurricane Katrina, and laments:

To permanently destroy millions of acres of Appalachia to extract maybe 20 years of coal is not only stupid, it is derangement at a scale for which we do not have adequate words, let alone the good sense and the laws to stop. . . . It is destroying the wonders of the mixed mesophytic forests of Northern Appalachia once and for all, including habitats for dozens of endangered species. . . . Coal companies' efforts to plant grass and a few trees here and there are like putting lipstick on a mutilated corpse. The fact of the matter is that one of the most diverse and beautiful ecosystems in the world is being destroyed along with the lives and culture of the people who have stayed behind. . . .[131]

Those ecosystems are being destroyed so that we may speed our arrival at the catastrophic 3°C or 4°C future, further upending ecosystems, which ramp up the impacts of climate change. And so on.

All the examples I have described in this chapter comprise a fair bit of wishful thinking and deck-chair rearranging unless we fundamentally re-envision how to structure societies that are equitable and sustainable and

130. Robert Costanza et al., *Changes in the Global Value of Ecosystem Services*, 26 Global Envtl. Change 152, 156 (2014).

131. David Orr, *The Carbon Connection*, 21 Conservation Biology 289 (2007).

prevent some small portion of the population from gluttonously consuming more than their share of earth's resources, thus emitting GHGs while sucking up the resources that nonhuman life requires as well and speeding up the vicious, reenforcing, civilization-destroying cycle of climate change and biodiversity loss.

If at a deep level, we fundamentally thought about these crises as intertwined, symbiotic, and synergistic, we'd be focusing on the root causes: there are too many of us, and some of us are too rich and simply want too much. All "wants" and "needs" require chipping away bits of the earth, require polluting the global atmospheric commons, require eroding the remaining vestiges of the planet's functioning ecosystems and component species. Most people are ecologically illiterate; we don't really understand or appreciate how or why human well-being requires a relatively stable atmosphere and biosphere. Alternatively, some of us understand that and don't care. To see and care about the intertwined crises of climate change and biodiversity, and to avoid (or at least survive) a 4°C future requires a fundamental, "deeply equitable" realignment of values from abuse of the earth toward reverence for the earth, with this reverence imbued in our personal ethical codes, and written into our laws. Deeply equitable policies and laws act in synergy to maximize the health and potential of all individuals, communities, and ecosystems. The equity is deep because values become rooted within each individual, because we fundamentally re-imagine our community responsibilities, and because we root these values and responsibilities in our policies and laws which, in turn, support values and actions promoting even deeper equity.[132]

Absent a turn toward reverence for the planet, and for the atmosphere and biodiversity that synergistically sustain us, we impel the shredding of human and nonhuman fabric wrought by the 3°C or 4°C world. Absent a fundamental appreciation that the synergistic effects of climate change and biodiversity loss threaten human existence, which would result in rapid, synergistic efforts to obviate both, it is hard to be optimistic about life—human and nonhuman—in the coming, chaotic, heated world.

132. David Takacs, *Forest Carbon Project and International Law: A Deep Equity Legal Analysis*, 22 Geo. Int'l L. Rev. 521 (2010).

America Erased

Michele Okoh

To the unrelenting commitment of Mayor Bobbie Jones, who has made it his mission to preserve and grow America's history, and to all the other community leaders working to ensure that America will not be erased.

Drought. Flooding. Extreme heat. Climate change has many tools for destruction, but no matter the disaster, in a 4 degree Celsius (°C) world, parts of the United States will be left uninhabitable.[1] Significant portions of the population will be forced to leave their homes due to climate disasters and will live their lives as internally displaced people.[2] These people will bring with them diverse cultural identities. They will also have left places of significant cultural and historical relevance.[3] The locations may be lost, but the people will endure.

The nature of this loss requires protecting the lives and health of these people, but it also requires protecting the unique cultures and identities interwoven into the tapestry of the U.S. identity. Whether one subscribes to the view of the United States as a melting pot or a salad, a crucial part of the American identity is the diversity of cultures adorning the fabric of this country. The erasure of these cultures is more than an isolated, confined loss; it is the wiping out of a critical part of the American identity.

Author's note: The author is grateful for the willingness of Mayor Bobbie Jones to share his insights and experience on one of America's great historic communities, the Town of Princeville, North Carolina. She further appreciates the comments and suggestions of Derek Warden and Christian Giusto. She is also thankful for the research assistance of Radhika Shah and Katie Thompson and for the feedback and support of the Environmental Law Collaborative.

1. J.B. Ruhl & Robin Kundis Craig, *4°C*, 106 Minn. L. Rev. 191 (2021).
2. *See Global Report of Internal Displacement 2021*, Internal Displacement Monitoring Ctr. (2021), https://www.internal-displacement.org/global-report/grid2021/downloads/IDMCGRID21FinalHQ.pdf?v=2.
3. *See* David G. Anderson et al., *Sea-Level Rise and Archaeological Site Destruction: An Example From the Southeastern United States Using DINAA (Digital Index of North American Archaeology)*, 12 PLoS One e0188142 (Nov. 29, 2017); Abby Neal, *Cultural Heritage Is a Necessary Component of Climate Solutions*, Envtl. & Energy Study Inst. (Aug. 14, 2020), https://www.eesi.org/articles/view/cultural-heritage-is-a-necessary-component-of-climate-solutions.

This chapter will assess whether the United States is prepared to prevent the loss of both health and culture associated with internal displacement due to climate change. First, this chapter will provide an overview and discuss the nature of the problem of internal displacement due to climate change. Second, the chapter will evaluate what actions the United States has taken to address expected climate change internal displacement within its own borders. Third, the chapter will focus on U.S. preparedness to protect its culture and history from being erased by climate change. This discussion will address the current U.S. approach to protecting its cultural and historical resources. Additionally, it will present insights from the mayor of a community facing the threat of having its culture and history erased by climate change so that the reader can better appreciate what the United States stands to lose culturally and historically due to climate change. Finally, the chapter will discuss what the preservation of these communities might look like once the connection to place is lost.

Overview of Internal Displacement Due to Climate Change

With increased impacts related to climate change, also come increased limitations on areas that are inhabitable on this earth. Since 1990, the Intergovernmental Panel on Climate Change (IPCC) has recognized that climate change's greatest impact may be on human migration.[4] Specifically, the U.S. Government Accountability Office (GAO) defines climate migration as the "preemptive movement of people and property away from areas experiencing severe climate change impacts" and recognizes it as "one way to improve climate resilience."[5] This definition includes both the relocation of entire communities and managed retreat (incremental relocation of communities and resources).[6] Climate change is increasingly becoming a significant driver of forced migration, both internationally and domestically. Migration is typically an adaptive response of last resort, exercised when other means of adaptation and government assistance are insufficient to meet immediate needs.[7] Although forced migration is far from a new phenomenon, climate change is altering the nature of this migration. Where conflict and violence once were

4. Oli Brown, *Migration and Climate Change*, International Org. for Migration (IOM) (2014), https://www.ipcc.ch/apps/njlite/srex/njlite_download.php?id=5866.
5. *Climate Change: A Climate Migration Pilot Program Could Enhance the Nation's Resilience and Reduce Federal Fiscal Exposure*, U.S. GAO (July 2020), https://www.gao.gov/assets/gao-20-488.pdf.
6. *Id.*
7. Brown, *supra* note 4.

the main drivers of forced migration, extreme weather has become the main driver of new displacements.[8]

Extreme weather events are responsible for the great majority of new displacements.[9] In 2017, 61% of displacement was caused by disasters (as compared to 39% caused by conflict).[10] The vast majority of these disaster-related displacements were due to extreme weather events, such as wildfires, hurricanes, and flooding. Out of the 18.8 million disaster-related displacements, 18 million were weather-related.[11] People are most likely to migrate to areas where they have connections, such as family and other means of social support.[12] Accordingly, the bulk of this migration has been internal displacement.[13]

Extreme weather-related events accounted for 22.3 million newly internally displaced persons in 2021 alone.[14] Internally displaced persons refer to those who have been forced to leave their homes due to violence, conflict, human rights violations, or disasters, but remain within their home country.[15] It is fairly typical for people to migrate within their own country,[16] and in cases of internal displacement, people are most likely to settle in places where they have ethnic, cultural, or historical connections.[17] Unlike other displaced persons who cross country borders, such as asylees and refugees, these internally displaced persons still have all the rights and protections of citizenship or residence that they had prior to displacement.[18]

Addressing Climate Change Internal Migration Proactively

As discussed in Clifford J. Villa's chapter, "Environmental Justice and the 4°C World," in addition to the nature of extreme weather events, vulnerability plays a significant role in how communities will be impacted by cli-

8. *Global Report on Internal Displacement 2022*, Internal Displacement Monitoring Centre (2022), https://www.internal-displacement.org/global-report/grid2022/ [hereinafter Internal Displacement Monitoring Centre 2022].
9. *Id.*
10. *Id.*
11. *Id.*
12. Brown, *supra* note 4.
13. *Global Report on Internal Displacement 2018*, Internal Displacement Monitoring Centre (2018), https://www.internal-displacement.org/global-report/grid2018/.
14. Internal Displacement Monitoring Centre 2022, *supra* note 8.
15. *Guiding Principles on Internal Displacement*, UNHCR The UN Refugee Agency (Sept. 2004), https://www.unhcr.org/43ce1cff2.pdf.
16. Brown, *supra* note 4.
17. *Id.*
18. *Handbook for the Protection of Internally Displaced Persons*, UNHCR The UN Refugee Agency (2010), https://www.unhcr.org/4c2355229.pdf.

mate change.[19] As noted in a report from the International Organization for Migration (IOM) Research Series: "A natural hazard (such as an approaching storm) only becomes a 'natural disaster' if a community is particularly vulnerable to its impact."[20] Ultimately, a community's vulnerability is "a function of its *exposure* to climatic conditions (such as a coastal location) and the community's *adaptive capacity* (the capacity of a particular community to weather the worst of the storm and recover after it)."[21] While a 4°C change will be "universally negative," the impacts of climate change are not linear.[22] Non-climate drivers affecting a community's vulnerability are also important to a community's ability to adapt to climate change.[23] The report noted that, "only through a structural understanding of the environment in the broader political and cultural context of a region or country can one begin to understand the 'role' it plays as a factor in population movement."[24] Additionally, these factors go beyond serving as mere drivers of vulnerability; they also need to be considered as part of an approach to risk reduction and supporting successful climate migration. The U.S. Global Change Research Program's (USGCRP's) *Fourth National Climate Assessment* identifies that "factors such as access to resources, culture, governance, and available information can affect not only the risk faced by different populations but also the best ways to reduce their risks."[25]

In fact, standards for the treatment of internally displaced persons have existed since 1998.[26] While these standards are not binding under international law, they are based on existing binding international law.[27] At a minimum, the United States should be prepared to follow these guidelines. The U.N. Human Rights Council recommends a human rights-based approach to addressing the needs of internally displaced persons.[28] This approach is important because generally, human rights are negatively impacted following a disaster due to "inadequate planning and disaster preparedness, inappropriate policies and measures to respond to the disasters, or simple neglect," not

19. Clifford J. Villa, *Environmental Justice and the 4°C World*, *in* Facing the Worst Climate Case: The Role of Law (forthcoming 2023).
20. Brown, *supra* note 4.
21. *Id.*
22. *Id.*
23. *Id.*
24. *Id.*
25. 2 U.S. Global Change Res. Prog., Fourth National Climate Assessment: Impacts, Risks, and Adaption in the United States 1312 (last updated Mar. 2021).
26. *Guiding Principles on Internal Displacement*, *supra* note 15.
27. *Id.*
28. Walter Kälin, Report of the Representative of the Secretary-General on the Human Rights of Internally Displaced Persons, *Operational Guidelines on the Protection of Persons in Situations of Natural Disasters*, U.N. Doc. A/HRC/16/43/Add.5 (Jan. 31, 2011).

by any "purposeful policies."[29] The outcome is characterized by both existing vulnerabilities within the population and the effectiveness of disaster planning and preparation, for both prevention and mitigation.[30]

The United States is not immune to climate change-related internal displacement. From 2008-2021, there were 10.5 million disaster-related internal displacements within the United States. Approximately 7 million were due to storms, 3 million were due to wildfires, and over half a million were due to flooding.[31] Adequately addressing global forced migration due to climate change means that the United States must also be prepared to manage its own resulting internal displacement.

U.S. Preparedness for Internal Displacement Due to Climate Change

Overall, the United States is ill-prepared to address climate migration within its borders. Currently, there is no official federal program aimed at preparing people for internal displacement within America.[32] According to a report from the GAO: "Federal programs generally are not designed to address the scale and complexity of community relocation and generally fund acquisition of properties at high risk of damage from disasters in response to a specific event such as a hurricane."[33] Additionally, despite the fact that many U.S. communities will face relocation due to climate change, the GAO reports "few communities in the United States . . . have considered or implemented climate migration as a strategy to improve their resilience."[34] For the few communities that have engaged in climate migration, the process has been slow due to the absence of a central federal authority to coordinate climate migration.[35] For example, it took Newtok, Alaska, 30 years and Isle de Jean Charles, Louisiana, 20 years to relocate in response to climate change.[36]

Additionally, the federal government's approach has been fragmented because there is no lead federal agency directing federal assistance for climate

29. *Id.*
30. *Id.*
31. *United States, IDMC,* INTERNAL DISPLACEMENT MONITORING CTR., https://www.internal-displacement.org/countries/united-states#internal-displacement (last visited Aug 1, 2022).
32. Carlos Martín & Alexander Williams, *A Federal Policy and Climate Migration Briefing for Federal Executive and Legislative Officials*, URB. INST. (Mar. 2021), https://www.urban.org/sites/default/files/publication/103796/a-federal-policy-and-climate-migration-briefing-for-federal-executive-and-legislative-officials_0.pdf.
33. *Climate Change: A Climate Migration Pilot Program Could Enhance the Nation's Resilience and Reduce Federal Fiscal Exposure, supra* note 5.
34. *Id.*
35. *Id.*
36. *Id.*

migration.[37] As of 2013, the GAO has included "Limiting the Federal Government's Fiscal Exposure by Better Managing Climate Change Risks" on its high-risk list of federal programs that are vulnerable to "fraud, waste, abuse, and mismanagement, or in need of transformation to address economy, efficiency, or effectiveness challenges."[38] The GAO concluded: "The federal government is not well positioned to address the fiscal exposure presented by climate change, and needs a government-wide strategic approach with strong leadership to manage related risks."[39] The federal government has made no progress since the GAO's 2019 high-risk report.[40]

Despite the importance of planning and preparation in migration outcomes, the United States has been primarily reactive in its approach to climate migration.[41] The federal government, through the Federal Emergency Management Agency (FEMA), typically waits for a disaster to occur to aid impacted communities.[42] This wait-for-a-disaster approach also occurs with disaster mitigation; the disaster declaration is the trigger.[43] Both the GAO and risk management best practices stipulate that the federal government should prepare for climate mitigation *before* a disaster occurs.[44] To address climate change migration, the federal government needs to move away from a reactive response focused on emergency response and shift to a proactive approach that accounts for vulnerabilities.

Because climate change is associated with extreme weather events, FEMA has become the default agency for addressing climate-related disasters. FEMA's authority to manage federal disaster relief programs arises from the Robert T. Stafford Disaster Relief and Emergency Assistance Act (Stafford Act).[45] The Stafford Act, however, does not explicitly address climate change.[46] Instead, the Stafford Act limits FEMA's response to instances

---

37. *Id.*
38. *Id.*
39. *High-Risk Series: An Update*, U.S. GAO (Feb. 2013), https://www.gao.gov/assets/files.gao.gov/assets/gao-13-283.pdf.
40. *Limiting the Federal Government's Fiscal Exposure by Better Managing Climate Change Risks*, U.S. GAO, https://www.gao.gov/highrisk/limiting-federal-governments-fiscal-exposure-better-managing-climate-change-risks (Aug. 17, 2022).
41. Martín & Williams, *supra* note 32; U.S. GAO, Disaster Resilience Framework 53 (2019) (GAO-20-100SP).
42. Martín & Williams, *supra* note 32.
43. *Id.*
44. *Climate Change: A Climate Migration Pilot Program Could Enhance the Nation's Resilience and Reduce Federal Fiscal Exposure*, *supra* note 5.
45. Stafford Act, Pub. L. No. 93-288, as amended (codified at 42 U.S.C. §5121 et seq.).
46. *See id.*

where the president issues either a major disaster declaration or emergency declaration in response to a state's[47] request.[48]

A major disaster declaration makes all of FEMA's programs available, while an emergency declaration has a broader application, but offers limited financial assistance. Some, but not all, effects of climate change are clearly identified as major disasters under the Stafford Act. Specifically, "any natural catastrophe (including any hurricane, tornado, storm, high water, wind-driven water, tidal wave, tsunami, earthquake, volcanic eruption, landslide, mudslide, snowstorm, or drought), or, regardless of cause, any fire, flood, or explosion" would constitute a major disaster as long as the president determines that the damage is "of sufficient severity and magnitude to warrant major disaster assistance under this chapter to supplement the efforts and available resources of States, local governments, and disaster relief organizations in alleviating the damage, loss, hardship, or suffering caused thereby."[49] If an incident does not rise to the level of a major disaster, the president can issue an emergency declaration whenever they determine "[f]ederal assistance is needed to supplement State and local efforts and capabilities to save lives and to protect property and public health and safety, or to lessen or avert the threat of a catastrophe in any part of the United States."[50] The Stafford Act, however, limits funds for emergency declarations to $5 million unless the president determines: (A) "continued emergency assistance is immediately required"; (B) "there is a continuing and immediate risk to lives, property, public health or safety"; and (C) "necessary assistance will not otherwise be provided on a timely basis."[51] Additionally, whereas all FEMA assistance is available during a major disaster declaration, the Act restricts what assistance FEMA may provide for an emergency declaration.

Despite the broadness of the two declarations, many climate disasters may not qualify for FEMA assistance as either a major disaster or emergency. Specifically, "Stafford Act declarations generally respond to rapid-onset events that cause a measurable amount of damage in a particular geographic area over a defined period of time."[52] The problem is that many impacts of climate change have unclear durations and cumulative damages that are dif-

47. "State" refers to "any State of the United States, the District of Columbia, Puerto Rico, the Virgin Islands, Guam, American Samoa, and the Commonwealth of the Northern Mariana Islands." 42 U.S.C. §5122(4).
48. *See* 44 C.F.R. 206.31.
49. 42 U.S.C. §5122(2).
50. *Id.* §5122(1); 44 C.F.R. 206.35.
51. 42 U.S.C. §5193(b).
52. *Climate Change, Slow-Onset Disasters, and the Federal Emergency Management Agency*, Cong. Res. Serv. (Dec. 1, 2022), https://crsreports.congress.gov/product/pdf/IN/IN11696.

ficult to define.[53] In addition to examples of extreme weather events given as examples under the Stafford Act, climate change also includes slow-onset, compound, or cascading disasters.[54] Damages from these types of disasters are difficult to connect to one discrete event.[55] Nevertheless, FEMA restricts its programs to exclude these types of disasters. Thus according to FEMA regulations: "No Federal assistance under the Act shall be approved unless the damage or hardship to be alleviated resulted from the disaster-causing incident which took place during the incident period or was in anticipation of that incident."[56]

The federal government's focus on disasters with identifiable durations and clearly attributable damages has excluded communities in need of climate migration assistance. For example, Newtok has had difficulty accessing disaster relief funds for climate migration. Newtok relocated due to slow-moving climate impacts associated with permafrost thawing and coastal erosion.[57] In 2016, President Barack Obama denied their request for assistance because he determined that slow-moving disasters did not qualify for aid under the Stafford Act.[58] Overall, the United States seems ill-prepared to address both tangible and intangible losses due to climate migration.

Recent U.S. Actions to Address Climate Migration

On February 4, 2021, President Joe Biden signed Executive Order No. 14013, Rebuilding and Enhancing Programs to Resettle Refugees and Planning for the Impact of Climate.[59] In addition to directing federal agencies to take "[s]teps to [i]mprove the [e]fficacy, [i]ntegrity, [s]ecurity, and [t]ransparency" of the U.S. refugee program and revoking specific Trump Administration executive actions that placed additional barriers to refugee resettlement, Executive Order No. 14013 also directs the National Security Advisor to prepare a report on climate change's impact on migration, including internal displacement. The executive order also stipulated that the report should, at a minimum, address collaboration with "localities to respond to migration resulting directly or indirectly from climate change."[60] In response, several

53. *Id.*
54. *Id.*
55. *Id.*
56. 44 C.F.R. 206.32(f).
57. *Climate Change: A Climate Migration Pilot Program Could Enhance the Nation's Resilience and Reduce Federal Fiscal Exposure*, *supra* note 5.
58. *Id.*
59. Exec. Order No. 14013, 86 Fed. Reg. 8839 (Feb. 4, 2021).
60. *Id.*

U.S. mayors issued a letter expressing their support and interest in assisting in the development of the report.[61]

Per Executive Order No. 14013, the U.S. government released on Oct. 21, 2021, the *Report on the Impact of Climate Change on Migration.* This report is monumental because it "marks the first time the U.S. [g]overnment is officially reporting on the link between climate change and migration."[62]

Ultimately, the report did not directly address internal displacement caused by climate change. Instead, it included in its recommendations that that the United States should "[c]onsider developing a complementary report that addresses the impacts of climate change on migration/relocation within the United States to include special consideration in areas of rapid climate change and dense populations."[63] Additionally, the report recognized that "a number of U.S. communities are already experiencing severe impacts from sea-level rise, permafrost thaw, drought, and wildfires."[64] In the United States, internal displacement is expected to be significant. A study from 2020 predicted that 13 million people would be displaced by 2100 from direct flooding due to sea-level rise alone.[65] Since then, predictions related to climate change have become more dire. Ultimately, the United States seems primed to deal with internal migration everywhere except for within its own borders.

Protecting Culture When Place Is Lost

In addition to a lack of preparedness to address protecting the health, safety, and well-being of those facing climate migration, America appears to be unprepared to protect its own cultural and historic resources. If the United States is to preserve its culture and history in the face of climate change, it must also shift its focus toward protecting the culture that resides within those people.[66] Yet it appears that much of the current approach to protecting culture and history is rooted in protecting *places*. The paragon of this

61. Steve Adler et al., *US Local Governments Call for Equitable and Inclusive Action on Climate Migration*, Mayors Migration Council (Apr. 22, 2021), https://www.mayorsmigrationcouncil.org/biden-climate-eo.
62. The White House, *Report on the Impact of Climate Change on Migration* (Oct. 2021), https://www.whitehouse.gov/wp-content/uploads/2021/10/Report-on-the-Impact-of-Climate-Change-on-Migration.pdf.
63. *Id.*
64. *Id.*
65. Caleb Robinson et al., *Modeling Migration Patterns in the USA Under Sea-Level Rise*, 15 PLoS One 1-15 (Jan. 22, 2020), http://dx.doi.org/10.1371/journal.pone.0227436.
66. *See* W. Neil Adger et al., *Cultural Dimensions of Climate Change Impacts and Adaptation*, 3 Nature Climate Change 112 (Nov. 11, 2012), available at https://www.nature.com/articles/nclimate1666.

approach is the National Historic Preservation Act. Places deemed worthy of preservation are listed on the National Register of Historic Places, which has historically not been racially and gender inclusive, thereby failing to reflect diversity in America.[67] Places that have been recently added to address this lack of diversity are especially vulnerable to climate change.[68]

Executive Order No. 13146 is an example of historic preservation beyond the National Historic Preservation Act. In the wake of Hurricane Floyd's devastation of Princeville, North Carolina, President Bill Clinton issued Executive Order No. 13146 to recognize the historical significance of Princeville as the first city founded in the United States by freed slaves and to create the President's Council on the Future of Princeville, North Carolina.[69] Unfortunately, memory is ephemeral, and until recently, the National Museum of African American History and Culture recognized Eatonville, Florida, as the first town chartered by black Americans.[70] This error has since been corrected, and Princeville's pride in being the first town chartered by black Americans endures.[71] Despite this previous inaccuracy, residents of Princeville are aware of their cultural significance and the value their community holds in American history.[72]

Many residents of Princeville were relocated following Hurricane Floyd in 1999, but the town was rebuilt.[73] Eventually, Princeville's population returned to its levels prior to Hurricane Floyd.[74] The town of Princeville had the option of a buyout, but ultimately, the town rejected it.[75] Princeville instead opted to rebuild its levees to protect it from the 100-year floodplain.[76]

Unfortunately, the 100-year flood came 83 years early with Hurricane Matthew in 2016.[77] Again, the town was flooded, destroying 450 homes.[78] The population was only 2,200 at the time of Hurricane Matthew.[79] The road to recovery has been long, with many residents not wanting to abandon

67. Neal, *supra* note 3.
68. *Id.*
69. Exec. Order No. 13146, 65 Fed. Reg. 12318 (Mar. 8, 2000).
70. Cynthia A. Grace-McCaskey et al., *Finding Voices in the Floods of Freedom Hill: Innovating Solutions in Princeville, North Carolina*, 11 J. Envtl. Stud. & Sci. 341 (May,2021), https://link.springer.com/article/10.1007/s13412-021-00701-5.
71. *Id.*
72. *Id.*
73. *Id.*
74. *Id.*
75. *Id.*
76. *Id.*
77. *Id.*
78. *Hurricane Matthew Recovery—Princeville*, Coastal Resilience Ctr., https://coastalresiliencecenter.unc.edu/crc-projects/hurricane-matthew-recovery/hurricane-matthew-recovery-engagement/hurricane-matthew-recovery-princeville/ (last visited Jan. 6, 2022).
79. *Id.*

the historical significance of Princeville.[80] Following Hurricane Matthew, North Carolina provided funding to purchase a total of 141 acres of neighboring land to relocate the most threatened parts of the town.[81] In a 4°C world, however, partial retreat will be insufficient.[82] The places communities value most will be lost.

Princeville is an example of cultural and historical resilience. When their history was forgotten by other Americans, the people of Princeville remembered who they were as a community. The attachment to place will endure, but in the face of destruction, governments can choose to invest not just in protecting places, but also in the people who take pride in that culture and history. Memories can be forgotten, however, and geography is a part of community identity.[83] Once communities are dispersed, the United States risks losing that community identity, and consequently, the history and culture associated with that community.

What We Are Losing: Insights From the Mayor of Princeville

On July 28, 2022, Mayor Bobbie Jones of Princeville, North Carolina, discussed what it would mean to lose a historic place like Princeville. At that time, Princeville was undergoing many positive changes aimed at protecting the city from the devastation of climate change. Since Hurricane Floyd and Hurricane Matthew, Princeville had received funding to upgrade its levees, and the U.S. Army Corps of Engineers was meeting monthly to update residents on the progress of their planning efforts. Mayor Jones reported that the city recently completed storm water improvements and that they were collaborating with North Carolina State University and the North Carolina Conservation Corps on flood prevention. The focus was on partial retreat and relocating nearby to the 53-acre and 88-acre plots of land that were purchased to secure the survival of Princeville. The previous night the community had come together to approve a "20-year vision plan." On the day of the interview, Mayor Jones learned that Princeville would receive a $12 million block grant to develop infrastructure on the 53 acres of land. Mayor Jones was looking forward to Princeville having a promising future, one where its people would not only continue to live, but thrive.

---

80. Grace-McCaskey et al., *supra* note 70.
81. *Id.* at 348.
82. Ruhl & Craig, *supra* note 1.
83. Jianchao Peng et al., *Place Identity: How Far Have We Come in Exploring Its Meanings?*, 11 Frontiers Psych. 294 (Mar. 10, 2020).

To Mayor Jones, serving as mayor was more than a job or a political office. It was a mission. According to Mayor Jones:

> To think about what our forefathers suffered and how they persevered. How they came to swamp land with absolutely nothing but their God-given gifts and talents, and they created Freedom Hill. From Freedom Hill to Princeville, to what we have today is an amazing story. What they did, we owe it to them today to make Princeville even better than what it is. That's my mission.[84]

Therefore, he and the people of Princeville continue to focus on bettering Princeville and finding ways to share its amazing story with the world. It is a story that Mayor Jones had to admit that he originally took for granted. He recounted:

> When leaving and living here, I had no idea what Princeville was. But now that I know, I wouldn't leave for anything in the world because this is rich history. It is up to us to get this rich history out to the world and let the world know the town of Princeville and how important it is. We need to support it.[85]

He hoped to preserve Princeville not only for its strong people and culture, but also for its significance to America. Mayor Jones emphasized:

> We have it on our entrance sign. "The first African American town chartered in the United States of America." A lot of people don't like that but that's the fact. That's why we're not down in the history books. Racism. But the things we are doing now will get us, maybe not in the history book, but people will know about us.[86]

He was particularly concerned about the relevance of Princeville's history to young people. According to Mayor Jones:

> Why is that important? Because, how do you know where you're going if you don't know where you came from? The town of Princeville was the beginning for all African Americans. The first town chartered. . . . All these odds were against us. . . . That's got to be strong, powerful people. I am so proud to be a part of it. I would not change who I am for anything in the world. . . . I want our young people to feel the same way because I believe they don't feel that now. . . . They don't know what our forefathers did for them. It's our job to reveal to them how special they are, where they've come from, and where they can go.[87]

84. Interview with Bobbie Jones, Mayor of Princeville, N.C. (July 28, 2022).
85. *Id.*
86. *Id.*
87. *Id.*

As emphasized by Mayor Jones, losing Princeville would be a loss that would not only affect the people of Princeville, but also the future generations. It would be a loss that would transcend the limits of place but would affect American culture as a whole. Princeville is an important part of American history. It is a history teeming with resilience, a quality desperately needed in a country facing the type of catastrophic change projected to result from climate change.

Welcome to the Metaverse: What Remains After a Physical Place Is Lost to Climate Change

Place is an important and complex aspect of individual and collective identity, but it is not the only source of identity. Geographic communities are just one type of community, just one classification existing among a multitude of identities.[88] Culture and history can be protected if a cultural/historical perspective is taken toward communities. The geography may be lost, but the community will remain, if protected. To protect this culture and history, the United States can choose to take an anticipatory or reactive approach to adaptation. The current approach is largely reactive, but an anticipatory approach is necessary to protect these resources against the advancing threat of climate change.[89]

Nevertheless, although necessary to protect community and culture, preserving these elements of America without a physical place to unify them is less than ideal. It requires the creation of a space that transcends the physical nature of place. Outside the United States, there have been advancements in addressing this problem through the metaverse.

As opposed to having a physical location to share, communities are now moving to virtual spaces. Tuvalu, a small island nation expected to be erased by climate change, is in the process of becoming the "World's First Digital Nation."[90] This entails the creation of a virtual copy of Tuvalu, one where its culture and history can be preserved despite its land being lost.[91]

88. Travis B. Paveglio et al., *Re-Conceptualizing Community in Risk Research*, 20 J. Risk Res. 931 (2017), http://dx.doi.org/10.1080/13669877.2015.1121908.

89. Shiv Someshwar, *Adaptation to Climate Change: Moving Beyond "Reactive" Approaches*, World Res. Inst., https://www.wri.org/our-work/project/world-resources-report/adaptation-climate-change-moving-beyond-reactive-approaches (last visited Jan. 6, 2022).

90. Jessica Cohen & Thomas McKenna, *Tuvalu Is Set to Become "The World's First Digital Nation" as the Climate Crisis Worsens*, Now This News, Nov. 15, 2022, https://nowthisnews.com/news/tuvalu-replicate-metaverse.

91. Lucy Craymer, *Tuvalu Turns to Metaverse as Rising Seas Threaten Existence*, Reuters, Nov. 15, 2022, https://www.reuters.com/business/cop/tuvalu-turns-metaverse-rising-seas-threaten-existence-2022-11-15/.

Tuvalu is not alone in its efforts to relocate to the metaverse. Seoul, South Korea, became the first major city to develop a public metaverse platform.[92] The city launched the Seoul Metropolitan Government metaverse platform to provide municipal services in 2023.[93] The city has a five-year plan to expand the platform to all municipal services.[94] Prior to Tuvalu's efforts, Barbados approved the first metaverse embassy in order to expand its diplomatic influence beyond the confines of its borders on Aug. 12, 2021.[95] Meanwhile, the United Arab Emirates (UAE) has taken several steps to extend its reach into the metaverse. The UAE plans to launch the world's first metaverse hospital[96] and Dubai's Virtual Assets Regulatory Authority as the first regulatory agency in the metaverse.[97] Additionally, Dubai has a strategy to create 40,000 jobs in the metaverse by 2030,[98] and the UAE Ministry of Economy has announced a new headquarters in the metaverse.[99]

With these efforts come significant financial investments and planning. If the United States waits to react to the loss of its places, then it will be too late. It is hard to copy a location, even in the metaverse, once it is gone.

Conclusion

Documents can be preserved. Oral histories can be recorded. But land, places that are slated to become uninhabitable in a 4°C world, cannot be saved from climate change. The failure of the United States to prepare for climate change migration within its own border threatens the health, safety, security, and overall well-being of its population, but it also jeopardizes losing significant

92. Thomas Maresca, *Seoul Launches Ambitious Metaverse Platform for City Services, Tourism*, UPI, Jan. 16, 2023, https://www.upi.com/Top_News/World-News/2023/01/16/Seoul-Metaverse-virtual-platform-launched/6531673859297/.
93. Rina Chandran, *Analysis: Seoul, Barbados Check Into Metaverse as Governments Eye Virtual Presence*, Reuters, Nov. 24, 2021, https://www.reuters.com/markets/currencies/seoul-barbados-check-into-metaverse-governments-eye-virtual-presence-2021-11-25/.
94. Cohen & McKenna, *supra* note 90.
95. Roy Lie Atjam, *Barbados to Establish the World's First Embassy in the Metaverse*, Diplomat Mag., Aug. 30, 2022, https://diplomatmagazine.eu/2022/08/30/barbados-to-establish-the-world-first-embassy-in-the-metavesre/.
96. *UAE Set to Launch the First Metaverse Hospital*, Med. Tourism Mag., https://www.magazine.medicaltourism.com/article/uae-set-to-launch-the-first-metaverse-hospital.
97. Alvin R. Cabral, *Dubai's Virtual Assets Regulator Becomes World's First Authority to Enter Metaverse*, Nat'l News, May 3, 2022, https://www.thenationalnews.com/business/technology/2022/05/03/dubais-virtual-assets-regulator-becomes-worlds-first-authority-to-enter-the-metaverse/.
98. Alkesh Sharma, *Sheikh Hamdan Approves New Phase of Dubai Metaverse Strategy*, Nat'l News, Nov. 24, 2022, https://www.thenationalnews.com/business/2022/11/24/sheikh-hamdan-approves-new-phase-of-dubai-metaverse-strategy/.
99. Luke Huigsloot, *UAE Ministry of Economy Opens Up New Headquarters in the Metaverse*, Cointelegraph, Sept. 29, 2022, https://cointelegraph.com/news/uae-ministry-of-economy-opens-up-new-headquarters-in-the-metaverse.

aspects of its own culture. If place cannot be saved, the metaverse provides an unsatisfactory answer for at least preserving this culture. Nevertheless, since the metaverse requires this data to be preserved for transference into this virtual space, even the metaverse cannot save the United States from its own failure to preserve its culture and history.

What will happen if America chooses to continue emphasizing place in its approach to protecting and preserving history and culture? If people lose both their geographic community and the proximity geography provides to one's social community, what culture and history will be lost? Will America take the anticipatory approach to preserving the culture and history existing within these communities? Or will America simply be *erased*?

Governance in a Warming World

Climate-Changed Communities

Sarah Fox

Changing environmental conditions have long caused population movement in the United States and globally. Historians believe that a severe drought likely contributed to the abandonment of settlements by the Anasazi people of the American Southwest.[1] A potato blight in Ireland in the mid-1800s led to widespread famine and emigration to the United States and elsewhere.[2] The Dust Bowl of the 1930s occurred after severe drought caused crop yields to plummet and giant dust storms to sweep over much of Kansas, Missouri, Oklahoma, and Texas, leading to a mass exodus of people from affected states.[3] And today, climate migrants in Central America have traveled to Mexico and the United States, hoping to escape environmental conditions that make it difficult to work or live.[4]

These population responses to climate change can be expected to accelerate, likely on orders of magnitude far larger than the country has previously experienced.[5] A world of high-level warming will bring sustained, major disruptions of many kinds. Environmental changes will continually impact and shift both the natural world and the structures built upon it. And those effects will alter how people live as severe weather, resource constraints, and economic realities shape new conceptions of geographically desirable land.

Author's note: Many thanks to my Environmental Law Collaborative co-authors for the engaging conversations that precipitated this publication, as well as the feedback and discussions as this chapter was being developed. Special thanks to Katy Kuh and Shannon Roesler for their thoughtful work as editors.

1. *See, e.g.*, Karin Klein, *Climate Change: Lessons From the Vikings and Ancient Cliff Dwellers*, L.A. Times., Aug. 2, 2013, https://www.latimes.com/opinion/opinion-la/la-ol-global-warming-war-violence-20130802-story.html.
2. Evan D.G. Fraser, *Social Vulnerability and Ecological Fragility: Building Bridges Between Social and Natural Sciences Using the Irish Potato Famine as a Case Study*, 7 Conservation Ecology 9 (2003), http://www.jstor.org/stable/26271945.
3. *See* Abrahm Lustgarten, *Climate Change Will Force a New American Migration*, ProPublica (Sept. 15, 2020), https://www.propublica.org/article/climate-change-will-force-a-new-american-migration.
4. *See, e.g.*, Abrahm Lustgarten, *The Great Climate Migration*, N.Y. Times, July 23, 2020, https://www.nytimes.com/interactive/2020/07/23/magazine/climate-migration.html [hereinafter Lustgarten, *Climate Migration*].
5. While this chapter will focus on shifts into and within the United States and the particularities of its governance system, similar migrations will of course happen globally.

While some amount of population movement is to be expected even with lower levels of climate change, at higher levels these shifts in many parts of the country will become extreme.[6]

Population shifts from areas negatively impacted by climate change to those better able to weather the new environment will lead to climate-changed communities. These kinds of movements in response to changing conditions can be expected to some degree at many levels, from intra-local movement between neighborhoods to interstate migrations that take people thousands of miles from home. But regardless of whether people are moving across town or across the country, these kinds of changes will be felt heavily, and differently, at the local level, and will require local responses. As Michelle Okoh discusses in her chapter, "America Erased,"[7] these shifts raise many questions about culture and identity, and how those aspects of personhood can be preserved in the face of community change.

Such questions of identity are interesting and rich. They also make necessary conversations about local governance, and whether and how local systems will be able to rise to the challenges facing them. Changing population size is not something new for local governments. Many of the tools that they already have, including zoning, regional planning, inter-local cooperation, development fees, and countless others, can and should be deployed in new ways. Even so, communities growing and shrinking in response to climate change will challenge our frameworks for population growth and, particularly, for population loss. The size of a community matters structurally, financially, and culturally. By considering these disparate kinds of impacts, it may be possible to prepare local governments to plan better for climate change.

Any such preparation requires, of course, that local governments have the authority to take needed actions. Ensuring local ability to act may require changes to state law in many jurisdictions. Beyond authority, the challenges facing communities warrant taking seriously the idea of changing jurisdictional boundaries to better reflect new environmental and population-based realities. Constructing a set of governance possibilities that includes flexibility in local boundaries alongside regional forms of government could promote a stronger network of inter-local cooperation and regional responsiveness. Local governments will also likely need greater fiscal freedom to respond to climate-induced changes in property values and population, which may require altering current constraints on local taxing and spending authority. Contemplating the changing population patterns and needs that high-level

6. *See, e.g.*, Lustgarten, *supra* note 3.
7. Michele Okoh's chapter, *America Erased,* begins on page 81.

warming will bring may help to highlight where current boundaries don't make sense in terms of governance, resource management, or community resilience. And considering the possibility of high-level warming now will better position local governments and their citizens to create communities better suited for life on a climate-changed planet.

Planning for Growth

A changing climate brings relative winners and losers. As is true for the rest of the world, some parts of the United States will become less fit for human habitation due to increased heat, flooding, fire risk, and related impacts. Other parts of the country will be comparatively better off. The higher the level of warming and the more extreme the climate impacts, the greater the differential is likely to be between climate secure and insecure regions. Similarly, neighborhoods within some cities will diverge in terms of livability. With this geographic difference will come geographic movement. As these changes in population occur, it is likely to be cities that bear the greatest impacts.[8]

Anticipated population growth in favorable climate areas brings with it many questions about how communities can and should look in a world of high-level warming. While growth is often a goal for local governments, growth does not guarantee civic success,[9] particularly when those population increases happen at a large scale. With increased community size comes the prospect of insufficient resources, overcrowding, and concomitant backlash from residents already in place if that change is not adequately planned. The last major American environmental migration during the Dust Bowl of the early 20th century led hundreds of thousands of residents from drought-affected areas in the United States to move to California and other parts of the American West.[10] In some places, this migration led to a 50% increase in the local population.[11] Those migrants were often met with scorn, ridi-

8. *See, e.g.*, Lustgarten, *supra* note 3; Lustgarten, *Climate Migration*, *supra* note 5:

   For all the ways in which human migration is hard to predict, one trend is clear: Around the world, as people run short of food and abandon farms, they gravitate toward cities, which quickly grow overcrowded. It's in these cities, where waves of new people stretch infrastructure, resources and services to their limits, that migration researchers warn that the most severe strains on society will unfold.

9. *See, e.g.*, Charles Marohn, *The Growth Ponzi Scheme*, Strong Towns (May 18, 2020), https://www.strongtowns.org/the-growth-ponzi-scheme (explaining some reasons why continual growth is not necessarily a success strategy for local governments).

10. *The Dust Bowl, California, and the Politics of Hard Times: A Child's Life*, State of Cal. Capitol Museum [hereinafter *A Child's Life*].

11. *The Dust Bowl, California, and the Politics of Hard Times: California's Reaction*, State of Cal. Capitol Museum [hereinafter *California's Reaction*].

cule, and prejudicial treatment.[12] Climate refugees leaving Central America and moving north are already facing similar kinds of backlash.[13] Thus, the questions for communities poised to receive new entrants who have been displaced by climate change are both pragmatic and existential.

And while climate growth can and will occur on a macro scale in terms of wholly new entrants to a local government, growth will occur at a micro scale as well, as climate change shifts housing preferences from one part of a city to another. For instance, in recent years, cities in the United States like Miami, Florida, and New Orleans, Louisiana, have seen preferences shift to—and housing costs correspondingly rise in—areas of those cities least likely to experience flooding.[14] As these patterns of growth occur within a community, they raise questions similar to those surrounding new entrants.

At a pragmatic level, those questions begin with: How do you house the necessary number of people in places that will themselves be safe from climate impacts? In Cinnamon Carlarne and Keith Hirokawa's chapter, "Decentering Dominance for Climate Change Adaptation in a Worst-Case Climate World," they offer vocabulary for describing the varying relationships that local governments may have with climate migrants. In their framework, recipient cities are places for whom population growth from climate migrants may be unwelcome, and climate havens are places that are making a concerted push to welcome new residents displaced by climate change. In some cities that have been mentioned as possible havens, like Buffalo, New York, and other parts of the so-called Rust Belt, housing stock is currently far from full. But to the extent that the number of entrants to the housing market begins to outstrip supply, climate change-induced growth may function as a gentrification spur, driving up housing costs and displacing those not able to afford the new market conditions. Environmental benefits carry the potential for this kind of impact[15]—and, as the Carlarne and Hirokawa chapter explains, relative climate safety may become one of the greatest large-scale environmental benefits of all. Thus, concerns about gentrification and housing costs, both within particular cities and across certain regions, loom

12. *See, e.g.*, *A Child's Life*, *supra* note 10 (describing prejudice faced by migrant children); *California's Reaction*, *supra* note 11: ("Townspeople labeled Dust Bowl migrants as "Okies," no matter where they were from. To them, Okies were ignorant, uneducated, dishonest, and strange.").

13. *See, e.g.*, Lustgarten, *supra* note 3; Lustgarten, *Climate Migration*, *supra* note 4.

14. *See, e.g.*, Casey Tolan, *High Ground, High Prices: How Climate Change Is Speeding Gentrification in Some of America's Most Flood-Vulnerable Cities*, CNN (Mar. 3, 2021), https://www.cnn.com/interactive/2021/03/us/climate-gentrification-cnnphotos-invs.

15. *See, e.g.*, Sarah Fox, *Environmental Gentrification*, 90 U. Colo. L. Rev. 803 (2019).

large. Accommodating growing numbers of people will require discussions about local housing policy,[16] and possible changes to zoning codes.

Beyond the mere fact of demand outstripping supply if housing policy does not accurately reflect the likely number of entrants, communities experiencing large numbers of entrants may also engage in a hardening of community borders through exclusionary zoning measures[17] that are designed to make entrance by new residents more difficult. As Carlarne and Hirokawa detail, the history of the United States is replete with examples of communities using land use controls to limit community growth in racist and otherwise exclusionary ways.[18] Concerns about growth also come with concerns about infrastructure and provision of an adequate supply of services for the community. And, finally, growth raises the question of how to expand in ways that do not degrade natural resources in areas where climate migrants and refugees establish a new home.[19] In all of those ways, growth due to relative climate attractiveness contains opportunities for some local governments but also many pragmatic challenges.

And as for more existential questions on both macro and micro scales, localities will have to contend with what it is that makes a community. What do increasing numbers of residents do to community identity, both for a city as a whole and in terms of the individual neighborhoods that make up a city? How do you preserve community identity and culture while making space for many new entrants—all of whom are bringing their own identities and cultures? These are not new problems for local governments, but the possibly large numbers of entrants in some places and the possible speed with which this transition will occur as various climate tipping points are reached means that climate change will alter communities in dramatic ways. It should also be anticipated that entrants to some communities will be received differ-

16. *See, e.g.*, Jeremy Deaton, *The Consequences of Being a Climate Refuge City*, Bloomberg CityLab Env't (Dec. 5, 2019), https://www.bloomberg.com/news/articles/2019-12-05/the-consequences-of-being-a-climate-refuge-city.

17. *See, e.g.*, 2 Patricia E. Sulkin, N.Y. Zoning Law & Prac. §20:02 (West updated Oct. 2022) (defining exclusionary zoning to mean "land use control regulations which singly or in concert tend to exclude persons of low or moderate income from the zoning municipality").

18. *See* Cinnamon P. Carlarne & Keith H. Hirokawa, *Decentering Dominance for Climate Adaptation in a Worst-Case Climate World*, [to be completed once page numbers are set] (referencing creation of white spaces, redlining, zoning, control of ecosystem services, and property rights as tools of dominion over space).

19. Parag Khanna & Susan Joy Hassol, *America's Next Great Migrations Are Driven by Climate Change*, Sci. Am. (Oct. 14, 2021), https://www.scientificamerican.com/article/americas-next-great-migrations-are-driven-by-climate-change:

> In the 21st century, we must shift from coastal to inland, from low to high elevation, and from resource-depleted to resource-rich areas—and we must do so sustainably, for our next habitat may well be our last chance to coexist with nature before there is nothing left to sustain us.

ently based on race, class, and socioeconomic status, along with whether the entrants are part of a large or small class of entrants. In some cases, constitutional and other anti-discrimination laws may protect against more overt forms of discrimination against climate entrants. Other race and class-based impacts, however, including access to housing, environmental amenities, public services and others may be harder to address with current laws.

Tools exist for local governments that have the foresight to plan for this kind of climate- change-induced growth and its attendant impacts and questions. It may be predictably difficult to incorporate long-term projections into current policy, and it may be attractive to encourage climate growth without engaging in accompanying planning.[20] But those local governments that engage now in thinking about measures like higher density affordable housing, disaster resilience, public transit, and preservation of green space and other natural resources that may help to preserve relative climate security will be the ones to benefit from climate growth. And communities that take on that challenge with full awareness of the ways in which dominance dynamics are playing out in their community response will be better-positioned to arrive at just and equitable patterns of growth.[21] Those that fail to take such actions face the risk of difficult transitions down the road for both existing residents and new entrants.

Planning for Loss

As described in the Introduction to this volume, high-level warming will mean extreme environmental change for much of the country and the world. That change will take varied and interconnected forms, including increased days of extreme heat and humidity, reduced water supplies, spread of non-native species, increased pests and bacteria, stronger storms, flooding, and many others. Many of those impacts will be dramatic enough that some people will overcome the—often very strong[22]—impulse to stay in place. Some local governments will experience loss from climate change as people reconsider the location of their primary home. Communities that rely

---

20. *See, e.g.*, Deaton, *supra* note 16 (quoting George Besch, a sustainability expert, as saying, "[y]ou can't just declare yourself a climate refuge, you know. You've got to work and earn it," and quoting Vivek Shandas, a professor of urban planning at Portland State University, as saying that Buffalo, New York's claims to being a climate haven may be "pretty premature . . . in part because we haven't really seen the preparation necessary for larger numbers of people").
21. *See* Carlarne & Hirokawa, *supra* note 18.
22. *See, e.g.*, Alexander B. Lemann, *Stronger Than the Storm: Disaster Law in a Defiant Age*, 78 La. L. Rev. 437, 457 (2018) (noting that natural disasters trigger "a set of emotional responses that often lead to an intense, frequently adversarial desire to rebuild," and attributing that impulse to rebuild and stay to overlapping factors including an act of revenge, a form of culture, and an act of resistance).

heavily on the environment for tourism or as vacation destinations may also be exceedingly vulnerable to largescale change. In some places, changing weather patterns and rising sea levels will erode beaches and eliminate or alter other natural features; in others, rising temperatures will mean higher levels of insects on land and algae in water. And in many, the habitat for many species will shift.[23]

Population patterns when it comes to climate change do not, of course, occur in a bubble. Questions of loss in the climate context will be impacted by other population trends. For instance, the opportunity for remote work, accelerated by the COVID-19 pandemic,[24] may spell greater opportunity for flexibility on location for some jobs. As occurred during the pandemic, those with sufficient job flexibility and resources may have greater incentive and ease to relocate. Moreover, the broader predictions of population decline in the United States mean that, even without climate change, many local governments in the country should be preparing for loss.[25]

The long fallout in Rust Belt cities over the course of the twentieth century shows the negative downward spiral that can occur from population loss in a region,[26] and many areas of the United States would be well-advised to have plans on loss in place for high levels of warming, in addition to the other demographic trends noted above. Current frameworks around local revenue authority and resource allocation make that kind of planned shrinking very difficult and poorly incentivized, however, as well as politically unpopular. Local governments in the United States often rely heavily on continued growth to finance their operations.[27] Property taxes, development fees, and, in some places, taxes on industries like tourism and real estate are all impor-

23. Steven Mufson et al., *2C: Beyond the Limit: Extreme Climate Change Has Arrived in America*, Wash. Post., Aug. 13, 2019, https://www.washingtonpost.com/graphics/2019/national/climate-environment/climate-change-america.

24. *See, e.g.*, Kim Parker et al., *COVID-19 Pandemic Continues to Reshape Work in America*, Pew Rsch. Ctr. (Feb. 16, 2022), https://www.pewresearch.org/social-trends/2022/02/16/covid-19-pandemic-continues-to-reshape-work-in-america (finding increases in working from home among those whose job is amenable to remote work).

25. *See, e.g.*, Daniel B. Rosenbaum, *Reforming Local Property for an Era of National Decline*, 70 Buff. L. Rev. 1115, 1131 (2022).

26. *See, e.g.*, Daniel Hartley, *Urban Decline in Rust-Belt Cities*, Fed. Rsrv. Bank Cleveland (May 20, 2013), https://www.clevelandfed.org/newsroom-and-events/publications/economic-commentary/2013-economic-commentaries/ec-201306-urban-decline-in-rust-belt-cities.aspx (describing cycles of population loss and reverse gentrification occurring in Buffalo, Cleveland, Detroit, and Pittsburgh).

27. *See, e.g.*, Charles Marohn, *The Growth Ponzi Scheme, Part 3*, Strong Towns (June 15, 2011), https://www.strongtowns.org/journal/2011/6/15/the-growth-ponzi-scheme-part-3.html (explaining problem of reliance on new development to finance local government).

tant sources of local revenue[28] that stand to be greatly diminished as climate change alters local natural environments and citizens depart for other areas.

The vulnerability of these sources of revenue in high-level warming scenarios means that many local governments in areas expected to suffer the most dramatic negative effects from climate change could face significant budget shortfalls. Beyond that, underlying this discussion is the premise that if an area is experiencing population decline attributable to climate change, it is being impacted by enough negative environmental impacts to cause people to leave. Thus, at the same time that population is declining, these local governments are also likely to face ballooning budgets from physical storm damage, crumbling infrastructure due to extreme temperatures, greater demand for emergency health services, and growing inequality and instability.[29]

These kinds of impacts from loss can come from residents exiting a local government fully. But, as with growth, loss is likely to occur on both an interlocal, macro level and an intralocal, micro level. Just as certain regions are more vulnerable to changing environmental conditions, different neighborhoods within localities will feel those impacts to varying degrees. In consequence, local officials may have to contend with conversations about growth and loss in tandem, within the same city, and to craft a community response to these new patterns. In the case of intralocal movement, resident exit will have fewer financial ramifications at the city level. Even so, on the loss side there remain many questions about service provision and resource allocation, and on the growth side many of the same issues mentioned above in terms of available housing, gentrification, and identity. Those questions, broadly, might be summarized as: who gets to leave, and who gets left behind? Who gets to stay, and on what terms? Exit, and the resources it requires, is not evenly achievable.[30]

At both a macro and a micro level, local governments and their citizens have the ability to plan, in advance, for loss. But here the questions begin once again. Will a city have to grapple with the loss of certain neighborhoods, because of physical impacts from climate change, unsuitability for adapta-

28. *See, e.g.*, Erin Scharff, *Cities on Their Own: Local Revenue When Federalism Fails*, 48 FORDHAM URB. L.J. 919, 928 (2021).
29. *See, e.g.*, Tim Robustelli & Shahin Vassigh, *How Miami Can Survive Climate Change*, SLATE: FUTURE TENSE (May 12, 2022), https://slate.com/technology/2022/05/miami-climate-change-survival.html.
30. *Cf.* Emily Badger, *COVID Didn't Kill Cities. Why Was That Prophecy So Alluring?*, N.Y. TIMES, July 12, 2021, https://www.nytimes.com/2021/07/12/upshot/covid-cities-predictions-wrong.html (noting, in the context of the COVID-19 pandemic, that "the 'end of cities' has often really meant the end of cities for a certain class of white professionals, not for residents of color who never left during the pandemic, or for low-wage workers who kept riding transit and going to work," and that "'Cities are over,' in other words, is a convenient conclusion if you have decided they are over *for you*") (emphasis in original).

tion, or difficulty of provision of services in a world of reduced resources? If neighborhoods are to be allowed to become depopulated, what protections might be put in place to prevent gentrification of other parts of the city and displacement of lower-income residents? What does loss of certain neighborhoods mean for local cultural heritage, and how do you best engage in placemaking while grappling with loss? Will certain geographic features or parts of the city be not just depopulated but physically lost due to rising sea levels or other flooding? If so, what does that mean for infrastructure, and for water supplies? Will protected buildings or historic districts need to be abandoned? How do you decide which ones—and what legal obligations might stand in the way of making that decision?

In some jurisdictions the losses that local governments will see in coming years might be better managed by adapting to more resilient planning, financial, and organizational models. Some scholars in the growing body of work on shrinking cities have advocated a number of different planning strategies for city decline, "including stronger building code enforcement, discouraging construction of new housing in high vacancy areas, land banking, swift rehabilitation or demolition of abandoned buildings, relocation assistance for residents in highly distressed areas, and relaxed zoning codes that allow for a greater variety of uses in declining areas."[31] Local resiliency might also be found by diversifying sources of revenue to the extent permitted by the state,[32] or in changing boundaries to better reflect current realities. And, ultimately, one of the biggest questions that will loom for some local governments is whether to maintain their incorporated status.

As discussed below, the ability to implement these kinds of policies depends on the extent of authority provided by states to their local governments. And even for local governments with the necessary authority, trying to raise revenue from a shrinking number of people may generate a downward spiral where ever-increasing taxes and fees for remaining residents become unsupportable. Thus, for many local governments, population loss will likely mean looking to the state and federal governments for some degree for additional resources.[33] Ultimately, even budget flexibility and creativity, as well as additional financial support, will not change the fact that some

31. *See, e.g.*, Payton Heins, *Embracing Smart Decline*, 6 Agora J. Urb. Plan. & Design, 1-6 (2012) (summarizing city decline literature); *see also, e.g.*, Rosenbaum, *supra* note 25, at 1161 (advocating for shifts in property law to a "callable fee" system to allow local governments greater flexibility in the event of decline).

32. *See* Scharff, *supra* note 28.

33. *See, e.g.*, Anna Marandi & Kelly Leilani Main, *The Next American Migration: What Cities Should Know About Climate Change and Populations on the Move*, Nat'l League of Cities (2022), at https://www.nlc.org/wp-content/uploads/2022/04/CS-Domestic-Climate-Migration-and-US-Cities-Report.pdf.

local governments in areas of large population outflow will have to reallocate and cut resources—to do less with less. This kind of rebudgeting is of course not unfamiliar to local governments who have been through recessions, the COVID-19 pandemic, and other major reworkings of financial expectations. High-level warming is similar to those local crisis points in many ways, but different in terms of scale and the extent to which it represents not just a difficult moment in time but a changed future.

Local governments and their citizens that are willing to seriously contemplate the climate-changed future now have the opportunity to bring to the table varied stakeholders to think about the future of the place in a way less likely to be possible once in the throes of real loss. Some comprehensive planning is already required of most local governments;[34] taking seriously the prospect of planning and incorporating realistic climate scenarios into those discussions would require communities to grapple more frankly with the question of loss. What that comprehensive planning process looks like will depend on the time scale used in a given jurisdiction. A typical time frame is 20 years, though states often vary from 10 to 30 years in required outlook.[35] Many local governments could benefit by looking beyond that time horizon for climate impacts such as extreme flooding. To address that need, some states like Florida have increased flexibility on the part of local governments to use different planning periods to address different aspects of planning such as sea level rise.[36] Other local governments like Norfolk, Virginia have adopted both a standard comprehensive plan as well as a broader, longer-range plan for 2100 and the climate realities expected to be in place at that point.[37]

---

34. Erwin S. Barbre, Annotation, *Requirement that zoning variances or exceptions be made in accordance with comprehensive* plan, 40 A.L.R.3d 372 (1971) ("The Standard State Zoning Enabling Act provides that zoning regulations 'shall be made in accordance with a comprehensive plan.' The enabling legislation of a majority of states includes this requirement or some variant thereof.").

35. *See, e.g.*, Christine Quattro & Thomas Daniels, *The Constellation of Plans: Toward a New Structure of Comprehensive Plans in US Cities*, 11 LAND 1767 (2022) (showing sample of comprehensive plan projections, with a variety of time horizons averaging rougly 20 years); *see also, e.g.*, 1 AMY H. GOINS ET AL., RI CLE LAND USE §5.1.2 (West 2017 & Supp. 2022) (requiring a 20-year time frame in Massachusetts); R.I. GEN. LAWS §45-22.2-12 (West 1956) (requiring 20-year planning horizon in Rhode Island).

36. *See, e.g.*, David L. Markell, *Emerging Legal and Institutional Responses to Sea-Level Rise in Florida and Beyond*, 42 COLUM. J. ENV'T L. 1, 26 (2016) (describing 2011 Florida legislation that "increases the flexibility of local governments to use different planning periods so that, for example, a local government could use a fifty-year coastal management element to address SLR, while using a ten-year planning period for the rest of the plan").

37. *See, e.g.*, CITY OF NORFOLK, NORFOLK VISION 2100, https://www.norfolk.gov/DocumentCenter/View/27768/Vision-2100---FINAL?bidId= (describing reason for developing Norfolk 2100 plan as related to the limitations of the 20-year timeline in the normal comprehensive planning process, and noting):

    Given the growing challenges of sea level rise, aging infrastructure, population growth, and

Even where longer timelines are possible in the planning process, human psychology may prove the ultimate stumbling block. Getting to a place where local leaders are willing and able to acknowledge and plan around a future of loss is likely to be exceedingly difficult. The United States has, for instance, millions of miles of shoreline that continues to be built and rebuilt in the face of rising sea levels and increasingly destructive storms. The psychology of entrenched interests, of home, of community, of culture, and the sheer desire to continue life as planned all present huge roadblocks to acceptance of this kind of loss before it occurs.

Acknowledging that political will may not currently exist in many places to contend with the reality of high-level warming does not change the fact that some cities will indeed face huge climate impacts that they will not be able to engineer their way around or move through with emergency relief funds from the federal and state governments.[38] As warming moves toward 2°C and beyond, those kinds of resources will simply not be available. Loss, whether experienced primarily in terms of population, physical infrastructure, neighborhood, community, culture, services, or other impacts, is likely to be a defining part of the future in many parts of the United States. Planning for that reality now could leave open avenues for adaptation and integrating conversations about growth and loss together on a national, regional, and local level.

Changed Boundaries for a Changed World

As the phrase climate change implies—and as the other authors of this book have made clear in each of their chapters—ultimately what we are facing is immense change: change in the natural environment, in physical infrastructure, in social relationships, in political capacity. These changes will test all levels of government, with the direct impacts being felt in many ways first and hardest at the local level. Confronting high-level warming and the questions of growth and loss that it presents should provoke questions about the adequacy of and support for local structures as they respond to our current and coming moment.

---

an uncertain and global economy, a vision focused on preserving the City as it is today does not provide the broad guidance that will be needed to both weather and meet the challenges of tomorrow. Vision 2100 seeks to fill that gap.

38. Whether federal relief funds will or should continue to be available for communities that have been continually destroyed by extreme weather events is beyond the scope of this chapter but a question worthy of discussion. *See, e.g.*, Lisa Grow Sun, *Smart Growth in Dumb Places: Sustainability, Disaster, and the Future of the American City*, 2011 B.Y.U. L. Rev. 2157, 2185 (2011) (detailing some of the ways that "public subsidization of disaster risk has not yet received the public scrutiny it deserves").

Taking on change at the local level has no shortage of difficulties, including limitations on local authority by state legislatures, inadequacy of resources, fractured responses, and myriad others. As noted, suggestions for how local governments might react to growth and loss often assume a certain amount of local autonomy. Local governments, however, act under grants of authority from the state. Those grants range from broad to exceedingly narrow. Thus, the ability of any one local entity to take action in response to its particular climate reality is highly variable.[39]

Moreover, climate change is a political and polarizing issue in many parts of the United States. It has become a flashpoint between many local governments that wish to take action on climate change and state governments that seek to halt any climate response.[40] Recent experience with the COVID-19 pandemic and the fractured state and local response to it offer a clear and concerning example of the chilling effect that lack of alignment between state and local governments can have on local attempts to adapt to conditions on the ground.[41] As Kevin Lynch notes in his chapter, "Preemption: Opportunities and Obstacles for Climate Adaptation,"[42] state governance dynamics may thwart attempts by local governments to deploy the tools they need to respond to climate change in real time. This may include environmental measures such as local governments attempting to transition to renewable forms of energy,[43] as well as those related to the broader climate transition

39. *See, e.g.*, Sarah Fox, *Localizing Environmental Federalism*, 54 U.C. Davis L. Rev. 133 (2020).

40. *See, e.g.*, Amy Turner, *When State Preemption of Local Climate Laws Undermines Equity*, Climate L. Blog (Mar. 5, 2021), https://blogs.law.columbia.edu/climatechange/2021/03/05/when-state-preemption-of-local-climate-laws-undermines-equity.

41. *See, e.g.*, Kim Haddow, *Preemption, Public Health & Equity in the Time of Covid-19*, *in* COVID-19 Playbook: Legal Recommendations for a Safer, More Equitable Future 76-79 (Public Health Law Watch Mar. 2021), https://static1.squarespace.com/static/5956e16e6b8f5b8c45f1c216/t/60995942ea2dbf3f3bc31788/1620662599928/COVIDPolicyPlaybook-v2_May2021.pdf.

42. *See* Kevin J. Lynch, *Preemption: Opportunities and Obstacles for Climate Adaptation*, to be completed once page numbers are set].

43. For instance, many local governments are facing current or threatned preemption of municipal bans on natural gas. Ella Nilsen, *Cities Tried to Cut Natural Gas From New Homes. The GOP and Gas Lobby Preemptively Quashed Their Effort*, CNN (Feb. 17, 2022), https://www.cnn.com/2022/02/17/politics/natural-gas-ban-preemptive-laws-gop-climate/index.html. Slightly beyond that, in 2022, lawmakers in Virginia introduced a bill that would "prohibit any 'public entity that provides natural gas utility service' from discontinuing service 'generally or to any commercial or industrial customers' without providing three years of notice, undertaking certain negotiations and in some circumstances offering the system up for auction to the highest bidder." *See* Sarah Vogelsong, *Proposal to Forbid Local Gas Bans Dropped in Senate*, Va. Mercury, Mar. 2, 2022, https://www.virginiamercury.com/2022/03/02/proposal-to-forbid-local-gas-bans-dropped-in-senate.

including policies on housing,[44] health,[45] land use,[46] and others. The threat alone of such preemption can exert a chilling effect on local action; for example, a 2018 survey found that 72% of health officials and 60% of mayors abandoned or delayed local policymaking efforts in the face of possible preemption.[47] And while local governments in many states can take a variety of actions, even local entities with authority to act may be organized in suboptimal ways. For instance, as discussed below, the lack of regional planning structures can hamper the ability of local governments to tackle complex inter-jurisdictional problems like those presented by high-level warming. All of these questions of authority, identity, and capacity present real challenges for local governments in responding to extreme climate change.

But local governance also presents some opportunities in taking on the disruptions of high-level warming. The structure of substate governments is not dictated by the federal Constitution. That document sets out the power sharing relationship between the federal government and the states, but does not mention local governments. Local governments, therefore, have long been subject to and constructed by the unique particularities of the state in which they are located.[48] Those constraints are to blame for many of the potential difficulties faced at the local level. Nevertheless, the lack of federally mandated structure also offers the potential for experimenting with different forms of government better positioned for a high levels of warming.

Political boundaries that have defined communities, resources, and authority for many years may no longer make sense in a warming world, whether because of population growth or loss, shifts in natural features and resource demands, or some combination of these changes.[49] And while local

44. *State Preemption of Equitable Housing Policies*, Local Solutions Support Ctr., (2022), https://www.supportdemocracy.org/equitablehousing/#zoning.

45. *See, e.g.*, Public Health Law Center at Mithcell Hamline School of Law, Dillon's Rule, Home Rule, and Preemption (2020), https://publichealthlawcenter.org/sites/default/files/resources/Dillons-Rule-Home-Rule-Preemption.pdf.

46. *See, e.g.*, Fla. Stat. §163.3177 (West 2021) (requiring every local government to "include in its comprehensive plan a property rights element to ensure that private property rights are considered in local decisionmaking"). While the law specifically states that private rights to "use, maintain, develop, and improve" property are subject to state law and local ordinances, these kinds of laws may signal a growing willingness on the part of the state to interfere in local land use policies. *See id.*

47. Lainie Rutkow et al., *Local Public Health Policymakers' Views on State Preemption: Results of a National Survey, 2018*, 109 Am. J. Pub. Health 1107-10 (2019).

48. *Cf.* Hunter v. Pittsburgh, 207 U.S. 161 (1907); *see also, e.g.*, Richard Briffault et al., Cases and Materials on State and Local Government Law (9th ed. 2021).

49. *See, e.g.*, Parag Khanna & Susan Joy Hassol, *America's Next Great Migrations Are Driven by Climate Change*, Sci. Am. (Oct. 14, 2021), https://www.scientificamerican.com/article/americas-next-great-migrations-are-driven-by-climate-change ("If we want the United States to remain meaningfully united, it may require graduating beyond our antiquated administrative boundaries of states and toward a system of resource zones and the infrastructures within and across them that enable the mobility of people, goods, and resources.").

boundaries are often difficult to shift as a matter of practice and entrenched interests, there do exist mechanisms for altering the shape and form of substate governments. Government boundaries should be part of the conversation about adapting to high-level warming. For example, local governments facing the prospect of dramatic population out-migration might consider disincorporation, potentially followed by annexation into another neighboring jurisdiction, or consolidation with other local entities. Disincorporation has historically been very rare.[50] In some states, however, population loss could carry with it the threat of losing local home rule authority.[51] Local governments unable to support a baseline level of services may also ultimately fare better by disincorporating and being either annexed by a neighboring municipality or coming under a county or other kind of regional governance structure. Those moves would themselves involve loss (loss of a government entity), but also perhaps loss of local community identity. But those kinds of changes could help to prevent loss in other ways, by offering resources to people living in the area, providing needed services, and better reflecting new environmental realities.

More broadly, new forms of regional planning and responsibility could be created to respond to the realities of high-level warming in the form of needs for infrastructure, medical and emergency responses, social services, schools, and other areas. This may be done formally, through the use of power-sharing arrangments. In many states, local governments with home rule authority may engage in a process of interlocal cooperation, allowing two or more entities to take on a task by sharing authority and resources.[52] For example, many inter-local transit authorities and other infrastructure-related agencies are already in existence.[53] Those kinds of regional responses may be accomplished without a loss of or change of official local boundaries. But they insert a layer of cross-boundary cooperation and support for regions or jurisdictions to blunt climate impacts, and their boundaries could be drawn in ways that reflect the current and changing needs of an area. Short

50. *See* Briffault et al., *supra* note 48, at 326.

51. *See, e.g.*, Nick Kachiroubas & Markus Beyer, *On the Bubble: What Happens to an Illinois Home-Rule Municipality When Its Population Drops Below 25,001?*, 4 Ill. Mun. Pol'y J. 191 (2019), https://las.depaul.edu/centers-and-institutes/chaddick-institute-for-metropolitan-development/research-and-publications/Documents/IMPJ_191-204_On_the_Bubble_copy.pdf.

52. *See, e.g.*, Briffault et al., *supra* note 48, at 643 (noting that "local government units engage in intergovernmental cooperative ventures for a number of reasons," and detailing examples and types of these forms of intergovernmental cooperation).

53. *See, e.g.*, Sheryll Cashin, *Localism, Self-Interest, and the Tyranny of the Favored Quarter: Addressing the Barriers to New Regionalism*, 88 Geo. L.J. 1985, 2029 (2000) (explaining that "transportation is regionalized in virtually all metropolitan regions, with some form of interlocal transit district overseeing the financing and operation of transportation services, particularly for mass transit").

of formal arrangements, local governments could also benefit from regional climate collaboration. Creating such networks would bring the benefit of shared information and resources, and could also help to ensure that adaptation efforts made in one jurisdiction do not undermine other adaptation or mitigation efforts elsewhere.[54]

Regional planning around climate change is already occurring in some areas of the United States. For example, the Southeast Florida Regional Climate Change Compact is a "partnership between Broward, Miami-Dade, Monroe, and Palm Beach Counties, to work collaboratively to reduce regional greenhouse gas emissions, implement adaptation strategies, and build climate resilience across the Southeast Florida region."[55] The Compact is the "first example where U.S. counties voluntarily committed to work at the regional scale to address climate change."[56] Though not a formally recognized legal entity,[57] the Compact has offered a structure through which the counties involved have coordinated on climate policy, developed a unified measure of anticipated sea level rise, and engaged in regional vulnerability and climate planning.[58] Implementation of the Compact falls to the many individual jurisdictions that are party to its provisions. California, which has legislation and executive orders requiring or encouraging climate action and planning at the state, local, and regional level,[59] has also seen a number of examples of regional planning surrounding climate change.[60] In addition to the efforts among local governments, California also has an Alliance of Regional Collaboratives for Climate Adaptation (ARCCA)—a collaborative body for regional planners.

The regional efforts seen to date have taken on several broad categories of work: convening, policy and planning, outreach and policy engagement, funding and development, and science and assessment.[61] Convening can play an important role in regional planning efforts by offering an organized way

54. *See, e.g.*, Xueqing Shan, *Coordinating Local Adaptive Strategies Through a Network-Based Approach*, 29 Duke Env't L. & Pol'y F. 183, 199 (2018) (highlighting benefits from coordination on adaptation as well as negative consequences of a lack of coordination).

55. *See What Is the Compact?*, Southeast Florida Reg'l Climate Change Compact, https://southeastfloridaclimatecompact.org/about-us/what-is-the-compact.

56. Sydnee Menees & Jessica Grannis, Lessons in Regional Resilience: the Southeast Florida Regional Climate Change Compact (2017), https://www.georgetownclimate.org/files/report/GCC-Lessons-in-Regional-Resilience-SE_FL_Compact-Jan_2017-v2.pdf.

57. *Id.*

58. *Id.*

59. Annie Bennett & Jessica Grannis, Lessons in Regional Resilience: Case Studies on Regional Climate Collaboratives (2017), https://www.georgetownclimate.org/files/report/GCC-Lessons-in-Regional-Resilience-Synthesis-Jan_2017.pdf.

60. *Id.*

61. *Id.* at 6.

for talking about regional issues that is often otherwise lacking.[62] Regional bodies have also provided technical assistance and recommendations that can help to guide and build capacity for the individual local governments involved.[63] Regional efforts can help in seeking out state and federal funding support, and can also pool funds to help spread resources for climate efforts across a region.[64] And these collaborations have also led to better regional data and climate assessments.[65]

These examples show the multilayered types of government responses that can and have been seen already with regard to climate change's impacts on communities. This kind of regional coordination could be helpful in areas facing population loss and population surges alike, offering flexibility and ways to mitigate impacts beyond jurisdictional boundaries. It may also be key in taking a much-needed broader look at development and its impacts on the environment. Where areas are growing, convening representatives from local governments in the region could help to ensure that expansions of the built environment in response to climate change are planned in a climate-sensible and sensitive way. And where areas are losing population, it may be possible to convert land in a region no longer needed or wanted for human population to uses that help to buffer some of the stronger climate impacts. For instance, the King County-Cities Climate Collaboration, another regional climate planning body in Washington, has committed[66] to supporting the transferable development rights (TDR) program in King County[67] where possible. That program creates a separate, alienable property right to develop for property owners in designated "send" areas. Those property owners can then sell their right to develop to those hoping to build in designated "receive" areas. With the purchase of TDR rights comes the ability to build at higher densities than would otherwise be permitted in the receiving zones.[68] Historically, TDR programs have been difficult to carry out on a regional basis.[69] But challenges with these kinds of boundary-cross-

62. *Id.*
63. *Id.* at 7.
64. *Id.* at 8-9.
65. *Id.* at 9-10.
66. King County-Cities Climate Collaboration, Joint Letter of Commitment: Climate Change Actions in King County, https://your.kingcounty.gov/dnrp/library/dnrp-directors-office/climate/joint-commitments-update-with-signatures-final.pdf.
67. *TDR Marketplace: Transfer of Development Rights*, King County, https://kingcounty.gov/services/environment/stewardship/sustainable-building/transfer-development-rights/market-info.aspx.
68. *Program Overview: Transfer of Development Rights*, King County, https://kingcounty.gov/services/environment/stewardship/sustainable-building/transfer-development-rights/overview.aspx.
69. *See Introduction to TDR Programs*, Geo. Climate Ctr., https://www.georgetownclimate.org/adaptation/toolkits/managed-retreat-toolkit/transfer-of-development-rights.html.

ing program are precisely why regional collaboration is likely essential for regions facing new climate realities.

The United States does not have a robust history of regional planning or governance. However, as emphasized throughout this book, the country is also facing unprecedented change. That may spur changes in governance structures that better fit and reflect the environmental and social conditions on the ground. The examples above offer a window into how and when regional collaboration may be possible, either on a formal or an informal basis. Those regional collaborations, and the changed understanding of boundaries that they reflect, may be key to responding to extreme climate change. They are valuable not only for the sharing of planning and resources, but also for the processes and connections they help to build.

Indeed, shifts in local governance structures may lead to the stable local foundations that are likely essential to weathering the changes high levels of warming will bring. Sarah Krakoff, for instance, has written about formulation of a planetarian identity as key to adapting behavior and laws to address climate change.[70] Her view of planetarian identity formation shares with other communitarian forms of environmental ethics both a faith in and sense of duty surrounding the ability of individual actors to act in environmentally responsible and significant ways, fostered at the local level.[71] In such a view, local community-building and governance matters because "there will be no solution to the world's environmental problems if we fail to focus on the livelihood and well-being of local communities throughout the world."[72] If it is at the local level that people learn to be citizens—as local government theorists going back to Alexis de Tocqueville have proposed[73]—then it is at the local level that people will re-learn how to be citizens of a world dramatically different from the one they are used to. The robustness and flexibility of local structures therefore matters not only for their ability to respond to needs of citizens but also for their ability to inculcate the values needed for those citizens and their governments to thrive in a climate-changed world.[74]

70. *See* Sarah Krakoff, *Planetarian Identity Formation and the Relocalization of Environmental Law*, 64 Fla. L. Rev. 87, 133 (2012).

71. *Id.* at 132-33.

72. *Id.* at 97.

73. *See, e.g.*, Federal Energy Regulatory Comm'n v. Mississippi, 456 U.S. 742, 790 (1982) (O'Connor, J., concurring) quoting Alexis de Tocqueville for his views on the importance of participation in local government to the functioning of American democracy, and noting that

> [c]itizens . . . cannot learn the lessons of self-government if their local efforts are devoted to reviewing proposals formulated by a faraway national legislature. If we want to preserve the ability of citizens to learn democratic processes through participation in local government, citizens must retain the power to govern, not merely administer, their local problems.

74. *See* Krakoff, *supra* note 70, at 92-93 noting that

> local climate action groups may be important solely because of the habits of living they

As with any conversation about local governments, generalizations are helpful only to a certain point. Each state has its own law about what local governments within its jurisdiction may do, and any conversation about the possibility for substate governments and governance structures must account for those unique legal aspects. As a result, helpful conversations about the substate experience of and response to high levels of warming should include the specific and variable environmental impacts that the place in question is expected to experience, the unique social conditions in that place, and the state laws in place that may constrain the substate response. Making that information, and the knowledge of how it intersects, widely known and available can help inform the many hard conversations that are to come for communities. Whether growing, shrinking, or otherwise changing, there is no one way to make the value judgments that will be required of communities faced with high-level warming. But regions and communities that have taken the time to consider their own climate-changed future and to foster the necessary conversations will be in a better position to adapt to life on a changing planet.

---

cultivate. Norms and behaviors reflecting less dependence on energy; more local knowledge about food, landscape, and weather; and greater reliance on friends and neighbors may be beneficial ends in themselves. In this scenario, the efforts of local climate action groups will not be enough to save the planet, or at least a planet with ecologies, cultures, and species that have evolved for the climate as we know it. But they might be enough to sow the seeds for life on a different planet that would nonetheless be worth living on.

Preemption: Opportunities and Obstacles for Climate Adaptation

Kevin J. Lynch

For Kaye Fissinger, one of the community leaders in Longmont, Colorado, whose tireless advocacy for her community inspired this chapter.

As high-level warming becomes more common, it is critical for human society to respond effectively and forcefully to meet the many challenges coming our way. We have to be prepared for a 1.5- to 4-degrees Celsius (°C) increase in temperature.[1] The scale of the coming change and the relatively short time frame in which it will occur both suggest that our society will need to respond in a highly coordinated and efficient way to best put our limited resources to work. This in turn will require all levels of government—local, state, regional, national, and international—to work in coordination toward achieving reasonable climate adaptation, for us to avoid the worst disruptions due to climate change. Preemption law can make a mess of all of this, as it has done in areas related to climate mitigation in recent years; but preemption done right can instead be a critical tool for effective climate adaptation.

This chapter will explore how we can get the best climate adaptation policies in place through a thoughtful, deliberate approach to the law of preemption. Although preemption is also an issue between the federal government and the states, this chapter will focus on state-level preemption. Sometimes preemption will be necessary to block wasteful or counterproductive efforts. Nevertheless, in general, preemption should be carefully limited to rare cir-

---

Author's note: I am grateful to the research assistance provided by Abigail Frische, as well as many helpful comments from Sarah Fox, Jessie Owley, Karen Bradshaw, Josh Galperin, Katy Kuh, and Shannon Roesler and of course to the organizers and participants in the 2021 gathering of the Environmental Law Collaborative for many helpful discussions and provocative questions.

1. As but one example, a recently published study estimates that inevitable melting of the Greenland ice sheet will trigger nearly a foot of global sea-level rise. Jason E. Box et al., *Greenland Ice Sheet Climate Disequilibrium and Committed Sea-Level Rise*, 12 Nature Climate Change 808 (2022).

cumstances, with a presumption to empower all levels of government to take action necessary to adapt to impending climate change. Various governments will not always get this right, but there is greater risk of mischief if courts or legislatures try to micro-manage climate adaptation policy at lower levels. Courts have proven themselves to be biased toward the status quo when they have applied preemption doctrine to climate mitigation, and can be expected to do the same for climate adaptation. Thus, this chapter proposes ways to narrow the opportunity for courts to interfere with important climate adaptation policies, instead putting the choices in the hands of elected representatives. Of course state legislatures and other elected officials will still make mistakes from a climate adaptation perspective. But at some point, for reasons that Josh Galperin explores more fully in "4Cs at 4°C: Counting, Contestation, Communication, and Consideration for Collectively Constructing Concepts of Climate Change,", we have to trust the democratic process[2] to produce good enough outcomes regarding climate adaptation, taking account of the unique circumstances and preferences in a particular area. Preemption law can enable us to get it right, so that local governments are not undermining critical state or national policies that require coordination across different jurisdictions,[3] yet retain an important role—perhaps even an expanded role in some respects, as suggested by Sarah Fox in "Climate-Changed Communities"—to allow for local decision making that can be better tailored to the unique needs and preferences of smaller communities of people. Thus, it is important that state legislatures be able to preempt local policies that would inhibit climate adaptation, but there should be a high bar for such preemption to be recognized by the courts. This approach thus gives greater autonomy to local governments to craft locally relevant solutions to the problem of climate adaptation, so long as they do not interfere with important goals at broader scales.

2. Perhaps this is too big of an assumption. Certainly, our democratic systems have thus far proved woefully inadequate to the challenge of climate mitigation. Something must change going forward if we are to get climate adaptation right. For the purposes of this chapter, however, I assume there are actors of goodwill who wish to respond to climate change in an effective manner. If our society collectively decides not to do this, then we must face the consequences.
3. As a contrary example from the housing policy context, local residents and elected officials in towns across Connecticut (and many other states) seek to block efforts to create affordable housing. *See, e.g.*, Lisa Prevost, *Town After Town, Residents Are Fighting Affordable Housing in Connecticut*, N.Y. Times, Sept. 4, 2022, https://www.nytimes.com/2022/09/04/realestate/connecticut-affordable-housing-apartments.html#:~:text=In%20the%20town%20of%20Fairfield,19%20units%20of%20affordable%20housing. This same type of dynamic, where existing distributions of wealth and property stand in the way of necessary changes for the good of society as a whole, can be expected to come up often in the climate adaptation context.

Preemption law, however, also poses a great threat to effective climate adaptation policy. Preemption law has been used in the past,[4] and almost certainly will be used in the future, to frustrate sensible and necessary climate policies due to the political influence of vested interests, such as industry and the concentration of property and wealth in a relatively small subset of the population. The powerful interests that are relevant to climate adaptation might be somewhat different than in the climate mitigation context, of course. For climate mitigation, the primary culprit is the fossil fuel industry and their supporters. For climate adaptation, instead we should be focused on undue influence from wealthy homeowners in climate-threatened areas, such as coastal areas or places at increasing risk of wildfire, who push for the use of society's resources to protect their property. Or we might be concerned about the influence of wealthy property owners in climate havens who might resist additional development and density in those areas. And of course traditional fossil fuel interests can still play a role here, as we are seeing the natural gas industry push for continued investment in distribution infrastructure that will saddle us with reliance on their product for decades to come.[5]

This chapter will explore how various actors in our political system could "get it right" on preemption and overcome the influence of powerful interests opposed to the necessary changes. What can well-intentioned state legislatures do to empower local government while preventing counterproductive local actions? What can well-intentioned judges do to ensure they do not protect the wealthy and powerful at the expense of public adaptation to climate change? What can the voters do if judges and legislatures fail them? This chapter will explore lessons from the climate mitigation context to identify potential solutions for getting preemption right for climate adaptation.

Brief consideration of some examples may be helpful to understand both the stakes of getting the preemption issue right and also how different approaches to preemption can lead to different outcomes regarding climate adaptation. As Fox notes, communities that are potential climate havens include some communities that currently have ample spare capacity in their housing stock—but that could quickly change. If those communities react to an influx of climate migrants by enacting exclusionary zoning measures, then that could drive up housing costs and lead to climate-based gentrifica-

4. *See, e.g.*, Erin Ryan, *The Twin Environmental Law Problems of Preemption and Political Scale*, *in* Environmental Law, Disrupted (Keith Hirokawa & Jessica Owley eds., ELI 2021) (noting the threat that preemption posed to state and local efforts to push back against the rollback of environmental protections at the federal level under the Trump Administration).

5. *See, e.g.*, Sam Brasch, *Xcel Energy Played a Leading Role in a Stealthy Plan to Defend Natural Gas in Colorado*, Colorado Public Radio (Feb. 27, 2023), https://www.cpr.org/2023/02/27/xcel-energy-coloradans-for-energy-access.

tion. This is an example that would benefit from express preemption to prevent local interests from interfering with the broader public good, in this case necessary and equitable migration of population to climate havens. On the flip side, local governments should retain flexibility to experiment with different approaches to building codes and infrastructure planning to promote resiliency and hardening of infrastructure in their communities. Active steps should be taken to protect that local autonomy so that judges do not swoop in at the behest of powerful and wealthy industries seeking to retrench the status quo, with findings of implied, field, or conflict preemption.

As explained more fully below, there are three main avenues for change to ensure that preemption law gets it right with respect to climate adaptation. First, legislatures at the state level should provide clear guidance to courts to foreclose broad and unjustified findings of implied or field preemption that block or delay necessary climate adaptation policies at the local level. Second, advocates should push for greater and more specific rights-based approaches to addressing climate change, such as environmental rights amendments in state constitutions or rights of nature that require all levels of government to respond to the crisis posed by a 4°C future. Finally, courts themselves can avoid recklessly and needlessly hobbling society's response to climate change by adopting a clear statement rule, holding that courts will defer to elected officials to develop climate adaptation policies and will only hold such a policy preempted upon finding a clear declaration of intent to preempt by the relevant state legislature. The first two avenues are promising areas for advocacy groups to focus their energy on in the near term, while the appointment and election of judges who will adopt this sensible and humble approach should be an advocacy priority.

Background on Preemption

Although the general outlines of preemption law are well known, I will first provide a brief recap of preemption law[6] as well as my thoughts on this topic. The doctrine of preemption refers to the idea that a higher authority of law will displace the law of a lower authority when the two come into conflict. Preemption law depends upon the relationship between various levels of government. The interplay between state and federal governments is regulated by

6. It is important to note that I am referring to different types and contexts of preemption than discussed as part of the toolbox needed for climate adaptation in J.B. Ruhl & Robin Kundis Craig, *4°C*, 106 Minn. L. Rev. 191, 265-69 (2021). Although federal mandates including an environmental floor to be implemented through cooperative federalism are likely to be important, I am more focused on less explicit forms of preemption, especially where courts will strike down local efforts at climate adaptation through implied, field, or conflict preemption.

the U.S. Constitution, with the federal government having only enumerated, but broad powers to regulate in certain spheres, such as interstate commerce. But the Supremacy Clause[7] and the Tenth Amendment combine to mean that the federal government may preempt contrary state laws in those areas that the federal government may regulate, but otherwise states have broad latitude in other areas.[8] The state-local government[9] relation is regulated by state constitutions, although generally local governments operate under powers delegated to them by the states,[10] and thus local governments are often subject to more strict preemption standards than are states. This relationship is controlled by the home-rule doctrine, which confers local autonomy over local issues. It is the state-local relationship that is the focus of this chapter.

There are several types of preemption that are generally recognized. First, express preemption occurs when the state government expressly declares its intent to preempt local government action on a particular matter. This only works so long as the issue is one within the authority of the state government, but if it is, express preemption will usually be recognized by the courts. Even in the absence of express preemption, courts will sometimes recognize preemption that is implied if the legislature's intent to preempt is implicit in the relevant law's structure and purpose.[11] Field preemption may also be found when state regulations entirely occupy the field in which the local government wishes to regulate.[12] Courts will also recognize preemption where the local government law conflicts with a state law.

Unfortunately, in my view, these formulations give many different opportunities for courts to find preemption, particularly in the areas of implied, field, or conflict preemption. Powerful industries often run to court and successfully obtain preemption rulings to block polices they object to and could not defeat in the legislative and political arenas.[13] Thus, as recommended

7. Congressional Research Serv., *Federal Preemption: A Legal Primer* (updated May 18, 2023), https://crsreports.congress.gov/product/pdf/R/R45825.
8. In one notable and relatively recent case in the environmental law context, the U.S. Supreme Court held that the Clean Air Act displaced any *federal* common-law right to seek abatement of greenhouse gas emissions from fossil fuel-fired power plants. American Elec. Power Co. v. Connecticut, 564 U.S. 410 (2011). That case, however, arguably did not foreclose application of *state* common law (nuisance, etc.) to address air pollution that contributes to climate change, and currently there are various attempts around the country to hold major polluters accountable. *See, e.g.*, Lesley Clark, *Colo. Governments Tell SCOTUS to Stay Out of Climate Fight*, E&E News (Aug. 11, 2022) (describing litigation in California, Colorado, Maryland, and New York).
9. It is outside the scope of this chapter, but I would note that the federal-local government relationship is a bit more complicated. *See, e.g.*, Nixon v. Missouri Mun. League, 541 U.S. 125 (2004).
10. Sarah Fox, *Home Rule in an Era of Local Environmental Innovation*, 44 Ecology L.Q. 575, 585 (2017).
11. *See, e.g.*, City of Golden v. Ford, 348 P.2d 951, 653-54 (Colo. 1960).
12. Rice v. Santa Fe Elev. Corp., 331 U.S. 218, 230 (1947) (discussing field preemption at the federal level).
13. See *infra* discussion of examples from Colorado regarding fracking.

below, legislatures who wish to exert greater control over what is and is not preempted should aim for as much clarity as possible. And where necessary, the people should utilize their rights to direct democracy to limit judicial preemption rulings that block or delay critical policies from being enacted. For example, in many states, but particularly in the western United States, ballot measures allow citizens to adopt state laws or amend their constitutions, and these procedures could be used to overturn bad preemption rulings by the courts or to handcuff courts from even making those mistakes in the first place.

Despite these criticisms, there are good policy reasons behind the law of preemption.[14] Some local variation can be useful in allowing diverse communities to express their own preferences in dealing with issues at the local level.[15] But local variation can cross a line where it interferes with unified state or national policy. In some instances, a unified policy is not essential,[16] and local considerations should prevail, especially in home-rule jurisdictions. In certain areas, however, the broader interest must trump local considerations. Climate adaptation will often be one of those areas due to the risk of crosswise policies that frustrate the broader goals of the state or nation.

In many states, preemption law has gone way off the rails, and home rule has been dramatically limited. Efforts to reinvigorate home rule,[17] while applicable broadly, would have many generally beneficial effects on climate adaptation policy at the local level. The National League of Cities recently convened many leading experts on preemption law to evaluate home rule and generate proposals for reforming home rule to adapt to the challenges faced in our modern society, resulting in the excellent report *Principles of Home Rule for the 21st Century*.[18] This report noted how states in the 19th century had asserted control over local governance, leading to a predominant view of local governments as formally legally subordinate to the states.[19] Although cities and metropolitan regions are typically the economic engines of nearly every state, in recent years "punitive preemption" has become more

14. Even advocates of strong home rule acknowledge that there is a legitimate role for states to play with respect to local authority. *See* National League of Cities, Principles of Home Rule for the 21st Century 26 (2020) [hereinafter National League of Cities]. This chapter adopts a similar approach, generally disfavoring preemption, but recognizing that it is important in key circumstances, adding climate adaptation to the list of areas where there may be significant inter-local spillovers.

15. Richard Briffault, *The Challenge of the New Preemption*, 70 Stan. L. Rev. 1995, 1998 (2018).

16. I wholeheartedly endorse the criticisms of unthinking reliance on "uniformity" to justify state preemption of local laws that were laid out in the home rule for the 21st century report, discussed *infra*.

17. Home rule is the term used to describe local self-government, which was enshrined in many state constitutions during the Progressive Era. David J. Barron, *Reclaiming Home Rule*, 116 Harv. L. Rev. 2255, 2296-321 (2003).

18. National League of Cities, *supra* note 14.

19. *Id.* at 9.

and more commonplace, whereby states enact legislation seeking to punish local governments and local officials over policy disagreements.[20] Ultimately the report makes several recommendations which are consonant with the principles laid out in this chapter, including that "local governments are vital places of self-governance and that local democracy should play a central role in state constitutional law."[21] Specifically, the report endorses the "presumption against state preemption principle"[22] that would have a tremendous beneficial impact on climate adaptation policy, if implemented.

Lessons From the Past: Preemption and Climate Mitigation Measures

Our efforts at climate mitigation have failed miserably, in part due to interference from preemption law. This is not to say that had we gotten preemption right, we could have prevented extreme climate change from occurring—of course that is not the case. But preemption law has been used to devastating effect by wealthy and powerful interests to frustrate even minor attempts to reduce greenhouse gas pollution and leave fossil fuels safely in the ground. This next section will examine how preemption law played a crucial role in fights over local regulation on fracking, including bans, in the 2010s. In some states, such as Colorado, preemption law was used to block local bans or moratoria, while in Pennsylvania, a relatively strong environmental rights amendment in the state constitution was key to supporting local regulation of fracking. What can these different outcomes tell us about potential legal options to get preemption law right in the climate adaptation context?

We will start in Colorado. Technological developments in the oil and gas industry, specifically horizontal drilling and hydraulic fracturing, led to a boom of oil and gas extraction in the United States in the 2010s.[23] Formerly productive oil fields such as the Denver-Julesberg Basin in Colorado, which had been extensively drilled in prior decades, became active again as these new technologies enabled the recovery of oil and gas from deeper and dif-

20. *Id.* at 14, 17.
21. *Id.* at 20.
22. *Id.* at 26.
23. *See* Kevin J. Lynch, *Regulation of Fracking Is Not a Taking of Private Property*, 84 U. CIN. L. REV. 38, 42-43 (2016). Horizontal drilling is a technology that enables a well to be drilled mostly vertically from the surface to the entry point of a reservoir, where the well then turns to continue horizontally through the reservoir in order to expose more of the rock formation to the well bore. Lynn Helms, *Horizontal Drilling*, 35 N.D. DEP'T MINERAL RES. NEWSL. 1, 1 (2008). Hydraulic fracturing, often used in combination with horizontal drilling, is the process by which large volumes of water are pumped down a well at high pressure in order to break apart the rock formation surrounding a well, releasing oil or gas that can be brought to the surface.

ferent types of rock formations such as shale.[24] In the years since the prior oil and gas booms (and busts), communities across the Front Range of Colorado had grown, especially suburban and exurban communities outside of the major population center around Denver. The growing population was on a collision course with the oil and gas industry, as companies pushed for "neighborhood drilling" while communities raised concerns about their health, safety, and the environment.[25] One of the earliest major developments came in fall 2012, when the residents of Longmont voted to amend their city charter to prohibit fracking within city limits. The fracking ban passed after a campaign by a local grass-roots organization called Our Health, Our Future, Our Longmont.[26]

The fight had been brewing for years, but the fracking ban struck like a thunderclap in Colorado and was faced with an immediate backlash from industry and state government officials.[27] Residents in Longmont had long been pushing the city council to adopt tighter regulations on the oil and gas industry. City leaders were afraid to go too far in regulating the industry, however, in part due to the experience in nearby Greeley, Colorado, where an earlier total ban on all oil and gas development had been struck down as preempted under state law.[28] Unsatisfied with the relatively modest regulations enacted by the city, residents organized primarily through Our Longmont to ban fracking through a ballot measure. Sixty percent of the voters approved the fracking ban.[29] Almost immediately, the Colorado Oil and Gas Association, an industry trade group, sued the city of Longmont, quickly joined by the Colorado Oil and Gas Conservation Commission as a plaintiff, along with a small oil and gas company interested in fracking in Longmont. The city, which never wanted a fracking ban in the first place, was left to defend the ballot measure against this onslaught.[30] Several environmental and con-

24. U.S. Environmental Protection Agency, The Process of Unconventional Natural Gas Production (Feb. 14, 2023), https://www.epa.gov/uog/process-unconventional-natural-gas-production.

25. Lynch, *supra* note 24, at 43-45.

26. Longmont City Charter, art. XVI (the charter amendment containing the fracking ban); *see also* Jefferson Dodge, *People of the Year: Longmont Anti-fracking Citizens' Group Our Longmont*, Boulder Wkly., Dec. 27, 2021, https://boulderweekly.com/news/people-of-the-year-longmont-antifracking-citizens-group-our-longmont (describing the local grassroots organization behind the fracking ban in Longmont).

27. Longmont v. Colorado Oil & Gas Ass'n, 369 P.3d 573, 577 (Colo. 2016) (describing how industry sued to challenge the ban quickly, with the state joining as a plaintiff).

28. Voss v. Lundvall Bros. Inc., 830 P.2d 1016 (Colo. 1992).

29. *See* Zahra Hirji, *Colorado: Judge Strikes Down Town's Fracking Ban*, Inside Climate News, July 25, 2014 https://insideclimatenews.org/news/25072014/colorado-judge-strikes-down-towns-fracking-ban (noting 60% support).

30. *See* Jack Healy, *With Ban on Drilling Practice, Town Lands in Thick of Dispute*, N.Y. Times, Nov. 12, 2012, https://www.nytimes.com/2012/11/26/us/with-ban-on-fracking-colorado-town-lands-in-thick-

servation groups, including not just Our Longmont but also the Sierra Club, Food & Water Watch, and Earthworks intervened (represented by the Environmental Law Clinic at the University of Denver, which I supervise), in the litigation so that someone actually in favor of the fracking ban would be included.

While the litigation over the Longmont ban was pending, several other communities looked to take similar actions, often through grass-roots organizing and the use of ballot measures. Voters in Boulder, Colorado, overwhelmingly approved their own fracking ban in 2013, with approximately 78% of voters in support.[31] Residents in Lafayette, Colorado, approved a Community Bill of Rights ordinance through the ballot measure process in November 2013.[32] The Lafayette law asserted rights of community self-governance and rights of nature and included an explicit ban on fracking. And finally the residents of Fort Collins approved their own ordinance through the ballot measure process, this time not banning fracking but merely putting in place a five-year moratorium[33] in order to allow the city to study the impacts of fracking, particularly in densely populated areas. State and industry plaintiffs challenged each of these local laws in court as preempted by state law.

Notable in the litigation was that the courts short-circuited a full defense of the fracking bans and the moratorium. The district court judge ruled against the Longmont fracking ban on summary judgment, after a rushed and limited period of discovery. This was even though prior cases in Colorado had indicated that developing a full factual record is critical to assessing whether an operational conflict exists between state and local law.[34] On appeal, the Colorado Supreme Court took the unusual and nearly unprecedented step of taking the case up before the Colorado Court of Appeals decided the initial appeal in the case.[35] Ultimately the Colorado Supreme Court in the *Longmont* and *Fort Collins* cases struck down both the ban and the moratorium as preempted by the Colorado Oil and Gas Conservation Act.[36] At virtually

---

of-dispute.html (noting the mayor's opposition to the ban and weariness at the prospect of defending it in court).

31. *See* Keith Coffman, *Three of Four Colorado Communities Vote to Ban, Suspend Fracking*, Reuters, Nov. 6, 2013, https://www.reuters.com/article/usa-fracking-colorado/three-of-four-colorado-communities-vote-to-ban-suspend-fracking-idUKL2N0IR0YG20131106.
32. *Community Rights Networks: State Community Rights Networks*, Community Envtl. Legal Defense Fund, https://celdf.org/where-we-work/community-rights-networks.
33. Voters in Broomfield, Colorado, narrowly defeated a similar moratorium proposal in 2013.
34. Board of Cty. Comm'rs v. Bowen/Edwards Assocs., 830 P.2d 1045 (Colo. 1992).
35. *Longmont*, 369 P.3d at 577: "Before hearing oral argument, however, a division of the court of appeals requested a transfer of this case to [the CO Supreme C]ourt.".
36. *Id.* at 585; *see also* Fort Collins v. Colorado Oil & Gas Ass'n, 369 P.3d 586, 593 (Colo. 2016).

every step in the litigation, the cities and citizen groups were prevented from making a full factual defense of their laws, as the courts instead rushed to strike down these democratically enacted laws at the request of industry and their allies in state government.

The litigation on the preemption issue in *Longmont* and the related cases centered on several key issues. First, was a ban or moratorium on fracking a local or statewide issue? The court concluded, largely on concerns related to the need for uniform regulation and the potential for extraterritorial impact, that the matter was not a local concern.[37] The court even cited a fear that the fracking ban in Longmont might create a "ripple effect" across the state by encouraging other municipalities to enact their own fracking bans,[38] and of course, this would be unacceptable. Second, what precisely was the state's interest? The court referred to various forms of the states' interest, including an interest in "the efficient and fair development of oil and gas resources in the state," in "regulating fracking," in "oil and gas development," and merely "fracking."[39] In this chameleon-like form, the state's interest could morph however necessary to support a finding of preemption. Notably, the court imputed these interests to the state even though the Colorado Oil and Gas Conservation Act never mentioned the concept of fracking. And finally, was there any conflict between the local laws and the Colorado Oil and Gas Conservation Act, which set up a structure for loose oversight of oil and gas extraction in the state? Here, the court looked to whether the local law would materially impede or destroy a state interest. Because the state's interest was defined narrowly as "fracking," a ban or even moratorium on fracking was found to be in operational conflict with state law.[40] As such, the court in 2016 struck down both the Longmont fracking ban and the Fort Collins moratorium as preempted by state law.[41]

Ultimately in Colorado, the lack of regulation on fracking and the continued expansion of "neighborhood drilling" became untenable, and the leg-

37. The court rejected out of hand arguments that the new technology should be evaluated anew, instead applying the same reasoning from over 20 years earlier in the *Voss* case. *Longmont*, 369 P.3d at 573.
38. *Id.* at 581.
39. *Id.* at 580, 581, 584, 585 (describing the different versions of the state's interest relied on by the court).
40. *Id.* at 580-81 (noting the state's interest in fracking and in regulating fracking). The Colorado Oil and Gas Conservation's express declaration was for the Oil and Gas Conservation Commission to

> foster the responsible, balanced development, production, and utilization of the natural resources in oil and gas in the State of Colorado in a manner consistent with protection of public health, safety, and welfare, including protection of the environment and wildlife resources.

Colo. Rev. Stat. §30-60-102 (2018). The Colorado Supreme Court read into this broad declaration a state interest in fracking. This is some of the language that was later amended by the state legislature.
41. *Longmont*, 369 P.3d at 573.

islature had to step in to update its laws. Unfortunately, the state suffered a series of accidents and explosions, including an explosion at a house traced to leaking flowlines from wells owned by Anadarko Petroleum, killing Mark Martinez and his brother-in-law Joe Irwin.[42] There was a series of egregious permitting decisions by the state, including one where a proposed multi-well site was moved for being too near to a school (attended by predominantly white children), only to be located even closer to another school (this time attended predominantly by Latino children).[43] These and other developments, along with the earlier preemption decisions, led to the passage of Senate Bill 19-181, which reformed Colorado's Oil and Gas Conservation Act.[44] The law changed the purpose of the relevant state agency from promoting oil and gas development to regulating it, strengthened requirements to protect public health and the environment, and explicitly stated that local governments could regulate fracking for health, safety, and environmental reasons, effectively undoing the earlier preemption rulings.[45] But the damage had largely been done at that point, as the fracking boom had spread across Colorado and many local governments felt compelled to agree to comprehensive drilling plans favorable to industry.

A similar battle played out quite differently in Pennsylvania. Fracking was booming in Pennsylvania even before it was in Colorado. There, as in Colorado, state officials and the oil and gas industry sought to impose uniform statewide rules for oil and gas development that would encourage and promote fracking, specifically through statewide zoning standards for oil and gas operations, enacted by the legislature in 2012.[46] As a result of this law, local governments were required to allow oil and gas development in every zoning district, even residential or other types of zoning where industrial activity would typically not be allowed. So effectively, the state had attempted to explicitly preempt local zoning laws from applying to oil and gas development. This time, instead of industry and the state suing to stop local restrictions, local governments were able to sue the state to challenge the constitutionality of this preemption law.

---

42. Grace Hood, *2 Years After a House Exploded Near a Firestone Oil and Gas Well, the Federal Report Is Finally Here*, CPR NEWS (Oct. 29, 2019, 8:11 AM), https://www.cpr.org/2019/10/29/ntsb-firestone-house-explosion-report.
43. The Daily Show, *That's Fracked: Can a Colorado School Combat Environmental Racism*, YOUTUBE (Feb. 1, 2019), https://www.youtube.com/watch?v=CsUJ0EcTSQM.
44. COLO. SENATE BILL NO. 19-181 (2019).
45. *Id.*
46. Robinson Twp. v. Commonwealth, 83 A.3d 901, 915 (Pa. 2013) (describing state law prohibiting any local regulation of oil and gas).

The difference, compared to Colorado at least, is that Pennsylvania has a state constitutional provision which requires the state to "conserve and maintain" public resources "for the benefit of all the people."[47] This environmental rights provision made all the difference in the preemption analysis by the court. Although lower courts in Pennsylvania had upheld the state law, ultimately the state Supreme Court found that state preemption of local zoning on oil and gas was unconstitutional.[48] The court found that the state as well as local governments were bound by the duty to conserve and maintain public resources. As a result, the state legislature did not have the power to remove local authority to carry out its constitutional obligations regarding the environment.[49]

There are several lessons to be drawn from the experience with regulation of fracking in Colorado and Pennsylvania. First, as is evident from the experience in Colorado, preemption law is a broad tool that enables judges to vindicate the interests of the wealthy and powerful even when those interests would otherwise lose in the political arena. Absent any measures to limit judicial discretion in this area, preemption will always lurk in the background, waiting to frustrate or delay sensible climate policies. Second, the Colorado example shows the perils of amorphous standards for conflict preemption. Although the *Longmont* court rejected industry attempts to claim implied or field preemption over fracking regulation, the ever-shifting version of the state's interest allowed the court to find a conflict, even though oil and gas development could occur in Longmont in compliance with both state and local law, so long as fracking was not employed. The court's willingness to divine a supposed state interest in fracking, when the legislature had not contemplated or even mentioned the term, underscores how readily courts rush to declare laws preempted. Third, and crucially, the Pennsylvania example shows how voters[50] in approving constitutional amendments can forestall harmful preemption decisions, even when the legislature attempts to

47. Penn. Const. art I, §27. The full provision reads:

> The people have a right to clean air, pure water, and to the preservation of the natural, scenic, historic and esthetic values of the environment. Pennsylvania's public natural resources are the common property of all the people, including generations yet to come. As trustee of these resources, the Commonwealth shall conserve and maintain them for the benefit of all the people.

48. *Robinson Twp.*, 83 A.3d at 901. The decision was 4-2, with a plurality of three justices basing its decision on the environmental rights provision, and a fourth concurring based on due process concerns. *Id.*

49. *Id.* at 985.

50. And similarly, legislatures could also forestall harmful court rulings on preemption; or judges themselves can resist calls from powerful interests to preempt laws that threaten the status quo.

expressly preempt local laws. Thus, there is hope that we can get the preemption issue correct in the climate adaptation context.

Getting Preemption Right in the Context of Climate Adaptation

How would the fight over preemption play out in the context of climate adaptation? Briffault's "new preemption" framing[51] is one way this might occur; state governments hostile to climate change science and policy or to fundamental changes in our social order might attempt to preempt local governments such as cities from developing not only locally tailored climate adaptation approaches but also attempts to implement an orderly and coordinated climate adaptation policy. States might attempt to preempt local building code[52] changes that would lead to more sustainable development and hardening of infrastructure, at least in areas where those changes might threaten vested interests such as the fossil fuel industry.[53]

Nevertheless, preemption law can also enable effective climate adaptation, if used appropriately. State preemption could therefore promote sensible climate adaptation policies against poor local choices. Think of the local government that chooses to squander resources in defending the indefensible, such as low-lying areas that will be unable to keep rising sea levels at bay or desert regions that promote more and more development that goes beyond the available water supply in the region. These types of wasteful activities might prove politically powerful at the local level, at least in the short term, but could be overcome through state-level preemption to ensure a more rational climate adaptation policy is implemented statewide.

Although there are many potential pitfalls related to preemption law which might delay or derail successful coordination of climate adaptation policies, preemption law done right carries a great deal of promise to ensure that all levels of government are working in concert towards a livable future

51. Briffault, *supra* note 15, at 1998. "New preemption" is defined as "sweeping state laws that clearly, intentionally, and at times punitively bar local efforts to address a host of problems." *Id.* at 1997. New preemption includes both punitive preemption desitned to punish local governments and officials, and nuclear preemption designed to blow up the ability of local governments to regulate unless given explicit state authorization. *Id.*

52. For examples of the types of changes to building codes that could have a big impact on climate adaptation, check out *Chapter 3: Land Use and Community Character*, Sustainable Dev. Code, https://sustainablecitycode.org/chapter/chapter-3 (last visited Nov. 28, 2023).

53. As an example, think of the battles in recent years where progressive local governments have banned natural gas hookups in new building construction, and the pushback from some states and the fossil fuel industry to preempt these local efforts at climate mitigation and adaptation. *See* Amy Turner, *Municipal Natural Gas Bans: Round 2 (The Evolution of State Preemption Law)*, Climate L. Blog (July 29, 2020), https://blogs.law.columbia.edu/climatechange/2020/07/29/municipal-natural-gas-bans-round-2-the-evolution-of-state-preemption-law.

as we attempt to adapt to a changing climate. There are several different ways that state legislatures, courts, and even the people through direct democracy can improve our chances of getting climate adaptation right. State legislatures could enact laws that would prevent courts from finding unwarranted preemption of local efforts, while at the same time ensuring that local governments do not frustrate a unified and coherent approach to climate adaptation. Several rights-based or other constitutional approaches can also prove useful both to encourage action by all levels of government and to foreclose potentially harmful preemption rulings. These include both existing rights and constitutional provisions, as well as avenues for advocacy to add or strengthen existing protections. And finally, courts, of course, have the ability to get this correct themselves and help rather than hinder society's response to the existential threat of climate change. Each of these possibilities will be explored in turn below.

At the state level, state legislatures could expressly direct state courts in how to apply the law of preemption in the climate adaptation context. Thus, a state might pass an overarching law laying out a rule of interpretation to guide state courts, for example, by stating that all laws of the respective state shall be interpreted to promote local authority to adapt to climate changes, unless specifically and expressly preempted by state law. Such a law would help to avoid the situation in Colorado where courts found a state interest in fracking despite no mention of fracking in any state statute. At the same time, state legislatures can and should pass statutes to expressly preempt local actions that frustrate the climate adaptation policies the state seeks to implement. For example, a state legislature might expressly preempt actions to rebuild in areas prone to climate disaster absent sufficient hardening of infrastructure in that location. Or state legislatures might expressly preempt local governments from engaging in exclusionary zoning designed to keep climate refugees from migrating there, either from within the state or from other parts of the country. State laws might even expressly state that they do not preempt specific local actions that the legislature seeks to encourage, such as development in more sustainable regions of the state or movement of infrastructure out of the areas most likely to suffer climate disasters.

State constitutional provisions can also provide even clearer directions to courts that they should not interfere with local actions to adapt to impending climate changes. Some states already have existing constitutional protections, such as Pennsylvania's environmental rights amendment.[54] A few other states have explicit environmental rights provisions, including Hawaii,

54. *See supra* note 29 and accompanying text.

Montana, and New York; however, constitutional rights for environmental protection are not nearly as common in the United States as they are in many other countries.[55] Many other U.S. states, however, have reference to "inalienable rights" which typically include enjoying and defending life and liberty, acquiring, possessing, and protecting property, and pursuing and obtaining safety and happiness.[56] These inalienable rights provisions could easily be read to cover protection of the environment and necessary adaptation to a changing climate.[57] Nevertheless, advocates who want to avoid the risk of adverse preemption decisions from courts would be wise to push for constitutional amendments that explicitly protect a right to a healthy environment, as in Pennsylvania's constitution.

Another approach would be a trans-substantive rule such as the Presumption Against State Preemption contained in the Model State Home Rule Constitutional Article put forward by the National League of Cities.[58] This presumption against preemption could also do a lot of good for climate adaptation even though it is not limited to that topic. The good news, in many states at least, is that constitutional amendments can be achieved through ballot measures even in the face of opposition from legislatures that might resist such actions.

In addition to human-centered rights based approaches, additional protections for the Rights of Nature would be helpful in the climate adaptation context. Many indigenous communities in North America have been leading the way on the Rights of Nature issue, either proposing amendments to tribal constitutions, enacting statutes on the rights of nature, or asserting these rights in efforts to stop harmful extractive activity.[59] These new legal actions are not creating any new rights, but rather codifying what these communities

---

55. Michael B. Gerrard, *Environmental Rights in State Constitutions*, Climate L. Blog (Aug. 31, 2021), https://blogs.law.columbia.edu/climatechange/2021/08/31/environmental-rights-in-state-constitutions.

56. *See, e.g.*, Cal. Const. art. I, §1.

57. Relatedly, state constitutions could be amended to clearly ground the responsibilities and obligations of the public trust doctrine in state law or expand its application for those states that have narrowly construed it. As I have written previously, the public trust doctrine can be used both as a sword to prod reluctant governments to act on climate issues and also as a shield against challenges to climate-related policies. *See* Lynch, *supra* note 23, at 79. Although attempts to limit fracking and oil and gas extraction are more related to climate mitigation, the same principles would apply to climate adaptation policies as well.

58. National League of Cities, *supra* note 14, at 53-61. This presumption embodied in a state constitution would bar implied preemption and raise the requirements on state preemption while setting clear standards for concurrent regulation by state and local governments.

59. *See, e.g.*, Erin Ryan et al., *Environmental Rights for the 21st Century: A Comprehensive Analysis of the Public Trust Doctrine and Rights of Nature Movement*, 42 Cardozo L. Rev. 2447, 2536-38 (2021) (cataloging approaches in recent years taken by Indigenous communities in the United States and Canada).

have always held to be true about nature and the connections between people and the environment.

Rights of Nature are also reflected in international contexts as well, such as the 2010 Universal Declaration of the Rights of Mother Earth.[60] In other countries, Rights of Nature are more explicitly incorporated into national constitutions. For example, in Ecuador the constitution was amended in 2008 to protect many environmental rights associated with nature and declare that nature has the right to exist, persist, maintain, and regenerate its vital cycles, and that all people and communities are empowered to enforce these rights.[61] Similar approaches have also been taken in other South American nations such as Colombia.[62] Elsewhere in New Zealand, the government granted legal personhood to Te Urewra National Park and the Whanganui River watershed, appointing them legal guardians.[63] Groups such as the Earth Law Center are working around the world, including in the United States, to spread and expand these Rights of Nature principles.[64] Similar to the human-centered rights approaches discussed previously, Rights of Nature would provide a substantive rule that would protect the right and obligation of all levels of government to adapt to a changing climate.

Lastly, it is important to note the role of courts in determining whether preemption applies and under what circumstances. Thus, courts can get this right, from a climate adaptation perspective. They just need a little help to do so. Some ways that courts can be neutered of their ability to cause mischief through preemption rulings would be constitutional amendments related to the environment or more specifically to climate change and adaptation. Legislatures can also provide more detailed guidance to courts in the form of laws that guide the courts in how to apply preemption law in this climate adaptation context. A state legislature could, for example, direct the courts as a general matter not to preempt local efforts to adapt to climate change unless expressly directed to do so by the legislature. This would take away the ability of courts to find broad, and often unjustified, implied, field, or conflict preemption to strike down important local efforts at climate adaptation.

60. Universal Declaration of Rights of Mother Earth, World Peoples Conf. on Climate Change & the Rts. of Mother Earth (2010), https://www.therightsofnature.org/universal-declaration.
61. Constitucíon Política de 2008 [C.P.] ch. VII (Ecuador).
62. Nicholas Bryner, *Colombian Supreme Court Recognizes Rights of the Amazon River Ecosystem*, International Union for Conservation of Nature (Apr. 20, 2018), https://www.iucn.org/news/world-commission-environmental-law/201804/colombian-supreme-court-recognizes-rights-amazon-river-ecosystem.
63. Te Awa Tupua (Whanganui River Claims Settlement) Act of 2017, subpt. 12 (N.Z.).
64. *What Is Earth Law?*, Earth Law Center, https://www.earthlawcenter.org/what-is-earth-law (last visited Nov. 28, 2023).

And of course courts could also just fix this problem on their own. I cannot say how likely this is, and I am not naive enough to think that many courts are likely to do this. Courts have the ability, however, to tweak their preemption doctrine within the confines of stare decisis[65] to respond to the existential threat of climate change. By recognizing the need for government to respond effectively in a coordinated fashion to climate change, courts (perhaps at the individual state level) could employ a clear statement rule,[66] effectively a presumption against finding preemption that is not express. With this presumption in place, courts would hesitate to find implied preemption or field preemption in the climate adaptation context, and they would avoid finding conflict preemption unless it was impossible to comply with both state and local laws.

How might this work in practice? Courts can declare that the baseline presumption is that all levels of government will need to do their part so that society can effectively adapt to climate change. And in order for the court to find preemption of a local effort at climate adaptation, it will require that the legislature clearly and expressly state that such local activity is preempted. This would respect the right of the legislature to say what is preempted and would cut back on courts expanding preemption beyond anything contemplated by the legislature in the past. It would also help to avoid the pitfalls of critical local policies getting delayed or even struck down by courts. In this context and many others, delay works in favor of the status quo and the wealthy and powerful. Delay in the context of climate adaptation can be deadly. Through a clear statement rule for climate adaptation preemption, courts would be saying that climate adaptation is crucial due to the existential threat climate change poses to our society, and unless the relevant legislative body has spoken clearly, they will presume that local efforts at climate adaptation are valid and will defer to elected officials to set policy rather than having unelected judges who lack any expertise dictate our climate policy.

---

65. Preemption law is often notoriously muddled and conflicting and thus provides ample room for courts to clarify and correct the doctrine. The Colorado Supreme Court in *Longmont* was candid in how convoluted and unclear its preemption decisions had become and attempted to clarify the doctrine in that case. *See Longmont*, 369 P.3d at 573: ("We begin our analysis by acknowledging the confusion that some of our prior preemption cases have engendered, and we address what we perceive to be the cause of that confusion.").

66. Courts make up clear statement rules all the time, as highlighted recently when the U.S. Supreme Court announced the so-called major questions doctrine, a clear statement rule reflecting a presumption against regulatory authority by the federal government in areas that significantly impact the economy. *See* West Virginia v. EPA, 597 U.S. ___ (2022) (naming for the first time the "major questions doctrine" even though it claimed support in earlier cases for this "doctrine"). It would be worth exploring in more detail whether preempting local or state authority over climate adaptation policies should be seen as a variation on the major questions doctrine.

Although courts have in the past recognized a "presumption against preemption,"[67] in practice they are quite eager to overcome this presumption especially if powerful and wealthy interests prefer preemption in a particular area.[68] This gloss on the presumption against preemption would reflect the appropriate humility that judges should show, would promote the rule of law rather than the rule of arbitrary judicial decisions, would promote democratic accountability for government policy, and would preserve the ability of state legislatures to override bad climate adaptation policies adopted by local officials. This is not a perfect solution and it would certainly allow some bad climate adaptation policies to go into place, depending on the politics of the jurisdiction surrounding a particular issue. But this approach is much preferable to judges taking this power for themselves, away from elected officials, by striking down climate adaptation policies as preempted absent a clear and express statement to that effect from the relevant legislature.

Conclusion

Adapting to all the changes that will come with a 4°C future is a monumental challenge and one that our system of government may not survive. Many of the flaws in our unique form of democracy here in the United States are highlighted in the area of preemption law. Special interests and powerful forces can manipulate our system to stymie effective public responses to the existential crisis of climate change. These interests have done so in the past and likely will continue to do so in the future. But if the politics around climate change can somehow be solved or at least improved enough to enable sensible climate adaptation policies to be adapted, then we have a chance to get it right with respect to preemption law. There are multiple different and complementary avenues for change to move us toward a rational preemption framework. Important changes can come from legislatures, courts themselves, and even the voting public in the form of ballot measures and constitutional amendments. These changes, if successfully and consistently implemented, can provide guidance to ensure our courts play an important

67. *See, e.g.*, Rice v. Santa Fe Elev. Corp., 331 U.S. 218, 230 (1947); Medtronic v. Lohr, 518 U.S. 470, 485-86 (1996). These cases are discussed in Ryan, *supra* note 4.

68. Some scholars argue that the presumption against preemption is inappropriate and therefore favor a more aggressive application of preemption law by the courts. *See, e.g.*, Caleb Nelson, *Preemption*, 86 Va. L. Rev. 225 (2000) (arguing that the Supremacy Clause of the U.S. Constitution undercuts the presumption against preemption); *see also* PLIVA Inc. v. Mensing, 564 U.S. 604 (2011) (citing Nelson in discussing the presumption against preemption). Formalistic approaches such as this threaten to do great damage in the climate adaptation context, if not cabined or rejected outright by judges, legislatures, and the people themselves.

role in enforcing a coordinated and efficient climate adaptation policy, while not unnecessarily frustrating or delaying important policies at the state or local level. The big question really is what will it take for us to solve the current political problems and overcome structural deficiencies in our political system. It may be that our society must truly hit rock bottom with respect to climate change before we can pick ourselves up and start to respond in a clear-eyed way to the crisis we are faced with. Nevertheless, for those already on board with the fight to respond to climate change, this chapter provides a road map of actions that can be taken now to improve our chances of rising to the challenge and adapting to a 4°C future.

Rhetoric Versus Reality After Winter Storm Uri

Melissa Powers

In February 2021, a blast of artic air descended upon Texas, where it lingered for nearly a week.[1] The freezing temperatures caused critical components of the Texas energy system to shut down, leaving millions of people without heat or power for days.[2] The imbalance between soaring energy demand and diminished supply also nearly caused a complete, uncontrolled grid blackout, which could have left parts of Texas without power for months.[3] While Texas avoided that particular catastrophe, Winter Storm Uri nonetheless exacted a terrible toll, including nearly 250 deaths and at least $130 billion in damages.[4]

In the midst of the Uri crisis, Texas politicians were quick to falsely attribute the energy outages to renewable sources and the non-existent Green New Deal, among other things,[5] while they downplayed the impacts of unwinterized natural gas infrastructure—which was in fact the leading cause of the outages.[6] Politicians also seemed to elevate political point-scoring and questions of state sovereignty above concerns for the people who had suf-

---

1. Joshua W. Busby et al., *Cascading Risks: Understanding the 2021 Winter Blackout in Texas*, 77 Energy Res. & Soc. Sci. 2-4 (June 2, 2021), https://www.sciencedirect.com/science/article/pii/S2214629621001997 [hereinafter Busby et al.].
2. *Id.* at 4.
3. *Id.*; Matt Largey, *Texas' Power Grid Was 4 Minutes and 37 Seconds Away From Collapsing. Here's How It Happened*, KUT90.5 (Feb. 24, 2021), https://www.kut.org/energy-environment/2021-02-24/texas-power-grid-was-4-minutes-and-37-seconds-away-from-collapsing-heres-how-it-happened.
4. Busby et al., *supra* note 1, at 4-5; Mitchell Ferman, *Texas Gas Companies Face Fines up to $1 Million for Failing to Prepare for Extreme Weather*, Tex. Trib., Aug. 30, 2022, https://www.texastribune.org/2022/08/30/texas-power-grid-natural-gas-weatherization-rules/; Federal Energy Regulatory Comm'n (FERC), North American Elec. Reliability Corp. & Reg'l Entities (NERC), The February 2021 Cold Weather Outages in Texas and the South Central United States (Nov. 16, 2021), https://www.ferc.gov/media/february-2021-cold-weather-outages-texas-and-south-central-united-states-ferc-nerc-and [hereinafter FERC Winter Outage Report].
5. Bryan Mena, *Gov. Greg Abbott and Other Republicans Blamed Green Energy for Texas' Power Woes. But the State Runs on Fossil Fuels*, Tex. Trib., Feb. 17, 2021, https://www.texastribune.org/2021/02/17/abbott-republicans-green-energy/. Some politicians blamed the crisis on poor management by the Electricity Reliability Council of Texas (ERCOT), which oversees the state's electricity system. In pointing the finger at ERCOT, they deflected attention from state regulators of the oil and gas industry.
6. Busby et al., *supra* note 1, at 3-4; FERC Winter Outage Report, *supra* note 4, at 10-17.

fered through days of sub-zero temperatures without energy.[7] Political framing of the problem carried through to the solutions Texas lawmakers and some regulators proposed, which included increasing the state's reliance on natural gas, penalizing renewable energy, and leaving critical infrastructure unweatherized.[8] Some of these proposals eventually became law,[9] which could result in Texas remaining vulnerable to future energy outages caused by severe weather.[10]

Technical reports released after Winter Storm Uri identified clear causes of the energy crisis.[11] Above all, they blamed a lack of winterization at power plants, natural gas wells, and natural gas pipelines.[12] Governance failures—including regulators' failure to mandate weatherization, inadequate energy planning, poor energy market design, and a lack of communication—also contributed to the crisis, as did the absence of alternative technologies available to consumers when grid-based energy service became unavailable.[13] The reports recommended several actions Texas lawmakers and regulators could take to prevent future energy crises during weather extremes. Some of these recommendations, predictably, emphasized the importance of weatherizing Texas's energy infrastructure.[14] Some recommendations targeted the gover-

7. Victoria Bekiempis, *Rick Perry Says Texans Will Endure Blackouts "To Keep the Government Out of Their Business,"* Guardian, Feb. 18, 2021, https://www.theguardian.com/us-news/2021/feb/18/rick-perry-texans-endure-blackouts-keep-government-out.
8. Russell Gold, *The Texas Grid Failure Was a Warm-Up*, Tex. Monthly, Feb. 2022, https://www.texasmonthly.com/news-politics/texas-electric-grid-failure-warm-up/.
9. An initial legislative proposal to invest in about 10 gigawatts of new and modified natural gas generation was defeated during the 2023 legislative session. *See* David Wallace-Wells, *Even in Texas, You Can't Stop the Green Revolution*, N.Y. Times, June 14, 2023, https://www.nytimes.com/2023/06/14/opinion/texas-green-revolution-fossil-fuels.html. However, Texas Senate Republicans referred a $10 billion funding package to state voters, who voted in favor of the Texas Energy Fund in November 2023. Of the $10 billion, approximately $7.2 billion is earmarked for natural gas power plants. *See* Mose Buchele, *Proposition 7 Would Provide Billions in Incentives for New Power Plants*, KUT News, Nov. 6, 2023, https://www.kut.org/energy-environment/2023-11-06/proposition-7-would-provide-billions-in-incentives-for-new-power-plants-in-texas; *see also* Robert Walton, *Texas Voters Approve $10B Energy Fund, With Most Going to Build Gas-Fired Power Plants*, Utility Dive, Nov. 8, 2023, https://www.utilitydive.com/news/texas-voters-approve-energy-fund-gas-power-plants-proposition-7/699110/.
10. *See* Michael E. Webber et al., *Two Years After Its Historic Deep Freeze, Texas Is Increasingly Vulnerable to Cold Snaps—And There Are More Solutions Than Just Building Power Plants*, The Conversation (Feb. 10, 2023), https://theconversation.com/two-years-after-its-historic-deep-freeze-texas-is-increasingly-vulnerable-to-cold-snaps-and-there-are-more-solutions-than-just-building-power-plants-198494.
11. Busby et al., *supra* note 1; FERC Winter Outage Report, *supra* note 4.
12. Busby et al., *supra* note 1, at 3-4; FERC Winter Outage Report, *supra* note 4, at 10-17.
13. Busby et al., *supra* note 1, at 6-8; *see also* Colleen M. Baker & James W. Coleman, *Paying for Energy Peaks: Learning From Texas' February 2021 Power Crisis*, 23 Transactions: Tenn. J. Bus. L. 463 (2022).
14. Busby et al., *supra* note 1, at 7; Erin Douglas et al., *Texas Leaders Failed to Heed Warnings That Left the State's Power Grid Vulnerable to Winter Extremes, Experts Say*, Tex. Trib., Feb. 17, 2021, https://www.texastribune.org/2021/02/17/texas-power-grid-failures/.

nance problems.[15] Others went further, emphasizing the reliability benefits that renewable energy, demand response, storage, and energy efficiency—the bedrocks of clean electrification—could provide.[16]

During the first three years following Winter Storm Uri, Texas had implemented some of these recommendations and disregarded several others. Notably, despite the proven unreliability of Texas' gas infrastructure and despite the market-driven growth of wind, solar, and battery storage in the state,[17] many politicians nonetheless promoted increased reliance on natural gas while they impeded natural gas weatherization or governance reforms.[18] These responses were not due to a lack of tools, knowledge, or resources to develop a cleaner and more reliable grid.[19] Instead, it appears that many state policymakers simply would not support or implement strategies that deviated from how they had chosen to frame Winter Storm Uri's energy crisis.

Sara Gosman has argued that discourse theory and policy framing could help elucidate how certain states view the problem of resilience and thus the policy solutions they consider viable.[20] Whereas the premise of traditional policymaking is that problems are self-evident and policy should focus primarily on the design of legal, technical, and economic solutions to those problems, discourse theory treats identification of the problem itself as an "act of interpretation and representation."[21] Policymakers allow their own biases and perceptions to influence how they define policy problems, and the resulting articulation of a problem necessarily leads to solutions that the policymakers deem acceptable.[22] Policy framing thus allows policymakers to ignore technical or legal recommendations that do not align with their chosen description of a problem.[23]

---

15. *See* Baker & Coleman, *supra* note 13; Busby et al., *supra* note 1. *See also* Alexandra Klass et al., *Grid Reliability Through Clean Energy*, 74 Stan. L. Rev. 969 (2022) (offering a series of recommendations for federal and regional grid governance).
16. Busby et al., *supra* note 1, at 6-8; Webber et al., *supra* note 10. Saul Griffith with Sam Calisch & Laura Fraser, Rewiring America: A Field Manual for the Climate Fight (2020) (describing the "electrify everything" approach); Mark Z. Jacobson et al., *Zero Air Pollution and Zero Carbon From All Energy at Low Cost and Without Blackouts in Variable Weather Throughout the U.S. With 100% Wind-Water-Solar and Storage*, 184 Renewable Energy 430 (2022) (explaining the resiliency benefits of electrifying everything).
17. *See* Nicolás Rivero, *Winter Storm Tests Texas Green Grid Upgrades*, Wash. Post (Jan. 14, 2024), https://www.washingtonpost.com/climate-solutions/2024/01/14/texas-grid-winter-storm-power-outage/.
18. *See* Gold, supra note 8.
19. *Id.*; Busby et al., *supra* note 1, at 7. Indeed, well before Winter Storm Uri, Texas had before it several evidence-backed recommendations for developing a more reliable and resilient grid, which it disregarded. Busby et al., *supra* note 1, at 7.
20. Sara R. Gosman, *Framing Energy Resilience*, 35 J. Land Use & Envtl. L. 1, 12 (2019).
21. *Id.* at 6.
22. *Id.* at 6-7.
23. *See id.* at 9-12.

Policy framing could explain how some Texas politicians understood Winter Storm Uri and thus how they chose to respond. But post-Uri developments in Texas may also reveal the limits of policy framing. Despite the opposition of many politicians, Texas added much more renewable energy, battery storage, and demand response to the electricity grid in the three years following Uri. Texas lawmakers had also failed to enact controversial legislative proposals to build several expensive new natural gas power plants that critics said would make the state's energy system more vulnerable to future storms.[24] It is too early to determine whether politicians' framing will eventually stifle clean energy growth or force more unreliable natural gas into the state's energy mix. But three years after Uri, many Texas politicians' statements appeared to be empty rhetoric rather than influential policy framing.

These developments in Texas may also offer lessons to those who fear that rhetoric will undermine efforts in other states to avoid or adapt to a 4°C future by integrating clean electrification into forward-looking state reliability and resiliency plans.[25] As much as Texas politicians tried to use blame-shifting and anti-renewable framing to suppress further clean energy development in the state, their efforts appeared incapable of overriding the market and regulatory dynamics that promoted the development of renewable energy and storage assets in the state. In addition, many of the statements were subject to fact-checking that diminished the power of the political rhetoric. While policy frames may indeed affect how problems are understood and thus revolved, their impacts can be checked.[26]

This chapter first describes how Winter Storm Uri crippled Texas' energy system and how Texas responded. Next, it examines Texas policymakers' responses to the storm through the lens of policy framing and assesses the extent to which that framing affected the state's post-Uri resilience efforts. The chapter concludes that clean energy advocates could learn from Texas' experiences and use policy framing to complement their efforts to accelerate the development of a clean and reliable electricity grid and prevent the worst climate case from becoming a reality.

---

24. Buchele, *supra* note 9. Ultimately, the legislators referred a ballot measure to voters. The ballot language indicated the innocuous-sounding "Texas Energy Fund" would simply "support the construction, maintenance, modernization, and operation of electric generating facilities." While a majority of voters approved the ballot measure, it is likely that most were unaware that more than 70% of the approved funding will support natural gas facilities. *Id.*
25. *See* Romany M. Webb et al., *Climate Risk in the Electricity Sector: Legal Obligations to Advance Climate Resilience Planning by Electric Utilities*, 51 ENVTL. L. 577 (2021).
26. *See* Gosman, *supra* note 20, at 12-13.

Winter Storm Uri and Its Aftermath

In 2021, Winter Storm Uri caused a days-long energy outage in Texas when escalating energy demand coincided with declining supplies of electricity and natural gas.[27] The mismatch between demand and supply almost led to a complete grid collapse, which could have left parts of Texas without power for months.[28] While grid managers narrowly avoided that catastrophe, they did so by curtailing power deliveries to millions of people throughout the state. In the end, hundreds of people died and Texas lost an estimated $130 billion in direct and indirect damages,[29] if not more.[30]

As Uri wreaked disaster, it quickly became clear that the grid failure might have been avoided through better governance and oversight.[31] Indeed, Texas utilities and regulators had failed to heed decade-old advice to winterize power plants and natural gas facilities.[32] When the unwinterized facilities began to fail during Uri's unrelenting, but not unprecedented, cold,[33] many Texas politicians denied that natural gas weatherization played a role in Uri's energy crisis and blamed renewable energy and a handful of individuals for what turned out to be a much more comprehensive regulatory failure.

After Uri, Texas politicians continued to bristle against expert recommendations for the state to use clean electrification as a critical component of ensuring future resilience to weather extremes.[34] Texas politicians instead allowed many natural gas facilities to remain unweatherized, sought to impose onerous obligations on renewable facilities, pursued the construction of 10,000 megawatts of new natural gas generation that most experts considered unnecessary, and disregarded demand-side measures that could make homes and businesses more resilient to future weather extremes.[35] In

27. Busby et al., *supra* note 1, at 2-4.
28. *Id.* at 4; Largey, *supra* note 3.
29. Busby et al., *supra* note 1, at 4-5; Ferman, *supra* note 4; FERC Winter Outage Report, *supra* note 4.
30. Chris Stipes, *New Report Details Impact of Winter Storm Uri on Texas*, Univ. Houston (Mar. 29, 2021), https://uh.edu/news-events/stories/2021/march-2021/03292021- hobby-winter-storm.php.
31. Busby et al., *supra* note 1, at 6-8; *see also* Baker & Coleman, *supra* note 13.
32. Busby et al., *supra* note 1, at 7; Douglas et al., *supra* note 14.
33. Busby et al., *supra* note 1, at 7.
34. *See id.* at 6-8.
35. *See* Nitish Pahwa, *Farewell Transmission*, Slate (Apr. 27, 2023), https://slate.com/business/2023/04/texas-power-grid-senate-plan-gas-fossil-fuels-renewables.html; Chris Tomlinson, *Grid Experts and Execs Slam $10 Billion Electricity Plan, Republicans Approve It Anyway*, Hous. Chron., Apr. 5, 2023, https://www.houstonchronicle.com/business/columnists/tomlinson/article/gop-electricity-grid-plan-slammed-passed-17875837.php; Christopher Harress, *Texas Is On a Crusade to Kill the State's Stunning Renewable Energy Progress*, Reckon (Apr. 11, 2023), https://www.reckon.news/news/2023/04/texas-is-on-a-crusade-to-kill-the-states-stunning-renewable-energy-progress.html; Saijel Kishan et al., *Republicans Fight a Solar Boom That's Made Texas King of Clean Energy*, Bloomberg, Apr. 19,

the midst of these political maneuverings, however, independent regulatory actions and market dynamics incentivized the addition of more renewables, storage, and demand response —the very technologies energy experts had stated would make the Texas energy system more reliable and secure—to the Texas electric grid. While it is too soon to predict whether Texas' energy system is prepared for another days-long extreme winter storm, the political response to Winter Storm Uri appeared to have less impact than anticipated.

This section first explains how Texas had ample forewarning of its energy system shortfalls and how it ignored advice to improve the resiliency of its energy system. It then describes the events of Winter Storm Uri, the ways in which Texas policymakers sought to scapegoat renewables as the primary causes, and how that framing affected the state's responses to Uri.

The Prelude to Uri

Uri was not the first storm that revealed the vulnerability of the state's gas-dependent energy system. In 2011, a decade before Winter Storm Uri, a cold front hit Texas, freezing natural gas wells and incapacitating power plants across the state.[36] A post-storm report prepared by federal energy agencies attributed these failures to inadequate energy system weatherization and advised Texas to winterize its energy infrastructure, particularly natural gas facilities.[37] Texas grid regulators and lawmakers ignored much of this advice.[38] Rather than mandate weatherization, regulators established voluntary "best practices" for electricity generators and left natural gas producers to their own devices.[39] Grid regulators believed their approach was validated when another cold spell hit Texas in 2018 and the power stayed on.[40] But the 2018 temperatures were neither as cold nor as long-lasting as the arctic

---

2023, https://www.bloomberg.com/news/articles/2023-04-19/texas-energy-going-solar-brings-gop-backlash#xj4y7vzkg (also linking the opposition to the political backlash against environmental, social, and governance practices). While they failed to pass legislation to achieve these goals, the Texas Senate secured voter approval of the Texas Energy Fund, which committed more than $7 billion to natural gas power plants and excluded clean energy resources from the fund. *See* Mose Buchele, *Proposition 7 Would Provide Billions in Incentives for New Power Plants,* KUT News, Nov. 6, 2023, https://www.kut.org/energy-environment/2023-11-06/proposition-7-would-provide-billions-in-incentives-for-new-power-plants-in-texas; *see also* Robert Walton, *Texas Voters Approve $10B Energy Fund, With Most Going to Build Gas-Fired Power Plants,* Utility Dive, Nov. 8, 2023, https://www.utilitydive.com/news/texas-voters-approve-energy-fund-gas-power-plants-proposition-7/699110/.

36. Busby et al., *supra* note 1, at 7; Douglas et al., *supra* note 14.
37. FERC & NERC, Report on Outages and Curtailments During the Southwest Cold Weather Event of February 1-5, 2011, at 10, 203-09 (2011), https://www.ferc.gov/sites/default/files/2020-04/08-16-11-report.pdf.
38. Busby et al., *supra* note 1, at 7.
39. Douglas et al., *supra* note 14.
40. *Id.*

temperatures that would hit Texas in 2021.[41] Winter Storm Uri revealed the insufficiency of the Texas voluntary approach.

The Texas Energy System's Failure During Uri

During Winter Storm Uri, arctic air caused Texas temperatures to drop below freezing for several days.[42] In response to the cold, Texans turned up their space heaters and furnaces, causing a dramatic spike in electricity and gas use.[43] For a few days, power plants and gas lines were able to meet the increased demand.[44] But the persistent cold, combined with poor contingency planning, made many power plants inoperable.[45] As water in thermal power plants and gas pipelines froze, power plants began to "rapidly trip offline."[46] At the worst moment, more than 50 gigawatts (GW)—nearly 49%—of the state's electricity-generation capacity became unavailable.[47] By way of comparison, the state's extreme winter planning scenario had anticipated a drop of only 14 GW.[48] The dramatic decrease in electricity supply combined with very high demand (which also exceeded the amount modeled in the state's extreme winter planning scenario) placed Texas only a few minutes away from a complete grid shut down.[49]

To avoid a catastrophic imbalance between electricity supply and demand, grid operators instituted load-shedding orders that suspended electricity delivery to millions of consumers.[50] Among the curtailed users were natural gas production facilities, which thus lacked electricity necessary to supply fuel to power plants, worsening the risk of a catastrophic grid failure.[51] Power cutoffs also affected millions of homes and businesses.[52] While the curtailments prevented the grid from completely shutting down and averted the need for a "black start" restoration of energy service that could have taken weeks or months—during which time millions of Texas would have been

---

41. *Id.*
42. Busby et al., *supra* note 1, at 2.
43. *Id.* at 2-3. Baker & Coleman, *supra* note 13, at 468; Andrea Zelinski, *What Went Wrong With Texas' Main Electric Grid and Could It Have Been Prevented?,* Tex. Monthly, Feb. 17, 2021, https://www.texasmonthly.com/newspolitics/what-went-wrong-with-texass-main-electric-grid-and-could-it-have-beenprevented.
44. Busby et al., *supra* note 1, at 3, fig. 1.
45. *Id.* at 4.
46. *Id.* at 3, fig. 1.
47. *Id.* at 4.
48. *Id.* at 2.
49. *Id.* at 4.
50. *Id.*; Baker & Coleman, *supra* note 13, at 466.
51. Busby et al., *supra* note 1, at 2-4; Baker & Coleman, *supra* note 13, at 468.
52. Busby et al., *supra* note 1, at 2-4; Baker & Coleman, *supra* note 13, at 468.

without any electricity—the curtailments still exacted an enormous cost.[53] An estimated 246 people died from hypothermia, asphyxiation, and other causes related directly to loss of electricity and heat.[54]

In the midst of the crisis, as available energy supplies were dropping, the Public Utility Commission of Texas (PUCT) attempted to use price signals in the wholesale electricity market to induce more electricity generation. In an effort to incentivize increased output from operable electricity generators, the PUCT issued emergency orders that unilaterally set the market price for all wholesale electricity sales at $9,000 per megawatt-hour (MWh) for four days, even though electricity had been clearing the market at closer to $1,200 per MWh.[55] The PUCT's decision had the effect of dramatically raising the costs of electricity,[56] but it did not substantially increase power production. Several wholesale energy suppliers earned record profits during the five-day storm,[57] which distribution utilities and their customers were obligated to pay. Within a few days, some distribution utilities paid more for wholesale electricity than they had previously paid during several previous years.[58] Some of their customers, including residential users who would normally pay about $80 per month, were charged more than $6,700 for a few days' worth of electricity usage.[59] Many distribution utilities, however, were unable to

---

53. Busby et al., *supra* note 1, at 4.
54. Patrick Svitek, *Texas Puts Final Estimate of Winter Storm Death Toll at 246*, Tex. Trib., Jan. 3, 2022, https://www.texastribune.org/2022/01/02/texas-winter-storm-final-death-toll-246/.
55. *Texas Court Invalidates PUC's Decision on Winter Storm Uri Electricity Prices* 5 (Apr. 17, 2023), https://www.energyby5.com/ercot-uri-decision.
56. Baker & Coleman, *supra* note 13, at 471. The PUCT's decision may have been designed to offset flaws in the pricing algorighms used in Texas energy markets. As Profs. Baker and Coleman explain, Texas employed an energy-only market, rather than both energy and capacity markets, to ensure that adequate electricity supplies are available to meet demand. When electricity demand increases in energy-only markets, price "adders" are often used to provide generators additional compensation to meet the escalating demand. The adders should, in theory, induce available (but expensive) generators to deliver power during periods of scarcity and send longer term price signals that encourage the construction of new electricity generation to serve future load. During Winter Storm Uri, market signals became crossed as electricity users were subjected to curtailment orders designed to prevent a grid shutdown; as power usage dropped due to the load shedding, the market algorithms automatically lowered the prices for electricity that cleared Texas' markets. Because the PUCT believed that lower prices were inconsistent with the price signals the market was designed to send, the PUCT reset market clearing prices at the maximum cap of $9,000 per MWh. *Id.* at 469-71. While these price signals may have aligned with the market design, they could not overcome the physical limitations preventing more energy production.
57. Busby et al., *supra* note 1, at 6.
58. Baker & Coleman, *supra* note 13, at 471.
59. Giulia McDonnel Nieto del Rio et al., *His Lights Stayed on During Texas' Storm. Now He Owes $16,752*, N.Y. Times, Feb. 20, 2021, https://www.nytimes.com/2021/02/20/us/texas-storm-electric-bills.html. *See also* Busby et al., *supra* note 1, at 6-7; Reese Oxner, *Texas Woman Who Received $9,300 Electricity Bill Files Class-Action Lawsuit Against Wholesale Electricity Provider Griddy*, Tex. Trib., Feb. 23, 2021, https://www.texastribune.org/2021/02/23/texas-electric-bill-griddy/ (describing how one woman who would normally have paid $200 ended up with a bill for more than $9,000 during the same time).

pass their full costs onto their customers and have since filed for bankruptcy.[60] While the PUCT's price adjustments had clear economic impacts, they did not achieve regulators' goals of inducing more power production. Price signals could not overcome the physical constraints on Texas's energy system.

Instead, the energy crisis ended when the storm passed and temperatures rose, allowing unweatherized plants to resume operations as energy demand decreased.

Political Responses to the Uri Crisis

Some Texas policy actors saw Winter Storm Uri as an opportunity for political messaging and point-scoring. Above all, politicians and right-wing media figures sought to blame renewable energy. Some Texas politicians wrongly pinned all of the blame for the crisis on wind generators,[61] and Fox News falsely blamed wind energy 128 times over 2 days for causing the energy outages.[62] Although wind production did drop during the storm, natural gas—not renewable energy—was by far the dominant cause of the outages, due to freezing at unwinterized natural gas power plants, a precipitous drop in natural gas production at unwinterized wells, and reduced deliveries of gas to power plants.[63] Yet, even after post-mortem analyses demonstrated that natural gas was the primary culprit, Texas politicians continued to blame renewables for the outages.[64]

Texas politicians, particularly Gov. Greg Abbott, also sought to shift most of the blame onto the board of ERCOT, the organization that manages the reliability of the state's electricity system. Two days into the storm, Governor Abbott tweeted that the "Electric Reliability Commission of Texas has been anything but reliable," and promised to review ERCOT's actions to

60. Erin Douglas & Emily Foxhall, *Appeals Court Says State Agency Set Electricity Prices Too High During 2021 Winter Storm*, Tex. Trib., Mar. 17, 2023, https://www.texastribune.org/2023/03/17/puc-appeals-court-uri-prices/.

61. Gold, *supra* note 8.

62. Teddy Gonzalez & Jillian Knox, *In the Dark: The Scapegoating of Renewables After Grid Failures*, 63 Nat. Resources J. 30, 31 (2023) (citing Rob Savillo, *Fox News and Fox Business Falsely Blamed Renewable Energy for Texas Blackouts 128 Times Over Two Days*, Media Matters (Feb. 18, 2021, 11:29 AM), https://perma.cc/HH5R-MFMB).

63. FERC Winter Outage Report, *supra* note 4, at 10-17. FERC attributed 96% of the fault to "freezing issues" at the generation plants, "fuel issues" associated with the inability to produce and deliver fuel to power plants, and "mechanical/electrical" issues that usually arose from the freezing and fuel supply failures. *Id.* at 15, fig. 3. Freezing wind turbines accounted for 22% of the capacity losses, while energy outages at gas plants caused 55% of the energy outages. *Id.* at 16, fig. 3. Natural gas was also 87% responsible for the "fuel issues" that contributed to the outages. *Id.* at 16.

64. Indeed, Texas regulators and utilities had been warned a decade earlier that the state's energy infrastructure needed winterization, after a 2011 winter storm caused power outages due to freezing pipelines and power plants. Ferman, *supra* note 4.

understand how it had failed.[65] While this could be seen as a state leader committing to investigate and correct a governance problem, commenters have noted it also could be considered a tactic to deflect responsibility, as it suggests that members of ERCOT had knowledge and agency the governor did not.[66] Indeed, in some interviews, Abbott suggested that he was not especially familiar with ERCOT (and, thus, presumably would not have been able to intervene earlier to ensure ERCOT performed better).[67] Finally, in other statements, Abbott emphasized that four of ERCOT's board members lived outside the state, hinting that their outsider status may have made them less concerned for the welfare of Texans and prompting all four to resign.[68]

At the same time, Texas politicians who have long viewed Texas' isolation from the interstate electricity grid as a point of pride categorically denied that isolation could make Texas more vulnerable.[69] Rick Perry, a former Texas governor and U.S. Secretary of Energy, was especially aggressive in his defense of the status quo. Even as electricity and water services remained out of service, and before families were able to bury their loved ones, Perry insisted that "Texans would [choose to] be without electricity for longer than three days to keep the federal government out of their business."[70]

While these are only a few snapshots of the political rhetoric and framing Texas policymakers used in the midst of Uri's electricity crisis, they are nonetheless illustrative of the narratives policymakers embraced in the midst of the storm. Above all, politicians sought to assign blame to a limited set of actors (particularly those at ERCOT) and energy sources (i.e., renewables). In so doing, they implicitly exonerated others causes. And they maintained the same views even after expert analyses provided a much clearer and more thorough description of the causes and contributors to the energy crisis.

What the Experts Said

In the wake of Winter Storm Uri, researchers and regulators identified several factors that contributed to the energy outages. Above all, despite the

65. Greg Abbott [@GregAbbott_TX], *Governor Abbott on Power in Texas* [Tweet], TWITTER, (Feb. 16, 2021), https://twitter.com/kwtx/status/1361766831275597826. *See also* Matthew Gerber et al., *Power Grid Politics: Winter Storm Uri and Texas Governor Greg Abbott's Image Repair Discourse*, 59 SPEAKER & GAVEL 35, 41 (2023)
66. Gerber et al., *supra* note 65, at 41.
67. *Id.* at 42.
68. *Id.*
69. Victoria Bekiempis, *Rick Perry Says Texans Will Endure Blackouts "To Keep the Government Out of Their Business,"* GUARDIAN, Feb. 18, 2021, https://www.theguardian.com/us-news/2021/feb/18/rick-perry-texans-endure-blackouts-keep-government-out.
70. *Id.*

decade-old recommendations to winterize energy facilities, the Uri energy crisis was attributed to Texas' failure to require winterization of power plants, gas production wells, and other infrastructure that was prone to freezing.[71] Texas regulators also failed in other aspects of oversight and emergency planning. They had not developed emergency cold weather energy scenarios for sutained periods of extreme cold, even though Texas had experienced similar cold weather events in the past.[72] Texas regulators also neglected some of the emergency measures they did have in place. For example, although Texas rules should have ensured that gas production wells that are considered "critical infrastructure" would continue to receive electricity during load-shedding events, the rules' efficacy hinged on well owners' compliance with a requirement to submit a one-page form identifying their wells as critical.[73] Many well owners had failed to submit the forms, and their regulators had failed to track compliance with the reporting requirement. Consequently, in the midst of the crisis, electricity service to many critical gas wells was curtailed.[74] The resulting reduction in natural gas deliveries to power plants, in turn, worsened the capacity shortfalls in the electricity system and brought the grid even closer to collapse.[75]

In addition, Texas arguably relied too heavily on incomplete energy market design and pricing signals to promote energy reliability without having regulatory backstops in place.[76] As discussed above, the markets allowed some wholesale electricity suppliers and several gas producers to earn enormous profits during the storm, but they did little to ensure sufficient supplies of electricity and gas.[77] Similarly, despite an abundance of evidence that dynamic pricing is generally ineffective at increasing building efficiency or preparing end users for extreme weather, Texas did little to encourage building retrofits or energy efficiency measures.[78] Indeed, even as the arctic front

71. Busby et al., *supra* note 1, at 3-4; FERC Winter Outage Report, *supra* note 4, at 10-17. FERC attributed 96% of the fault to "freezing issues" at the generation plants, "fuel issues" associated with the inability to produce and deliver fuel to power plants, and "mechanical/electrical" issues that usually arose from the freezing and fuel supply failures. *Id.* at 15, fig. 3. Freezing wind turbines accounted for 22% of the capacity losses, while energy outages at gas plants caused 55% of the energy outages. *Id.* at 16, fig. 3. Natural gas was also 87% responsible for the "fuel issues" that contributed to the outages. *Id.* at 16.
72. Busby et al., *supra* note 1, at 2-4.
73. *Id.*; Baker & Coleman, *supra* note 13, at 468.
74. *Id.* Busby et al., *supra* note 1, at 2-4.
75. *Id.*
76. Baker & Coleman, *supra* note 13, at 469-71 (describing dysfunction in the wholesale energy markets); *see also* Andrew N. Kleit, *The Texas Electricity Two-Step*, 46 Regulation 18, 18-20 (Fall 2023) (explaining how Texas' energy-only market failed in incentivize sufficient generation capacity).
77. Gold, supra note 8.
78. Busby et al., *supra* note 1, at 7.

was descending on Texas and despite ample time to prepare consumers for electricity shortfalls, Texas officials barely communicated warnings to the public.[79] Many people were therefore not adequately prepared for the days of energy outages they ultimately experienced.

Finally, researchers attributed some of the harms experienced during Winter Storm Uri to the isolation of Texas' electricity system from the rest of the country's. Unlike the rest of the lower 48 states, Texas has chosen to keep its electricity system physically—and therefore legally—separate from the interstate transmission system.[80] This separation prevented Texas from accessing electricity supplies from other states that were less affected by Uri's cold weather or that had winterized energy facilities.[81]

Texas' Responses to Uri

In the three years following the Uri crisis, Texas politicians and regulators took several actions to prevent future energy outages. While some of these actions aligned with the experts' recommendations for designing a more resilient grid, state political leaders were reluctant to follow other recommendations, particularly those that would impact natural gas production and use in the state, despite growing concerns about natural gas's reliability during extreme weather.[82] Because Texas has not since experienced another extended cold-weather event like Winter Storm Uri, it is unclear whether the state's energy system is prepared for another major winter storm. But energy experts warn that several critical vulnerabilities remain.

Post-Uri expert recommendations focused, not surprisingly, on winterizing the state's natural gas system, from production wells to power plants. While state regulators did order gas-fired power plants to winterize,[83] legislation passed after the storm required weatherization only of gas production facilities that were "prepared to operate during a weather emergency."[84] The Railroad Commission of Texas, which regulates the oil and gas industry, then developed rules that exempted from weatherization requirements any

79. *Id.*
80. Baker & Coleman, *supra* note 13, at 469. If Texas were to interconnect its electric grid to the rest of the interstate system, Texas would lose regulatory authority over its wholesale energy markets and interstate transmission, both of which are subject to FERC jurisdiction instead. *Id.*
81. *Id.*; Busby et al., *supra* note 1, at 7-8.
82. *See* Sherin Elizabeth Varghese, *US Energy Regulator Recommends Revising Reliability Standards for Extreme Weather,* Reuters (Sep. 20, 2023), https://www.reuters.com/business/energy/us-energy-regulator-recommends-revising-reliability-standards-extreme-weather-2023-09-21/.
83. See Shelby Webb, *Investigation: Texas Failed to Crack Down on Gas After Grid Crisis,* EnergyWire (Jul. 20, 2023), https://www.eenews.net/articles/investigation-texas-failed-to-crack-down-on-gas-after-grid-crisis/.
84. *See* Gold, supra note 8.

facilities that were not planning to operate during weather emergencies, effectively allowing gas companies to opt out of the requirements.[85] A loud public outcry sent the Railroad Commission back to the drawing board, but energy experts were skeptical that the subsequent rules would ensure that an adequate amount of natural gas wells and pipelines will be sufficiently winterized before the next big winter storm.[86] This skepticism was driven in part by the Railroad Commission's repeated assertions, despite evidence to the contrary, that insufficient winterization of gas wells and pipeline infrastructure did not contribute to Uri's electricity outages, as well as the commission's attempts to blame electricity service cutoffs for all of the gas supply shortfalls.[87] Doubts about the winter preparedness of the gas system seemed to be well-founded when Texas gas production dropped by 20% during a cold spell in December 2022.[88]

Texas resisted other changes that could forestall future energy outages. Invoking an unsubstantiated fear of losing regulatory autonomy, Texas politicians rejected out-of-hand any proposal to increase Texas' interconnections with the interstate grid.[89] In addition, despite increasing energy demand driven by population growth, Texas refused to pass mandatory energy efficiency or conservation standards. While Texas promoted a voluntary demand response program that encourages energy conservation during peak periods, it was not clear if these efforts would sufficiently mitigate peak energy demand during extended extreme weather, particularly since the state's rising population had already increased the risk that available energy supplies would be insufficient to meet the resulting load growth. During the December 2022 cold spell, for example, although temperatures were 10 degrees warmer than during Winter Storm Uri, electricity demand was higher.[90] Moreover, demand response programs induce short-term reductions in energy consumption and do not address the state's need for improved building efficiency through insulation

85. *Id.*
86. *Id.*; *see also* Jacqueline L. Weaver, *The Railroad Commission's New Duties to Keep Texans Warm: Winter Storm Uri Forces Change*, State Bar of Texas, 46 Oil, Gas & Energy L. Section Rep. 15-27 (Mar. 2022); Webb, *supra* note 83.
87. Gold, supra note 8. As Gold notes, gas supplies were disrupted days before any electricity blackouts began. *Id.*
88. Garret Golding, *Texas Electrical Grid Remains Vulnerable to Extreme Weather Events*, Fed. Reserve Bank Dallas (Jan. 17, 2023), https://www.dallasfed.org/research/economics/2023/0117; *see also* Webb, *supra* note 83.
89. *See* Reese Oxner, *Texas Could Connect to National Power Grids Without Losing Autonomy, Former Grid Regulator Says*, Tex. Trib., Feb. 15, 2022, https://www.texastribune.org/2022/02/14/texas-national-power-grids/. Former state and federal energy regulators have argued that Texas has authority under federal law to extend its interstate connections, which would also allow Texas energy companies to profit from exporting more electricity, without ceding regulatory power to FERC. *Id.*
90. *See* Golding, *supra* note 88.

and other physical retrofits. If load growth outpaces demand response participation and Texas experiences another storm like Uri, outages could again leave many Texans in the dark and cold.

Finally, and contrary to many of the recommendations in the post-Uri expert reports, many Texas politicians sought to increase natural gas electricity generation and reduce the role of renewables in the state. In particular, legislators drafted bills to prevent new renewables from being developed in the state, to authorize construction of 10,000 MW of new natural gas capacity, and incentivize even more natural gas plants.[91] These bills were defeated in the 2023 Texas legislative session,[92] but the Texas Senate then referred a $10 billion Texas Energy Fund, which earmarked more than $7 billion for new natural gas power plant development, to Texas voters. While voters approved the funding in November 2023, it appears that many believed it would improve energy reliability overall, rather than natural gas specifically.[93] Some Texas energy insiders doubt that the fund can be administered in a way that will push substantial new natural gas electricity into the market, so its efficacy remains to be seen.

Notwithstanding these various actions, the Texas grid added far more wind and solar power and battery storage in the three years following Uri.[94] Experts attribute this growth to a favorable regulatory regulatory that predated Uri, and they believe these new energy sources have made the energy system more resilient.[95] Indeed, several news stories published in the years following Uri specifically attributed the state's more reliable energy system to these clean energy sources.[96] Ultimately, although Texas politicians were able to leverage the Uri energy crisis into more funding for fossil fuels, it is unclear whether this funding can overcome the market and regulatory forces that have enabled continued growth of renewables and energy storage in Texas.[97]

91. Pahwa, *supra* note 35; Tomlinson, *supra* note 35.
92. Wallace-Wells, *supra* note 9.
93. Buchele, *supra* note 9.
94. *See* Sasha von Oldershausen, *The Freeze Has Thawed. The Grid Survived. What Was Different this Time?*, Tex. Monthly (Jan. 19, 2024), https://www.texasmonthly.com/news-politics/ercot-power-grid-2024-freeze/.
95. *Id.*; Rivero, *supra* note 17.
96. *See* von Oldershausen, *supra* note 94; Ella Nilsen, *Wind and Solar Are Propping Up the Texas Power Grid Amid a Brutally Long Heat Wave*, CNN (Jul. 8, 2023), https://www.cnn.com/2023/07/28/business/texas-renewable-energy-heat-wave-climate/index.html.
97. Webber et al., *supra* note 10.

Policy Framing After Energy Crises

What lessons can one take from Texas' political and rhetorical response to Winter Storm Uri, and do these responses suggest that policy framing plays a critical role in energy resilience? Discourse theory suggests that policymakers' framing of Winter Storm Uri would strongly influence the actions Texas took in response.[98] In reality, however, policy framing seemed to only go so far in affecting how the state responded to the energy crisis, perhaps because energy scholars, professionals, and the media challenged many of the falsehoods Texas politicians made about the causes Winter Storm Uri. Winter Storm Uri may thus illustrate how misleading policy frames can be overcome by competing, evidence-backed, and sustained narratives, which, in combination with existing regulatory and market structures, can enable a transition to a clean and resilient energy system and stave off the worst-case climate scenario.

This section thus considers the role that policy framing may play in accelerating or impeding such a transition. It first describes the theory and processes of policy framing in the energy reliance context. Next, it details the ways in which Texas policy actors employed policy framing during and after Winter Storm Uri. Finally, this section examines the limitations of that policy framing in Uri's wake.

Policy Framing and Energy Resilience

Traditional policy analysis often assumes that the problem to be solved is obvious and that policy work should focus on identifying viable solutions. Social scientists, however, have long recognized that the identification of problems is a highly contested and often subjective component of policymaking.[99] Through policy framing, policy actors create an understanding of the problem and a model for subsequent actions in light of the problem they have identified.[100] In other words, whereas traditional policymaking often starts by asking: "What's to be done?," policy framing first asks: "What's the problem represented to be?" That representation will often embed or dictate how policy actors choose to respond to the problem.[101]

98. *See* Gosman, *supra* note 20.
99. *See* Gosman, *supra* note 20, at 6-7.
100. Merlijn van Hulst & Dvora Yanow, *From Policy "Frames" to "Framing": Theorizing a More Dynamic, Political Approach*, 46 Pub. Admin. 92, 98 (2016).
101. *Id.* at 96.

Policy framing involves three distant acts: (1) making sense of the situation; (2) naming the problem; and (3) telling a story about the problem.[102] At its simplest level, sense-making is the process of figuring out what has happened or is happening.[103] This process is not, however, a purely objective or empirical exercise. In many cases, the process of making sense of a problem includes normative judgments about not just what is happening but about what "ought to be."[104] Once a policy actor has made some sense of the issue, the actor next names it.[105] Naming involves three steps: (1) selecting the features that warrant attention; (2) naming those features; and (3) and categorizing them.[106] In other words, "actors 'name' the problem by highlighting characteristics of the policy issue that are consistent with their understanding and creating labels that reflect these characteristics."[107] Through naming the relevant characteristics of a problem, policy actors choose which characteristics they consider relevant and which are outside of the established frame.[108] The last part of policy framing is the storytelling, through which actors use stories to both define the problem and prescribe the solutions.[109] These stories often "attribute blame or praise and suggest causes of harm or success."[110] In so doing, they become avenues for policy actors to use discourse as a means of wielding power.[111]

As Sara Gosman has argued, policy framing has allowed policy actors to narrowly define the issue of energy resilience as one involving threats to continuous energy supply from climate change.[112] By naming climate change as the threat and energy supply as the victim, so to speak, policy actors are able to ignore the energy sector's contribution to climate change (and thus the energy sector's self-inflicted harms).[113] This, in turn, justifies energy resilience strategies that focus on protecting energy infrastructure from climate-related extreme weather events, rather than on replacing fossil fuel infrastructure with clean energy systems that will not worsen climate change.[114] Just as policy framing has helped define what resilience means in relation to climate

102. *Id.* at 97.
103. *Id.*
104. *Id.* at 98 (quoting Martin Rein & Donald Schon, *Problem Setting in Policy Research*, *in* Using Social Research in Public Policy Making 235, 240 (C.H. Weiss ed., 1977).
105. *See* van Hulst & Yanow, *supra* note 100, at 99; Gosman, *supra* note 20, at 7.
106. *See* van Hulst & Yanow, *supra* note 100, at 99.
107. Gosman, *supra* note 20, at 7.
108. *Id.*
109. *Id.*; van Hulst & Yanow, *supra* note 100, at 100-01.
110. *See* Van Hulst & Yanow, *supra* note 100, at 101.
111. *Id.*
112. Gosman, *supra* note 20, at 8.
113. *Id.* at 8-12.
114. *Id.*

change, so might policy framing help explain how Texas politicians sought to respond to Winter Storm Uri.

Framing Winter Storm Uri

When the three distinct acts of policy framing—sense-making, naming, and storytelling—are applied to Winter Storm Uri, some of Texas' initial responses to Winter Storm Uri begin to make some sense.[115] This is not to say that Texas' responses were evidence-backed or objectively sound. To the contrary, Texas politicans ignored many of the experts' recommendations for improving the reliability and resilience of its energy system. But, when one considers how leading Texas policy actors defined and then described the causes of Winter Storm Uri, it becomes clearer why they would reject the experts' advice.

The first step of policy framing, making sense of a situation, often involves "a normative leap from what *is* to what *ought to be*."[116] Sense-making involves more than objective observations of events to arrive at factual conclusions; in making sense of a situation, policy actors use their prior knowledge and values to reach an understanding of events that aligns with the actors' existing views.[117] In the case of Winter Storm Uri, many of the Texas politicians and media figures that sought to blame the disaster on wind energy and renewables had long histories of climate denialism and antipathy toward renewable energy.[118] Some politicians and regulators had either worked for or with the natural gas industry for a long peried, or had received campaign donations from the sector, and thus came predisposed to favor the gas industry when attempting to make sense of the situation by assigning blame.[119] Other policy actors were in regulatory roles overseeing natural gas facilities or designing energy markets.[120] If natural gas were primarily to blame for the energy out-

115. *Id.* at 97.
116. *See* van Hulst & Yanow, *supra* note 100, at 98 (emphasis in original).
117. *Id.*
118. Harress, *supra* note 35; *see also* Emily Foxhall, *Texas Utility Commission Chair Raises Threat of Summer Power Outages and Pushes for More Gas-Powered Electricity*, Tex. Trib., May 3, 2023, https://www.ksat.com/news/texas/2023/05/04/texas-utility-commission-chair-raises-threat-of-summer-power-outages-and-pushes-for-more-gas-powered-electricity/; Joshua Fetcher, *Texas Energy Officials' Proposal to Overhaul the Power Grid Is Drawing Skepticism*, Tex. Trib., Nov. 18, 2022, https://www.texastribune.org/2022/11/18/texas-power-market-overhaul-puc-winter-storm/; Zoe Parker, *Texas Legislators Should Consider Alternatives to Strengthen Grid Reliability Before Gambling on PCM*, Utility Dive (Apr. 26, 2023), https://www.utilitydive.com/news/texas-legislature-grid-reliability-performance-credit-mechanism/648226/.
119. *See* Gold, supra note 8.
120. Martin Farrer et al., *U.S. Conservatives Falsely Blame Renewables for Texas Storm Outages*, Guardian, Feb. 17, 2021, https://www.theguardian.com/us-news/2021/feb/17/conservatives-falsely-blame-renewables-for-texas-storm-outages. *See also* Busby et al., *supra* note 1; Baker & Coleman, *supra* note 13.

ages, then, by extension, so were these regulators. The prior dispositions of these policy actors and media figures almost certainly influenced their decision to blame renewables for the energy outages.

Similarly, many Texas politicians have long viewed Texas' isolation from the interstate electricity grid as a point of pride and federal regulation as overly intrusive.[121] These beliefs translated into politicians rejecting arguments that isolation could increase the state's vulnerability.[122] They had no reason to seek further information or a deeper understanding of the risks that independence may have presented by exacerbating the outages. Politicians' prior knowledge and beliefs predisposed them to a narrative that blamed the outages on unreliable renewables and not on Texas' isolated grid.

Many Texas policy actors also seemed to make sense of Uri by treating it as a freak accident rather than a portend of the future in a climate-altered world. Had these individuals accepted the reality of climate change, which is projected to cause many more extreme cold weather events, they may have followed the decade-old recommendations to winterize Texas energy infrastructure. Instead, even after Winter Storm Uri, Texas energy regulators downplayed the risks of future cold weather extremes. For example, they commissioned a grid reliability study that assumed all future winter storms will be less severe than Uri.[123] Whether this reticence to engage with worst-case scenario planning was a result of climate denialism or some other embedded instinct is unclear. Nonetheless, by making sense of Winter Storm Uri by treating it as an outlier, Texas policymakers were able to justify their disregard of expert advice.

The second phase of policy framing, naming, involves more than assigning labels; through naming, "policy actors draw disparate elements together in a pattern, selecting some things as relevant or important and discarding, backgrounding or ignoring others."[124] Texas politicians did not just name renewables as the primary culprits responsible for Uri; they also excused others. Perhaps most notable were the Railroad Commission's continued assertions that unwinterized natural gas production facilities bore no respon-

---

121. Victoria Bekiempis, *Rick Perry Says Texans Will Endure Blackouts "To Keep the Government Out of Their Business,"* Guardian, Feb. 18, 2021, https://www.theguardian.com/us-news/2021/feb/18/rick-perry-texans-endure-blackouts-keep-government-out.

122. *Id.*

123. *See* Robert Walton, *E3 Defends Texas Market Analysis as Early Comments on Reliability Proposals Turn Negative*, Utility Dive (Dec. 14, 2022), https://www.utilitydive.com/news/e3-texas-reliability-market-proposals-puc-comments-ercot/638713/. The consultancy that prepared the grid reliability study refuted some of the criticisms of the study's design and assumptions. In particular, they insisted that extreme weather estimates were adequately incorporated into the analysis, even though Winter Storm Uri's specific conditions were not. *Id.*

124. *See* van Hulst & Yanow, *supra* note 100, at 99.

sibility for the energy outages.[125] It is hardly surprising, then, that the Railroad Commission's proposed rules would have allowed most gas wells to remain unwinterized in the future.

Finally, in the last phase of policy framing, policy actors use storytelling to create a compelling and coherent narrative. Even if it is not true or logical, the storytelling process helps both the audience and the policymaker to develop an understanding of the underlying causes of and thus optimal solutions to the identified problem. The overarching story that Texas politicians told was narratively coherent: due to the unchecked growth of unreliable renewable resources and the failure of a few out-of-state regulators, Texas lacked adequate electricity to meet the load. The story was compelling in part because it fit into long-held views about the unreliability of renewable energy. It did not matter that the story was largely untrue. Indeed, the political story of Winter Storm Uri—i.e., what and whom was to blame—seemed more important to some politicians than the human toll.[126] And once the story of Uri focused on political point-scoring and blaming, politicians sought to use Uri as an opportunity to open a new front in the emerging culture wars against renewables, rather than to identify strategies to make citizens safe.[127] In short order, for many political leaders in Texas, the story of Winter Storm Uri became a story of political power and partisan views, rather than a story of energy planning, grid governance, and protecting human lives from future extreme weather events.

Rhetoric versus Reality

And yet, political leaders' framing appeared to have only limited impacts on the actual governance and operation of the state's energy system and its energy mix. In the three years following the Winter Storm Uri, wind, solar, and battery storage in the state increased,[128] thanks largely to a favorable regulatory and market structure. Anti-renewable, pro-natural gas bills failed to pass during the 2023 legislative session,[129] and state lawmakers were only able to secure funding to subsidize natural gas through a ballot initiative that made no mention of gas.[130] Even the Railroad Commission had to revise

125. Gold, supra note 8.

126. *See* Bekiempis, *supra* note 121, discussing Rick Perry's comment that Texans would prefer to remain without power than to have an interstate grid connection. Sen. Ted Cruz (R-TX) was also criticized for using the outages as an opportunity to vacation in Mexico, rather than as a chance to assist Texans without power.

127. *Id.*

128. *See* von Oldershausen, *supra* note 94.

129. *See* Wallace-Wells, *supra* note 9.

130. *See* Buchele, *supra* note 9.

its first set of proposed rules to provide at least some oversight over the gas system's winterization.[131] Although the stories politicians had told about Uri did influence some policy changes, they could not fundamentally disrupt the state's energy system.

There are likely several reasons why. First, the regulatory system in Texas favors the development of economically viable energy resources, and renewable resources fit that description.[132] Not only is it relatively easy to site renewable energy in the state, but the state's growing population has created a strong appetite for increased energy supplies from all resources, including renewables.[133] Upending that entrenched system would have required substantial legislative and regulatory reforms. Second, and perhaps more importantly, politicians' framing did not go unchallenged. The media provided thorough coverage of Winter Storm Uri during and immediately after the energy outages, and the media has maintained a focus on the reliability of the Texas energy system since. Scholars, market participants, and regulators have also kept their attention trained on the issue, helping to to fact-check the political rhetoric. In addition, the fact that Winter Storm Uri affected so many people in such devastating ways likely made issues related to the energy system much more salient than they would have been in the past. Since Uri, Texans have received multiple warnings about potential energy outages during extreme weather events. The sustained public interest in the issue has exposed Texans to more information and fact-checking, perhaps diminishing the power of political rhetoric.

Of course, the post-Uri story in Texas is not over, and it is too soon to know whether or not the policy frames used by Texas politicians will have a greater effect in the future on the Texas energy mix and reliability. Nonetheless, three years after Uri, the rhetoric had failed to create a new reality in Texas.

Conclusion

Texas' experiences with Winter Storm Uri reveal the ways in which policy actors might seek to use framing to affect our understanding of, and thus response to, major climate-related events. Through factually baseless or exaggerated claims, Texas policy actors tried to deter energy system reforms that would improve reliability and advance clean electrification. A fair amount of

---

131. *See* Weaver, *supra* note 86.
132. *See* Dionne Searcey, *How Texas Kept the Lights On in the Recent Deep Freeze*, NY Times (Jan. 17, 2024), https://www.nytimes.com/2024/01/17/climate/texas-grid-renewables-gas-freeze.html?searchResultPosition=1.
133. *Id.*

this framing appeared to be influenced by climate denialism, there is a risk that political actors in other states could pursue similar framing approaches when and if they face their own energy crises.

But just as frames can be created, they can be revised.[134] In Texas, the false narratives were subject to regular evidence-backed challenges, which seemed to limit the political force of the anti-renewable rhetoric. The experience in Texas may therefore provide lessons for those seeking to promote grid reliability through clean electrification. Clean energy advocates should develop their own accurate narratives that help the public make sense of future energy outages and the roles that fossil fuels play in worsening climate change and, often, increasing grid vulnerability.

As climate change worsens, severe weather events and energy outages are likely inevitable. Doubling down on fossil fuels in the name of reliability is not. Somewhat unexpectedly, the experiences in Texas may provide some lessons for preventing misleading and partisan rhetoric from undermining the transition to a clean and reliable grid.

134. *See* Gosman, *supra* note 20, at 12.

The Tyranny of Baselines

Jessica Owley, Karen Bradshaw,
Keith H. Hirokawa, & Robin Kundis Craig

Many environmental law paradigms focus on fixed points. Sometimes the fixed points are in the past, and environmental laws call upon us to look at a baseline or previous state of nature and compare our actions against it. Other approaches call for us to consider an ideal state and develop strategies regarding how to reach it. In a 4 degree Celsius (4°C+) world, both strategies fail. Adhering to baselines is meaningless and striving for goals that are unachievable may lead to paralysis. Our chapter explores an alternative mode for moving forward with an approach that minimizes suffering.

Facing the Worst Climate Crisis: The Role of Law

In summer 2021, members of the Environmental Law Collaborative (ELC) gathered to explore how we could carve a path forward for environmental law in the context of intense climatic change. We found ourselves repeatedly frustrated by both past and potential uses of laws in the climate change context. Although law should serve as a reliable tool to govern how we manage crises, we have struggled with both the role that law has played in facilitating the climate crisis and the potential of law to provide a thoughtful and protective response to climate change. For example, initially environmental scholars, policymakers, and activists focused on slowing climate change through mitigation. We sought ways to reduce global warming through decarbonization strategies, geoengineering, and other ideas. Climate change mitigation remains critical and should not be set aside, but exclusive scholarly focus there has delayed discussion of climate change adaptation. Many mitigation efforts focused on saving the world we know, while adaptation has always accepted that the world we know is lost and that climate change is transforming the world into an unfamiliar and potentially hostile place. When people could still believe that mitigation efforts could completely avoid any need to adapt, discussing climate change adaptation was taboo because doing so acknowledged defeat. Suggesting that we would adapt to climate change instead of mitigating climate change rankled.

Perspectives have evolved. Mitigation now focuses on avoiding the worst aspects of climate change and on stabilizing the climate, eventually reducing greenhouse gas concentrations in the atmosphere; however, some amount of adaptation is now unavoidable. Nevertheless, even once ecological conditions made it clear that adaptation could be ignored no longer, discussions of adaptation were constrained by mitigation goals. As Robin Kundis Craig and J.B. Ruhl explain, our mitigation-centered adaptation approach constrained adaptation discussions to +2°C scenarios, even as we grew to understand that limiting warming to 2°C was unlikely.[1]

While it is important to avert the climate crisis, we can't ignore the need for a legal regime that forces us to prepare for survival. The devastating effects of climate change are already happening—people are un-homed by wildfires, displaced by flooding, and dying from unprecedented heat. Climate change is here. It is brutal. And it is in large part the consequence of law. Our legal framework propels us toward high-level warming in large part because of our state-endorsed lack of action and because of laws that encourage emission-heavy consumption. We suffer climatic changes while the law fails to bear more than a hint of that crisis. Thus, an essential legal obstacle is the failure to face what's coming. The time has come to stop pumping the brakes and instead lean into the spin to minimize the damage.

This chapter delves into a feature that permeates our environmental laws and conservation strategies: the environmental baseline. These baselines lie beneath our laws and policies and often interfere with, or even prevent, efforts to prepare for climate change. Baselines are counterproductive in the face of optimistically assumed warming of 1.5-2°C and deeply dangerous in the context of high-level warming. Variously referred to as paradigms, ideals, and constructs, we employ environmental baselines in everyday life as a means of interacting with nature: baselines might help us to identify healthy relationships, favorite meals, or even unsafe driving conditions.[2] In

1. J. B. Ruhl & Robin K. Craig, *4°C*, 106 Minn. L. Rev. 191 (2021).
2. Arguably, the pervasiveness of nature ideals is in large part due to the manner in which we have equated nature with wild or wilderness and imbued the wilderness construct with values typically reserved for our most meaningful elements of identity; as Bill Cronon writes, "To gain such remarkable influence, the concept of wilderness had to become loaded with some of the deepest core values of the culture that created and idealized it: it had to become sacred." William Cronon, *The Trouble With Wilderness; or, Getting Back to the Wrong Nature, in* William Cronon, Uncommon Ground 69, 73 (1995). Yet, sociologists Peter Berger and Thomas Luckmann have argued that reliance on "social constructions" is unavoidable, at least because we can never escape nature:

> Man is biologically predestined to construct and inhabit a world with others. This world becomes for him the dominant and definitive reality. Its limits are set by nature, but once

environmental law, fixed points of reference in a living, ever-changing earth can be helpful in understanding human interactions with our natural environments. Sometimes, baselines serve as important descriptive markers for human health impacts and water quality standards or as the means to measure rates of change in the environment. Environmental baselines are, however, often used in a more unwitting, yet very dangerous way: we standardize picturesque landscapes, species populations, ecosystem processes, and other environmental circumstances to serve the purposes and goals of environmental law, thereby ignoring present circumstances and the unattainability of ideals.

Law, in this sense, is a maladaptation. This chapter examines this circumstance of law, including the tendency in law to remain loyal to particular environmental baselines despite how counterproductive or damaging such loyalty might be. The fundamental question is: *Do baselines or ideal states of nature—including our present or recently past realities—make sense when we are making decisions for a world we can't yet envision?* This chapter explores the benefits and problems with baselines, showing why conscious engagement with baselines is crucial to environmental policymaking in a climate change era. Baselines are counterproductive in the face of optimistically assumed warming of 1.5-2°C and deeply dangerous in the context of high-level warming

Tyranny of the Baselines

Where do current legal structures fail us? This chapter is not an attempt to outline all of the collective climate failures and challenges in law. Instead, it wrestles with one institutional failure that has proved particularly pernicious on multiple scales: the embedded use of environmental baselines, or ecological ideals, as a basis for valuing stasis and change in the environment. This section discusses the normative use of baselines in environmental law, illustrates the problems created by the baseline approach, and suggests some ways to counteract those problems.

---

constructed, this world acts back upon nature. In the dialectic between nature and the socially constructed world, the human organism itself is transformed. In this same dialectic, man produces reality and thereby produces himself.

Peter L. Berger & Thomas Luckmann, The Social Construction of Reality 168 (1966).

Baseline Problem Number One: Status Quo Bias

A first baseline concern is how often we set the status quo as our baseline without confronting the appropriateness or the justice of the status quo. Arguably, the pressure and persuasion of the status quo underlies most deliberative practices. Thomas Kuhn, in his work on paradigm shifts and the self-perpetuating character of "normal science" in scientific discourse, argued that "a paradigm governs, in the first instance, not a subject matter but rather a group of practitioners."[3] Acceptance of a paradigm constitutes induction into a profession, a process in which even new practitioners become defenders of the status quo. Hence, Timothy Luke describes the process of eco-managerialism, in which students seek out natural resource management training with an intention to engage in conservation, often prompted by a deep relationship with and respect for ecosystems, but quickly fall into line with an educational program designed to estimate the value of forests in terms of board-feet of lumber, water diversions in cubic feet per second, and wetland function in terms of mitigation ratios.[4]

In like manner, deliberative practices such as law generally condition participants to operate within the confines of a dominant paradigm. Without regard for the substance of the law and its relation to human and ecological needs, law uses rigid doctrines that break instead of bend. Moreover, law in the United States is premised on the idea that once an issue has been decided, it need not be revisited. This principle, known as stare decisis,[5] facilitates a reliance on the stability of law, particularly the notion that law will be followed (and enforced) to protect the comforts that come with such expectations. In addition, legal educators train new lawyers to identify dominant law, rather than the way that law should (or could) be.[6]

Nevertheless, as in the example of climate change, new information that challenges the dominant legal paradigm has assaulted the propriety of legal standards that brought us to the present moment. Climatic shifts—bringing

3. Thomas Kuhn, The Structure of Scientific Revolutions 180 (1962).
4. Timothy W. Luke, Eco-Managerialism: Environmental Studies as a Power/Knowledge Formation, Lecture at York University (Oct. 3, 2002) (transcript available at http://aurora.icaap.org/index.php/aurora/article/view/79/91). In the context of climate change, the work of Law Students for Climate Accountability makes transparent how prestigious law schools pipeline students to positions at private firms—high paying and traditionally high status—that are deeply engaged in promoting the positions and interests of the status quo fossil fuel industry. Law Students for Climate Accountability, https://www.ls4ca.org/.
5. *See* John Paul Stevens, *The Life Span of a Judge-Made Rule*, 58 N.Y.U. L. Rev. 1, 1 n.2 (1983) (explaining that the term comes from the phrase stare decisis et non quieta movere, translated as, "let the decision stand and do not disturb things which have been settled").
6. *See* Duncan Kennedy, Legal Education and the Reproduction of Hierarchy: A Polemic Against the System (2004).

drought, storms, sea-level rise, and ecosystem and human migration—appear to undermine the status quo as a result of the attribution of climate change to land use and pollution past practices. It is in the treatment of such emerging and realized needs that preservation of the status quo has a particularly pernicious impact on justice. As Allan Hutchinson explains, an approach to adjudication that does not challenge established baselines "deal[s] with the deprived and disadvantaged in society by simply pretending they do not exist."[7] In contrast, thinking about the impacts of paradigm discourse in law can have a liberating effect, as Douglas Litowitz comments: "Changes in the law can be instigated by those willing to think of the other of the legal system, those who practice what Thomas Kuhn has called 'revolutionary science' by swimming against the tide of 'normal science.'"[8]

Private land conservation and the rise of conservation easements illustrate how a status quo bias can limit creative solutions to environmental problems. For decades, the essential idea of a conservation easement was to preserve the status quo.[9] Used chiefly as a tool to stop development, the essence of a conservation easement is keeping land in its current undeveloped state. Over time, conservationists have learned to use the tool more creatively, but it has been slow-going and the changes have not been radical. For example, working landscapes are increasingly protected with conservation easements, forcing such agreements to acknowledge that there could be active uses of the land and changes to accommodate shifting agricultural practices or ecosystem needs.[10] Such acknowledgments do not challenge the fundamental idea of a conservation easement as just keeping the current situation in place. Champions of the tool argue that treading water is sometimes the best we can do in the environmental realm.

This same dilemma applies to habitat conservation. In *Weyerhaeuser v. U.S. Fish & Wildlife Service*, the U.S. Supreme Court constrained the ability of conservation agencies to establish critical habitat in areas not currently occupied by the species.[11] The U.S. Fish and Wildlife Service (FWS) noted that the "near eradication" of the endangered dusky gopher frog habitat made it hard to find adequate critical habitat. For this reason, the FWS also

7. Allan Hutchinson, *The Last Emperor?*, *in* READING DWORKIN CRITICALLY 21 (Alan Hunt ed., 1992).
8. DOUGLAS E. LITOWITZ, POSTMODERN PHILOSOPHY AND LAW 178 (1997).
9. *See* Jessica Owley, *Neoliberal Land Conservation and Social Justice*, 3 IUCN ACAD. ENVTL. L. E-J 6 (2012); Jessica Owley, *Changing Property in a Changing World: A Call for the End of Perpetual Conservation Easements*, 30 STAN. ENVTL. L.J. 121 (2011)
10. *See, e.g.*, Jess R. Phelps & David P. Hoffer, *California Carbon Offsets and Working Forest Conservation Easements*, 38 UCLA J. ENVTL. L. & POL'Y 61 (2020); Jessica Owley et al., *Climate Change Challenges for Land Conservation: Rethinking Conservation Easements, Strategies, and Tools*, 95 DENV. L. REV. 727, 747 (2018).
11. Weyerhaeuser Co. v. U.S. Fish & Wildlife Serv., 139 S. Ct. 361 (2018).

included lands that could be made habitable in the future. In rejecting the FWS' anticipatory habitat protection approach, the Court called into question the ability of the FWS to plan for habitat protection in a changing world.[12] It tied the hands of an agency who might wish to incorporate future environmental conditions in its conservation regime.

Are we saving space for nature?[13] Baseline biases can constrain our approach to habitat conservation. We seek to stem habitat destruction instead of working to expand habitat. But protecting current habitat is not enough in the face of climate change. Wildlife habitat is increasingly impacted by disasters like fires, floods, and droughts. Human migration and pressure on land for infrastructure could lead to even greater threats to habitat based on climate change pressures.[14] Our current approach to mitigation for habitat loss often exacerbates this problem.

Notice the role of compensatory mitigation here. For example, the "no-net-loss-of-wetlands" policy suggests that we currently have the desired amount of wetlands. In general, 1:1 ratios for habitat conversion are only set up with the idea of preserving the status quo, not improving the status quo. And the truth is that a 1:1 ratio doesn't preserve the status quo.[15] Created habitat is not guaranteed to be as high quality as lost habitat.[16] We are only guessing (increasingly educated guesses) at how habitat will react to replacement strategies. As Karrigan Bork explains, we have "left ourselves a narrow margin of safety in all kinds of systems, from infrastructure to agriculture to environmental protection."[17] Our strategy can't be stuck on preserving what we currently have. Instead, we need to shift from preservation to building and maintaining rich natural environments. First, preserving what we have

---

12. *See* J.B. Ruhl, *What Is Habitat?*, 34 Nat. Resources & Env't 52 (2019); Isabella Kendrick, Note, *Critical Habitat Designations Under the Endangered Species Act in an Era of Climate Crisis*, 121 Colum. L. Rev. 81 (2021).
13. Karrigan Bork, *Leaving Room for Nature, in* Karrigan Bork et al. (Environmental Law Collaborative), *Adapting to a 4°C World*, 52 Envtl. L. Rep. 10211, 10218 (Mar. 2022) [hereinafter Bork, *Leaving Room for Nature*] .
14. Jessica Owley, *Climate-Induced Human Displacement and Conservation Lands*, 58 Hous. L. Rev. 665 (2021).
15. R. Eugene Turner et al., *Count It by Acre or Function—Mitigation Adds Up to Net Loss of Wetlands*, 23 Nat'l Wetlands Newsl. 5 (2001); *see also* Sophus Olav Sven Emil zu Ermgassen et al., Perspective, *The Role of "No Net Loss" Policies in Conserving Biodiversity Threantened by the Global Infrastructure Boom*, 1 One Earth 305, 311 (2019) (discussing no-net-loss policies in the context of biodiversity offsets and finding evidence that

    offsetting policies have been designed to by policymakers and influenced by the private sector to "sell" the narrative that infrastructural expansion and environmental protection can go hand in hand without a deep reflection on the considerable barriers to achieving true [no net loss] in practice or place-based nature of biodiversity and cultural value.

16. Jessica Owley, *Preservation Is a Flawed Mitigation Strategy*, 42 Ecology L. Currents 1 (2015)
17. Bork, *Leaving Room for Nature*, *supra* note 13.

may be impossible, and it will be expensive. Second, preserving what we have may be undesirable. Our status quo has given privilege to certain communities and certain landscapes and has not been equitable or strategic.

Baseline Problem Number Two: They Perpetuate Inequalities

We fight to maintain the status quo, but the status quo is not where we should desire to be. Baselines that maintain the status quo are problematic as a matter of process, but they are especially sinister as a substantive concern. Adherence to a baseline grounds us in past models and seldom pushes us to go either behind or beyond the baseline. Sometimes, baselines are established that ignore inequalities. In both contexts, we need to reflect on the propriety of maintaining a status quo that was designed by the privileged to prop up the privileged. At present, landownership statistics are best described as the result of generations of segregation and oppression. As Sarah Krakoff explains, law in the United States has "helped transform an all-indigenous landscape into a 'blank space' on the map."[18] In the meantime, infrastructure and other public investments (such as hazardous waste facility siting) provide immense benefits to privileged communities, but are not equitably distributed to all communities. Our strategy should not focus on preserving current circumstances as the basis for a baseline, particularly when what we currently have isn't desirable. Indeed, even the law's current obsession with sustainability should make us pause and consider what it is that we are seeking to sustain.

In other instances, avoiding perpetuating inequality requires calling out current baselines as wrong. In a deeply complementary example of the dangers of problematic baselines, local histories championed in local comprehensive plans seldom celebrate the lives and accomplishments of people of color and disadvantaged communities: reading local comprehensive plans that illustrate the wonderful lives of those with privilege, but without also identifying non-privileged needs and histories, gives the impression that people of color do not even live there.[19] In such a scenario, the question becomes how to replace expectations set on the past with competing visions for the future.

In general, any baseline that ignores a history of state-sponsored inequities is likely to reproduce them. Avoiding consideration of redlining practices of the past might relieve us of the duty to reverse the discrimination that

18. Sarah Krakoff, *Not Yet America's Best Idea: Law, Inequality, and Grand Canyon National Park*, 91 U. Colo. L. Rev. 559, 569 (2020).

19. *See* Keith H. Hirokawa, *Race, Space, and Place: Interrogating Whiteness Through a Critical Approach to Place*, 29 Wm. & Mary J. on Race, Gender, & Soc. Just. 279, 305 (2023).

resulted in racialized and disadvantaged communities. Refusing to recognize the role of intergenerational wealth on mobility will leave us unprepared for both internal and external climate migration. Omitting the roles of people of color in the history of communities will punctuate a history of telling certain people that they do not belong. Baselines designed from a position of privilege tend to exclude the disadvantaged; such baselines do not serve disadvantaged communities.

Baseline Problem Number Three: We Spend Too Much Time Fighting Over Them

In many instances, U.S. environmental laws begin by establishing baseline conditions in the environment in which we live, work, and play. Under some laws, existing baseline conditions are protected by "anti-backsliding" policies[20] or set the basis for determining whether proposed changes conflict with or better serve background conditions.[21] In other instances, baselines are used to establish critical habitat conditions for a given species for the purpose of restoration and species survival. In many (if not most) of these instances, the baseline is idealized and propped up as a regulatory goal.[22] As a consequence, debates over metrics are complicated and mired in fears of the high costs of a baseline that is set too far into the past or future.

Occasionally, we end up stuck in the weeds of "how to measure" and use complication and complexity as excuses for not moving forward. One might recall decades of aggressive dialogue on the predictive capacity of our climate change models, the difficulties in measuring sea-level rise, or storm surge frequency in our futures.[23] Sometimes, baselines or metrics language have been used to manipulate projects so that they appear more or less impactful.[24]

20. As one example, the federal Clean Water Act (CWA) prohibits both "backsliding" in permit renewals—that is, the use of less-stringent effluent limitations, 33 U.S.C. §1342(o), 40 C.F.R. §122.44(l)—and the loss of any use of a waterway that existed in 1975. 40 C.F.R. §§131.12(a)(1) (prohibiting degradation that destroys an existing use), 131.3(e) (defining "existing uses" to be "those uses actually attained in the water body on or after November 28, 1975, whether or not they are included in the water quality standards").
21. Keith H. Hirokawa, *Making Sense of a "Misunderstanding of the Planning Process": Examining the Relationship Between Zoning and Rezoning Under the Change-or-Mistake Rule*, 44 Urb. Law. 295, 304-05 (2012); Karen Bradshaw, *Settling for Natural Resource Damages*, 40 Harv. Envtl L. Rev 211, 244 (2016)
22. Melinda Taylor & Holly Doremus, *Habitat Conservation Plans and Climate Change: Recommendations for Policy*, 45 Envtl. L. Rep. 10863 (Sept. 2015).
23. Myles Allen et al., *Scientific Challenges in the Attribution of Harm to Human Influence on Climate*, 155 U. Pa. L. Rev. 1353 (2007).
24. Todd S. Aagaard, *Environmental Harms, Use Conflicts, and Neutral Baselines in Environmental Law*, 60 Duke L.J. 1505, 1523 (2011) (explaining that baselines are susceptible to manipulation).

At a recent environmental law conference, the manager of a biodiversity conservation project complained about the time and money taken up by baseline assessment: *"We got 5 years of funding for a project to protect biodiversity in northern Cambodia. Three years in and we have spent almost all of our time and money on just determining the baseline conditions."* A lack of scientific information could mean that baseline studies are needed to understand conditions, but where the cost of the baseline studies leave no room for environmental protection efforts, the model is flawed.

To illustrate the complexity of baselines in the regulatory arena, consider an example from federal agencies and a local municipality working jointly to expand an airport. When trying to assess whether to add another runway to an airport, all agree that we need to assess the environmental impact of that new runway (as required by the National Environmental Policy Act (NEPA) and state law). But from where (or when) should we measure the probable changes that will occur from the expansion? Do we focus on the environmental impacts from the added air travel that will come with a new runway? Should we consider the baseline to be the current number of flights that navigate the airport in an exceptional year (full capacity), the average number of flights to and from the airport, or even global or national flight frequencies? Is the baseline to the number of flights anticipated if a new runway isn't built? As this example illustrates, there are often many metrics—or baselines—that one can choose to define the scope of environmental impact from a project.

To make matters worse, we aren't even that good at baselines. Shifting baseline syndrome, discussed further below, illustrates one error we make with baselines when we misunderstand and underestimate previous environmental conditions. As Craig has explained, the law also biases what people view as natural versus unnatural conditions.[25] When a human-engineered environmental crisis happens, it creates undesirable changes, which forces us to figure out how to recover. Yet, when some environmental crises get labeled "natural," we consider them to be an acceptable part of the baseline conditions. The debate over whether climate change is natural or anthropogenic fits well into this conundrum. If we understand that climate change is having devastating effects on our socioecological systems, does it matter whether we put the label "natural" on it?

We do not have an amazing track record of understanding how our socioecological systems operate (consider poor understanding of oceans, failures

25. Robin Kundis Craig, *Perceiving Change and Knowing Nature: Shifting Baselines and Nature's Resiliency*, *in* Environmental Law and Contrasting Ideas of Nature: A Constructivist Approach 87 (Keith Hirokawa ed., 2014).

at wetland restoration, etc.). Our environmental laws seem to be premised on an idea that we will be able to understand the world and obtain the information we need to make thoughtful decisions (see NEPA), but there is little support for those contentions on a broad scale. When we struggle to obtain the right information, baselines are unreliable.[26]

Baseline Problem Number Four: Baselines Are Sticky

In part, fights over baselines are persistent and intractable because they are embedded into so many regulatory regimes in ways that determine the costs of regulatory compliance. That is, the baseline adopted can determine the outcome of the project, meaning the assessment of whether the environmental impact is an acceptable trade off for the social benefit of a project or the degree of mitigation that will reduce project impacts relative to the ideal ecological conditions.

Problems also emerge because decisionmakers often feel stuck with baselines established early in a project. A baseline freezes a standard at a fixed point of time, then stays constant over subsequent periods. Changed information or conditions can make the baselines adopted at early stages less relevant, or even inappropriate, as the project progresses. Yet, the mental tethering to written baselines can hinder creative, adaptive approaches that might better meet the needs of the evolved project over time.[27]

For example, with respect to climate policy, when did +2°C become an acceptable goal for climate change mitigation? Many people believe it to be the wrong goal, but once established in the Paris Agreement (which says we agree on +2°C even though we think it should be +1.5°C), policymakers ran with it. Regardless of the initial debate, it is now the measurement we use. It is the goal of our policies even when we know that it is the wrong goal. By agreeing to use a particular baseline for the Paris Agreement—such as +2°C—were negotiators being pragmatic?[28] How could one excuse the loss of human life and inequitably distributed harms from higher temperatures? Moreover, as Ruhl and Craig point out, this baseline for climate change *mitigation* very effectively bled into climate change *adaptation* as well, inducing

26. *See id.* at 89; Bradley C. Karkkainen, *Bottlenecks and Baselines: Tackling Information Deficits in Environmental Regulation*, 86 TEX. L. REV. 1409 (2008).

27. Richard Delgado, *Our Better Natures: A Revisionist View of Joseph Sax's Public Trust Theory of Environmental Protection and Some Dark Thoughts on the Possibility of Law Reform*, 44 VAND. L. REV. 1209, 1218-23 (1991)

28. *See* Arden Rowell & Josephine Van Zeben, *A New Status Quo? The Psychological Impact of the Paris Agreement on Climate Change*, 7 EUR. J. RISK REG. 49 (2017), doi:10.1017/S1867299X00005377 (explaining how the choice of 2 degrees set a "psychologically powerful baseline against which future policy failures can be measured").

governments at all levels to plan for—and invest in—adaptation as though a 2°C increase in global average temperature was some kind of hard limit on what their adaptation necessities will be.

Shifting Baselines—Changing the Goal Posts

A common technique used when facing a daunting goal or task is to set sights lower. Realizing I am not going to be able to run a full marathon by next year, perhaps I should shift my goal to a half marathon. If I do it right, I will even tell everyone that a half marathon was always my goal. I will get praised for what I accomplished, and no one will be disappointed that I didn't run the full marathon. Given some time, I may even convince myself that my goal was always just the half marathon. In our personal and professional lives, this realignment of goals may be a healthy and practical choice by making our goals more realistic and more achievable. But when we convince ourselves to stick to what we currently view as achievable policy goals and fail to push, we do harm.

Shifting baselines allow us to ignore reality. Paradoxically, they also let us respond to reality, by adjusting to what is achievable instead of chasing impossible goals. There is a constant tension between maintaining an ideal that forces us to heights that may otherwise not be possible: ("I will run the whole marathon") and pragmatically putting resources toward attainable outcomes: ("I will run a half marathon"). It is difficult, if not impossible, to retrospectively assess whether changing the baseline was the right decision. Had I tried to run the whole marathon, might I have suffered an injury from muscle over-use that would have prevented me from running at all? If I complete the half marathon, am I failing to fulfill my potential? And consider the decision making behind these baseline processes. In setting the +2°C goal for the Paris Agreement, developed countries focused on what level of sacrifice was tolerable for them. Developing countries fought back on the framing, arguing instead the discussion should have focused on what they need for survival. This highlights the complexity of baselines in the climate context: Do I decide to set my exercise goals or diet based on what is comfortable for me or do I base it on what my doctor tells me I need to do to stay healthy?

With baselines we can make the law both too easy and too hard to change. The choices complicate decision making and hamper reaching the optimal solutions. This same pattern is a greater concern when it is a government entity making environmental policy. Consider some examples.

Contaminated Sites

Realizing the expense of cleaning up Rocky Flats (a contaminated area near the Denver airport), the federal government changed its goal of cleaning up the land to the level where it would be safe for residences.[29] Instead, they turned the area into a national wildlife refuge. This allowed the government to save cleanup costs because the standards for recreational use of the land are less stringent than those for residential use.

Carbon Reduction

When some countries realized that they would not meet their goals under the Kyoto Protocol, they changed their goals or decided to just drop out. Much like the would-be marathon runner who realizes they will not complete the race and thus, decides not to run it, Canada withdrew from the collective attempt to reduce emissions.[30] Canada decided it was better not to be a part of the treaty than to be violating it. There were no penalties because it was a voluntary agreement.

Russia and former Eastern bloc countries were able to meet their goals because of economic struggles during the recording/accounting periods.[31] They met their first-round commitments,[32] but they didn't undertake the systemic changes needed to address carbon emissions in the long term. When their economies improve, they emit high levels of pollution, skipping over the opportunity for a more environmentally promising pathway forward because the metrics/baselines didn't require it.

29. For a detailed personal history of the Rocky Flats site, see KRISTEN IVERSON, FULL BODY BURDEN: GROWING UP IN THE NUCLEAR SHADOW OF ROCKY FLATS (2012).
30. Ernest C. Nwanguma, An Analysis of the Rationale for Canada's Withdrawal From the Kyoto Protocol and the Possible Impacts on the Canadian Oil and Gas Industry (2016) (dissertation, Memorial University of Newfoundland), https://research.library.mun.ca/12407/1/thesis.pdf (asserting that Canada withdrew because it was unable to meet its commitments while exploiting its oil sands); Taylor Hathaway-Zepeda, *Qualifying Kyoto*, 26 HARV. INT'L REV. 30 (2004) (explaining that Canada was not likely going to be able to meet its commitments).
31. Kathryn Harrison & Lisa McIntosh Sundstrom, *The Comparative Politics of Climate Change*, 7 GLOBAL ENVTL. POL. 1 (2007).
32. Igor Shishlov et al., *Compliance of the Parties to the Kyoto Protocol in the First Commitment Period*, 16 CLIMATE POL'Y 768 (2016), doi: 10.1080/14693062.2016.1164658.

Fisheries

Fisheries provide a classic example of "shifting baseline syndrome," a phrase coined by Daniel Pauly in the 1990s.[33] Pauly described a phenomenon where each generation of fisheries scientists forgets what the oceans looked like in prior generations. The scientists accept their lot as given because they did not realize their potential. They collectively forget the amount of, how many types, and how big those fish used to be, and instead use the current status of fisheries in management decisions, such as in setting the total amount of fish that can be caught. The circumstance of truly robust fisheries is lost to generational amnesia, requiring historical reconstruction.

After being articulated by Pauly, many confirmed this trend in studies of various fisheries around the world. Pauly argued that the solution to the shifting baseline syndrome was more historical analysis and taking past conditions into account in planning. In some places, these historical analyses have indeed helped to change the goals of fisheries management—but in others they did not.[34] Did our laws create an obstacle to his recommended approach?

Over time as wildlife populations dwindle, we set our baselines at lower and lower population levels. The baselines that inform our policies reflect our limited memory of historic baselines, making current, low population levels seem "normal" and thus an acceptable basis for baselines. With species, we set a goal of not losing any more and only belatedly embrace the goal of ecosystem recovery.

Consider the McCloud River. After the 1940s, dams blocked the salmon returning to the river. There have not been salmon in the McCloud River for nearly 100 years.[35] Karen Bradshaw, a co-author of this chapter, is a fourth-generation resident of the small town near the river. Yet, despite this strong connection to the waterway and a keen interest in the ecology of the river, Bradshaw had no understanding that there were salmon in the river historically. In contrast, the Winnemem Wintu Indian Tribe, an indigenous government, has retained a baseline understanding of the river that should include salmon. In 2022, the Winnemem Wintu worked with a group of

33. Daniel Pauly, *Anecdotes and the Shifting Baseline Syndrome in Fisheries*, 10 Trends Ecology & Evolution 430 (1995).

34. In some areas, like the coral scientists in the Florida Keys, the phenomenon is not observed. Education and communication can help overcome this bias. M. Muldrow et al., *Shifting Baseline Syndrome Among Coral Reef Scientists*, 7 Human. & Soc. Sci. Comm. 1-8 (July 20, 2020), https://doi.org/10.1057/s41599-020-0526-0.

35. California Dep't of Fish & Wildlife, *Partners Return Winter-Run Chinook Salmon Eggs to McCloud River: Drought Action Moves Endangered Salmon Back Into Their Historical Habitat for First Time Since Construction of Shasta Dam* (July 12, 2022), https://wildlife.ca.gov/News/partners-return-winter-run-chinook-salmon-eggs-to-mccloud-river#gsc.tab=0.

state and federal agencies to restore salmon to the river. For the first time in 80 years, salmon will swim in the McCloud River.

This small example highlights a vital point in environmental policymaking—the importance of diverse inputs in baselines and policymaking more broadly. Although Bradshaw is an environmental expert in the academic sense and deeply invested in the McCloud River, her expertise did not include the traditional importance of the salmon on the river. Traditional ecological knowledge fills a vital gap in a broader understanding. Her ideas of baseline conditions and desired states was improved by information about how other community members viewed the river. The Winnemem Wintu brings to the table information that an environmental law scholar did not have—an accurate understanding of the historic basis of what the river "should" look like. By incorporating diverse senses of expertise—that of agency biologists, for example, along with that of lawyers and adjacent landowners—stakeholders were able to co-create an understanding of the McCloud River's ecological health that incorporates salmon, something that many stakeholders did not even know was lost.

Vaccinations and the Regulatory Shifting Baseline Syndrome

In her recent article, Craig, one of the authors of this chapter, identified another type of shifting baseline syndrome.[36] In the fisheries example, we saw that scientists, fishers, and policymakers gradually forget what a healthy fishery looks like. The opposite, however, can occur in some regulatory contexts. Using the example of measles, Craig explains that vaccines were a victim of their own success. Because vaccines had so successfully controlled measles, some families began to question the value of vaccination, especially in contrast to risks—real or perceived—from the vaccine itself. Without a lived experience of how bad measles could be, the vaccination started to sound more dangerous than the disease it was designed to prevent.[37] Measles outbreaks in 2015 and 2019[38] and outbreaks of polio in September 2022 in New York[39] hopefully will remind legislatures that vaccination mandates continue

36. Robin Kundis Craig, *The Regulatory Shifting Baseline Syndrome: Vaccines, Generational Amnesia, and the Shifting Perception of Risk in Public Law Regimes*, 21 Yale J. Health Pol'y, L. & Ethics 1 (2022).
37. *Id.* at 22-47.
38. *Id.* at 33-34.
39. The cases involved unvaccinated individuals becoming infected by what is known as circulating vaccine-derived poliovirus, which "occurs when local immunity to poliovirus is low enough to allow prolonged transmission of the original weakened virus in the oral polio vaccine. As the virus circulates and more genetic changes occur, the virus can regain its ability to infect the central nervous system and cause paralysis." *United States Confirmed as Country With Circulating Vaccine-Derived Poliovirus*, Ctrs. for Disease Control & Prevention (Sept. 13, 2022), https://www.cdc.gov/media/releases/2022/

to serve very real public health goals, and that it is only rarely (basically, only for smallpox)[40] that vaccines can eliminate a dread disease entirely.

In Craig's example, regulatory success led to a societal failure. The perverse result is that when we make the world better, people think calls for continued action—even, in some cases, to keep an existing regulatory regime in place—are overreacting. If I lose a lot of weight, do I decide I don't really need to keep exercising? If I see success from my antibiotics, do I stop taking them because they make my stomach hurt?

Craig draws upon this definition of generational amnesia: Individuals setting their perceptions from their own experience and failing to pass their experience onto future generations.[41] Intergenerational memory or intergenerational forgetting relies not only on individuals, but also upon cultural practices (such as storytelling, oral histories, and ceremonies) that are at odds with capitalistic focus on short-term maximization. If one is pursuing the common neoliberal goal of deregulation, the question becomes how generational amnesia—the loss of collective memory—serves to advance that goal. Nevertheless, because law itself is a memory institution—a record of problems deemed bad enough to warrant legal intervention—Craig questions whether some are "rhetorically deploying the syndrome to ground their legal argument."[42] From the Supreme Court's decisions on voting rights to Congress' and other legislatures' decisions to deregulate businesses, we see evidence of arguments that "we solved the problem so we can move on to other things. Let's lift the restrictions." The regulatory shifting baseline syndrome also resonates with some privatization concerns, where the government stops paying attention to a problem because the private sector is working on it.[43]

Avoiding Baselines

The Resiliency Conundrum

In rejection of past paradigms, scholars and policymakers have variously called for embracing sustainability and resiliency as alternative approaches to our current static laws. The line between them is not always clear, and

---

s0913-polio.html. Notably, vaccination prevents this process, and hence the infections were evidence of the regulatory shifting baseline syndrome.

40. Craig, *supra* note 37, at 31.
41. *Id.* at 5-6.
42. *Id.* at 21.
43. *See* John D. Echeverria, *Regulating Versus Paying Land Owners to Protect the Environment*, 26 J. LAND RESOURCES & ENVTL. L. 1, 44 (2005) (explaining how the private tool of conservation easements can crowd out public conservation efforts).

"sustainability" and "resilience" mean different things to different people. The choice of approach becomes even muddier because both approaches purport to rely on some of the same tools, such as adaptive management. While this chapter cannot resolve the debate, it does note a primary distinction in assumptions between most approaches to sustainability—especially sustainable development—and the resilience approaches founded on the Stockholm Center's ecological resilience models: resilience approaches far more readily embrace the fact that change is the baseline reality of both ecosystems and social-ecological systems, whereas sustainability tends to orient toward achievement of a steady-state reality that can be perpetuated indefinitely.[44]

Resilient ecosystems have both the tolerance for change and the ability to recover from disturbance. Resilience thinking acknowledges that ecological (and social) systems are subject to both gradual changes and sudden disturbances.[45] Recognizing system complexity along with the interdependence of social and ecological systems, resilience thinking encourages consideration of different reactions and interactions that may take place.[46] This approach can work well in a 4°C world. Instead of trying to adhere a landscape to an established baseline, resilience thinking considers a shifting world within a set of parameters. It also recognizes differences among ecosystems. Resilience thinking instructs us to consider each landscape on its own terms, building an understanding of what changes are likely to occur and assessing the level of long-term impacts that could be triggered, acknowledging also that changes are occurring at multiple scales, e.g., soil microbes, vegetation, watershed, climate simultaneously.

Resilience thinking can also be limiting, however, especially when translated into management goals. For example, while ecological resilience models incorporate tipping points, ecological thresholds, and transformations into new states, "managing for resilience" often means attempting to enhance the resilience of the current ecosystem to maintain its current configuration in the face of increasing disturbance.[47] Thus, efforts are taken to maintain current ecosystem types and prevent "flipping the system." Additionally, while resilience thinking presumes change it also assumes researchers understand

44. Melinda Harm Benson & Robin Kundis Craig, The End of Sustainability: Resilience of the Future of Environmental Governance in the Anthropocene 33-78 (2017). *See also* Jessica Owley, *Property Constructs and Nature's Challenge to Perpetuity, in* Environmental Law and Contrasting Ideas of Nature: A Constructivist Approach 64 (Keith Hirokawa ed., 2014).

45. Brian Walker & David Salt, Resilience Practice 304 (2012).

46. Carl Folke, *Resilience: The Emergence of a Perspective for Social-Ecological Systems Analyses*, 16 Global Envtl. Change 253 (2006).

47. *See, e.g.*, Craig R. Allen et al., *Managing for Resilience*, 17 Wildlife Biol. 337, 341 (2011) (describing managing wildlife for resilience as seeking to maintain system identity even when subject to a wide range of conditions and increasing the ability of the system to cope with change).

socioecological systems well enough to set parameters that will foster resilient systems. The ecological resilience model, however, just as easily allows for management based on guided transformation, accepting the fact the systems *will* change in the near future and constructing management to help ensure that when ecosystems transform, they flip into alternate but still productive states. Viewed from this perspective, the question is not whether ecological resilience is the best framework but rather: Why have current managers failed to embrace their potentially crucial roles in transformations?

Environmental Assessment and Planning

This chapter describes the way using fixed points, baselines, and the status quo in the law hamper our ability to do "the next right thing." We argue that we should set aside these frameworks that are keeping us frozen in place and instead develop new ideas that center goal-oriented collaboration. When we make personal decisions about our lives, we often think about what we want life to look like and then craft a plan for how to get there. Goals can be on a big scale (I want to be a veterinarian, I want to be able to retire at age 65) or small scale (I want to be able to go to the beach this weekend, I want to have shorter hair). With our goal in mind, we then set a path. We might not always reach our goals, or we might change our targets, but the goal is usually the starting point. The debate then can be about what is the right path to get there.

Others may take different, more measured approaches that focus on starting points (I don't know what career I want, but college seems a good place to start) or embrace the contingency of the future (I am not sure what my future holds, but maybe it is good to save money in case I want to use it for something). While this path-focused approach may work well, success is more frequent with a goal-oriented approach. Focusing on the path is dependent on the hope that the path itself determines the desired result, even if we don't know what that result may be.

As we move beyond the personal, we can think about environmental policies in similar ways. The Clean Water Act (CWA) is a goal-oriented law.[48] It sets a goal of fishable and swimmable waters. It then details mechanisms to achieve that goal. We can, of course, argue over whether the mechanisms are correct, but at least we know where it is headed. Judges and regulators frequently hearken back to the goal of the CWA when trying to assess the details. NEPA is a path-focused law—or at least it has become one. Courts

48. 33 U.S.C. §1251(a) (2012).

have interpreted NEPA to impose only a procedural mandate.[49] Thus, we have no law that calls for maximizing environmental benefits.

Little in the law mandates the protection of ecosystem health or ecosystem services. Instead, we have media-specific (water/air) and agency-specific (organic) acts that give us real mandates. In environmental assessment, we fight over what the baseline should be so we can assess the impacts of our proposed projects. Maybe instead we should plan more holistically. What do we want our world to look like? What are the projects that help us get there? How much does this project take us away from the goal? We should measure environmental impacts by considering whether, and by how much, the project will advance or detract from our goal of a healthy environment. Instead of asking how much carbon a project emit or how many acres of open space will be lost compared to today's levels, let's do a planning process where we set our goals. How much will this reduction in open space hamper our goals? Of course, this is not a simple change to make and will require us to confront difficult but important questions of who sets the goals and how. Our current framework fails to interrogate how the goal of maintaining the status quo perpetuates inequalities. These concerns should be addressed explicitly.

Collaborative Governance as Path Forward

Old environmental laws were necessary for responding to the crises of their time but are often insufficient for dealing with the crisis of this moment, again noting that the portions of environmental law that keep toxics and other pollutants out of the environment remain critical to reducing stressors to overstressed systems. Even so, our current environmental laws almost entirely fail to address the climate crisis. How, then, should we move forward?

Law clearly needs to evolve to deal with climate change and a changing planet. It takes disciplined effort to distinguish those laws that keep us maladapted by embedding stasis from those—like vaccination mandates and limitations on how many toxics we release into the environment—that need to stay in place to produce the best future possible despite the changes that are coming. This double-visioned perspective on how we evaluate existing law, however, allows for narrative competition and disagreements about which category certain laws fall into.

49. Anglers of the Au Sable v. U.S. Fisheries Serv., 565 F. Supp. 812, 823 (E.D. Mich. 2008) ("NEPA's mandate is merely procedural; it does not require particular outcomes").

An alternative solution derives from traditional ecological knowledge, particularly indigenous systems of maintaining historic information about the ecological conditions of a particular landscape over time. The oral histories, songs, dances, and traditions of some indigenous groups maintain a collective memory of a historic baseline species population even if the population is largely diminished or even destroyed.[50] This preserved cultural memory of historic population levels avoids the problem of artificially lowered baselines, creating a historically rooted baseline across generations, even in periods of species decline. This fixed point creates an ideal place to return to for future generations.

In envisioning the possible amidst the climate reality, we can transcend the status quo and create new realities that encompass better conditions. To be clear, this is not an overly optimistic, Pollyanna-ish approach to environmental law. Many will suffer because of climate change effects. Nevertheless, when planning new futures, we should recognize the potential to achieve outcomes that restore and repair past harms, including harms that some may deny or refuse to acknowledge. Doing so relies upon more inclusive environmental policymaking.

Fortunately, pockets of scholarship examining different tools can be woven together to create a new, more comprehensive tapestry of "environmental law" to displace the status quo with a legal system that is more inclusive, comprehensive, and responsive to climate change. New governance, collaborative analysis, and collaborative governance are crucial stepping stones that link where we are to where we need to go.[51] The time for moving from baselines to new, more expansive and flexible understandings of environmental outcomes and possibilities has arrived. Craig, for example, has

---

50. For example, the WoLakota project of the Rosebud Sioux Indian Tribe seeks to restore buffalo to roaming freely across the landscape, as they did historically. *See* https://www.wolakotaproject.org/. Although no living member of the Rosebud Sioux Indian Tribe can remember a time when buffalo roamed freely across their lands, ceremonies, oral histories, and traditional education have maintained a collective memory of the time when this was the norm. Despite the intentional eradication of buffalo from the plains by colonial settlers—as a direct attempt to eradicate not only the buffalo, but also the indigenous populations that relied upon them—the Sioux have maintained a baseline that includes the buffalo. This shared vision has informed current environmental policymaking of reintroducing buffalo to the plain in a manner consistent with wildlife (as opposed to livestock) that reflects an uninterrupted cultural understanding of a baseline.

51. For a discussion in governance trends, see Karrigan Bork & Keith H. Hirokawa, *Trends in Local Ecosystem Governance*, 3 FRONTIERS CLIMATE 1 (2021).

already explored this possibility in the concept of "trickster law,"[52] delineating three aspects to this new approach. First,

> trickster law seeks not . . . to use natural resources to the maximum extent deemed possible and desirable, but rather . . . employs a precautionary approach to human use of natural resources and seeks to minimize anthropogenic stressors, such as pollution (especially nutrients and toxics), on social-ecological systems.[53]
>
> Second, "trickster law acknowledges that some transformations are and will increasingly become unavoidable . . . and thus encourages anticipation of, and planning for, these transformations before they become social-ecological crises."[54]
>
> Finally, building on the adaptive governance literature's emphasis on polycentricity, "trickster law creates space for new voices and new values that can help societies cope with a changing world."[55]

Cinnamon Carlarne discussed boundaries in her contribution to ELC's collaborative essay, saying: "Law codifies and fixes boundaries."[56] She focuses on ecological boundaries, noting that "in a stubbornly stasis-oriented world,"[57] shifting boundaries of many types (political, ecological, psychological) challenge how we think about the role of law. How can we use the climate crisis to reimagine the role of law in addressing ecological challenges? How can we erode no-longer-fixed boundaries to reflect the changing, living earth?

In her ELC essay contribution, Karen Bradshaw suggests that environmental law scholars look to the instruction from Disney movies to just "do the next right thing" in this period of crisis and uncertainty.[58] We exist in a time in which there are no predictable or objectively correct answers. Changes are unfolding faster than Congress or agencies can act, particularly with the seemingly perpetual litigation that comes with regulatory attempts. Dealing with disaster necessarily means "small groups of people working together in localized ways."[59]

---

52. Robin Kundis Craig, *Trickster Law: Promoting Resilience and Adaptive Governance by Allowing Other Perspectives on Natural Resource Management*, 9 Ariz. J. Envtl. L. & Pol'y 140, 149-56 (2019) (providing three examples of how new voices—including indigenous voices—have changed natural resource management in beneficial ways).
53. *Id.* at 148.
54. *Id.*
55. *Id.*
56. Cinnamon P. Carlarne, *The Mutable Boundaries of a Worst-Case Climate World, in Adapting to a 4°C World, supra* note 13, at 10222.
57. *Id.* at 102224.
58. Karen Bradshaw, *Climate Change Lessons From a Disney Princess, in Adapting to a 4°C World, supra* note 13, at 10225.
59. *Id.* at 10226.

Stakeholder collaborations provide a model for moving forward. Localized solutions among divergent stakeholders can incorporate more diverse inputs into federal policymaking, produce innovative solutions, act responsively to rapidly changing conditions, and shield agency action from litigation that creates delays and drains resources from key objectives.[60] In this period of polarization, accepting that there are competing views and understanding but then moving on to solutions and shared visions is crucially necessary. Luckily, there exist thousands of existing stakeholder collaborations and a robust legal framework for Congress, agencies, and courts relying upon the collaborative analysis created by this tool. They have long been undertheorized by environmental law and administrative law scholars focusing upon a few key laws, but collaborations may hold a key, missing component to climate adaptation. A crucial aspect of stakeholder collaborations is that they advance a goal we advocate for in this chapter: letting go of a single, fixed baseline and embracing values of ecological responsibility.

Ultimately, we suggest that too stubborn a hold to particular baselines renders law unable to do the work of mediating the human relationship with nature. Principles of ecological responsibility and ethics that recognize that humans are only one species among the many on this planet may be more useful than the scientifically oriented, number-driven laws of the past. Although such a proposal may be met with critiques of being "unscientific" or "touchy feely," collaborative responsibility may offer greater insights than we get from attempts to cling to unrealistic baselines and governance approaches that build from a small group of people. Indeed, a clear-eyed approach requires less exactitude and more engagement with the diverse, difficult, and fuzzy questions of how we as a species are supposed to interact with one another and our natural environments in these changing times.

Governance tools must focus on overcoming polarization through improved communication. Co-creating policy is crucial. Adversarial approaches (such as the "timber wars" pitting environmentalists against loggers) are wasteful and counterproductive, just as slashed-earth policy in family law cases wastes resources and harms everyone. Much in the way that family law experts advocate mediation instead of litigation, so too should environmental law policymakers consider the benefits of policymaking that shifts from time-consuming, expensive litigation towards collaborative solutions. Many in our community shudder at cooperating with industry, assuming that collabora-

60. Keith H. Hirokawa & Jonathan Rosenbloom, *Local Variation to Lead the Disruption of Contemporary Environmental Law, in* Environmental Law, Disrupted 203 (Keith Hirokawa & Jessica Owley eds., 2021).

tion means acquiescence in a degraded world and industrial domination and destruction of the natural environment. This is not the case. Instead, we argue, true collaboration incorporates voices that the past century of environmental policymaking has overlooked by incorporating environmental justice and traditional ecological knowledge as decision-making tools of equal validity as the long-favored economic considerations that have dominated cost-benefit driven environmental analysis. While they may have a way to go, resource collaborations have achieved this integration in ways that the political process has not.[61] Mediation and negotiation strategies will be more fruitful than litigation and, in any event, will facilitate the stakeholder ownership of climate solutions in ways that competition cannot.

Now is the time to bring on the bold ideas. We must search for and embrace the unconventional. What we are doing isn't working. Clinging to the laws, worldviews, and governance tools that landed us in the present situation cannot produce the needed new answers. Many are too afraid to let go of the pieces we do have, leading to reactionary clinging to old and broken ideas. While people may critique environmental statutes, no one wants to get rid of them because of the fear of what may come next. We see the courts invoking the Framers to lock in a stagnant version of the U.S. Constitution instead of stopping to ask what would most serve our planetary needs. Let's step outside the worn and unproductive roads we've been walking.

If our goal is to minimize suffering and maximize flourishing given the climate reality, what does the law look like? Luckily, answers exist. There is some room for optimism: more inclusive decision making that incorporates historically excluded perspectives can produce better outcomes. Ecofeminism incorporates notions of community and care that integrate feminist worldviews and perspectives into modern understandings of the interaction with the environment.[62] Yet, ecofeminist constructs have been almost entirely excluded from federal law and policymaking. Similarly, environmental justice studies have exposed the valuable insights of historically marginalized populations into how to improve their own—and broader—wellbeing, which are suppressed through racist, majoritarian policies.[63] Recent presidential efforts to incorporate traditional ecological

61. *See* Karen Bradshaw, *Stakeholder Collaboration as an Alternative to Cost-Benefit Analysis*, 2019 B.Y.U. L. Rev. 655, 661-69 (2020) (presenting a case study of the Western Arctic Caribou Herd Working Group stakeholder collaboration that is working to prevent caribou herd collapse whereas prior, top-down wildlife management efforts had failed); Charlie Facemire & Karen Bradshaw, *Biodiversity Loss, Viewed Through the Lens of Mismatched Property Rights*, 14 Int'l J. Commons 650, 656-57 (2020) (comparing top-down U.S. Bureau of Land Management wild horse management efforts with the FWS' use of stakeholder collaboration to manage wild horses).

62. Cinnamon P. Carlarne, *Environmental Law & Feminism*, *in* The Oxford Handbook of Feminism and Law in the United States (Martha Chamallas et al. eds., 2022).

63. Clifford J. Villa, *Remaking Environmental Justice*, 66 Loy. L. Rev. 469 (2020).

knowledge into environmental policymaking suggest that federal agencies not only can, but must, incorporate indigenous understandings into modern laws.

New governance tools, laws, and legal pathways are also emerging to bridge where we are to where we need to go. The vast, but unrecognized, network of collaborative governance for public lands and natural resource management is increasingly influencing scholarly understanding of environmental law and administrative law. Private environmental governance allows corporations, trusts, nongovernmental organizations, and individuals to achieve valuable environmental aims without the sometimes time-constraining process of promulgating regulation or enacting laws.[64]

Conclusion

When the ELC met in 2021 to explore the paradigm shift of a +4°C world, a small group of legal scholars began the process of co-creating new environmental futures. This chapter begins with a framework for contemplating the role of baselines in a world defined by uncertainty. We posed a central question to guide this chapter: Do baselines or ideal states of nature—including our present or recent past realities—make sense when making decisions for a world we can't yet envision? In a stone-soup writing process that unfolded over the years, the co-authors drew upon our deep pockets of individual expertise across substantive topics to form an answer. An observation emerged that a fixation on a particular baseline might inaccurately reflect the potential of an ecosystem. The climate crisis invites and necessitates new approaches. We advocate for a forward-looking set of laws focused on goal setting, which might include historical understandings of individual landscapes informed by traditional ecological knowledge and science.

Current American environmental laws call for "restoration" of previous states[65] alongside "protecting,"[66] "preserving," and "maintaining"[67] current

---

64. Sarah Light, *The Law of the Corporation as Environmental Law*, 71 Stan. L. Rev. 137 (2019).
65. *See, e.g.*, Comprehensive Environmental Response, Compensation, and Liability Act (CERCLA) §107(f), 42 U.S.C. §9607(f) (discussing natural resources restoration under CERCLA; U.S. EPA, Natural Resources Damages: A Primer, https://www.epa.gov/superfund/natural-resource-damages-primer#restorations (last visited June 29, 2023) (stating that natural resource damage awards should only be used for "restoration or replacement of the injured natural resource" and explaining that restoration seeks to "return injured resources to baseline conditions."
66. The 30 x 30 protected areas goal fits right into this paradigm as do many modes of park-like preservation actions. *See* Blanca Begert, *30 x 30 Is Conservation's Flashy New Goal. Now Countries Need to Figure Out What It Actually Means*, Grist (Jan. 9, 2023), https://grist.org/article/30x30-is-conservations-flashy-new-goal-now-countries-need-to-figure-out-what-it-actually-means/ (explaining that the goal of "protecting" land has been set without agreement on what we can and should be protecting).
67. For example, the CWA's mission is "to restore and maintain the chemical, physical, and biological integrity of the Nation's waters." 33 U.S.C. §1251. *See also* Ahjond Garmestani et al., *Untapped Capacity*

conditions.[68] We seek to "eliminate" pollutants.[69] The law assumes that the current or previous states of being are the desirable ones. NEPA asks us to look at the no-action alternative (as though that would be the better environmental condition). While we acknowledge the benefits of restoration, protection, and maintenance, we seek to engage in a discussion of what it would look like if our laws instead used verbs like foster, support, enhance, or seek. How could we move to a more forward-looking state of action?

Ultimately, the future of environmental law might, like this book and this chapter, grow from a series of conversations of interested parties considering a single issue. Inspired by J.B. Ruhl and Craig, we started the conversation by asking how the law should adapt to a +4°C world. Next, we marshaled a group of scholars with diverse expertise and experiences to answer the related questions of how baselines help and hamper a world of change unfolding at multiple levels. Collectively, we have explored the status quo of law as it exists and imagined new environmental laws that might facilitate what is possible instead of merely maintaining what exists. In this way, this chapter—and the process underlying it—reflects the capacity of humans to explore new potentials and possibilities collectively and collaboratively. Like the outcome, the process argues that the work of our generation of environmental law thinkers is to employ new tools, methods, and mindsets to address the problems of our time.

---

for Resilience in Environmental Law, 116 PROC. NAT'L ACAD. SCI. 19899, 19900 (2019) (pointing out the "mismatch between existing environmental laws and social-ecological systems" built on 1970s' laws seeking "to improve, preserve, and maintain ecosystems in current or historic regimes").

68. The National Park Service Organic Act for example calls for conserving park resources so they can be enjoyed in the same way as current users with a goal of leaving them "unimpaired for the enjoyment of future generations." Act to Establish a National Park Service (Organic Act) of 1916, 39 Stat. 535, 54 U.S.C. §100101.

69. 33 U.S.C. §1251.

4Cs at 4°C: Counting, Contestation, Communication, and Consideration for Collectively Constructing Concepts of Climate Change

Joshua Ulan Galperin

Constructive criticism of the nation's environmental laws has been mounting over the past few decades.[1] One major line of criticism is that the laws are inadequate for addressing the most pressing environmental challenge: climate change. This argument addresses the shortcomings of specific regulatory tools and highlights the need to draw from a more diverse toolbox to combat climate change.[2] Another line of criticism argues that the very purpose, organizing principles, and framework of environmen-

Author's note: Many thanks to all the other authors in this volume whose brilliance gave me the necessary outlook and enthusiasm for putting this chapter together. Thanks also to Sara Kuebbing and Dan Simberloff for help with the scientific perspective on the balance of nature. To Joshua Briggs. And to Joey Jaroz for the excellent research assistance, many years ago and for a very different purpose, that ended up supporting this chapter.

1. *E.g.*, Frederic D. Krupp, Opinion, *New Environmentalism Factors in Economic Needs*, Wall St. J., Nov. 20, 1986, https://www.wsj.com/articles/SB117269353475022375; James L. Huffman, *Protecting the Environment From Orthodox Environmentalism*, 15 Harv. J. L. & Pub. Pol'y 349 (1991); Douglas A. Kysar, Regulating From Nowhere: Environmental Law and the Search for Objectivity (2010); David Schoenbrod et al., Breaking the Logjam: Environmental Protection That Will Work (2012); Michael P. Vandenbergh, *Private Environmental Governance*, 99 Cornell L. Rev. 129 (2013); Joshua Galperin, Op-ed, *"Desperate Environmentalism" Won't Save the Environment*, L.A. Times, Oct. 29, 2015, http://www.latimes.com/opinion/op-ed/la-oe-galperin-environmental-desperation-20151029-story.html; E. Donald Elliott & Daniel C. Esty, *The End of Environmental Externalities Manifesto: A Rights-Based Foundation for Environmental Law*, 29 N.Y.U. Envtl. L.J. 506 (2021).
2. *E.g.*, Irma S. Russell, *Streamlining NEPA to Combat Global Climate Change: Heresy or Necessity?*, 39 Envtl. L. 1049 (2009) (assessing whether the National Environmental Policy Act hinders projects that are necessary for mitigating climate change); Michael P. Vandenbergh & Jonathan M. Gilligan, Beyond Politics: The Private Governance Response to Climate Change 3 (2018) (explaining that public environmental laws alone cannot solve climate change); J.B. Ruhl & James E. Salzman, *What Happens When the Green New Deal Meets the Old Green Laws?*, 44 Vt. L. Rev. 693 (2020) (addressing how current environmental laws will impede climate-friendly projects).

tal law are inappropriate for both mitigating and adapting to climate change.[3] This second line of argument asserts that we need to reimagine the purpose of environmental law to minimize the harms of climate change. *How we search* for the purposes of environmental law is the focus of this chapter.

It did not start with Christopher Stone, but Stone's groundbreaking 1972 article, *Should Trees Have Standing?*, imagined an eco-centric basis for environmental law in which "we give legal rights to forests, oceans, rivers and other so-called 'natural objects' in the environment—indeed, to the natural environment as a whole."[4] The purpose of this expansion of environmental rights was to push cultural and institutional change that would result in better environmental protection.[5] Fifty years on, environmental thinkers are still searching for frameworks to support environmental protection often with an intense focus on climate change. In *After Nature*, for example, Jed Purdy traces a centuries-long history of lurching environmental ideology.[6] Purdy concludes that in a new age, the Anthropocene, new approaches are necessary.

With each critique comes a constructive alternative. This chapter will focus, as a case study, on the concept of "balance of nature." Balance of nature is a framework claiming that nature rests in a harmonious balance and human interference disrupts that balance. Imbalance is the mark of environmental harm. Scientists know that this is not an accurate description of the natural world, yet it has long underpinned environmental decision making and remains a dominant concept in environmental thought. In recent decades, however, as with other environmental ideologies that seek to establish a purpose, structure, and set of tools for environmental governance, many have critiqued the balance of nature and proposed alternatives like "resilience" as a driving principle for environmental protection.[7]

Each new proposal for framing and organizing environmental policy implies that environmental protection needs a fixed ideology and from that point criticizes one ideology before replacing it with another. As climate change has become the dominant concern in environmental protection, much of this ideological find-and-replace has focused on identifying envi-

3. *E.g.*, Melinda Harm Benson & Robin Kundis Craig, The End of Sustainability: Resilience and the Future of Environmental Governance in the Anthropocene (2017).
4. Christopher D. Stone, *Should Trees Have Standing?—Toward Legal Rights for Natural Objects*, 45 S. Cal. L. Rev. 450, 456 (1972).
5. *See id.* at 495.
6. Jedediah Purdy, After Nature: A Politics for the Anthropocene (2015).
7. *E.g.*, Robert L. Fischman, *Letting Go of Stability: Resilience and Environmental Law*, 94 Ind. L.J. 689 (2019); Robin Kundis Craig, *Learning to Live With the Trickster: Narrating Climate Change and the Value of Resilience Thinking*, 33 Pace Envtl. L. Rev. 351, 372 (2016); Daniel B. Botkin, Discordant Harmonies: A New Ecology for the Twenty-First Century (1994).

ronmental creeds that are appropriate for human-caused climate change.[8] This chapter will argue that the critiques of environmental law are right, but the constructive proposals are almost always, and almost necessarily, wrong.

Instead of searching for an ideology tailored to environmental law, effective environmental protection should not emerge from an essentialist view of nature but from a foundation that ought to underlie any governance endeavor: democracy. Put differently, we need to decide together how to govern the environment and not cling to essentialism that purports to tell us how to behave. There is no immutable law that tells us how to govern nature. We must do the hard work of making those decisions ourselves. Science provides the *is*, but not the *ought*, of environmental decision making. A concept like the balance of nature is not an accurate description of the natural world,[9] but we could, for better or worse, collectively decide that it should nevertheless guide our decision making. This focus on collective, democratic, environmental governance is not an entirely novel approach,[10] but it is one that deserves more attention and specificity, especially in a swiftly warming world.

Environmental governance is not only about stopping threats but also about living with change. As we hurtle toward a 4 degree Celsius (°C) future we must consider how we structure democratic institutions to allow us to self-govern in an unprecedented climate.[11] And that brings us to the 4Cs. This chapter does not offer all the answers but sets out a framework for assessing democratic governance at 4°C by focusing on four aspects of collective decision making: (1) counting; (2) contestation; (3) communications; and (4) consideration.

This chapter first describes the balance of nature principle as arguably the most prominent example of the search for predetermined environmental protection goals. It then frames the balance of nature, as with other essentialist frameworks, as democratic mythmaking or storytelling that helps give weight to social goals that are fundamentally untethered from any objective or empirical source of right and wrong. Next, the chapter explores how such social agreements can emerge from democratic institutions and presents the 4Cs as a vision of democracy to help guide environmental decisionmaking at 4°C. The chapter concludes by offering nascent ideas for how we can struc-

8. Fischman, *supra* note 7; Craig, *supra* note 7; Purdy, *supra* note 6.
9. *E.g.*, Frank N. Egerton, *Changing Concepts of the Balance of Nature*, 48 Q. Rev. Biology 322 (1973).
10. Purdy, *supra* note 6; Kysar, *supra* note 1.
11. As the introduction to this volume notes, the extent of climate change my not reach 4°C. In this chapter, I use 4°C as a symbol of significant and possibly catastrophic climate change without asserting that we will necessarily reach that level of warming. The point is that the earth and politics that take place upon the earth, will look different in a warmer world.

ture democratic institutions in a 4°C world that will allow us to generate the beliefs necessary for effective environmental governance in a new world.

The Balance of Nature and Other False Promises

The notion that natural systems are harmoniously balanced—that plants, animals, nutrients, light, water, all elements are precisely coordinated—goes back centuries.[12] This "balance of nature" concept "has been a theoretical fundamental concept in ecology."[13] It has also been a baseline for environmental law, helping policymakers articulate what is good—systems in balance—and what is bad—systems where human interference has thrown off the balance.[14] The trouble is, the concept of the balance of nature is wrong. It always has been. And scientists have long recognized this.[15]

The balance of nature is not the only ideological framework that environmental thinkers have proposed to guide environmental behavior. Some frameworks establish the goals of environmental action while others assert the best tools for such action, regardless of goals. Among the frameworks are some that are specific to environmental law and others that are more general but with a specific impact on environmental policy. The so-called Gaia hypothesis and related superorganism theory are other concepts that emerged from ecology.[16] Lawyers and economists invented welfare economics and cost-benefit analysis.[17] Religions have offered dominion and providence to command environmental thinking.[18] Philosophers and political theorists have tried to draw a line between the public and private spheres of action.[19] But "balance of nature" seems to persist despite decades and arguably centuries of empirical rejection, making it a potent case study.[20] This section

12. Egerton, *supra* note 9, at 324; Daniel Simberloff, *A Succession of Paradigms in Ecology: Essentialism to Materialism and Probabilism*, 43 Conceptual Issues Ecology 3, 30 (1980).
13. Egerton, *supra* note 9, at 324; *See also* Oswald J. Schmitz: The New Ecology: Rethinking Science for the Anthropocene (2017).
14. Fischman, *supra* note 7, at 690; *see* Alejandro E. Camacho, *Assisted Migration: Redefining Nature and Natural Resource Law Under Climate Change*, 27 Yale J. on Reg. 171, 245 (2010).
15. *E.g.*, Schmitz, *supra* note 13; P.R. Ehrlich & L.C. Birch, *The "Balance of Nature" and "Population Control,"* 101 Am. Naturalist 97, 106 (1967) ("The notion that nature is in some sort of "balance" with respect to population size . . . is demonstrably false.").
16. P.J. Boston, *Gaia Hypothesis, in* Encyclopedia of Ecology (2008); Egerton, *supra* note 9, at 327.
17. Joshua Ulan Galperin, *Environmental Governance at the Edge of Democracy*, 39 Va. Envtl. L.J. 70, 103 (2021).
18. Purdy, *supra* note 6.
19. *E.g.*, David Singh Grewal & Jedediah Purdy, *Introduction: Law and Neoliberalism*, 77 L. & Contemp. Probs. 1, 1 (2015); Jody Freeman, *The Private Role in Public Governance*, 75 N.Y.U. L. Rev. 543, 588 (2000).
20. Daniel Simberloff, *The "Balance of Nature"—Evolution of a Panchreston*, 12 PLoS Biology 1, 3 (2014) ("Yet, the idea of a balance of nature lives on in the popular imagination, especially among conservationists and environmentalists.").

therefore briefly describes the balance-of-nature idea, how the concept has influenced environmental policymaking, the scientific critique of the balance of nature, and its eventual rejection among environmental scholars.

Ecologist Daniel Botkin has offered one of the most complete critiques of the balance-of-nature concept,[21] and he has also offered one of the most complete definitions:

> Briefly stated, the Balance of Nature myth has three basic features: First, Nature, undisturbed by human influences, achieves a permanency of form and structure that persists indefinitely. Second, this permanent condition is the best condition for Nature: best for other creatures, best for the environment, and best for humans. Third, when disturbed from this perfect state, Nature is capable of returning to it.[22]

The balance of nature influenced early environmental law. Jonathan Weiner puts it most bluntly: "Much of the environmental law adopted in the past has been based on an ideal of preserving nature in a stable balance, of preserving nature against change—an ideal that is increasingly out of step with the new scientific understanding of ecosystems."[23]

The "new scientific understanding" to which Weiner refers—and to which I will return in just a moment—is the repudiation of the "balance of nature." This view recognizes that nature exists in constant flux, that systems are subject to regular disturbances that change their characteristics, that those disturbances (if disturbance is even the right word) come from human actions but also nonhuman factors, and that even while systems can rest in temporary states of stability, the stable states are not inherently better or more representative of the "correct" conditions for a given system.[24] Writers have referred to the alternative paradigm as "flux of nature"[25] and "dance of nature"[26] among other names.

For many, abandoning the balance of nature required adopting a new organizing principle. As Wiener wrote, if we don't have the balance of nature to assure us, "we need to find a better way."[27] "Sustainability" has been a

21. Daniel B. Botkin, Discordant Harmonies: A New Ecology for the Twenty-First Century (1994).
22. Daniel B. Botkin, *Adjusting Law to Nature's Discordant Harmonies*, 7 Duke Envtl. L. & Pol'y F. 25, 26 (1996) (citation omitted).
23. Jonathan Baert Wiener, *Law and the New Ecology: Evolution, Categories, and Consequences*, 22 Ecology L.Q. 325, 333-34 (1995).
24. Simberloff, *supra* note 20, at 3.
25. *Id.*
26. Judy L. Meyer, *The New Dance of Nature: New Concepts in Ecology*, 69 Chi.-Kent L. Rev. 875, 875 (1994).
27. Jonathan Baert Wiener, *Beyond the Balance of Nature*, 7 Duke Envtl. L. & Pol'y F. 1, 18 (1996).

major contender, focusing on the renewability of resources and weighing conservation against economic growth.[28] Adaptive management, "in which law follows a self-consciously evolutional process: promulgation, experimentation, evaluation, and revision" is another.[29] Karrigan Börk has turned to ecological sciences in an attempt to import the concept of "reconciliation" into environmental law.[30] Reconciliation explicitly rejects the idea of restoring any fundamentally "natural" balance and instead recommends focusing environmental protection on human-dominated systems without any reference to historic ideals.[31] Robert Fischman and Robin Kundis Craig each suggest a resilience and adaptive management framework that recognizes the dynamism of natural systems and the inevitability of change, but seeks to blunt and slow change to manageable transitions in terms of quality and speed.[32] In short, the toppling of one environmental creed begins a search for something new to fill the gap.

It is important to note that the "new" scientific understanding, even as Wiener wrote in 1995, was not new. In roughly 1855, Alfred Russel Wallace made the following observation:

> Some species exclude all others in particular tracts. Where is the balance? When the locust devastates vast regions and causes the death of animals and man, what is the meaning of saying the balance is preserved. . . . To human apprehension there is no balance but a struggle in which one often exterminates another.[33]

In 1930, Charles Elton wrote that "[the] 'balance of nature' does not exist and perhaps never has existed."[34] Although the term and concept lingered, "the predominant view by ecologists of the 1960s saw the whole notion of balance as, at best, irrelevant and, at worst, a distraction."[35]

Despite these scientific rejections, the *concept* of balance permeated environmental thinking and created a shared goal for how we would govern the environment. Mischaracterizations about nature informed that goal, which makes it wrong in a manner of speaking, but simply because it is scientifically

---

28. Fred P. Bosselman & A. Dan Tarlock, *The Influence of Ecological Science on American Law: An Introduction*, 69 Chi.-Kent L. Rev. 847, 860, 872 (1994).
29. Wiener, *supra* note 27, at 21; A. Dan Tarlock, *The Nonequilibrium Paradigm in Ecology and the Partial Unraveling of Environmental Law*, 27 Loy. L.A. L. Rev. 1121, 1139 (1994).
30. Karrigan Bork, *Governing Nature: Bambi Law in a Wall-E World*, 62 B.C. L. Rev. 155 (2021).
31. *Id.* at 170-71.
32. Fischman, *supra* note 7, at 697-99; Craig, *supra* note 7, at 352.
33. Simberloff, *supra* note 20, at 2 (citing H. Lewis McKinney, *Alfred Russel Wallace and the Discovery of Natural Selection*, 21 J. Hist. Med. & Allied Sci. 333 (1966)).
34. Charles Sutherland Elton, Animal Ecology and Evolution 17 (1930).
35. Simberloff, *supra* note 20, at 3.

wrong does not mean it is invalid as a goal. Goals are not commands from nature revealed by scientists, they are democratic agreements forged in the social and legal institutions that bring us together and allow us, sometimes force us, to encounter the ideas of others. Accordingly, as we peer into the future and see the too-real prospect that 4 degrees of warming will subjugate our institutions and upend our environmental principles, we should avoid worries about the "right" basis for environmental law and instead worry about how we can continue to set collective environmental goals as the world crumbles around us.

Setting Goals

Perhaps it is fairer to say that even without a 4°C future it would be better to understand environmental protection as a matter of collective goal-setting rather than a search for some exogenous commandments about the proper relationship between law and the environment. In the 4°C future, the institutions that facilitate democratic engagement may flounder, making it harder to generate or maintain environmental protection ideals. And certainly, the rapid and dramatic environmental changes that 4°C will bring will demand new, or at least newly scrutinized, ideals. Such ideals may arise without careful planning or forethought, but they do not arise from nothing.

Democratic institutions, broadly conceived, are critical to the law in large part because they engender the collective notions, like the balance of nature, that guide lawmaking.[36] As Craig has said, the "permeation of the law by cultural narrative []occurs in environmental law in the emerging laws and policies to cope with climate change."[37] This section thus looks at the role of cultural narrative, myth, collective ideas, whatever we may call it, in lawmaking. The next section more closely examines the role of institutions in generating those ideas.

Although we could use many names, "myth" is probably the most recognizable term to describe the big stories we tell that reflect our shared ideals.[38] Myths are usually false, or at least inaccurate, stories.[39] As the prior sec-

36. Craig, *supra* note 7, at 356-57 (citing Christine Metteer Lorillard, *Stories That Make the Law Free: Literature as a Bridge Between the Law and the Culture in Which It Must Exist*, 12 Tex. Wesleyan L. Rev. 251, 251 (2005)). *See also* Charles A. Reich, *The Law of the Planned Society*, 75 Yale L.J. 1227 (1966).

37. Craig, *supra* note 7, at 358.

38. Although I use the term "myth" to help describe the concept of collective ideas and democratic goal-setting, I do not mean to wade into the vast literature on the meaning and making of myth. I use the term here as a metaphor, which I hope will help to highlight the idea that stories and broad agreements of various kinds help to shape law.

39. Albert C. Lin, *Myths of Environmental Law*, 2015 Utah L. Rev. 45, 45.

tion demonstrates, the balance of nature story fits that criterion. Moreover, a myth, even when false, expresses "belief tenaciously held by its adherents."[40] Again, the prior section explains that even after the scientific dismissal of the balance of nature, many still adhere to the belief. But myths are not just false and persistent stories. They are stories, regardless of their truth or honesty, that "express important values and beliefs."[41]

The uncertainty inherent in environmental problems allows these collective stories to "flourish."[42] Albert Lin, therefore, was able to identify several prominent myths in environmental law, including sustainability, cost blindness,[43] the trivial role of individuals in environmental damage, the effectiveness of commodification and pollution trading, and the success of environmental mitigation.[44] These are specific stories and therefore somewhat different from the balance of nature. They are about effectiveness and consequences rather than existential questions. These examples are about *how* we do environmental protection while other myths, like the balance of nature, are about *why* and *to what end*.

There are countless other *how* myths in the law. Myths about the usefulness of *Miranda* warnings or the effectiveness of incarceration are stories about what works.[45] We collectively accept these stories as a sort of "cultural forgiveness" to help us stomach the difficult choices we make—they help us believe in win-win solutions rather than hard trade offs.[46] Stories about corporate personhood or the "reasonable person" are tales that we generally acknowledge are not true in any empirical or objective sense, but we make them real for legal purposes.[47] They are heuristics that make life more efficient or reflect ever-changing social norms. "Legal fictions," we call them.

Other legal yarns are more in line with the balance of nature because they seem to reflect what we believe. They structure our thinking and help define our ambitions rather than merely softening the blow of difficult choices like sending a human being to prison or giving away their money because they were negligent. There is, for instance, a story that tells us some things are

40. *Id.* at 72.
41. *Id.* at 71.
42. *Id.* at 75.
43. *Id.* at 45.
44. *Id.* at 46.
45. *Id.* at 77.
46. Thanks to my research assistant Joshua Briggs (Haub Law '24) for coining the phrase "cultural forgiveness" as an variant of "scapegoating theory." *See* Bradley C. Bobertz, *Legitimizing Pollution Control Through Pollution Control Laws: Reflections on Scapegoating Theory*, 73 Tex. L. Rev. 711 (1995) (arguing that pollution control law is a form of ritualized scapegoating in which the law provides a simple solution—regulating and therefore scapegoating big polluters—for a complex problem, and in so doing signaling that everybody else is absolved of responsibility).
47. Lin, *supra* note 39, at 72.

"private" and therefore sacrosanct while other things are "public" and therefore violable.[48] The myth of "public interest" posits that government need not make difficult choices about what goals to pursue because it is possible to define and calculate an objective "public interest" to orient government efforts.[49] This story emerges from the Progressive and New Deal eras, and helped society square its distaste for big government with demands for government intervention. The government might not seem so big if the goals to which it trod were not the mere choices of politicians or bureaucrats but were instead undeniable, measurable, and objective "public interests."[50] For those who do not believe in the objective public interest, the pluralistic public interest similarly says that government need not make the important decisions because various private organizations representing the full swath of public needs will negotiate and eventually present the government with the best path forward.[51]

With a specific focus on climate change policy, Craig and Melinda Benson look outside the cannon of European-American narratives that typically drive U.S. lawmaking and instead consider an archetype found in many other cultures, that of the "trickster."[52] "[W]hether the trickster takes the name of Coyote, Raven, Iktomi the Spider-Man, or several others[,]" the "trickster tales teach humans to expect the unexpected and that change—good or bad—is just part of life."[53]

Interestingly, the trickster story has something vital in common with other myths; it is a tale that tells people we are not always in control.[54] These stories share the core belief that we may be able to avoid hard choices. We can avoid hard choices because there are external forces at work. Whichever story emerges as the dominant myth, when it comes to lawmaking, at least, the narrative reassures us that government isn't making hard choices. Most myths help us believe that to govern effectively, we only need to focus on the margins because the big picture is already settled.

The balance of nature is a "big" myth like these others and it serves the same purpose. By assigning "nature" the real decision-making authority, the story allows us to avoid making hard choices about what to protect. The bal-

48. Galperin, *supra* note 17, at 89-93.
49. *See, e.g.*, Reich, *supra* note 36, at 1235; Galperin, *supra* note 17, at 104-05.
50. *See, e.g.*, Reich, *supra* note 36, at 1235; Galperin, *supra* note 17, at 104-05.
51. *See, e.g.*, Theodore J. Lowi, The End of Liberalism: The Second Republic of the United States (40th Ann. ed. 2009) (arguing that government hides its role by delegating decision making to private parties).
52. Benson & Craig, *supra* note 3.
53. Craig, *supra* note 7, at 384.
54. *Id.* at 385.

ance of nature tells us that what we must protect is the harmony of natural systems. Hard to do, perhaps, but easy to define the goal and thus avoid the threshold conflict.

All types of stories will need to change at 4°C, but these big ones may be most important, most necessary, to our perseverance. Collective stories can allow us to create collective goals, and that is exactly what the balance of nature has done. It has been a way to articulate the idea that human activity can harm the natural world. In the balance of nature story, "harm" means unbalancing natural systems. This is a useful concept insofar as it has allowed us to rally around a vision of nature and a strategy—reducing human impacts—that has had great success.[55] But when we embrace this, or any story, uncritically, or we do not see the myth as a myth, then we fail to hear, confront, and react to other stories that can also become part of our shared beliefs.

The problem is not the stories. We need stories. Nor is the problem inaccuracies or falsehoods. In law and policy, we sometimes need stories to help us fill the gap from uncertainty to action. The problem is that some narratives may be helpful while others may drive us off a cliff.[56] The balance of nature myth doesn't prevent us from dealing with environmental problems. To the contrary, it gives us a simple, understandable, and actionable framework—reduce human impacts and return natural systems to prehuman status.

But the balance of nature myth does prevent us from fully understanding environmental problems as human defined rather than fundamental, objective, immutable imbalances. In this respect, the tale allows us to ignore the importance of working together in democratic fora that allow us to build new stories and, I hope, stronger civic bonds. We have to avoid letting stories lull us into a sense of inevitability. We have to make sure we understand how they arise. We have to embrace the way they are made so we have some control over them, especially as the world warms. In other words, we need to develop a myth about our mythmaking. That is the focus of the next section.

The 4Cs

As the last section shows, we need to tell big stories because we need a way to communicate and understand shared beliefs and goals. At the same time, if we believe these shared stories are fundamentally and immutably true, they

55. Lin, *supra* note 39, at 46 ("[T]he laws in which the myths are embedded have dramatically reduced pollution, improved environmental quality, and protected valued resources.").

56. Greg Grandin, The End of Myth: From the Frontier to the Border Wall in the Mind of America 4 (2019).

can become ineffective or they can hide problems that need our attention. Thus, we need stories to be both dynamic and at least somewhat transparent. We also need stories that arise from the whole of society and not a narrow selection of only the most powerful voices. Although we tend to think of democracy as a structure of government, it is also a form of governance—of collective decision making. As such, democratic institutions are an important part of telling the stories, and perhaps more equitable stories, that articulate and motivate shared goals.

This section will explore this claim in two ways. First, it will propose four characteristics, the 4Cs, that make institutions democratic and therefore capable of contributing to productive mythmaking: (1) counting (majoritarianism); (2) contestation (individualism); (3) communication (reason-giving); and (4) and consideration (deliberation).[57] Second, it will describe how climate change may impact existing institutions.

Defining Democracy

I propose that we should embrace a more complex, robust, and, I hope, satisfying democracy. This view brings together the 4Cs. It is a view that may have particular use in generating social norms that can help repair and sustain our civic and environmental relationships.

The easiest, and perhaps most common, view of democracy says that democracy is just about counting, that is, about majoritarianism in which people vote and the government acts based on the preferences counted in that voting.[58] People vote for representatives and can use the majoritarian vote to oust those representatives if they choose.[59] Majoritarianism helps signal the sense of the people, install leaders, and, at least in theory, hold leaders accountable to majoritarian demands.[60] Yet, counting alone is insufficient to make an institution truly democratic. As Vandana Shiva cautions, democracy is not just about the big spectacles like elections: "[I]t is about what we do in between."[61] Counting is a spectacular driver of governance, but it is too

57. Galperin, *supra* note 17, at 85-89.
58. *E.g.*, Jean-Jaques Rousseau, The Social Contract (Maurice Cranston trans., Penguin Publishing Group 1968) (1762); Alexander M. Bickel, The Least Dangerous Branch: The Supreme Court at the Bar of Politics 16 (1962); John Hart Ely, Democracy and Distrust: A Theory of Judicial Review 4-5 (2d ed. 1980); Lisa Schultz Bressman, *Beyond Accountability: Arbitrariness and Legitimacy in the Administrative State*, 78 N.Y.U. L. Rev. 461, 478 (2003).
59. Bressman, *supra* note 58, at 462; Phillip Pettit, Republicanism: A Theory of Freedom and Government 185 (1997).
60. Edward Rubin, *The Myth of Accountability and the Anti-Administrative Impulse*, 103 Mich. L. Rev. 2073, 2119 (2005).
61. Vandana Shiva, Earth Democracy: Justice, Sustainability, and Peace 4 (2015).

thin on its own. First, majoritarian counting provides no space for individual rights. Second, counting is an action, basing governance on the will of the majority, but counting alone provides no fora for developing that will, for articulating demands.

Individual contestation is the second aspect of a democratic institution. Individual contestation requires that individuals, even in an otherwise collective effort, are not lost.[62] Individual contestation means that people, as individuals, rather than simply as a part of a voting bloc, are able to engage and influence decision making. When an individual has the opportunity to contest, to voice their opinion, that is a minimum level of individualism, but this democratic feature generally requires slightly more. It requires an opportunity to voice one's opinion in a formal space where there is a definable way in which the voice may impact decision making. Thus, individual contestation can come in many forms, including suing or petitioning, both of which require a formal response and, if successful, can have a direct influence on decisionmaking.

Communication of reasons, reason-giving, is the next important aspect of a democratic institution. When an institution makes a decision and does not communicate a reason for that decision, the decision is, by definition, arbitrary.[63] A purely majoritarian system could be an arbitrary system. People could vote for a popular candidate and that candidate could govern without any responsibility to explain their actions. But a robust democratic system demands that decisionmakers communicate reasons. Reasons allow people to consider how to vote, when or whether to petition or sue, and reasons help each of us to understand what others are thinking so we can confirm or recalibrate our own thinking.

Consideration or deliberation is the final pillar of democratic institutions. Consideration simply means that decisionmakers deliberate, consult, or discuss options before making a final decision.[64] Consideration fits nicely with reasoned communication because stated reasons can be the subject of deliberate consideration. As with each other aspect of democratic practice, we may demand the most careful consideration in the operations of government institutions. But just as people and policymakers vote, sue, and communicate reasons, so too does consideration exist in government and nongovernmental

62. *See*, Maggie McKinley, *Petitioning and the Making of the Administrative State*, 127 Yale L.J. 1538, 1559 (2018) (noting "avenue[s] for political participation distinct from the vote").

63. Henry S. Richardson, Democratic Autonomy: Public Reasoning About the Ends of Policy 36-37 (2002); *Arbitrary*, Dictionary.com, https://www.dictionary.com/browse/arbitrary (last visited June 15, 2023).

64. *Deliberation*, Dictionary.com, https://www.dictionary.com/browse/deliberation (last visited June 15, 2023).

venues. People deliberate through public debates, and protests, for instance, in the process of "democratic will formation."[65]

This multifaceted process must produce new ideas, not just replicate what already exists.[66] For example, communication and consideration are central to litigation.[67] One party will communicate reasons for bringing a lawsuit in the complaint, the other party will consider those reasons and then formulate an answer. The parties will present arguments, respond to those arguments, and ultimately there will be some resolution. The process begins as an individual contestation, but it requires reason and consideration. That interactive process is very unlikely to change either party's mind in the grand sense—neither will decide they are in the wrong—but it does force parties to dwell on the perspectives of the other and create new arguments in response. This is thoughtful confrontation, and though litigation is meant as a dispute resolution process rather than a politically generative process, thoughtful confrontation does generate ideas, even if they are simply ideas about how to best advocate one's position.

The notice-and-comment rulemaking process provides a more plainly democratic example because it is expressly about policymaking. There, Congress sets goals and standards for agency action. An agency considers those goals and then proposes a rule, which is a form of communicating a reason as a proposed rule presents action and provides a voluminous explanation for why that rule is necessary, is sound policy, and has legal authority. The public is invited to provide comment on the rule, which is a form of public reason-giving. The commenters can explain why they support or oppose a rule and offer alternatives. Agency officials must then consider those comments, integrate them into a new rule, or reject them. In so doing, the agency must respond to comments and communicate a reason for why it is or is not acting on the public input. Regardless of whether this process significantly changes the policy, like litigation, it is a necessarily relational process that forces people to think about and respond to the perspectives of others, and therefore, it is a process that generates something new. That something may be small and insignificant by itself, but it is real, and in the aggregate, it may influence how we see the world.

---

65. Richardson, *supra* note 63, at 180.

66. Jedediah Purdy, *The Politics of Nature: Climate Change, Environmental Law, and Democracy*, 119 Yale L.J. 1122, 1135-36 (2010) (citing Charles Taylor, *Interpretation and the Sciences of Man*, *in* Philosophical Papers: Philosophy and the Human Sciences 15, 37 (1985)).

67. *See* Melissa Mortazavi, *Tort as Democracy: Lessons From the Food Wars*, 57 Ariz. L. Rev. 929, 931 (2015).

This is a vision of democracy that at least to some extent, reflects many shared ideals such as equity, participation, respect, and transparency. It is also a system that has the benefit of forcing people to recognize the presence and opinions of other people and, in so doing, asking us to think about our own presence and opinions, thereby generating something new. That something, when repeated over and over, might be the basis of a new story.

To wit, 4C's democracy is a tool for generating shared goals. Because democracy and myths are expressions of values and not descriptions of the world, it is not necessary that myths are accurate in their details, only that they reflect shared goals. In environmental policy, the balance of nature story plays exactly this role. It is incorrect, but that does not mean it is wrong. It is not wrong if there is a process for considering the story and for revising it as we choose. Democracy provides one such process. And that could be the end of the chapter.

But at 4°C, we will need new stories. We already need new stories. This discussion of democracy provides an avenue for considering how to intentionally contribute to new stories. But what happens if, at 4°C, it is not only our stories that need reinvention, but also our democratic institutions?

Crumbling Democracy

"Even well-functioning democratic governance systems will need to adapt in order to manage a 4°C world effectively, and the United States' current default to an extreme version of individualistic democracy will not serve us well."[68] Without regurgitating all the ongoing threats to democracy and current systemic weaknesses,[69] we can anticipate how climate change might impact democratic institutions. Mass migrations will change the political geography of the United States, upending political expectations and creating population densities that may overwhelm local institutions.[70] Extreme weather may keep us indoors and otherwise change the ways in which we communicate.[71] There will be increased competition for space and resources,[72] which will strain and probably sever whatever civility remains in our system. The truly global problem of climate change will reduce the effectiveness of local institutions and even of our national governance structures, reducing trust and engagement.[73] The universality of climate change

68. J.B. Ruhl & Robin Kundis Craig, *4°C*, 106 Minn. L. Rev. 191, 280 (2021).
69. *See id.* at 278-79.
70. *Id.* at 228.
71. *Id.*
72. *Id.*
73. *Id.* at 245.

further complicates democracy because there are no global mechanisms for democratic engagement, no mechanisms that allow sufficient respect for the agency of future generations, those in different political jurisdictions, and no mechanisms that engage non-human animals.[74]

The U.S. Supreme Court decision in *West Virginia v. U.S. Environmental Protection Agency* helps illustrate some aspects of how climate change threatens democracy by entrenching the so-called major questions doctrine into the legal canon.[75] The major questions doctrine asserts that "in certain extraordinary cases" courts cannot allow federal agencies to promulgate regulations unless Congress has provided extremely clear authority in the text of the statute.[76]

This doctrine appears to shift power from administrative agencies to Congress, and to an extent it does that. But it also shifts power away from Congress. Specifically, the major questions doctrine shifts power away from past congresses, which drafted laws like the Clean Air Act, with clear intent but open-textured language. It transfers that power from Congress to judges. Where the Court intends to shift power away from agencies and to Congress, the Court seems to believe it is facilitating democracy by empowering Congress.[77] In fact, the Court is putting an emphasis on one aspect of democracy—the vote-counting majoritarianism that animates Congress—and deemphasizing other aspects of democracy, such as the structures of administrative policymaking that promote consideration, communication, and contestation. Moreover, requiring Congress to make extraordinarily clear textual delegations of authority, rather than relying on the values and goals that Congress has clearly articulated in the overall scheme of a statute, undermines the reasoned and deliberative signaling of legislation in favor of a very thin and formalistic version of majoritarian democracy. Because climate change is too big for the Court, it is already, at least in this subtle way, weakening our democratic institutions and working against democracy.

Conclusion: Constructing Democratic Institutions

"Americans overestimate the resilience of our democracy to our peril . . . ."[78] The resilience of our system, however, may increase if Americans can learn to believe in a more robust democracy. I have tried to articulate an optimistic,

74. Purdy, *supra* note 66, at 1132-33; Kysar, *supra* note 1, at 148-49.
75. 142 S. Ct. 2587 (2022).
76. *Id.* at 2609.
77. *See id.* at 2612-13.
78. Ruhl & Craig, *supra* note 68, at 278.

satisfying, productive, and realistic interpretation of and vision for our democratic system. To those who think this vision is not a good reflection of how we self-govern today, that is because my vision may be a democratic myth. If so, it is a myth we need. One that can help trace a silver lining around the devastation that climate change will bring: As the last part illustrated, climate change disrupts our institutions, but in so doing it will provide an opportunity to rebuild better democratic structures.

I have laid out a model that is not a total reimagining nor a fanciful invention. It is a pragmatic assessment of the best parts of our current system, and as we think about how to survive at 4°C, we should pay close attention to the 4Cs of the institutions that will help us sustain ourselves.

What might these institutions look like? That is the real challenge. It is simple enough to say that they should combine counting, contestation, communication, and consideration and that there should be a variety of institutions with different balances among the 4Cs. It is harder to envision specific new institutions, but a few ideas come to mind.

First, scale will become more acutely important in the 4°C future. Climate change, of course, is a quintessentially global problem but my focus is not so much on the best scale for addressing climate change. My focus is on the best scale for building institutions to engage people in all types of self-governance. People need access to institutions, which counsels in favor of local presence. People also need to know that institutions can be powerful and effective, which counsels for national institutions. These competing considerations suggest that institutions must have a local presence but wield federal power.[79] Empirical research demonstrates that people find local and regional offices of federal agencies to be effective for connecting people to the federal government.[80] These institutions will likely have majoritarian characteristics because Congress will have empowered them, and the president and presidential appointees will oversee them. They should welcome direct individual contestation that requires participants to communicate reasoned arguments and not only impassioned shouts. There are examples of such institutions like the U.S. Department of Agriculture's (USDA's) county committees, which implement federal law at the county level and could serve as a model.[81] Regardless of their form, the decisionmakers must be transparent

79. Joshua Ulan Galperin, *The Life of Administrative Democracy*, 108 Geo. L.J. 1213 (2020) (describing the locally elected federal administrators of the U.S. Department of Agriculture county committees).
80. Joshua Galperin & E. Donald Elliott, Providing Effective Notice of Significant Regulatory Changes: Final Report to the Administrative Conference of the United States 76-77 (2022).
81. *See* Galperin, *supra* note 79.

in their considerations and their conclusions, responding to public input and articulating how that input influences government action.

Second, the 4°C future is likely to change our proximity to one another, at the same time pushing us closer in space and further apart in our relationships. Climatic changes will make certain parts of the United States almost uninhabitable, sending hundreds of millions of people into the remaining regions in which people can comfortably survive.[82] When people live in tighter quarters, the intensity of current stresses may increase—for example, more traffic, more crowded public transit, and more competition for natural resources. Therefore, it will be increasingly important that institutions allow people to see each other as people, not as anonymous others. Although deeply flawed, the court system nevertheless deserves some praise for already providing a considered and individualized forum that demands respect for the presence of others, even in the most antagonistic circumstances.[83] Other institutions, with less built-in antagonism, will also be necessary. For instance, notice-and-comment rulemaking in the federal administrative state provides opportunities for *agonistic* (as opposed to antagonistic) contestation.[84] It does not pit parties directly against each other but instead seeks, at least in an idealized description, to produce reasoned policy that furthers Congress' established value judgments. It benefits from disagreement and different perspectives, but it does not finally resolve a dispute between specific parties. Like the courts, however, new institutions of this nature should focus on communicated reasons and considered interaction that addresses individual demands.

The third and final point is that institutions should help people imagine the world they want. I have no doubt there are ways to do this well beyond my imagination, but two strategies come to mind. First, policymaking institutions should provide opportunities for open-ended engagement in addition to opportunities to give input on policy proposals. This already happens in the form of administrative petitions or listening sessions, for example. But agencies might expand these events to make them more interactive. Rather than simply hearing what people have to say, creating conversation between people may spark ideas that would not otherwise arise.

Second, the focus here has been on traditional institutions of dispute resolution and policymaking. Where it may seem to have strayed into the

---

82. Karrigan Börk et al., *Adapting to a 4°C World*, 52 ENVTL. L. REP. 10211, 10216 (Mar. 2022).
83. *See* Joshua Ulan Galperin, *Value Hypocrisy and Policy Sincerity: A Food Law Case Study*, 42 VT. L. REV. 345, 373 (2018).
84. Daniel E. Walters, *The Administrative Agon: A Democratic Theory for a Conflictual Regulatory State*, 132 YALE L.J. 1, 15 (2022).

abstract and idealistic is my focus not just on democratic engagement in the business of government but also on lateral democratic engagement with each other. The purpose of a robust 4Cs democratic system is to hold up a mirror to ourselves and encourage us to see each other as equal partners in creating the future. But democratic government institutions can go beyond even this. They can help us see each other and see into the future.

Parks are an example. They are also democratic institutions, and they will need special attention in the warming world. The balance of nature may be a story whose time has passed. This has led others to question the purpose of parks that seem designed to capture a vignette of balance, a pristine space that is only a human creation and not a representation of "real" nature.[85] Whether or not we decide that balance is the myth we want to maintain, we need to have experiences that help us create shared visions of nature. Parks are one way to provide these experiences and visions, and an expansive and diverse park system will give us a diverse and expansive bookshelf from which to pull new stories.

The goals we set for environmental protection are just that: goals *we* set. We have always set environmental goals, but we have often convinced ourselves that those goals are not a matter of choice, but instead are inflexible forces of nature. The balance of nature story is one such example, in which we have imagined the natural world in a stable harmony that we upset and only our absence would rebalance. This is a myth, not a scientific reality. Many have recognized this and sought to replace balance of nature with new foundations for environmental protection. These efforts to replace old myths are important, but it is also important to recognize that myths themselves are inescapable. They are also valuable so long as we recognize that they are myths and we take responsibility to reshape them to serve our kaleidoscopic needs. Climate change, however, breaks the repetition and symmetry of our needs and demands a new kind of myth—not a myth about the natural environment, but a myth about mythmaking, a story that guides our process for mythmaking.

Sociologists, anthropologists, and storytellers have much to say about mythmaking, but lawyers have a responsibility too. Government institutions like courts, administrative agencies, and even public spaces like parks provide the fodder for democratic practice. These institutions provide the 4Cs. They offer majoritarian motivation and oversight (counting), platforms for individualist dispute (contestation), coherent reason-giving (communica-

85. *See* Wiener, *supra* note 27, at 7 (describing the national park system as an example of the manifestation of the balance of nature idea).

tion), and transparent, multiparty deliberation (consideration). These are the ingredients of democratic practice and can be the source of the democratic myth we need to cope with 4°C. The 4Cs can empower us to embrace collaborative governance, to see our role, and to see the role of our neighbors, turning them from mysterious, one-dimensional enemies to complicated allies, if not friends. The 4Cs may help us persevere as climate change undermines our persistent environmental stories, and they can be the basis for questioning and creating new stories.

Perhaps we decide we want to observe the balance of nature ideal to gauge environmental progress. Perhaps we decide we want to apply rights for natural systems. Perhaps we decide we want to engineer more resilient or economically productive ecologies. What is important is that we recognize that we are *deciding* and that we build institutions that invite us to make these decisions deliberately and together.

Equity and Justice in a Warming World

Environmental Justice Beyond 2°C

Clifford J. Villa

In spring 2022, the largest wildfire recorded in state history raged across the Sangre de Cristo Mountains in northern New Mexico, devastating forests, valleys, and the communities who depend upon the abundant natural resources of the area. In many cases, the Hermits Peak/Calf Canyon Fire impacted local families who have lived around Mora and San Miguel Counties for centuries, descending from Spanish colonists who settled in the area before the first English colony was founded in Virginia.[1] Generations of families living off the land in geographic isolation created a unique culture, mixing Hispanic and Indigenous bloodlines,[2] embracing communal irrigation and agriculture,[3] and even preserving the use of 16th-century Spanish.[4]

These unique communities, one after another, were placed on alert for mandatory evacuations as the fires burned for weeks across May and June 2022. By the time the fires were finally contained by the summer monsoons, there was remarkably no loss of human life among community members, but more than 350 homes and other buildings had been damaged or destroyed,[5]

Author's note: Thanks to Hannah Shotwell, University of New Mexico (UNM) School of Law Class of 2023, for outstanding research assistance for this chapter. The author dedicates this work to all New Mexicans impacted by the fires of 2022, with gratitude for sharing your stories and with admiration for your grit and determination to rebuild and continue a way of life. Nothing in this chapter reflects legal advice to any individual party, and views expressed in this paper reflect those of the author alone and not necessarily official positions of UNM or the U.S. Environmental Protection Agency.

1. Simon Romero, *"Burning Down a Way of Life": Wildfire Rips Through a Hispanic Bastion*, N.Y. Times, May 5, 2022, https://www.nytimes.com/2022/05/05/us/new-mexico-wildfires.html.
2. *See* Simón Ventura Trujillo, *The Long, Wondrous Life of Ventura Chávez, 1926-2013*, *in* Vanessa Fonseca-Chávez et al, *Querencia*: Reflections on the New Mexico Homeland 20-22 (2020) [hereinafter *Querencia*].
3. Eric Romero, *Southwestern Acequia Systems and Communities: Nuturing a Culture of Place*, 61 Nat. Resources J. 169 (2021).
4. Garland D. Bills & Neddy A. Vigil, The Spanish Language of New Mexico and Southern Colorado 5 (2008) (noting that "New Mexican Spanish" may "trace[] its presence in New Mexico to the arrival of Oñate's colonists in 1598").
5. Tim Wallace & Nadja Popovich, *A "Perfect Recipe for Extreme Wildfire": New Mexico's Record-Breaking, Early Fire Season*, N.Y. Times, June 1, 2022, https://www.nytimes.com/interactive/2022/06/01/climate/new-mexico-wildfires.html.

and innumerable animals and family possesions were lost.[6] As one community leader explained, "We lost more than a beautiful landscape. We lost . . . a way of life."[7]

The Hermits Peak/Calf Canyon Fire, while the largest now on record for New Mexico, was only one of at least six wildfires burning across the state in spring 2022.[8] The New Mexico wildfires reflect the convergence of trends including historic drought[9] and increasing springtime temperatures due to human-caused climate change.[10] The connection between climate change and wildfire risk has been acknowledged for decades. In 1992, with its first assessment report, the Intergovernmental Panel on Climate Change (IPCC) predicted matter-of-factly that "[l]osses from wildfire will be increasingly extensive."[11] Losses from the Hermits Peak fire were specifically anticipated at least 10 years in advance by a local U.S. Forest Service ranger who in 2012 observed the potential for a "catastrophic" fire in the area.[12]

That catastrophic fire came to pass in 2022, at a time when the public can clearly see that climate change is no longer just a theory, but a fact.[13] In the last four decades, average temperatures have risen significantly across the United States, with Alaska and New Mexico among the fastest warming states.[14] Since 1970, average temperatures in New Mexico have risen 3.5 degrees Fahrenheit (°F)—or nearly 2 degrees Celsius (°C). The international scientific community has urged world leaders to contain global

6. *See* Karin Brulliard, *One Month In, New Mexico's Largest-Ever Fire Fuels Anger and Despair*, Wash. Post, May 17, 2022, https://www.washingtonpost.com/nation/2022/05/17/new-mexico-largest-fire (detailing the statements of Fire Chief Isaac Herrera, who acknowledged no loss of human life, but personal loss of two horses in the fire).
7. Paula Garcia, *Our Homeland Is Burning—Now What?*, Santa Fe New Mexican, May 7, 2022, https://www.santafenewmexican.com/opinion/my_view/our-homeland-is-burning-now-what/article_43e87570-ce13-11ec-b372-d30a91013d29.html.
8. Romero, *supra* note 1.
9. According to one recent report, the ongoing drought in the American Southwest ranks as the most severe in 1,200 years. A. Park Williams et al., *Rapid Intensification of the Emerging Southwestern North American Megadrought in 2020-2021*, 12 Nature Climate Change 232, 232 (Mar. 2022) (concluding that "2000-2021 ranks as the driest 22-yr period since at least 800 C.E").
10. Wallace & Popovich, *supra* note 5.
11. IPCC, Climate Change: The 1990 and 1992 IPCC Assessments 88 (June 1992), https://www.ipcc.ch/site/assets/uploads/2018/05/ipcc_90_92_assessments_far_full_report.pdf.
12. Alicia Inez Guzmán, *Crowning Fury: New Mexico Wildfire Reignites Long-Standing Tensions*, Rolling Stone, June 8, 2022, https://www.rollingstone.com/culture/culture-features/new-mexico-fire-forest-service-1364071/ (comments of U.S. Forest Service ranger Steve Romero).
13. Steven Mufson et al., *2°C: Beyond the Limit: Extreme Climate Change Has Arrived in America*, Wash. Post, Aug. 13, 2019, https://www.washingtonpost.com/graphics/2019/national/climate-environment/climate-change-america/?itid=lk_interstitial_manual_6.
14. *Earth Day: U.S. Warming Rankings*, Climate Cent. (Apr. 20, 2022), https://www.climatecentral.org/climate-matters/earth-day-warming-rankings. According to this 2022 assessment, Alaska was determined to be the fastest warming state (+ 4.3°F), followed by Delaware (+3.5°F) and New Mexico (+3.5°F). *Id.*

warming above pre-industrial levels to 1.5°C ideally, and to 2°C at worst.[15] Current trajectories, however, suggest we may shoot past 2°C of global warming this century and enter a world of 3-4°C or beyond,[16] where "radical changes in . . . ecological systems will likely trigger tipping points in social systems, as well."[17]

Taking a sober assessment of continued global warming, legal scholars have emphasized the need for immediate action on both climate mitigation and climate adaptation, requiring hard decisions that may challenge core values of the past. On the climate mitigation side, according to Columbia Law School Prof. Michael Gerrard: "Every scenario for staying even at a fall-back position of 2 degrees at century's end includes the all-out construction of renewable energy projects," with the United States in particular requiring a "World War II-scale mobilization."[18] To achieve construction on this scale will require trade offs. Professor Gerrard observes: "Society has run out of time to save everything we want to save, and to mull things over for years."[19] We no longer have 10 years to wait for the approval of transmission lines, nor 4.5 years to go through the environmental impact statement process under the National Environmental Policy Act.[20] For the siting of wind farms, solar arrays, or transmission lines, we may have to "intrude into the critical habitat of an endangered species."[21] We may have to exercise federal preemption for state and local siting decisions, and we may have to "reform public participation" to accelerate renewables development.[22]

Likewise, on the climate adaptation side, Profs. J.B. Ruhl and Robin Kundis Craig, in their provocative article, *4°C*,[23] observe an "existential threat to democratic governance" from global climate change and posit

---

15. IPCC, Global Warming of 1.5°C, at 4-5 (2018).
16. J.B. Ruhl & Robin Kundis Craig, *4°C*, 106 Minn. L. Rev. 192, 198-99 (2021) (citing studies indicating that "the increase in global average temperature will . . . probably exceed 3°C this century," requiring adaptive measures to prepare for "an increase in global average temperature at least as high as 4°C").
17. As just one example that Ruhl & Craig provide here, an increase of 7.5°C by 2070, which could occur under current trajectories, would place "one-third of the world's population . . . in an annual temperature range" presently found in less than 1% of the world's land mass, "mostly in the Saharan desert." *Id.* at 199-200.
18. Michael B. Gerrard, *A Time for Triage*, 39 Envtl. F. 38 (2022). For a quick sense of the scale of the required mobilization, Professor Gerrard, drawing upon existing studies, estimates that the United States will have to close all coal-fired power plants and build the equivalent of 100 nuclear power plants or large wind farms *every year* until 2050 in order to meet new demands for electricity while meeting goals for reducing carbon emissions. *Id.* at 39.
19. *Id.* at 40.
20. *Id.*
21. *Id.*
22. *Id.* at 40, 42.
23. Ruhl & Craig, *supra* note 16, at 195.

the need for a reframing of established approaches to climate adaptation. Beyond the "Three Rs" of *resist*, *resilience*, and *retreat*, Ruhl and Craig suggest the urgent need for *redesign*,[24] a process of radical transformation that may require "letting go" of closely held beliefs, expectations, and goals.[25] Facing a future where "human suffering is likely to increase dramatically," the authors urge us to "ask uncomfortable questions" and consider even the most politically unpopular measures in order to preserve democracy through the cascade of change to come.[26] For Ruhl and Craig, necessary measures might include community relocation and "repurposing public lands for new human settlements."[27]

The "trade offs" and "letting go" as we confront the looming 4°C world raise fundamental concerns for environmental justice, which has long emphasized the inequitable distribution of environmental protection across classes including race and income. If global climate change will increasingly affect everyone on the planet, should we still try to focus attention on low-income people or communities of color? Can the "World War II-scale" development of renewable energy be squared with environmental justice principles of fair treatment and meaningful community involvement? To save our skins in the warming world, is concern for environmental justice now anachronistic, another luxury that requires letting go?

This chapter will consider that question, ultimately concluding that even in the face of a dramatically changing climate, concerns for environmental justice must continue to guide our actions. It first introduces basic concepts of "environmental justice." The chapter then considers climate change impacts on communities that are *not* traditionally the focus of environmental justice concerns. Next, it investigates the disproportionate impacts of climate change on the unique communities impacted by the 2022 wildfires in northern New Mexico. The chapter concludes by recognizing the need to consider the impacts of climate change on all communities, including those communities that are traditionally the focus of environmental justice concerns.

Environmental Justice Defintions

Recognition of the disproportionate impacts of environmental pollution on communities of color gave rise to a movement for "environmental justice"

24. *Id.* at 200-01.
25. *Id.* at 244.
26. *Id.* at 276.
27. *Id.*

that took hold more than 30 years ago[28] and remains stronger than ever today.[29] Environmental justice remains famously subject to varied understandings and definitions.[30] Early conceptions focused on race, giving rise to charges of "environmental racism."[31] In 1994, President Clinton's Executive Order No. 12898 explicitly extended environmental justice to protection of low-income and Indigenous peoples.[32] In 2023, President Biden's Executive Order No. 14096 expanded the definition of environmental justice to encompass "disability" plus consideration of other factors including "climate change," "cumulative impacts," "the legacy of racism," as well as "cultural and subsistence practices."[33]

Modern definitions point to systemic roots of environmental inequity[34] or encourage examination of the various factors that may make certain groups more vulnerable than other groups to adverse environmental impacts.[35] Modern definitions may also emphasize more equitable distribution of not just environmental burdens but also of environmental benefits.[36] Some scholars suggest that environmental justice will always elude settled definitions,[37] while other scholars, including environmental justice pioneer Charles Lee,

---

28. *See* Clifford J. Villa, *Remaking Environmental Justice*, 66 Loy. L. Rev. 469, 481-89 (2020).
29. *See* Clifford J. Villa, *No "Box to Be Checked": Environmental Justice in Modern Legal Practice*, 30 N.Y.U. Envtl. L.J. 157, 159 (2022) (observing "the renewed emphasis on environmental justice across the states, in Congress, and now atop the agenda for the Biden administration . . . .").
30. *See* Robert R. Kuehn, *A Taxonomy of Environmental Justice*, 30 Envtl. L. Rep. 10681, 10681 (Sept. 2000) (acknowledging that "'[e]nvironmental justice' means many things to many people").
31. *See* Richard J. Lazarus, *"Environmental Racism! That's What It Is,"* 2000 U. Ill. L. Rev. 255.
32. Exec. Order No. 12898, 59 Fed. Reg. 7629 (Feb. 16, 1994) (applying order to "minority populations and low-income populations" as well as "Native American programs").
33. Exec. Order No. 14096, 88 Fed. Reg. 25251 (Apr. 26, 2023).
34. *See, e.g.*, G. Bolte et al., *Environmental Justice: Social Disparities in Environmental Exposures and Health: Overview*, *in* Encyclopedia of Environmental Health 459, 461 (J.O. Nriagu ed., 2011):

    > Environmental justice, environmental equity, and environmental racism are different phrases that describe and explain central features of the environmental justice movement, focusing on the disparate impact of hazardous waste sites and other polluting facilities located in or near distressed neighborhoods with high concentrations of ethnic minorities and economically disadvantaged populations.

35. *See, e.g.*, Villa, *supra* note 28, at 518 (defining "environmental justice" to require consideration of "race, color, ethnicity, national origin, income, age, gender, sexual orientation, health condition, or any other potential factor of vulnerability").
36. *See* Charles Lee, *Evaluating EPA's Definition of Environmental Justice*, 14 Envtl. Just. 332, 336 (2021) (defining "environmental justice" as striving to "ensure the equitable and just distribution of resources and benefits in a manner that prioritizes communities experiencing the greatest inequities, disproportionate impacts, and unmet needs").
37. *See, e.g.*, Rachael E. Salcido, *Retooling Environmental Justice*, 39 UCLA J. Envtl. L. & Pol'y 1, 7 (2021) ("The definition of environmental justice will remain incomplete because it is fundamentally an ongoing movement."); David Schlosberg, *Reconceiving Environmental Justice: Global Movements and Political Theories*, 13 Envtl. Pol. 517, 534-35 (2004) ("An environmental justice movement can be unified, but it cannot be uniform. An insistence on uniformity will limit the diversity of stories of injustice, the multiple forms it takes, and the variety of solutions it calls for.").

maintain that the definition of environmental justice "can have important implications for environmental justice practice and is not a trivial matter."[38]

For purposes of environmental justice practice, the U.S. Environmental Protection Agency (EPA) has maintained a definition of environmental justice for more than twenty years that focuses on achieving "fair treatment" and "meaningful involvement." Specifically, EPA defines environmental justice to mean "the fair treatment and meaningful involvement of all people regardless of race, color, national origin, or income with respect to the development, implementation and enforcement of environmental laws, regulations and policies."[39] As Lee observes: "EPA's definition of environmental justice is perhaps the singularly most cited in existence today."[40] More than just cited, EPA's framework of "fair treatment" and "meaningful involvement" has been adopted and codified widely across the states. California and New York, for example, embrace "fair treatment" and "meaningful involvement" explicitly in state legislation,[41] while New Mexico and Washington adopt EPA's definition of environmental justice essentially verbatim in state law and policy, respectively.[42]

"Fair treatment" implies a substantive dimension to environmental justice, what Robert Kuehn refers to as "distributive justice,"[43] considering the distribution of environmental impacts or benefits across given subpopulations. "Meaningful involvement" reflects Kuehn's "procedural justice,"[44] recogniz-

38. Lee, *supra* note 35, at 337. *See also* Julie Sze & Jonathan K. London, *Environmental Justice at a Crossroads*, Socio. Compass 1331, 1347 (2008) ("These are no mere semantic or linguistic questions.").
39. *Environmental Justice*, U.S. EPA, https://www.epa.gov/environmentaljustice (Jan. 10, 2023).
40. Lee, *supra* note 35, at 332.
41. California passed its first piece of environmental justice legislation in 1999, which among other things required the California Environmental Protection Agency to conduct its programs "in a manner that ensures the fair treatment of people of all races, cultures, and income levels . . . " Cal. Pub. Res. Code §71110 (1999). In 2019, California amended its statutory definition of environmental justice to include "meaningful involvement." A.B. 1628, §3, 2019-2020 Reg. Leg. Sess. (Cal. 2019), *amending* Cal. Gov't Code §65040.12(e)(2) (2020):

> For purposes of this section, "environmental justice" means the fair treatment and meaningful involvement of people of all races, cultures, incomes, and national origins, with the respect to the development, adoption, implementation, and enforcement of environmental laws, regulations, and policies.

In New York, the state passed legislation in 2019 that among other things, established a statewide policy "that all people, regardless of race, color, religion, national origin or income, have a right to fair treatment and meaningful involvement in the development, implementation and enforcement of laws, regulations and policies that affect the quality of the environment." N.Y. Envtl. Conserv. Law §48-0101 (McKinney 2020).

42. Washington Healthy Environment for All Act, 2021 Wash. Sess. Laws ch. 314, §2(8) (defining "environmental justice"). In New Mexico, there remains no statutory definition of "environmental justice," but the website of the New Mexico Environment Department embraces EPA's definition of environmental justice verbatim. *See Equity*, N.M. Envtl. Dep't, https://www.env.nm.gov/general/environmental-justice-in-new-mexico (last visited July 15, 2022).
43. Kuehn, *supra* note 30, at 10681.
44. *Id.*

ing that community members must have real opportunities to participate in environmental decisions that affect them. With fair treatment and meaningful involvement forming twin pillars of environmental justice, as commonly conceived, the question remains: fair treatment and meaningful involvement *for whom?* This question will be explored in the sections that follow.

Environmental Justice—For All?

Beyond "fair treatment" and "meaningful involvement," EPA's definition of environmental justice applies expressly to "all people."[45] While environmental protection for all people may be a laudable goal, the "all people" definition of environmental justice drew condemnation from environmental justice advocates, as well as from EPA's Inspector General when it was crafted by EPA during the Bush/Cheney Administration.[46] The "all people" definition reflected a deliberate program of "de-emphasizing minority and low-income populations,"[47] rejecting a conception of environmental justice as a program of affirmative action with racial preferences.[48] Nevertheless, despite the initial condemnation it provoked, the "all people" definition of environmental justice remains firmly in place today.

Perhaps unwittingly, "all people" opened the door to an inclusive conception of environmental justice as a program intended to protect all people—*all of them*—including children, the elderly, the homeless, the undocumented, and members of the LGBTQ community.[49] At the same time, "all people" also allows claims to environmental justice from communities and individuals far removed from the original aims of the environmental justice movement. This may be particularly true when applying the environmental justice lens to the impacts of climate change.

Global climate change affects everyone, but it does not affect everyone equally, leading scholars and activists to raise concerns for "climate justice." According to one simple conception, "[c]limate justice can be defined generally as addressing the disproportionate burden of climate change impacts on

45. *Environmental Justice*, *supra* note 38.
46. *See generally* Villa, *supra* note 28, at 496-98.
47. U.S. EPA, Off. of the Inspector Gen., EPA Needs to Consistently Implement the Intent of the Executive Order on Environmental Justice 10 (2004) (Report No. 2004-P-00007) (citing Memorandum from Christine Todd Whitman, Administrator, U.S. EPA, to Assistant Administrators et al., "EPA's Commitment to Environmental Justice" (Aug. 9, 2001)).
48. Villa, *supra* note 28, at 496.
49. For one groundbreaking inquiry into environmental justice for transgender people, see Zacary E. Wilson-Fetrow, *Meaningless Involvement: How Traditional Modes of Involvement Exclude Transgender People From Environmental Justice*, 48 Ecology L.Q. 843 (2021).

poor and marginalized communities."[50] While this conception of climate justice appears to agree with original notions of environmental justice, the "all people" definition of environmental justice could apply equally to the disproportionate impacts of climate change on the "poor and marginalized"—or on the rich and powerful—or on any group in between. In fact, claims of disproportionate burdens from climate change may be asserted by many groups not traditionally associated with environmental justice. Such claims may appear in a variety of contexts, as indicated below.

Hurricanes

In 2005, Hurricane Katrina provided one early and jolting vision of life in our warming world. The hurricane winds, levee failures, and anemic Federal Emergency Management Agency (FEMA) response to Hurricane Katrina resulted in infamously disproportionate impacts among the black population of New Orleans.[51] Systemic race discrimination placed black people in harm's way and frustrated recovery efforts. But in terms of disproportionately affected groups, "people 75 years old and older were the most affected population cohort."[52] Researchers studying the mortalities after Hurricane Katrina suggest that older people were least likely to leave their homes and most likely to have impaired ability to avoid floodwaters.[53]

In 2017, Hurricane Maria struck a devastating blow to Puerto Rico, destroying infrastructure already weakened by years of poverty and neglect, and causing untold suffering across the island.[54] While official estimates of the death toll from Hurricane Maria suggested that only 64 lives were lost,

50. Rachel Jean-Baptiste et al., *Recent Developments in Climate Justice*, 47 ENVTL. L. REP. 11005, 11005 (Dec. 2017). For a more vigorous description of climate justice concerns, see the IPCC, CLIMATE CHANGE 2014: IMPACTS, ADAPTATION, AND VULNERABILITY, SUMMARY FOR POLICYMAKERS 6 (2014):

> People who are socially, economically, culturally, politically, institutionally, or otherwise marginalized are especially vulnerable to change change and also to some adaptation and mitigation responses (*medium evidence, high agreement*). This heightened vulnerability . . . is the product of intersecting social processes. . . . Such processes include, for example, discrimination on the basis of gender, class, ethnicity, age, and (dis)ability.

51. For an inside view of the disproportionate impacts of Hurricane Katrina, from pioneers of the environmental justice movement, see ROBERT D. BULLARD & BEVERLY WRIGHT, THE WRONG COMPLEXION FOR PROTECTION 74-78 (2012) (describing "the lethargic and inept emergency response after Hurricane Katrina [as] a disaster that overshadowed the deadly storm itself.").
52. Joan Brunkard et al., *Hurricane Katrina Deaths, Louisiana, 2005*, 2 DISASTER MED. & PUB. HEALTH PREPAREDNESS 215, 215 (2008). *See also* Myles Maltz, *Caught in the Eye of the Storm: The Disproportionate Impact of Natural Disasters on the Elderly Population in the United States*, 27 ELDER L.J. 157, 157 (2019) (noting that "elderly individuals over the age of sixty represent[ed] 71% of the fatalities in Hurricane Katrina . . . ").
53. Brunkard et al., *supra* note 51, at 219-20.
54. *See, e.g.*, Daniel Farber, *Response and Recovery After Maria: Lessons for Disaster Law and Policy*, 87 REV. JUR. U.P.R. 743, 753-54 (2018).

later studies placed the loss of life at well over 1,000 victims.[55] It may be that most victims of Hurricane Maria were Puerto Ricans, classified as a "minority" population under federal regulations,[56] and thereby indicating that Hurricane Maria had disproportionate impacts on a minority population.[57] Puerto Ricans, however, are hardly a minority in Puerto Rico, making this conclusion based on race or ethnicity less useful than inquiries into *why* some Puerto Ricans lived and others died. Of "excess deaths" attributed to Hurricane Maria, studies indicated that two of the strongest indicators for mortality were diabetes and heart disease.[58] Knowing these indicators of mortality as evidenced by Hurricanes Katrina and Maria, should environmental justice now encompass concerns for age as well as all manner of life-threatening preexisting conditions, including diabetes and heart disease?

Floods

Flooding, both inland and coastal, is another concern with our warming world. In August 2017, for example, the flooding associated with Hurricane Harvey was unprecedented. The hurricane stalled into a tropical storm and lingered for days, eventually dropping some 24.5 *trillion* gallons of water over Houston and southeast Texas.[59] It was a record for any single storm event in the United States, with over 203,000 homes damaged or destroyed.[60] And yet, within one year of the storm, 92% of flood victims were able to return to their homes. As commentators observed: "Resource-rich communities

---

55. Nishant Kishore et al., *Mortality in Puerto Rico After Hurricane Maria*, 379 N. Eng. J. Med. 162, 162 (2018) (estimating 4,645 "excess deaths"); Raul Cruz-Cano & Erin L. Mead, *Causes of Excess Deaths in Puerto Rico After Hurricane Maria: A Time-Series Estimation*, 109 Am. J. Pub. Health 1050, 1052 (2019) (estimating 1,205 excess deaths).
56. *See, e.g.*, 24 C.F.R. §81.2 (2021) (defining "Minority" to include "a person of Cuban, Mexican, Puerto Rican, South or Central American, or other Spanish culture or origin, regardless of race").
57. Puerto Ricans, of course, *are* a minority population in the continental United States, and that minority status may have contributed to troubling indications of discriminatory treatment by the U.S. government. *See, e.g.*, Charley E. Willison et al., *Quantifying Inequities in U.S. Federal Response to Hurricane Disaster in Texas and Florida Compared With Puerto Rico*, 4 BMJ Global Health 1 (2019) (concluding that "the federal response was faster and more generous across measures of money and staffing to Hurricanes Harvey and Irma in Texas and Florida, compared with Hurricane Maria in Puerto Rico"); Danny Vinik, *How Trump Favored Texas Over Puerto Rico*, Politico (Mar. 27, 2018) (observing, among other things, that "[n]ine days after Harvey, the federal government had 30,000 personnel in the Houston area, compared with 10,000 at the same point after Maria").
58. *See* Cruz-Cano & Mead, *supra* note 54.
59. Andrea Giampetro-Meyer & Nancy Kubasek, *Harvey: Environmental Justice and Law*, 31 Fordham Envtl. L. Rev. 37, 40 (2020).
60. *See* Blake Hudson, *Land Development: A Super-Wicked Environmental Problem*, 41 Ariz. St. L.J. 1123, 1123 (2019).

returned to normal relatively quickly, while communities of color and low-income communities were still a mess one year later."[61]

Hurricane Harvey had, in fact, inundated vast expanses of the Houston metropolitan area, with floodwaters at one point covering 70% of Harris County.[62] Both rich and poor neighborhoods were affected. By some measures, limited studies have indicated that floods have disproportionate impacts *on the rich*. As one study of flooding around Miami and Houston concludes: "We find that areas burdened by high magnitude/low frequency/sudden onset/low divisibility hazards, such as neighborhoods in 100 year flood zones, are likely to house more affluent residents who desire the benefits associated with the risks."[63] The benefits these affluent residents may seek include "beach access and open water views."[64] If such affluent residents, with their beachfront properties, really do experience disproportionate impacts from flooding, should they too be able to claim protection under the banner of environmental justice?

Extreme Heat

In late June 2021, an unprecedented heat wave swept across the Pacific Northwest, with all-time high temperatures recorded in British Columbia, Oregon, and Washington. According to one preliminary report, excessive heat—including a temperature of 116°F on June 28—was directly responsible for 54 deaths in the Portland metro area.[65] Of these deaths, 18.5% were people ages 60 or older.[66] According to the report:

> Lack of air conditioning was a key driver in mortality. Whereas about 80 percent of people in the Portland area have some level of air conditioning in their homes . . . none of those who died had central air, and only eight people had a portable air conditioning unit in their home.[67]

Significantly, and defying traditional notions about environmental justice and climate justice, the preliminary report found that recorded deaths from

61. Giampetro-Meyer & Kubasek, *supra* note 58, at 39.
62. Hudson, *supra* note 59, at 1124.
63. Sara Grineski et al., *Hazardous Air Pollutants and Flooding: A Comparative Interurban Study of Environmental Justice*, 80 GeoJournal 145, 155 (2015).
64. *Id.*
65. Multnomah Cnty., Preliminary Review on Excessive Heat Deaths 7 (June 2021), https://www.multco.us/file/100354/download.
66. *Id.*
67. *Id.* at 9.

the extreme heat in Portland were 92% white and 63% male.[68] So, should environmental justice now include protection for older white men?

Wildfires

As indicated in the Introduction, the IPCC has long recognized that one consequence of climate change will be "increasingly extensive" losses from wildfire.[69] As predicted by the IPCC, wildfires in recent years have indeed been increasing in frequency and magnitude.[70] And, as with other impacts from climate change, there may be disproportionate impacts from increasing wildfires that are surprising.

In fall 2017 (the same year as Hurricane Harvey and Hurricane Maria), northern California experienced the worst wildfire season in state history to date. The Tubbs Fire leveled city blocks in Santa Rosa, ravaged wine country in Napa and Sonoma Counties, and resulted in at least 40 deaths.[71] The Tubbs Fire, however, was soon eclipsed the next fall by the Camp Fire, which roared through the town of Paradise, California, and surrounding areas, destroying 18,800 structures and killing 85 people.[72] Of those who died in the Camp Fire, only six were under the age of 50.[73] The Camp Fire accordingly had an overwhelmingly disproportionate impact on older people, most of whom were white.[74]

68. *Id.* at 7.
69. IPCC, *supra* note 11, at 88 and accompanying text.
70. For one excellent introduction to wildfire management, see Karen M. Bradshaw, *A Modern Overview of Wildfire Law*, 21 Fordham Envtl. L. Rev. 445 (2010).
71. *Remembering the Victims of the North Bay Fires*, Press Democrat, Dec. 27, 2017, https://www.pressdemocrat.com/article/news/remembering-the-victims-of-the-north-bay-fires/.
72. MacKenzie Thurman, *Fighting Fire with Fire-Hardened Homes: The Role of Electric Utilities in Residential Wildfire Mitigation*, 122 Colum. L. Rev. 1055, 1059 (2022). For a truly gripping account of the Camp Fire, based upon interviews with dozens of survivors, responders, and scientists, see Alister Gee & Dani Anguino, *Last Day in Paradise: The Untold Story of How a Fire Swallowed a Town*, Guardian, Dec. 20, 2018), https://www.theguardian.com/environment/2018/dec/20/last-day-in-paradise-california-deadliest-fire-untold-story-survivors.
73. Katherine Skiba, *One Year Ago: California's Deadliest Wildfire Ravaged Town of Paradise*, AARP (Oct. 15, 2019), https://www.aarp.org/politics-society/history/info-2019/paradise-camp-fire-anniversary.html.
74. *See generally* Laura Newberry et al., *Many Victims of California's Worst Wildfire were Elderly and Died In or Near Their Homes, New Data Show*, L.A. Times, Dec. 13, 2018), https://www.latimes.com/local/lanow/la-me-ln-paradise-fire-dead-map-20181213-story.html. *See also QuickFacts: Butte County, California*, U.S. Census Bureau, https://www.census.gov/quickfacts/fact/table/buttecountycalifornia/BPS030221. For demographic data before the Camp Fire, indicating a county population that was 82.2% "white alone," see California Dep't of Housing & Cmty. Dev., State of California Proposed Action Plan for Disaster Recovery 46, fig. 35 (June 2020), https://www.hcd.ca.gov/community-development/disaster-recovery-programs/cdbg-dr/cdbg-dr-2018/docs/draft_2019_state_cdbg_disaster_recovery_action_plan_for_2018_disasters_english.pdf.

The impacts observed from the Camp Fire appear consistent with impacts of other wildfires across the western United States. Several studies have attempted to identify population segments most at risk from wildfires. One study, published in 2016, assessed wildfire hazards across the continental United States and concluded that areas with "high wildfire potential [are] associated with the lowest average social vulnerability scores," as measured by factors including ethnicity (Hispanic), race (Black), education (English as a second language), poverty, and age (people under 5 years or 65 and older).[75] In a more recent study published in 2022, researchers examined wildfire hazards associated with 16.7 million single-family residences across eleven states of the western United States.[76] The research method considered both modeled wildfire hazards, as well as actual proximity to large wildfires (defined as fires encompassing 1,000 acres or more) between 2011-2018 (including both the Tubbs Fire and the Camp Fire). The study found that areas with "[h]igh fire hazard . . . have higher per capita income, a lower percentage of residents below the poverty line, a higher percentage of white residents, and a lower perentage of black and Hispanic residents."[77]

In light of these findings, the 2022 study observed that "[a]s in high amenity yet high hazard coastal areas, it is likely that spatially correlated wildland amenities (e.g., tree cover, views, and access to recreational opportunities) make properties in high wildfire hazard areas desirable for higher income households."[78] In short, many rich people like to live and play in the mountains. While this conclusion may not come as a surprise to many outdoorsy readers of this chapter, it does challenge conventional assumptions of environmental justice and climate justice that locate disproportionate impacts of climate change on low-income individuals and communities of color. So, environmental justice now includes people who drive Range Rovers and own second homes in Colorado?

At first glance, impacts of the 2022 Hermits Peak/Calf Canyon Fire in the mountains of northern New Mexico might appear consistent with some of the findings above. The wildfires did indeed damage or threaten second homes and vacation properties. After the presidential disaster declaration on May 4,

75. Gabriel Wigtil et al., *Places Where Wildfire Potential and Social Vulnerability Coincide in the Coterminous United States*, 25 INT'L J. WILDLAND FIRE 896, 901-02 (2016). For an introduction to social vulnerability theory and the pioneering work of geographer Susan Cutter, see Robert R.M. Verchick, *Disaster Justice: The Geography of Human Capability*, 23 DUKE ENVTL. L. & POL'Y F. 23, 47-48 (2012).

76. Matthew Wibbenmeyer & Molly Robertson, *The Distributional Incidence of Wildfire Hazard in the Western United States*, 17 ENV'T RES. 1 (May 26, 2022). The western states consisted of Arizona, California, Colorado, Idaho, Montana, Nevada, New Mexico, Oregon, Utah, Washington, and Wyoming.

77. *Id.* at 4.

78. *Id.* at 6.

2022, fire victims were invited to apply for federal assistance from FEMA.[79] Two months later, however, 29% of applications had been denied by FEMA, for reasons that commonly included lack of proof that the damaged home was an applicant's "primary residence."[80] There were many other reasons, of course, that FEMA may have denied these applications for assistance.[81] At the same time, the Hermits Peak/Calf Canyon Fire also demonstrates reasons why we still need a framework of environmental justice to address the coming challenges of the 4°C world, as the next section will explore.

Environmental Injustice and Northern New Mexico Wildfires

Scholars have recognized this conundrum: the more inclusive the movement for environmental justice, the more it risks dilution and disorientation.[82] One answer to this dilemma may be to take a closer look at the particular circumstances of each affected community, to include its intersecting characteristics,[83] as well as its vulnerability and resilience.[84]

In the communities impacted by the Hermits Peak/Calf Canyon Fire in northern New Mexico, people lost more than second homes. Many victims lost primary residences and much more, including family homes that had been passed down for generations and working ranches tracing back to the original Hispano settlers. While the studies noted above suggest that

79. *See* U.S. EPA, *New Mexico Wildfires and Straight-line Winds* (Mar. 18, 2023), https://www.fema.gov/disaster/4652.

80. Patrick Lohmann, *FEMA Reverses Course on "Safe-to-Occupy" Home After Pressure. But What About Everyone Else?*, Source N.M. (July 7, 2022, 4:00 AM), https://sourcenm.com/2022/07/07/fema-reverses-course-on-safe-to-occupy-home-after-pressure-but-what-about-everyone-else.

81. *See* Patrick Lohmann, *30% of New Mexicans Seeking FEMA Help Got Denial Letters, But They Can Still Get Aid*, Source N.M. (June 14, 2022, 5:00 AM), https://sourcenm.com/2022/06/14/30-of-new-mexicans-seeking-fema-help-got-denial-letters-but-they-can-still-get-aid (identifying reasons including insurance coverage and lack of proof of home damage).

82. *See, e.g.*, Sze & London, *supra* note 37, at 1347 ("But, if environmental justice can mean almost anything, does it risk a dilution and even loss of meaning and purpose?").

83. *See generally* Stacia S. Ryder, *A Bridge to Challenging Environmental Inequality: Intersectionality, Environmental Justice, and Disaster Vulnerability*, 34 Soc. Thought & Res. 85, 86 (2017):

> Intersectionality theorizes that based on various identity characteristics, individuals may be oppressed and differentially impacted by a combination of interconnected societal structures . . . . By utilizing an intersectional framework to merge disaster vulnerability and environmental justice, we can treat these factors as they exist, enmeshed, in this case, in the context of environmental inequality and oppression. (Internal citations omitted.)

84. "Resilience" may be defined generally as "the capacity of systems to rebound from a disturbance and reestablish equilibrium." Laurie Ristino, *Surviving Climate Change in America: Toward a Rural Resilience Framework*, 41 W. New Eng. L. Rev. 521, 522 (2019). It is also often described informally as the capacity to "bounce back" from adverse events. *See, e.g.*, Mary Ellen Ternes, *Personal Resilience*, 36 Nat. Resources & Env't 3 (2022) (opining that "[a]s environmental lawyers, we think of resilience as the ability to bounce back"); Sarah E. Jenkins, *What Happens Next: Metaphor in Disaster Recovery Policy*, 2015 B.Y.U. L. Rev. 151, 167 (2015) (observing that "[c]ontemporary discussions of disaster resilience" refashion the definition "as an ability to 'bounce back'").

wildfires and floods may disproportionately impact affluent individuals and white people, the northern New Mexico fires of 2022 urge reexamination of this theory, revealing important qualifications and exceptions. For example, while studies have indicated that coastal areas prone to flooding are primarily populated by affluent, non-Hispanic whites, other studies have found that *inland* flood zones may be over-represented by racial and ethnic minorities.[85] Concerning wildfires, while high-hazard areas in the western United States may host disproportionate numbers of affluent, non-Hipanic whites, the same studies, observed closely, also reveal that the *highest* fire hazard areas may be associated with the lowest property values, occupied by disproportionate numbers of poor people, older residents, and Native Americans.[86]

The northern New Mexico fires illustrate these important observations. Far from affluent, counties of northern New Mexico that were devastated by the 2022 fires represented "the last refuge of the rural poor."[87] In fact, according to the U.S. Census Bureau, Mora County is one of the poorest counties in one of the poorest states in the United States.[88] It is also one of the most ethnically diverse, with an Hispanic population of 81%, and over 60% of households speaking a language other than English.[89] Given these intersecting characteristics, the 2022 northern New Mexico wildfires created unique concerns, demonstrating the disproportionate impacts of climate change on low-income individuals and communities of color. This section will evaluate three of these concerns.

Heirs Property

Heirs property is inherited land that lacks legal documentation, such as a deed or title, that establishes clear ownership.[90] Heirs property is common

85. Marilyn C. Montgomery & Jayajit Chakraborty, *Assessing the Environmental Justice Consequences of Flood Risk: A Case Study in Miami, Florida*, 10 Envtl. Resource Letters 1, 9 (2015).
86. Wibbenmeyer & Robertson, *supra* note 75, at 4. *See also* Wigtil et al., *supra* note 74, at 904 ("Nine per cent of housing units in high-wildfire-potential areas also had high social vulnerability"). For examples of disproportionate impacts of wildfires on Indigenous peoples, see Ariel Iannone Román, *West Coast Fires Disproportionately Affect Indigenous Communities*, Cultural Survival (Sept. 23, 2020), https://www.culturalsurvival.org/news/west-coast-fires-disproportionately-affect-indigenous-communities ("In California, the Slater fire has burned down the homes of Karuk Tribal members and Tribal staff and the Red Salmon complex fire is burning an area that is sacred to the Karuk Peoples.").
87. Garcia, *supra* note 7.
88. *QuickFacts: Mora County, New Mexico*, U.S. Census Bureau, https://www.census.gov/quickfacts/fact/table/moracountynewmexico/P.
89. *Id.*
90. Scott Pippen, Shana Jones, & Cassandra Johnson Gaither, U.S. Forest Serv., Identifying Potential Heirs Properties in the Southeastern United States: A New GIS Methodology Utilizing Mass Appraisal Data vii (2017) [hereinafter Identifying Properties].

among rural black landowners in the South,[91] low-income neighborhoods with high concentrations of Latino and black homeowners,[92] Native tribal lands,[93] *colonias* along the U.S.-Mexico border,[94] and rural white Appalachian communities.[95] While heirs property may result from many circumstances, at least one of them is racial discrimination: in the Deep South, heirs property often reflects the Jim Crow era, when black people were excluded from protections of the legal system.[96]

Lack of clear title in an heirs property may impair the ability of disaster victims to obtain federal financial assistance after a disaster declaration.[97] In 2017, for example, the problem of heirs property impeded homeowner efforts to obtain disaster assistance following Hurricane Maria.[98] Recognizing this problem after Hurricane Maria, FEMA began to accept other forms of proof of ownership for purposes of disaster assistance in Puerto Rico.[99] Addressing heirs property on a national level, FEMA, under the Biden Administration, formally changed its policy in 2021, allowing disaster survivors to use alternate forms of documentation to establish home ownership.[100] This welcome change in FEMA policy reflects recognition of the disproportionate impacts of climate change on poor people and communities of color. It also demonstrates how progress towards fair treatment of these communities may be made when disproportionate impacts are both recognized and directly addressed.

---

91. Michelle Chen, *Black Lands Matter: The Movement to Transform Heirs' Property Laws*, NATION (Sept. 25, 2019), https://www.thenation.com/article/archive/heirs-property-reform.
92. Heather K. Way & Ruthie Goldstein, *Heir Property Owners and Federal Disaster Aid Programs: Opportunities for a More Equitable Recovery When Disaster Strikes*, 30 J. AFFORDABLE HOUSING & CMTY. DEV. L. 343, 469 (2022).
93. Jessica A. Shoemaker, *Like Snow in the Spring Time: Allotment, Fractionation, and Indian Land*, 2003 WIS. L. REV. 729 (2003).
94. *See* Heather K. Way, *Informal Homeownership in the United States and the Law*, 20 ST. LOUIS U. PUB. L. REV. 113 (2010).
95. Cassandra Johnson Gaither, *"Have Not Our Weary Feet Come to the Place for Which Our Fathers Sighed:" Heirs' Property in the Southern United States* (2016) (E-GEN. TECH. REP. SRS-216).
96. *"The Real Damage:" Why FEMA Is Denying Disaster Aid to Black Families That Have Lived for Generations in the Deep South*, WASH. POST, July 11, 2021, https://www.washingtonpost.com/nation/2021/07/11/fema-black-owned-property.
97. *Id. See also* RORY FLEMING ET AL., SEA GRANT N.C., SPLITTING HEIRS: THE CHALLENGES POSED BY HEIRS' PROPERTY OWNERSHIP TO COASTAL RESILIENCE PLANNING (2016), https://cdm16062.contentdm.oclc.org/digital/collection/p16062coll9/id/284309.
98. Ivis Garcia, *The Lack of Proof of Ownership in Puerto Rico Is Crippling Repairs in the Aftermath of Hurricane Maria*, 44 A.B.A. HUM. RTS. 20 (2021).
99. Clifford J. Villa, *Es FEMA El Problema? Hurricane Maria and the Slow Road to Recovery in Puerto Rico*, LEGAL PLANET (May 17, 2018), https://legal-planet.org/2018/05/17/guest-blogger-cliff-villa-es-fema-el-problema-hurricane-maria-and-the-slow-road-to-recovery-in-puerto-rico/.
100. *DHS Announces Changes to Individual Assistance Policies to Advance Equity for Disaster Survivors*, U.S. DEP'T OF HOMELAND SECURITY (DHS) (Sept. 2, 2021), https://www.dhs.gov/news/2021/09/02/dhs-announces-changes-individual-assistance-policies-advance-equity-disaster.

One challenge remaining with heirs property may be training FEMA employees on the existence and application of the new policy. There also appears to be a significant need to educate the affected public on the new policy. The problem of heirs property was raised directly by the fires in northern New Mexico, where generations of Hispanic families have handed down property without formal titles. In visits to the areas affected by the 2022 fires,[101] the author heard concerns about proper documentation commonly expressly by community members; however, no one appeared to be aware of the change in FEMA policy. As one affected community member simply explained: "We are told [FEMA] might cover damages from the fire if you have the right documentation."[102]

While the "right documentation" may remain a mystery to many community members, community advocates familiar with the change in FEMA's policy on heirs property can help. Despite continuing challenges of implementation, the change in FEMA's policy on heirs property is certainly a step in the right direction. It is also proof that environmental justice can continue to provide a useful framework for addressing challenges in our warming world.

Food Justice

The IPCC has recognized that global food security transitions "from high to very high risk [] between 2°C and 2.7°C."[103] In our 4°C world, as contemplated in the opening of this chapter, we must assume that food security is at some form of extreme risk. In addition to crop failures and other challenges to food production, food supplies may be directly destroyed by climate-related disasters. In the aftermath of Hurricane Katrina, one particularly gruesome component of the ensuing cleanup was the collection and proper disposal of tens of thousands of refrigerators left without electricity and containing food left to rot for weeks in the heat.[104] For many people, the loss of food in one's refrigerator may not mean much, especially considering the amount of food waste Americans produce ordinarily.[105] But for others, especially in low-income communities and communities of color, the loss of fresh

101. Among other direct communications, the author visited the affected areas and spoke with community members on June 25 and July 23, 2022.
102. Garcia, *supra* note 7.
103. IPCC Special Report: Climate Change and Land 19 (2019).
104. *See generally* U.S. EPA, Off. of the Inspector Gen., EPA Provided Quality and Timely Information on Hurricane Katrina Hazardous Material Releases and Debris Management (May 2, 2006) (Rep. No. 2006-P-00023).
105. *See* U.S. EPA, Off. of Res. Conservation & Recovery (2020) (Wasted Food Report, Rep. No. 530-R-20-004).

food may pose a significantly greater burden. For poor people affected by the fires in northern New Mexico, their "assets consist of mobile homes . . . and freezers full of meat from our small herds of cattle or last season's hunt."[106] These community members depend directly on the natural resources around them, including elk harvested in season as well as cattle run on private lands and public grazing allotments.

Unfortunately, current FEMA policy fails to recognize the value of food lost to any community members during disasters.[107] Instead, FEMA encourages people who lose food in disasters to seek assistance from voluntary organizations.[108] Food assistance may also be available from other federal or state agencies, through programs such as the U.S. Department of Agriculture's (USDA's) Supplemental Nutrition Assistance Program (SNAP).[109] For a short time, some victims of the northern New Mexico fires were eligible for assistance from the Disaster Supplemental Nutrition Assistance Program (D-SNAP).[110] Recipients of SNAP or D-SNAP may purchase food at some local stores through use of an Electronic Benefits Transfer (EBT) card.[111] For example, at the Family Dollar in Mora, New Mexico, fire victims could use EBT cards to purchase food including hot dogs and frozen pizza.[112] Nevertheless, the substitution of healthy, natural foods (including wild game) for store-bought, processed foods may pose significant concerns for environmental justice and what has more recently come to be known as food justice.

Like the varying definitions of "environmental justice," food justice is also subject to varying constructions. Food justice "aspires to establish healthy food as a fundamental right"[113] and recognizes a right for "all persons [to obtain] at all times a culturally acceptable, nutritionally adequate diet."[114]

106. Garcia, *supra* note 7.

107. FEMA's policy is explicit: "Food loss is not covered by FEMA's Individual and Households Program (IHP)." *You Asked: What Expenses Can FEMA Reimburse Me For?*, FEMA (May 11, 2022), https://www.fema.gov/fact-sheet/you-asked-what-expenses-can-fema-reimburse-me.

108. *Id.*

109. *Supplemental Nutrition Assistance Program (SNAP)*, USDA, Food & Nutrition Servs., https://www.fns.usda.gov/snap/supplemental-nutrition-assistance-program (last visited July 15, 2022).

110. *See Disaster Supplemental Nutrition Assistance Program Frequently Asked Questions*, N.M. Hum. Servs. Dep't, https://www.hsd.state.nm.us/disaster-food-benefits-available-for-victims-of-new-mexico-wildfires (last visited July 15, 2022).

111. *What Is Electronic Benefits Transfer (EBT)?*, USDA, Food & Nutrition Servs., https://www.fns.usda.gov/snap/ebt (Feb. 2, 2023).

112. *New Mexico Food Retailers Accepting EBT Card*, Helping Ams. Find Help, https://helpingamericansfindhelp.org/new-mexico/new-mexico-food-assistance/new-mexico-food-stamps-stores-near-you (last visited July 16, 2022).

113. Danielle M. Purifoy, *Food Policy Councils: Integrating Food Justice and Environmental Justice*, 24 Duke Envtl. L. & Pol'y F. 275, 379 (2014).

114. Deborah N. Archer & Tamara C. Belinfanti, *We Built It and They Did Not Come: Using New Governance Theory in the Fight for Food Justice in Low-Income Communities of Color*, 15 Seattle J. Soc. Just. 307, 310 (2016).

Related concerns for "food sovereignty" promote "'the right of peoples to healthy and culturally appropriate food . . . and their right to define their own food and agriculture system.'"[115] Whether hot dogs and frozen pizza from the local Family Dollar are "nutritionally adequate" for family sustenance is questionable. But the question of whether such foods are also "culturally appropriate" for a small Hispanic community that has lived off the land for centuries raises deeper concerns for food justice and food sovereignty. In any event, FEMA's complete failure to accord *any* value to a freezer full of meat demonstrates why concern for environmental justice, to include food justice, must remain an essential part of our approach to survival in the warming world. The IPCC has warned that global warming will bring food scarcity. But for supplies of healthy food that communities succeed in producing, policy options must be developed to protect such supplies and to provide compensation for significant losses.

Querencia

Beyond concerns for heirs property and food justice, the fires in northern New Mexico revealed concerns about the impacts to culture and spiritual well-being tied uniquely to the land. In northern New Mexico, people speak of *querencia*,[116] described by Rudolfo Anaya as "love of home, love of place."[117] Northern New Mexico scholar Eric Romero defines *querencia* as "a powerful sense of place" combined with "adherence to principles of land stewardship."[118] *Querencia* can be seen in the care that community members have taken in managing their natural resources for generations—and seen now in their grief as they contemplate the fires "burning down a way of life that's lasted hundreds of years."[119]

115. Allison Condra, *Food Sovereignty in the United States: Supporting Local and Regional Food Systems*, 8 J. Food L. & Pol'y 281, 298 (2012) (quoting 2007 Nyéléni Declaration). Importantly, advocates for food sovereignty distinguish this interest from food security, which operates within "the current corporate and international food regime." *Id.* at 296. EBT cards for use at the local Family Dollar operate within the "corporate and international food regime," potentially providing food security while denying food sovereignty.

116. "We've lived there so long because of our querencia." Romero, *supra* note 1 (quoting local resident Paula Garcia).

117. Rudolfo Anaya, *Querencia, Mi Patria Chica*, *Foreword* to Querencia (Univ. of New Mexico Press 2020). Prior to his passing in 2020, Rudolfo Anaya was recognized as a founder of contemporary Chicano literature, embracing heritage and traditions from both Hispano and Native American cultures in the American Southwest. *See* Simon Romero, *Rudolfo Anaya, a Father of Chicano Literature, Dies at 82*, N.Y. Times, July 5, 2020, https://www.nytimes.com/2020/07/03/books/rudolfo-anaya-dead.html#:~:text=Rudolfo%20Anaya%2C%20a%20writer%20whose,He%20was%2082.

118. Eric Romero, *Southwestern Acequia Systems and Communities: Nuturing a Culture of Place*, 61 Nat. Resources J. 169, 171 (2021).

119. Romero, *supra* note 1 (quoting state historian Rob Martinez).

Up in the mountains of northern New Mexico, this way of life includes raising animals,[120] grazing cattle,[121] collecting firewood,[122] harvesting timber from the forests,[123] and growing food crops using centuries-old irrigation systems. Experiments in economic development have attempted to alleviate chronic poverty while preserving local culture.[124] The value of protecting local culture for promoting community resilience in the face of our changing climate has been recognized within academic literature,[125] by nongovernmental organizations,[126] and by government agencies. For example, in a draft paper released during the Obama Administration, the U.S. Department of Homeland Security (DHS) observed that

> [p]romoting the protection of cultural heritage is necessary because of its intrinsic historic or artistic value and because it provides the fundamental spiritual and psychosocial support and sense of belonging communities need during the disaster recovery phase.[127]

The cultural heritage of northern New Mexico, developed over centuries and shaped by extraordinary hardships including previous fires and foreign invasions,[128] produced communities of profound resilience. Volunteer firefighters from the communities saved family homes and rescued pets.[129] Other

120. *Id.* (quoting local resident Miguel Martinez: "I left behind 25 goats, 50 rabbits, 10 chickens, and two dogs," after he escaped advancing flames with just the clothes on his back).
121. Brulliard, *supra* note 6.
122. Guzman, *supra* note 12 (outlining, Mora native and attorney, Antonia Roybal-Mack's complaint that the U.S. Forest Service has limited the traditional collecting of firewood from the forest, allowing the buildup of fuels that contributed to the fires in 2022).
123. Brulliard, *supra* note 6.
124. *See* Kristina Gray Fisher, *Reclaiming Querencia: The Quest for Culturally Appropriate, Environmentally Sustainable Economic Development in Northern New Mexico*, 48 NAT. RESOURCES J. 479, 505-08 (2008) (discussing Tapetes de Lana, a non-profit organization established in Mora, New Mexico, to promote development of small businesses involved with production of wool from local sheep and alpacas).
125. *See, e.g.*, Sidney Shapiro, *An Ounce of Prevention*, *Preface* to FROM SURVIVING TO THRIVING: EQUITY IN DISASTER PLANNING AND RECOVERY iv-vi (2018) (observing that "social resilience . . . is enhanced by strong social networks . . . and policies that recognize and account for the varied needs and capacities of different communities and populations").
126. As noted by the National Association for the Advancement of Colored Peoples (NAACP): "A key aspect of community resilience is social cohesion. . . . To have a community that works well together in times of crisis, there must be strong relationships, trust, and spirit of cooperation, unity, and mutuality to mitigate the shocks of a disaster." NAACP ENV'T & CLIMATE JUST. PROG., IN THE EYE OF THE STORM: A PEOPLE'S GUIDE TO TRANSFORMING CRISIS & ADVANCING EQUITY IN THE DISASTER CONTINUUM 18 (2018), https://naacp.org/resources/eye-storm-peoples-guide-transforming-crisis-advancing-equity-disaster-continuum.
127. DHS, MITIGATION FRAMEWORK LEADERSHIP GRP., DRAFT INTERAGENCY AGENCY CONCEPT FOR COMMUNITY RESILIENCE AND NATIONAL-LEVEL MEASURES 8-15 (2016), https://www.adaptationclearinghouse.org/resources/fema-noaa-draft-interagency-concept-for-community-resiliencecoindicators-and-national-level-measures.html.
128. *See* Romero, *supra* note 1 (presenting state historian testimony that invading American forces burned Mora, New Mexico, to the ground in 1847 during the Mexican-American War).
129. Antonia Roybal-Mack, Editorial, *Neglected Rural Communities Unprepared for Disaster*, ALBUQUERQUE J., May 24, 2022, https://www.abqjournal.com/2501924/neglected-rural-communities-unprepared-

community members, some who lost everything in the fires, volunteered to work in emergency shelters and food distribution centers.[130] Most remarkably, and in contrast to the most tragic consequences from the devastating fires in northern California, not one life appears to have been lost in the biggest fire ever recorded in New Mexico.[131] In part, that amazing fact may reflect lessons learned by emergency responders from previous disasters.[132] But it is also a testament to the unique culture of *querencia* in northern New Mexico, where communities have existed sustainably for centuries by taking care of the land and each other.

Conclusion

One lesson we may learn from the New Mexico fires of 2022 is the continuing need to consider the particular circumstances of individual communities, including both their vulnerabilities and their resilience. The communities of northern New Mexico affected by the Hermits Peak/Calf Canyon Fire may be poor by many economic measures, but they are also rich in culture, cohesion, and natural resources. As we contemplate the 4°C world, policymakers and emergency responders must comprehend and commit to protecting unique strengths. At the same time, we must also be prepared to provide assistance where and how it is truly needed—perhaps not for *all people*, to include the wealthy owners of beachfront condos, but perhaps for *some people*, to include those who may depend on firewood and full freezers to survive a harsh winter.

As legal scholars have noted, serious efforts to address climate change mitigation and adaptation will require "difficult trade offs" and "letting go" of some of what we consider precious. We may have to let go of some cars and trucks and air travel and old power plants and public lands that are

for-disaster.html.

130. Annette McGivney, *"Nothing To Go Back To": The Way of Life Lost to New Mexico's Historic Fire*, Guardian, May 18, 2022, https://www.theguardian.com/us-news/2022/may/18/new-mexico-wildfire-hermits-peak-calf-canyon (recounting stories of fire victims and volunteers, including Andrew Vigil, who "lost everything in the fire").

131. *See supra* note 3, and accompanying text. Tragically, on July 16, 2022, four emergency responders were killed in a helicopter crash after responding to a new wildfire in northern New Mexico. April Rubin, *Four Killed in New Mexico Helicopter Crash After Responding to Wildfire*, N.Y. Times, July 17, 2022, https://www.nytimes.com/2022/07/17/us/helicopter-crash-new-mexico.html. The following week, in the same area, flash flooding accelerated by the burn scars resulted in the deaths of at least two people. Mike Ives, *Two Dead and 1 Missing After Flash Flooding in New Mexico*, N.Y. Times, July 23, 2022, https://www.nytimes.com/2022/07/22/us/new-mexico-flash-floods.html.

132. Within the emergency response community, an essential doctrine is reflection and collection of "lessons learned" following each major disaster. *See, e.g.*, FEMA, 2017 Hurricane Season After-Action Report (July 12, 2018), https://www.fema.gov/sites/default/files/2020-08/fema_hurricane-season-after-action-report_2017.pdf.

needed for wind and solar development. We may have to let go of endless deliberations before siting decisions. But unless we are to abandon any claim to democracy and ideals of "equal protection," we will still need environmental justice to guide our actions into the future. On this point, there appears no disagreement.

For Professor Gerrard, the pursuit of "World War II-scale mobilization" of renewable energy may encounter impediments posed by "environmental justice concerns."[133] But that is not to say that concerns for environmental justice must be jettisoned. Rather, "we will need to *reform* public participation . . . to keep it from paralyzing clean energy development."[134] How those reforms should take shape will require careful consideration,[135] but may be guided at least in part by the common environmental justice framework of fair treatment and meaningful involvement.

For Ruhl and Craig, as we prepare to adapt to the 4°C world, equity remains a fundamental principle for the redesign process. They stipulate that any successful redesign must maintain "opportunities and support for individuals and communities that otherwise face significant risks of being ignored, overrun, forgotten, left behind, or otherwise further marginalized."[136] In the warming world, marginalized communities may be ignored, as they have been historically, or they may be embraced for their special strengths and identified for assistance when needed. If we do climate change mitigation and adaptation right, we might have a more just society—and a safer one.

Ruhl and Craig observe in conclusion: "We can do better to prepare the nation for the path to 4°C."[137] It will take sacrifices—and it will take all of us. We will need artists, engineers, lawyers, and health professionals,[138] as well as governance on all levels, the private sector, and community organizations. No one person needs to do it all. But we will still need some people to keep an eye on traditional concerns for environmental justice—to include low-income individuals and communities of color—to continue remedying

133. Gerrard, *supra* note 18.
134. *Id.* at 40, 42 (emphasis added).
135. For ideas and actions on permitting reform under the Biden Administration, see FACT SHEET: Biden-Harris Administration Releases Permitting Action Plan to Accelerate and Deliver Infrastructure Projects On Time, On Task, and On Budget, White House (May 11, 2022), https://www.whitehouse.gov/briefing-room/statements-releases/2022/05/11/fact-sheet-biden-harris-administration-releases-permitting-action-plan-to-accelerate-and-deliver-infrastructure-projects-on-time-on-task-and-on-budget.
136. Ruhl & Craig, *supra* note 16, at 202.
137. *Id.* at 282.
138. For an exploration of the roles that health professionals may play in helping to prepare communities for the climate future, see *Building Resilience Against Climate Effects (BRACE) Framework*, Ctrs. for Disease Control & Prevention (Oct. 31, 2022), https://www.cdc.gov/climateandhealth/BRACE.htm.

mistakes of the past and helping us avoid mistakes in our future. Preparing for the 4°C future may require letting go of some old notions and modes of inquiry, but it may also require holding onto culture, history, and lessons from the past.

Avoiding Performative Climate Justice

Katrina Fischer Kuh

Open-eyed assessment of the potential for and on-the-ground realities of high-level warming (significantly beyond 2 degrees Celsius (2°C)) supports the implementation of extraordinary and immediate mitigation and adaptation measures and portends that even with such measures, climate impacts will strain adaptive capacity to the breaking point and beyond, resulting in significant societal dislocation and loss and damage. In the context of adaptation to high-level warming, societies will transition from a steady state punctuated by the need to manage periodic emergencies to a near-constant state of managing extreme conditions. Today's climate impacts and those on the horizon increasingly infuse mitigation and adaptation efforts with urgency, causing policymakers to contemplate or issue formal declarations of a climate emergency and to streamline review processes to aid the rapid deployment of mitigation and adaptation infrastructure and technology. In both contexts—the implementation of extraordinary mitigation measures and adaptation to high-level warming—urgency and need have the potential to create injustice and sideline or overwhelm efforts to reduce existing injustice.[1]

Emergency as the contextual backdrop for law and policymaking—whether experienced, formally declared, or simply perceived and anticipated—can create or exacerbate injustice. High-level warming will produce successive and deepening domestic climate emergencies (resulting in internal

---

Author's note: With many thanks to readers and editors, including Cinnamon Carlarne, Keith Hirokawa, Frederick Mauhs, Gabrielle Mickel, Michele Okoh, and Clifford Villa.

1. As other chapters in this book, including those authored by Cinnamon Carlarne and Keith Hirokawa, Robin Kundis Craig, and Clifford Villa attest, it is challenging to precisely define justice and injustice in the context of climate change. Broadly, "climate justice fundamentally is about paying attention to how climate change impacts people differently, unevenly, and disproportionately, as well as redressing the resultant injustices in fair and equitable ways." Farhana Sultana, *Critical Climate Justice*, 188 GEOGR. J. 118 (2022). Climate change, standing alone, is a profound injustice. Indigenous peoples are being subjected to the unintended, but catastrophic consequences of a colonial system of extraction and capitalism that has already deeply harmed them. In thinking about justice and high-level warming, this chapter uses the term "justice" broadly with particular concern for how high-level warming and our responses to it may exacerbate existing injustice—produced by colonization; racial, gender, and other forms of discrimination; and economic inequality—and/or complicate efforts to remedy it.

displacement, food insecurity, and political instability), triggering scarcity and struggle that could sap the motivation and capacity to attend to justice. The best intentions—for example, to manage internal migration to support successful relocation by low-income communities, avoid climate gentrification, and prevent receiving locations from adopting discriminatory policies, tricky tasks in the best of times—may yield to the urgency of other, more pressing adaptation needs. Justice may be treated, as described aptly by Clifford Villa in "Environmental Justice Beyond 2°C," as a "luxury that requires letting go."

At least for now, exhortations to climate justice abound. We are in a moment of intense climate policymaking and justice is often central in these discussions and the laws and policies they produce.[2] But today's concern for justice and the adoption of justice provisions may not be sufficient. The key question is whether the commitment to justice today, and the provisions to protect justice that are adopted to advance that commitment, can and will endure as the pressures of high-level warming intensify. Without staying power, justice measures in climate policy may prove to be performative gestures that make us feel better today but do little to substantively advance justice tomorrow—and in particular under high-level warming.

Incorporating precommitments to rough justice into mitigation and adaptation law, triggered and enforceable through automatic processes and made in the relative cool of now as opposed to the heat of later, could help to make a present-day commitment to climate justice more enduring (stickier). Key aspects of a precommitment might include that it should be: (1) sticky (not easily reversed—set out in statute as opposed to an executive order, for example); (2) automatic (trigger a clear and measurable outcome or duty that is not dependent on the exercise of discretion); and (3) early (the commitment should be made prior to the circumstance(s) in which it would be implemented). Such "precommitment strategies"[3] are unlikely to achieve fully just outcomes and should be accompanied by myriad other mechanisms for advancing justice, but they could help to prevent least just outcomes.

---

2. *E.g.*, Alexandria E. Dolezal, *Power to the People: Distributing the Benefits of A Clean Energy Transition Through Equitable Policy, Legislation, and Energy Justice Initiatives*, 106 Minn. L. Rev. 2441 (2022).
3. Richard Lazarus uses the term precommitment strategies to describe asymmetric institutional design features that he recommends incorporating into federal climate change legislation to prevent the repeal or weakening of mitigation commitments. Richard J. Lazarus, *Super Wicked Problems and Climate Change: Restraining the Present to Liberate the Future*, 40 Envtl. L. Rep. 10749 (Aug. 2010). This chapter explores the basic concept of a precommitment strategy—making policy commitments harder to overlook or undo in the future—in the context of climate change justice, including at the subnational level.

The precommitment strategy discussed herein seeks to maximize the effectiveness of efforts to advance justice in climate change policy, while also acknowledging that they are incremental and, standing alone, likely insufficient. Climate change law, the focus here, is an area of rapid and significant lawmaking where the nexus to climate change is obvious and there are serious efforts being made to respect and advance climate justice in new laws. Ultimately, however, the prerogative to gird our laws and policies for the uphill climb for justice under high-level warming extends far more broadly and will need to incorporate broader social policy, such as entitlement reform.[4] Another approach to limit injustice in the turmoil to come is to strive to enter it with the least amount of carry-over injustice, or injustice that we produced and tolerated even in times of relative stability and relative plenty by focusing on achieving what Robin Kundis Craig refers to in "Survival Equity and Climate Change Triage: How to Decide Who Lives and Who Dies" as "day-to-day" equity. This suggests the promise of approaching climate change through a social justice lens in the style of the Green New Deal and also the need for more radical social and legal reforms. The justice provisions embodied in climate change policy and examined in this chapter are incremental in that they attempt to advance justice within traditional legal and policy frameworks. It may be that much stronger medicine is needed to meaningfully advance justice, particularly in the context of high-level warming, and that these incremental approaches have an opportunity cost in that they "forestall[ ]. . . serious consideration" of necessary but deeper change.[5] However, if the justice aspects of current climate policy—incremental though they be—are *also* ineffective, that would compound the harm.

This chapter first sketches the contours of precommitment strategies by identifying examples of precommitment strategies in existing climate change law and contrasting them with other approaches for advancing justice that are not sticky, automatic, and early, and thus would not be considered precommitments. It then contemplates whether and why sticky, automatic, and early precommitments to justice may be an important strategy to advance

4. Andrew Hammond, *On Fires, Floods, and Federalism*, 111 Cal. L. Rev. 1067 (2023) (discussing climate adaptation of public benefit programs).

5. Richard Delgado, *Our Better Natures: A Revisionist View of Joseph Sax's Public Trust Theory of Environmental Protection, and Some Dark Thoughts on the Possibility of Law Reform*, 44 Vand. L. Rev. 1209, 1226 (1991). *See also id.* at 1221:

> Most serious reform movements fail because society prefers incremental rather than wide-ranging change. In a version of the maxim that "bad money drives out good," we are almost invariably drawn to doomed, moderate approaches . . . when society needs more sweeping, ambitious ones. We resist precisely the medicine that could save us. We turn to strong solutions only when it is either too late, or when our thinking has advanced so far that the solutions seem commonplace and tame.

justice goals in anticipation of and at high levels of warming. It concludes by analyzing the use of precommitments to justice in the context of the expedited siting and construction of renewable energy infrastructure.

What Is a Precommitment to Justice?

Many climate change laws and policies reference and seek to advance justice goals.[6] The approaches to incorporating justice goals into climate change law vary widely, however, and not all measures constitute a precommitment to justice. A precommitment to justice should be sticky (not easily reversed—set out in statute as opposed to in an executive order, for example), automatic (trigger a clear and measurable outcome or duty that is not dependent on the exercise of discretion), and early (the commitment should be made prior to the circumstance(s) in which it would be implemented). These three attributes—stickiness, automaticity, and earliness—may help to create precommitments to justice that are more likely to endure as we seek to advance justice in laws and policies being designed now to mitigate and adapt to climate change. Each of these attributes is further explained and connected to the climate exigency/justice nexus below.

Sticky

The stickier a measure is, the less easily it can be reneged. This may be important to make it harder to trade off justice to achieve other goals, including mitigation and adaptation, as described more fully *infra*. Evaluating the stickiness of different mechanisms for adopting climate justice policies is easy at a high level of generality and much trickier when examined more closely. In broad strokes, it is easy to see that a statute requires greater time, political will, and process to undo or bypass than an executive order or agency guidance and constrains the scope of permissible agency regulation. Agency regulations are also somewhat enduring, tethered to the permissible interpretation of an authorizing statute and subject to process and judicial review for their amendment.

Even a statute can, of course, be waived or changed, particularly in the face of perceived emergency (see the example of the border wall *infra*). Con-

6. For example, the legislative findings prefacing New York's Climate Leadership and Community Protection Act exhort that "[a]ctions undertaken by New York State to mitigate greenhouse gas emissions should prioritize the safety and health of disadvantaged communities, control potential regressive impacts of future climate change mitigation and adaptation policies on these communities, and prioritize the allocation of public investments in these areas." N.Y. Envtl. Conserv. Law §43-B, art. 75, Refs & Annos (McKinney 2021).

stitutions are harder to change than statutes. Federal or state constitutions could be amended to explicitly advance climate justice. This is perhaps possible in some states, but extremely unlikely at the federal level. Climate justice might also be advanced through interpretations of existing state or federal constitutional text, although the room for climate justice within existing understandings of the scope of federal constitutional rights is questionable.[7]

On the face of it, a measure designed to advance climate justice would probably be more enduring in a statute than in a regulation and in a regulation than in an executive order. But it is complicated. A statute may be readily undone by new legislation in the face of shifting public priorities after a climate disaster. Are there ways to orient or draft statutes to make it less likely that the political winds will shift against them? Regulations, too, can sometimes be "sticky," or difficult to rescind.[8] Even executive orders, easily undone with the stroke of a pen by a governor or president, can sometimes prove enduring. No administration, even those the overall posture of which has not seemed particularly supportive of environmental justice, has withdrawn the executive order on environmental justice first issued by President William J. Clinton: Executive Order No. 12898, *Federal Actions to Address Environmental Justice in Minority Populations and Low-Income Populations* (EJ EO).[9] And, although the robustness with which the EJ EO has been implemented has waxed and waned significantly over time, it can be understood as an important part of a broader and ongoing instantiation of environmental justice (EJ) principles.[10] In some contexts, measures may be most enduring

---

7. Katrina Fischer Kuh & James R. May, *Can the Constitution Save the Planet?*, *in* DEMOCRACY IN A HOTTER TIME: CLIMATE CHANGE AND DEMOCRATIC TRANSFORMATION (David W. Orr ed., MIT Press 2023).
8. Richard J. Lazarus, *The Super Wicked Problem of Donald Trump*, 73 VAND. L. REV. 1811, 1836 (2020) (describing various ways in which executive climate action, including agency rulemakings, produced during the Obama Administration had "significant staying power and, unlike presidential executive orders, cannot be so easily reversed."); Aaron L. Nielson, *Sticky Regulations*, 85 U. CHI. L. REV. 85, 116 (2018) (explaining how the procedures attendant in rulemaking can make regulations enduring or sticky because "even if the agency wanted to change the scheme in the future, it would be difficult to do so—the same procedures that make it hard to create policy also make it hard to rescind policy.") (citation omitted).
9. Federal Actions to Address Environmental Justice in Minority Populations and Low-Income Populations, 59 Fed. Reg. 76299 (Feb. 16, 1994): ("[E]ach Federal agency shall make achieving environmental justice part of its mission by identifying and addressing, as appropriate, disproportionately high and adverse human health or environmental effects of its programs, policies, and activities on minority populations and low-income populations.") [hereinafter Environmental Justice].
10. For an account of the progressive development and strength of EJ despite a lack of explicit grounding in federal environmental statutes, *see* Clifford J. Villa, *No "Box to Be Checked": Environmental Justice in Modern Legal Practice*, 30 N.Y.U. ENVTL. L.J. 157, 180 (2022) (describing the "emergence of legal principles for environmental justice, including the requirement for conducting an adequate EJ analysis") [hereinafter Villa, *No "Box to Be Checked"*].

when they inculcate values, perspectives, and expectations that cannot be readily altered through changes in the text of specific laws or policies.

Thus, while stickiness is an important attribute to aspire to in adopting climate justice measures, understanding what is most likely to be sticky or enduring warrants thoughtful interrogation. One important consideration may be to recognize, pulling from Joshua Galperin's analyses in "4Cs at 4°C: Counting, Contestation, Communication, and Consideration for Collectively Constructing Concepts of Climate Change," the value of democratic process. Although no measure is truly enduring for all time, putting in place processes that surface, define, make clear, and allow for democratic input on trade offs to the greatest extent possible may have great value.[11]

Automatic

Automatic measures are clear and concrete. The more automatic a measure is, the less dependent its implementation is on the exercise of discretion. This will make it harder for a measure to be slighted in implementation, both because agencies presumably try to satisfy clear requirements and because noncompliance will be easier to discern and enforce. This may become particularly important as governments and agencies find themselves running to stay in place, stretching budgets and expending significant effort to satisfy minimum obligations in the face of climate chaos.

The federal EJ EO provides a useful example of how discretion in implementation can limit effectiveness. The EJ EO exhorts agencies to "make achieving environmental justice part of its mission," but has few automatic, or clear and substantive, requirements.[12] While EJ principles have continued to develop, increasingly finding a foothold in subnational laws, environmental reviews, statutes, and constitutional law,[13] the EJ EO itself has proved difficult to directly implement and enforce, particularly under less enthusiastic administrations.[14] The U.S. Inspector General lamented in 2004 that "EPA has not fully implemented Executive Order 12898 nor consistently

11. *See generally* Keith H. Hirokawa & David Dickinson, *The Costs of Climate Disruption in the Trade Offs of Community Resilience*, 41 W. New Eng. L. Rev. 455, 461 (2019) (emphasizing the importance of anticipating and identifying trade offs in the context of ecosystem services).
12. *See* Environmental Justice, *supra* note 10, at 76299.
13. Villa, *No "Box to Be Checked," supra* note 10, at 191 ("While there is still no federal regulation that requires agencies to conduct an EJ analysis, courts have invalidated federal and state actions for failure to fully analyze EJ concerns and incorporate EJ analysis into decision-making.").
14. Uma Outka, *Fairness in the Low-Carbon Shift Learning From Environmental Justice*, 82 Brook. L. Rev. 789, 804 (2017) ("The lack of integration between environmental justice and substantive law and policy has allowed EJ to be positioned as a secondary—even cursory—concern, addressed as a matter of procedure.")

integrated environmental justice into its day-to-day operations"[15] and the U.S. Government Accountability Office (GAO) observed, in 2019, that most agencies "have not shown clear progress toward achieving their environmental justice goals and the purpose of the executive order."[16]

Early

And a commitment that is adopted early, before the full pressure of exigency arises, is less likely to bargain-down justice by unfairly weighing it against crisis needs.[17] Requirements to immediately direct funding to EJ communities (like the establishment of mandatory statutory minima in terms of the share of benefits to be provided to disadvantaged communities, as employed in both New York's Climate Leadership and Community Protection Act (CLCPA), discussed below and the Inflation Reduction Act)[18] can be understood to be early in the sense that the funding, and the benefits it creates, happen now and cannot be clawed back. The allocation of such funds advances not only climate justice, but also day-to-day equity. Successful green job uptake that produces economic benefits can help to reduce greenhouse gas (GHG) emissions and make communities more resilient to climate impacts. Taken together, the criteria of automaticity and earliness caution against relying on balancing tests in implementing approaches designed to protect justice. A statutory provision allowing an agency to forego fulsome EJ participation requirements upon finding that the need for the construction of mitigation infrastructure significantly outweighs potential disparate impacts may grow from a rarely used exception to the default as urgency increases and agencies race to meet statutory deadlines.

Moreover, engaging with justice earlier in time may help forecast future trade offs between justice and other values that—at least in anticipation of crisis as opposed to within it—appear sufficiently unpalatable that simply

15. Office of Inspector General, U.S. EPA, EPA Needs to Consistently Implement the Intent of the Executive Order on Environmental Justice i (Mar. 1, 2004), https://www.epa.gov/office-inspector-general/report-epa-needs-consistently-implement-intent-executive-order (last visited July 21, 2022).

16. U.S. GAO, Environmental Justice Federal Efforts Need Better Planning, Coordination, and Methods to Assess Progress 17 (Sept. 2019).

17. *See generally* Uma Outka, *Fairness in the Low-Carbon Shift Learning From Environmental Justice*, 82 Brook. L. Rev. 789, 792 (2017) ("[E]nvironmental justice can and should inform the transition's trajectory *early* to achieve robust integration of the movement's core principles with legal and physical infrastructures for a low-carbon energy sector.").

18. For a summary of Inflation Reduction Act provisions directing benefits to disadvantaged communities, see Environmental Justice (EJ) Provisions of the 2022 Inflation Reduction Act, Harvard Environmental & Energy Law Program, https://eelp.law.harvard.edu/2022/08/ira-ej-provisions/ (last visited Apr. 4, 2023).

recognizing the future trade off creates impetus to avoid the need for trade off in the first instance. One important contextual aspect of the timing dynamic here is that it is the fact that we are *already very late* in our mitigation efforts, which creates the need for extraordinary (fast, without fulsome participation and review, reliant on unproven technologies with potential risks) mitigation and adaptation and raises the specter of sacrificing justice to avoid other harms. An even deeper and earlier approach to justice would have been to start mitigating seriously decades ago or to have remedied existing societal injustices because "[t]he best way to prevent social disadvantage from becoming deadly during disasters is to eliminate the disadvantage, rather than merely focusing on the disaster situation."[19]

Identifying Precommitments

This section surveys approaches to justice embedded within climate change law and policy from different states to identify and contrast approaches that do and do not constitute precommitments to justice. New York's CLCPA provides both an example of a precommitment to justice as well as examples of more typical efforts to advance justice that might prove less durable in the face of high-level warming. The statute provides that disadvantaged communities "shall receive no less than thirty-five percent of the overall benefits of spending on clean energy and energy efficiency programs," giving statutory force to the recognition that EJ includes equitable distribution of benefits.[20] This precommitment is automatic, sticky, and early—a clear duty, enshrined in statute, and decided prior to the distribution of funds.[21]

The CLCPA's establishment of mandatory statutory minima in terms of the share of benefits to be provided to disadvantaged communities offers an interesting way of incorporating automaticity into climate justice measures. There can be a tension between clear and objective legal mandates and the need for flexibility in policy to adapt to a changing climate. The CLCPA's mandatory statutory minima, however, preserves significant flexibility in terms of the scope and type of mitigation and adaptation measures, while protecting just distribution of benefits. Below, I raise the possibility of using a similar approach to prevent the disproportionate siting of industrial-scale renewable energy in EJ communities by setting a statutory ceiling.

19. Daniel A. Farber, *Disaster Law and Inequality*, 25 Law & Ineq. 297, 320 (2007).
20. N.Y. Envtl. Conserv. Law §75-0117 (McKinney 2021).
21. This is not to say that the statutory command is entirely clear and automatic. For example, it is proving complicated to define which communities are considered "disadvantaged communities" and how to define and count benefits.

The CLCPA contains many other mechanisms for incorporating justice into mitigation and adaptation policy, some of which come close to a pre-commitment to justice by mandating a relatively clear duty and others that require too much judgment or discretion in their application to be considered automatic. For example, in developing regulations to implement statewide GHG emission limits, the New York State Department of Environmental Conservation (NYSDEC) is required to "[e]nsure that activities undertaken to comply with the regulations do not result in a net increase in co-pollutant emissions."[22] Because facilities that produce GHGs and co-pollutants are disproportionately located in EJ communities, this requirement should help to avoid a situation where climate mitigation measures exacerbate existing injustice by exposing those populations to even more non-GHG pollution. The bar on an increase in co-pollutants constitutes a relatively clear statutory command, but the need to evaluate whether and how the department's regulations prompt an increase in co-pollutants introduces some uncertainty about the automaticity of the command—whether its violation would be clear and the command readily enforceable. The provision nonetheless comes close to a precommitment to justice. The statute also exhorts the department to "[p]rioritize measures to maximize net reductions of greenhouse gas emissions and co-pollutants in disadvantaged communities."[23] This charge is not sufficiently clear to constitute a precommitment. (Perhaps use of the statutory minimum strategy described above—requiring that a set percentage of net reductions occur in disadvantaged communities—would be a more reliably effective alternative?) All of the CLCPA's efforts to advance justice through mitigation and adaptation policy are laudatory and welcome; provisions that satisfy the elements of a precommitment may, however, prove especially durable and valuable as we face high-level warming.

Massachusetts' climate statutes provide other examples.[24] Some approaches from Massachusetts do not (at least fully (yet)) satisfy the criteria for a pre-commitment to justice, but there is a clear trend over time toward strengthening of justice measures and reason to be optimistic that broad, statutory justice commitments may become embedded in more automatic regulatory provisions. For example, the 2008 Global Warming Solutions Act requires the submission of road map plans for how the state will meet identified emis-

22. N.Y. Envtl. Conserv. Law §75-0109 (McKinney 2021)..
23. *Id.*
24. Massachusetts passed the Global Warming Solutions Act in 2008, 2008 Mass. Acts ch. 298, and has since built on that statute, including most notably through An Act Creating a Next-Generation Roadmap for Massachusetts Climate Policy, 2021 Mass. Acts ch. 28, and An Act Driving Clean Energy and Offshore Wind, 2022 Mass. Acts ch. 179.

sion reduction limits, and in 2021, Massachusetts amended the law through the Next Generation Roadmap Act to require that the plans shall "summarize the steps taken by the commonwealth to improve or mitigate economic, environmental and public health impacts on low- or moderate-income individuals and environmental justice populations."[25] It also directs the Energy and Environmental Affairs secretary to develop programs and issue rules to meet emission limits and implement the road map and provides that these "regulations shall achieve required emissions reductions equitably and in a manner that protects low- and moderate-income persons and environmental justice populations."[26]

These commands reside within statutory text, but they are vague and defer details to development through agency regulation. This renders the statutory justice policy neither sticky nor automatic. The state regulatory process may, of course, lead to the development of rules that implement the statute in a justice-enhancing manner. The *Massachusetts Clean Energy and Climate Plan for 2025 and 2030* includes a full chapter on *Ensuring Just Transition in the Commonwealth*, identifies numerous policies designed to advance climate justice (such as community-based air quality monitoring), and explains that "[e]very policy designed to achieve the GHG emissions reduction targets has been developed with a lens that focuses on delivering positive outcomes for environmental justice populations."[27] Similarly, the Clean Energy and Climate Plan for 2050 includes as Chapter 2 *Centering Environmental Justice* and outlines an intention to "set a minimum threshold for investments that benefit EJ populations and low- to moderate-income residents."[28] The broad statutory command may ultimately produce a regulatory regime that satisfies more of the criteria of a precommitment to justice; the likelihood of this is increased by the strong justice provisions governing environmental review. Thus, at present, the statutes alone do not create a precommitment but there is reason to be optimistic that the broad statutory commands will sharpen into strong and specific regulation.

Other aspects of Massachusetts' statutory climate law come closer to or could be considered precommitments to justice. The Next Generation Roadmap Act significantly enhances the consideration of EJ in environmental review. It requires the preparation of an environmental impact report for

25. Mass. Gen. Laws Ann. ch. 21N, §5 (West 2022).
26. *Id.* §6.
27. Massachusetts Clean Energy and Climate Plan for 2025 and 2030, xi (June 30, 2022), https://www.mass.gov/info-details/massachusetts-clean-energy-and-climate-plan-for-2025-and-2030.
28. Massachusetts Clean Energy and Climate Plan for 2050, 12 (Dec. 2022), https://www.mass.gov/info-details/massachusetts-clean-energy-and-climate-plan-for-2050.

projects likely to cause damage to the environment that are located within one mile of an EJ population (five miles for projects that impact air quality); prohibits categorical exemptions from review for projects "located in a neighborhood that has an environmental justice population"; and mandates that reports consider cumulative impacts (existing unfair or inequitable environmental burdens on the EJ population).[29]

The law augments these enduring, automatic and early procedural requirements with additional measures related to environmental review which, while not independently rising to the level of precommitments to justice, are strengthened by the fact that they are anchored in the precommitment to conduct EJ-sensitive review. The additional measures include broad exhortations to the secretary to "consider the environmental justice principles . . . [and] reduce the potential for unfair or inequitable effects upon an environmental justice population" and to "establish standards and guidelines for the implementation, administration and periodic review of environmental justice principles by the executive office of energy and environmental affairs and its agencies."[30]

The law also specifies a source and minimum amount of funding (at least $12 million annually) to be directed to the Massachusetts Clean Energy Center (MassCEC), a quasi-public economic development agency.[31] The funding is to be used to implement a clean energy equity workforce and market development program for certified minority-owned and women-owned small business enterprises, individuals residing within an EJ community, and current and former workers from the fossil fuel industry. The source and amount of funding are specified in the statute; thus, despite the necessity of the MassCEC developing details for disbursement, the core justice function is thus largely enduring and automatic because disbursement must conform to the statutory parameters. It is also early in the sense that equitable distribution of the benefits of the green energy transition is considered coincident with the adoption of policy spurring that transition. This provision thus satisfies the prerequisites of a precommitment to justice.

---

29. Mass. Gen. Laws Ann. ch. 30, §62B, E.

30. *Id.* ch. 30, §62K. EJ principles are defined as

> principles that support protection from environmental pollution and the ability to live in and enjoy a clean and healthy environment, regardless of race, color, income, class, handicap, gender identity, sexual orientation, national origin, ethnicity or ancestry, religious belief or English language proficiency, which includes: (i) the meaningful involvement of all people with respect to the development, implementation and enforcement of environmental laws, regulations and policies, including climate change policies; and (ii) the equitable distribution of energy and environmental benefits and environmental burdens.

Id. ch. 30, §62.

31. *Id.* ch. 23J, §13.

This review of different measures incorporating justice goals into climate change law and policy reveals a variety of approaches. Some measures incorporate justice in a way that is sticky, automatic, and early and can thus be considered precommitments to justice. Other measures reference and seek to advance justice but lack one or more of the attributes of a precommitment. The next section offers reasons why efforts to advance justice in the context of high-level warming may be most likely to endure and produce benefits if structured as precommitments to justice.

Why Precommitments Are Important Under High-Level Warming

The three identified attributes of a precommitment to justice—that it be sticky, automatic, and early—may help to protect justice goals from ceding to exigency. Climate exigency will take many forms and, in all of them, will be more pronounced for high-level warming. The prospect of high-level warming, underscored by the dislocation of the climate impacts that will precede it, renders immediate, large-scale, and effective mitigation interventions urgent and paramount. Sudden climate disasters (fires, floods, heatwaves) will become increasingly frequent and severe and generate immediate, overwhelming needs. And slower moving climate-caused or climate-exacerbated phenomena (such as desertification, drought, migration, sea-level rise) will create other emergencies—conflict, border pressure, famine. We will find ourselves running to stand still, spending ever more time, attention, and resources fixing what we've broken (transplanting individual branches of coral by hand as reefs diminish, fortifying dams to withstand unpredictable and unprecedented snow melts).

High-level warming and the path to it will thus exert pressures on society, resources, and institutions that are acute, intense, and grinding. By the time we reach high-level warming, our society and governing institutions will be under immense strain: "Each disaster compounds pressures on vulnerable populations, fractures the foundations of already weakened social and political systems, exposes the limits of the rule of law, and reveals the cumulative impact of intersecting social, political, economic, and ecological crises."[32] And experience suggests that exigency readily overwhelms justice.

Sacrifice of justice is regularly accepted as a trade off in the context of preparing for, avoiding, or addressing future disaster or emergency, particularly when government action is infused with a sense of urgency. The perceived

32. Cinnamon P. Carlarne, *From Covid-19 to Climate Change: Disaster & Inequality at the Crossroads*, 12 San Diego J. Climate & Energy L. 19, 27 (2021).19, 27 (2021) [hereinafter *From Covid-19 to Climate Change*].

need for immediate government action to address a pressing policy issue can cause decisionmakers to bypass procedural and other safeguards designed to protect justice values. For example, the perceived need for border security led to the passage of legislation authorizing the Secretary of the U.S. Department of Homeland Security (DHS) to "waive all legal requirements . . . to ensure expeditious construction of the barriers" along the U.S.-Mexican border,[33] as well as a presidential declaration of emergency "that the southern border presents a border security and humanitarian crisis that threatens core national security interests and constitutes a national emergency" because "[t]he southern border is a major entry point for criminals, gang members, and illicit narcotics."[34] DHS has repeatedly invoked its authority to waive the requirements of environmental and other statutes when constructing sections of border wall.[35] The construction has caused significant environmental impacts and spurred outcry from indigenous groups who contend that it interferes with their religious and cultural practices.[36]

When such trade offs in the face of exigency occur, the welfare of marginalized communities and individuals is often the easiest to give up. Disadvantaged communities may be sacrificed to prevent harm to wealthier white communities:

> Putting the vulnerable in harm's way to protect the privileged is a common theme in the history of disasters. During the Great Mississippi Flood of 1927, as floodwaters threatened New Orleans and levees protecting the city faltered, city elders met to devise a plan to save New Orleans. At their urging, Louisiana's Governor ordered levees downstream of New Orleans dynamited,

---

33. REAL ID Act of 2005, Pub. L. No. 109-13, div. B, tit. I, §102, 119 Stat. 231, 306.
34. *Declaring a National Emergency Concerning the Southern Border of the United States*, 84 Fed. Reg. 4949 (Feb. 15, 2019), *terminated by Termination of Emergency With Respect to the Southern Border of the United States and Redirection of Funds Diverted to Border Wall Construction*, Pres.Proclamation No. 9844, 85 Fed. Reg. 8715 (Jan. 15, 2021).
35. *E.g.,* Determination Pursuant to Section 102 of the Illegal Immigration Reform and Immigrant Responsibility Act of 1996, *as amended*, 83 FR 3012-01Fed. Reg.R 3012-01 (May 15, 2020): ("Accordingly, pursuant to section 102(c) of IIRIRA, I hereby waive in their entirety, with respect to the construction of roads and physical barriers . . . the following statutes"). The Determination goes on to explicitly waive application of 24 statutes, including the National Environmental Policy Act, Archeological Resources Protection Act, Safe Drinking Water Act, Administrative Procedure Act, Native American Graves Protection and Repatriation Act, and the American Indian Religious Freedom Act.
36. Manzanita Band of Kumeyaay Nation v. Wolf, 496 F. Supp. 3d 257, 269 (D.D.C. 2020) (declining to grant a preliminary injunction to prevent construction of border wall after waiver of statutory review requirements; "[o]n this record, the Court finds no reason to deviate from the clear intent of the IIRIRA to ensure expeditious construction of the barrier projects. The Court acknowledges the Kumeyaay'sKumeyaay"s efforts to preserve their culture and religious practices."). *See also* Teo Armus, *"You don't Ddon't Control the border':Bborder'": Indigenous Groups Protesting Wall Construction Clash With Federal Agents*, WASH. POST, Sept. 23, 2020, https://www.washingtonpost.com/nation/2020/09/23/border-wall-construction-protests/ (last visited July 5, 2022).

sparing the city by diverting flooding into the predominantly poor, Black communities to the south.[37]

A similar dynamic is at play when communities with greater political voice and means construct sea walls or other flood controls that displace water onto less powerful neighboring communities. Post-disaster, EJ communities are vulnerable to being saddled with hosting debris landfills and other locally undesirable land uses related to cleanup and rebuilding efforts.[38]

More generally, it is easy to imagine that the trade offs occasioned by government resource scarcity will tend to exacerbate injustice. Governments faced with mounting costs to maintain basic infrastructure and services (bridges, roads, power) may see social support programs, crucial to vulnerable populations, as dispensable, or at least more so.[39] And agencies faced with time and resource constraints and struggling to meet core, mandatory tasks may find it easier to neglect or short time-consuming processes aimed at protecting justice, particularly to the extent that they are not mandatory or subject to significant discretion, than to falter on more clearly defined deliverables.

The easy acceptance of trade offs that disproportionately impact disadvantaged communities and individuals mirrors the tacit acceptance of existing inequity, which shapes the disproportionate impacts from disaster and its aftermath and gives rise to other sobering incursions on justice. As has been frequently recognized, poor and historically disadvantaged communities will have fewer resources and opportunities to protect themselves from harm, recover from losses, and/or access government aid. In the words of Cinnamon Carlarne, whose own chapter in this book, with Keith Hirokawa, explores justice through the lens of climate dominance, "disaster streams along existing pathways of inequality, deepening those inequalities as it flows."[40]

Breakdowns in civil authority in the immediate wake of disaster can be particularly dangerous for racial minorities. After Hurricane Katrina, town police officers in the majority white community of Gretna fired their weapons over the heads of evacuees attempting to flee New Orleans on foot by crossing a bridge to Gretna, blocking access to thousands. As described by

37. Lisa Grow et al., *Disaster Vulnerability*, 63 B.C. L. Rev. 957, 1020 (2022) (citations omitted).

38. *Id.* at 1022: ("Because they typically have less political voice, vulnerable neighborhoods are often targeted for disaster-related, undesirable land uses, such as new landfills necessitated by debris cleanup, which aggravate existing environmental justice issues, or temporary post-disaster housing, which taxes already strained infrastructure.") (citations omitted).

39. Imagine budgetary choices between after school programs and funding needed to upgrade or repair storm-damaged highways. Congress already experienced long delays authorizing disaster welfare funding after a series of climate-fueled natural disasters in 2018. *See* Hammond, *supra* note 4 (describing delays in congressional appropriations for disaster relief and the practice of now requiring budget offsets for relief spending).

40. *See From Covid-19 to Climate Change, supra* note 32, at 39.

the *Chicago Tribune*: "Atop the bridge to Gretna, under the strain of an unprecedented crisis, the thin veneer of American civilization peeled back for a moment to reveal the atavistic, tribally protective impulses coursing beneath."[41] "No one in America today can realize the collapse of civil authority that happened in this area after Katrina," said Ronnie Harris, Gretna's mayor for the past 23 years. "People think, 'That can't happen here.' Well, it did happen. It was a return to basic human nature, a clannish feeling. You clung to people you know, people you trust and what's familiar and comfortable to you."[42] Although officials offered race-neutral explanations for the decision, such as Gretna's lack of supplies, racial geography provides important context:

> [T]he Gretna incident can be understood not simply as intentional discrimination against the evacuees, but as a racially territorial defense of Gretna's white space. . . . [S]patial context helps to structure the social meaning and consequences of race itself. Because at the time of the hurricane, New Orleans was predominantly black and Gretna was mostly white, the officials on the bridge likely assumed that the black evacuees were not from Gretna. The racial meaning of the two places allowed the police to sort who did and did not "belong" on the bridge according to their racialized spatial grouping and in a way that reinforced cultural norms of white privilege and power.
>
> ***
>
> [R]acially identifiable space triggers racial associations that incite a sense of belonging and proprietary power. Space takes on social and cultural meaning that in turn stimulates territorial reactions. Thus, the racialized associations with New Orleans itself helped to construct the image of the evacuees as (poor, black) "looters." Prior to the incident on the bridge, New Orleans was stereotyped by Gretna officials as a site of black poverty and crime. This racial stigma was then mapped onto the Katrina evacuees, creating perceptions that they were a racial horde encroaching on the white space of Gretna, rather than people merely seeking safety and dry land. Coming from a black space that had been stamped as "dangerous," the black evacuees—at least in the eyes of Gretna officials—became presumptively dangerous themselves. Race, therefore, surfaces in the town officials' class-loaded efforts to keep a particular kind of black person out of Gretna—the poor who come from the dangerous black city. The evacuees' racial profile is partially constructed based on their presumed geographical association with (poor, black) New Orleans.[43]

41. Howard Witt, *Katrina Aftermath Still Roils Gretna*, Chi. Trib., Sept. 4, 2008, https://www.chicagotribune.com/nation-world/chi-gretna_wittsep04-story.html (last visited June 29, 2022).
42. *Id.*
43. Elise C. Boddie, *Racial Territoriality*, 58 UCLA L. Rev. 401, 408-09, 450 (2010) (citations omitted).

Notably, "[m]uch of the violence that actually occurred following Katrina was committed by individuals [vigilantes and police] who subscribed to the myth that their neighbors and fellow citizens would degenerate into animals and who thus employed violent measures to protect themselves—or their property—against this perceived threat," and who "believed that the largely poor, black survivors of Katrina were all potential looters and rapists."[44] And it is not uncommon for entire groups, often racial minorities, to be scapegoated in the face of societal challenges.

All of this suggests that the strain and exigencies of high-level warming will exacerbate existing injustice, give rise to new challenges to justice, and make it even harder to commit resources and orient law toward preventing and rectifying injustice. That should prompt us to structure institutions, laws, and programs to create a precommitment to justice that is more likely to endure.

Expedited Renewables Siting and a Precommitment to Justice

New York adopted the Accelerated Renewable Energy Growth and Community Benefit Act of 2020, also known as "New York's expedited renewables siting law" to expedite the siting of major renewable energy projects, or those with capacity of 25 megawatts or more.[45] The effort to speed the deployment of renewable energy projects is motivated by the recognized urgency of rapid climate mitigation and exemplifies the types of trade offs that extraordinary mitigation will increasingly reflect.[46] As explained below, the law reflects a clear concern for justice as evidenced by numerous justice provisions, but the nature of those provisions creates some doubt about their durability and strength, i.e., whether they will prove to be empty gestures or meaningful commitments to justice.

To expedite siting and development of major renewable energy projects, New York's expedited renewables siting law creates a streamlined permit process and also establishes a program (the Build-Ready Program) through which a state agency will identify sites, prepare them for renewable energy

44. Lisa Grow Sun, *Disaster Mythology and the Law*, 96 Cornell L. Rev. 1131, 1148 (2011).
45. L. 2020, c. 58, pt. JJJ, §1, codified as N.Y. Pub. Auth. §1900. (Apr. 3, 2020).
46. *See generally* J.B Ruhl & James Salzman, *What Happens When the Green New Deal Meets the Old Green Laws?*, 44 Vt. L. Rev. 693, 718 (2020) (identifying the "trade offs that will be necessary" in the energy transition and admonishing that we "must acknowledge that these trade offs exist and integrate solutions at the front end of the mobilization. Waiting for them to become salient and deciding what to do about them then is simply poor governance."); Shelley Welton & Joel Eisen, *Clean Energy Justice: Charting an Emerging Agenda*, 43 Harv. Envtl. L. Rev. 307, 359 (2019) (explaining how expedited siting laws for renewables reduce traditional process methods of protecting EJ).

projects, and auction development rights to private renewable energy developers.[47] With respect to permit application and review, the statute mandates a strict timeline for application review, exempts major renewable energy projects from myriad state laws (including environmental review under New York's environmental review statute), preempts local authority and zoning if the implementing agency (the Office of Renewable Energy Siting (ORES)) determines that it is unduly burdensome "in view of the CLCPA targets and the environmental benefits of the proposed major renewable energy facility,"[48] and limits judicial review of ORES decisions.[49] The law directs ORES to promulgate regulations setting installation standards and conditions for similar installations. With respect to government site identification and preparation, the statute authorizes the New York State Energy Research and Development Authority (NYSERDA) to prepare "build-ready sites," or sites teed up for quick construction of a renewable energy facility because all permits, property interests, agreements, and/or other authorizations necessary have already been obtained.

Build-Ready Sites

Large wind and solar installations typically need significant acreage, which would tend to direct them away from some EJ communities in urban areas. Nonetheless, the statute provides that priority shall be given to "previously developed sites, existing or abandoned commercial sites, including without limitation brownfields, landfills, former commercial or industrial sites, dormant electric generating sites, or otherwise underutilized sites," which could encourage the creation of build-ready sites at locations in EJ communities.[50]

---

47. The Build-Ready Program is slated to sunset (expire and be deemed repealed) on December 31, 2030.
48. Section 94-c, Subsection (5)(e)):

    [T]he office may elect not to apply, in whole or in part, any local law or ordinance which would otherwise be applicable if it makes a finding that, as applied to the proposed major renewable energy facility, it is unreasonably burdensome in view of the CLCPA targets and the environmental benefits of the proposed major renewable energy facility.

49. N.Y. Exec. Law §94-c (McKinney 2021):

    Notwithstanding any other provision of law, including without limitation article eight of the environmental conservation law and article seven of the public service law, no other state agency, department or authority, or any municipality or political subdivision or any agency thereof may, except as expressly authorized under this section or the rules and regulations promulgated under this section, require any approval, consent, permit, certificate, contract, agreement, or other condition for the development, design, construction, operation, or decommissioning of a major renewable energy facility with respect to which an application for a siting permit has been filed. . . .

50. *See generally* Uma Outka, *Renewable Energy Siting for the Critical Decade*, 69 U. Kan. L. Rev. 857, 866-67 (2021)):

    This kind of development can revitalize areas with long dormant sites, including those with a history of contamination. . . . At the same time, it can have the effect of bringing fa-

The long history of siting locally undesirable land uses disproportionately in EJ communities suggests the need for caution. The statute and implementing regulations evidence sensitivity to EJ concerns. The justice-oriented measures are not, however, sufficiently enduring, automatic, or early to constitute a precommitment to justice.

In selecting build-ready sites, the statute provides that one consideration "may include" the "potential impacts of development on environmental justice"[51] and the statement of legislative intent identifies "protect[ing] environmental justice areas from adverse environmental impacts" as a goal of the relevant programs.[52] The statute directs NYSERDA to develop procedures and protocols for the establishment and transfer of build-ready sites which must include "a preliminary screening process to determine, in consultation with the department of environmental conservation, whether the potential build-ready site is located in or near an environmental justice area and whether an environmental justice area would be adversely affected by development of a build-ready site."[53] The statute further directs NYSERDA to "assess the need for and availability of workforce training in the local area of build-ready sites to support green jobs development with special attention to environmental justice communities," but programs and financial support for the local workforce and under-employed populations are left "subject to available funding."[54]

These justice provisions, while laudable in spirit and intent, recognize justice, but it is not clear that they create an enduring commitment to protect it. The provisions are relatively sticky, in the sense that they are contained directly in the statutory text. But they leave significant discretion to the agency in implementation; that is, they are not automatic. It is perhaps little solace that NYSERDA will identify adverse effects on EJ communities when selecting build-ready sites since it is only invited (not mandated) to weigh those effects. Fast forward and imagine an agency pressed to meet increasingly steep deliverables on renewables construction to satisfy ever more urgent mitigation efforts and it is not hard to envision justice falling by the wayside. And the exhortation to give "special attention to environmental justice communities" in providing workforce training is somewhat hollow if

cilities closer to more populated areas, raising equity considerations in some instances and increasing the likelihood of local opposition, depending on the size and scale of the project proposed.

51. N.Y. Pub. Auth. Law §1902.
52. *Id.* §1900.
53. *Id.* §1902.
54. *Id.*

contingent upon the availability of funding which, for the reasons discussed above, we can expect to be in increasingly short supply over time.[55]

Permit Application and Review

The justice protections are also limited for permitting, which would include sites selected and leased by project developers from willing landowners outside of the build-ready program. The expedited permit rubric set forth in the statute does not mandate EJ constraints, representing a significant change from the preexisting siting regime. Under the siting regime previously applicable to major renewable energy projects, and still applicable to fossil fuel power plants, the underlying statute explicitly required EJ review and cumulative impact analysis for air quality.[56] New York's expedited renewables siting law doesn't have a similar requirement. Moreover, New York has since significantly strengthened its EJ requirements, both substantively and procedurally,[57] and now prohibits issuance of a permit for a new project if "the project will cause or contribute more than a de minimis amount of pollution to a disproportionate pollution burden on the disadvantaged community."[58] But, as noted above, New York's expedited renewables siting law exempts major renewable energy projects from these requirements.[59] This further enlarges the gulf between the limited EJ review required for large renewable projects and that required for other projects subject to SEQRA.

ORES promulgated a *regulation* requiring that an appendix analyzing EJ be included in every permit application.[60] But there isn't anything in the statute compelling EJ review. The code provision setting forth the major renewable energy development program, which instantiates the expedited review process for major renewable energy projects, does not explicitly reference EJ. The statutory text directs ORES to adopt "a set of uniform standards and conditions for the siting, design, construction and operation of each type of major renewable energy facility" and instructs that these standards and conditions "be designed to avoid or minimize, to the maximum

55. Contrast this with the statute's creation of a dedicated endangered and threatened species mitigation bank fund to be filled with proceeds from "revenues received pursuant to the provisions of section 11-0535-c of the environmental conservation law." N.Y. State Fin. Law §99-hh (McKinney 2021).
56. N.Y. Pub. Serv. Law §164).) (McKinney 2021).
57. For an overview of these changes, see Michael B. Gerrard & Edward McTiernan, *New York Adopts Nation's Strongest Environmental Justice Law*, N.Y.L.J. (May 10, 2023, https://scholarship.law.columbia.edu/faculty_scholarship/3936 (last visited May 19, 2023).
58. Environmental Conservation Law (ECL) §70-0118.
59. N.Y. Exec. Law §94-c(6) (McKinney 2021).
60. N.Y. Comp. Codes R. & Regs. tit. 19, §900-2.20.

extent practicable, any potential significant adverse environmental impacts related to the siting, design, construction and operation of a major renewable energy facility."[61] The law references a public comment period[62] and states that judicial review shall be permitted for, among other things, determining whether the siting decision was "[m]ade pursuant to a process that afforded meaningful involvement of citizens affected by the facility regardless of age, race, color, national origin and income."[63] The statute also requires that a "host community benefit" be provided to the host community, but leaves it to the public service commission to establish a procedure that will determine what the host community benefit will be in any particular instance.[64] Protections for EJ communities are therefore anchored in the ORES regulation and specifically the requirement that applicants include an EJ appendix with their application for a permit.

Review of the required EJ appendix prepared and submitted by applicants suffers from a lack of automaticity. Applicants must file an exhibit that identifies and evaluates "significant and adverse disproportionate environmental impacts of the facility on an Environmental Justice (EJ) area"; identifies "specific measures the applicant proposes to take" to avoid, minimize and offset such impacts "to the maximum extent practicable"; and includes "[a] qualitative and, where possible, quantitative analysis demonstrating that the scope of avoidance, mitigation and offset measures is appropriate given the scope of significant and adverse disproportionate environmental impacts of the facility resulting from its construction and operation."[65] Since there is no justice-specific charge to ORES in the statute, ORES retains wide discretion to decide whether the avoidance, mitigation and offset measures are "appropriate" and whether and how to weigh impacts on EJ communities in application determinations.

Despite the lack of compulsory statutory protection, there are good reasons to expect that at least in the near-term, NYSERDA and ORES will be attentive to justice considerations. There is a strong culture of con-

61. N.Y. Exec. Law §94-c (McKinney 2021).
62. *E.g., id.*, §§5(c) and (d).
63. *Id.* §5(g)(2)(F).
64. Accelerated Renewable Energy Growth and Community Benefit Act (AREGCBA) §20(c)(2)) provides:

> Such [Public Service Commission] proceeding shall determine the amount of such discount, credit, compensatory or environmental benefit based on all factors deemed appropriate by the commission, including the expected average electrical output of the facility, the average number of customers within the renewable host community, and the expected aggregate annual electric consumption within such renewable host community, *the potential impact on disadvantaged communities*, and the role of utilities, if any, in implementing any aspect of such program. (emphasis added).

65. N.Y. Comp. Codes R. & Regs. tit. 19, §900-2.20.

cern for EJ in New York, which is reflected in and buttressed by myriad laws and policies. New York adopted the strongest EJ law in the country in 2023 (although major renewable energy projects are exempted from its requirements),[66] New York law calls for the establishment of a permanent EJ advisory group,[67] state agencies in New York have long been required by law to develop and be "guided" by an EJ policy,[68] and the NYSDEC's environmental permit review process and application of the State Environmental Quality Review Act must consider EJ under Commissioner Policy 29 adopted in 2003.[69] A Climate Justice Working Group is advising on implementation of the Climate Leadership and Community Protection Act, New York's core climate mitigation law, which, as explained above, contains important precommitments to justice.

Yet, in the context of siting major renewable energy facilities, the legal anchor for EJ slipped from a statutory mandate to ORES' regulatory discretion. This may be indicative of the tendency, predicted above, that EJ values may cede as concern over global warming grows. Indeed, the slippage occurred—that is, New York's expedited renewables siting law was enacted—at a time when the New York Legislature and the governor were extremely concerned that the existing legal infrastructure for siting renewable energy projects was overly solicitous of local concerns, that valuable time in the renewables build-out had been lost, and that the process was in urgent need of "streamlining."[70] Here, the trade off is reduced community process and, since the adoption of New York's 2023 EJ law, reduced protection from disproportionate impacts in disadvantaged communities in favor of speed of renewables build-out.

This weakening of justice protections in the context of renewable energy siting in New York may not be unduly troubling even to those deeply concerned about preventing environmental injustice for a variety of reasons. There is a widespread sense that the need for justice protections is low in this context because renewables projects, for reasons of geography, are unlikely to gravitate toward traditional EJ communities and, if they do, to have few locally undesirable impacts. There is also confidence in New York's strong

66. Cumulative Impacts Bill, ch. 49, 2023 N.Y. Laws ; N.Y. Senate Bill No. 8830, §9, 246th Sess. (2023) (enacted); Env't Conserv. §§8-0105, 8-0109, 8-0113, 70-0107, 70-0118.]

67. N.Y. Envtl. Conserv. Law §48-0105.

68. *Id.* §48-0109.

69. NSYDEC, Commissioner Policy 29 Environmental Justice and Permitting (Mar. 19, 2003), https://www.dec.ny.gov/regulations/36951.html (last visited May 18, 2023).

70. *See* Frederic M. Mauhs, *Preempting Local Zoning Codes Fuels Opposition to Renewable Energy in New York*, 94 NYSBAJ 44, 45 (Mar./Apr. 2022) (describing how New York's expedited renewables siting law was born out of Albany's frustration with local opposition to renewable energy projects, stymying their buildout).

culture of concern for EJ and a sense that the political landscape is unlikely to change dramatically. And fast renewables deployment may prove beneficial to EJ communities by causing earlier retirement of fossil fuel-fired plants and limiting the harms of climate change, to which such communities are especially vulnerable.

You do not have to disagree with these intuitions (indeed, I share the sense that expedited renewables siting in New York is ultimately likely to be (overall) beneficial for traditional EJ communities!) to be concerned about how the slippage of justice protections occurred. Instead of setting out the above-described considerations explicitly, thereby allowing the underlying intuitions to be challenged and tested, the adoption and structure of the expedited siting law obscured the loss of justice protections, effectively employing gestures to justice to gloss over the loss of more meaningful protections. This creates a few potential harms, including the possibility that the same justice trade off approach will be uncritically imported into other contexts thereby allowing for the expedited siting (without strong justice protections) of other more worrisome infrastructure; that comfort with this type of approach will encourage misplaced reliance on "soft" justice protections likely to erode over time; and that the failure to acknowledge the loss of justice protections forestalled creative thinking about ways to avoid the need for trade off (in this case, preserve strong justice protections without slowing renewables deployment).

There is a risk that New York might adopt the same exemption approach to the siting of other climate infrastructure without fully cognizing the justice implications of doing so. Even if there no real on-the-ground harm from the loss of justice protections in the context of renewable energy siting, we should be very careful not to copy and paste this exemption-style approach to other contexts, like the siting of transmission lines, that have far greater local impacts.

Additionally, we should be wary of relying on "soft" protections, grounded in culture and prevailing political commitments, particularly over longer time periods. Even though New York's culture of respecting justice is strong, there are countervailing pressures on agencies facing monumental mitigation tasks on strict deadlines. It is imperative to consider the implementation of mitigation laws in the years and decades to come, as the urgency of the transition to renewables heightens, demands on government multiply, budgets shrink, and on-the-ground conditions deteriorate.

Finally, obscuring the loss of justice protections with gestures toward justice prevents creative thinking about ways to strengthen justice protections without unduly slowing renewable project development. For example, with respect to New York's expedited renewables siting law, the requirement for applicants to describe EJ impacts could, without jeopardizing time and creating undue delay, be enshrined in the statute instead of resting on a requirement set forth in regulation. The statute could also identify a ceiling (indexed to the proportion of build-ready sites or permits authorized in EJ areas), the exceedance of which would automatically trigger review by the Climate Justice Working Group.

After all, if you are *really* confident that these facilities won't be disproportionately sited in EJ communities, this shouldn't slow anything down, right? And there is no drag on renewables deployment that would be created by providing for dedicated funding commitments—the promise of job training could be coupled with identification of a dedicated funding source. We should take advantage of the existence of political will to advance EJ principles in the relative "cool" of now to lock-in meaningful precommitments to justice instead of settling for gestures toward justice that may not endure.

Conclusion

Significant lawmaking is underway to build climate change policy, particularly at the state level. Advancing climate justice is often understood as a key goal of these efforts. Mounting climate exigency will, however, make it progressively harder to attend to justice. This suggests the need to pay special attention (now) to designing measures to advance climate justice that will be more likely to endure in the face of increasing urgency, shifting priorities, resource scarcity, and societal strain. Otherwise, we risk adopting climate policy with gestures toward justice that make us feel better today but do little to protect justice tomorrow. Specific recommendations from applying a precommitment lens include embedding automatic guardrails into statutory text (like the CLCPA's establishment of mandatory statutory minima in terms of the share of benefits to be provided to disadvantaged communities); embracing approaches that provide immediate funding to EJ communities; avoiding balancing tests; and locking in reliable funding streams for justice measures. The precommitment lens would also encourage continued efforts to strengthen justice policies as they evolve over time. Even without a clear statutory command, a well-reasoned rulemaking can produce regulations that endure. As Villa describes, over time, even the most fragile legal foothold (an executive order) can grow and evolve into extensive and more meaningful laws, policies, and practices.[71]

71. *See* Villa, *No "Box to Be Checked," supra* note 10 (describing the legal and practical evolution of environmental justice).

Survival Equity and Climate Change Triage: How to Decide Who Lives and Who Dies

Robin Kundis Craig

In one of many foreshadowings of what climate change means for the future, heatwaves in June and July 2022 raged in most of the Northern Hemisphere, i.e., within most of the world's "rich" countries, as well as in many that are not so well off. "In June and July 2022, heatwaves struck Europe, North Africa, the Middle East, and Asia, as temperatures climbed above 40 degrees Celsius (104 degrees Fahrenheit) in places and broke many long-standing records"[1] (see Figure 1). In June, southern France reached 104°F (40°C), setting a record.[2] Japan broke temperature records that have persisted since 1875,[3] while the United Kingdom hit 104°F (40°C) for the first time since temperatures have been recorded.[4]

> In Western Europe, which was already experiencing severe drought, the heatwave fueled fires that raged across Portugal, Spain, and parts of France. In Portugal, temperatures reached 45 degrees Celsius (113 degrees Fahrenheit) on July 13 in the town of Leiria, where more than 3,000 hectares (7,400 acres) had burned. More than half of the country was on red alert as firefighters battled 14 active fires.[5]

Author's note: I want to thank the organizers of the Environmental Law Collaborative 2021 for including me and for choosing to feature 4°C, and to thank the editors of this book for their efforts and patience. The author may be reached at robinkcraig@gmail.com.

1. *Heatwaves and Fires Scorch Europe, Africa, and Asia*, NASA EARTH OBSERVATORY (July 13, 2022), https://earthobservatory.nasa.gov/images/150083/heatwaves-and-fires-scorch-europe-africa-and-asia.
2. Payton Major et al., *3rd Heat Wave Grips the South This Summer, and Experts Say It Will Get Worse*, CNN (July 7, 2022, 1:02 PM), https://www.cnn.com/2022/07/07/weather/excessive-heat-us-south/index.html [hereinafter *It Will Get Worse*].
3. *Id.*
4. Elise Hammond, *These Three Things Are Making Record-High Temperatures Possible in the UK, According to Scientists*, CNN (July 19, 2022, 4:05 PM), https://www.cnn.com/europe/live-news/uk-europe-heatwave-fires-news-071922-intl-gbr/index.html.
5. NASA EARTH OBSERVATORY, *Heatwaves and Fires Scorch Europe, Africa, and Asia*, (July 13, 2022), https://earthobservatory.nasa.gov/images/150083/heatwaves-and-fires-scorch-europe-africa-and-asia.

As wildfires in Europe caused at least 40,000 people to evacuate their homes, "[a] staggering 34 weather stations broke the 101.7 degrees threshold in Britain, logging temperatures higher than anything Britain has ever observed."[6]

Figure 1: Heatwaves and Fires in the Eastern Hemisphere, July 13, 2022

Darker colors indicate higher temperatures.

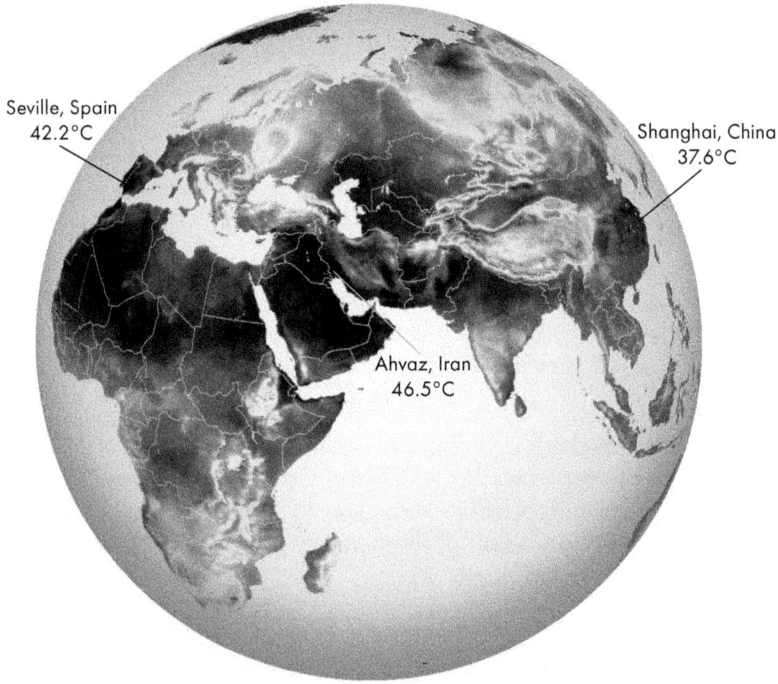

Source: NASA Earth Observatory, https://eoimages.gsfc.nasa.gov/images/imagerecords/150000/150083/eurasia_geos5_2022194_lrg.jpg

6. Matthew Cappucci & Meryl Kornfield, *Extreme Heat Prompts Alerts in 28 States as Texas, Oklahoma Hit 115*, Wash. Post, July 20, 2022, https://www.washingtonpost.com/climate-environment/2022/07/20/heatwave-us-record-oklahoma-texas/ [hereinafter *Extreme Heat*].

Some other notable records included:

- "In Italy, the record heat contributed to the July 3 collapse of a portion of the Marmolada Glacier in the Dolomites. The avalanche of snow, ice, and rock killed 11 hikers."[7]
- "In North Africa, Tunisia has endured a heatwave and fires that have damaged the country's grain crop. On July 13 in the capital city of Tunis, the temperature reached 48 degrees Celsius (118 degrees Fahrenheit), breaking a 40-year record."[8]
- "In Iran, temperatures remained high in July after reaching a scorching 52 degrees Celsius (126 degrees Fahrenheit) in late June."[9]
- "In China, the summer has brought three heatwaves that have buckled roads, melted tar, and popped off roof tiles. The Shanghai Xujiahui Observatory, where records have been kept since 1873, recorded its highest temperature ever: 40.9 degrees Celsius (105 degrees Fahrenheit) on July 13, 2022."[10]

Also in China, the heatwave broke a bridge in half in the city of Quanzhou in the southern Fujian province.[11]

Life was no less uncomfortable in the United States. By the end of the first week of July 2022, much of the Southeast was already in its third dangerous heat wave of the year, with high humidity exacerbating the impacts of the record temperatures.[12] By July 20, 28 states had issued extreme heat alerts to their citizens, with 200 million Americans experiencing temperatures in the 90s or higher over the course of three days.[13] The event prompted President Joe Biden to announce that climate change is an emergency.[14] About a week later, triple-digit temperatures arrived in the Pacific Northwest, prompting heat advisories and warnings for 13 million.[15] Portland, Oregon, and Seattle,

---

7. *Heatwaves and Fires Scorch Europe, Africa, and Asia*, NASA Earth Observatory (July 13, 2022), https://earthobservatory.nasa.gov/images/150083/heatwaves-and-fires-scorch-europe-africa-and-asia.
8. *Id.*
9. *Id.*
10. *Id.*
11. *Caught on Camera: Bridge Buckles in Scorching Heat*, CNN (July 26, 2022), https://www.cnn.com/videos/world/2022/07/26/china-heat-wave-quanzhou-bridge-buckle-jiang-ovn-intl-hnk-vpx.cnn.
12. *See It Will Get Worse*, *supra* note 2.
13. *See Extreme Heat*, *supra* note 6.
14. *Id.*
15. Isabella Grullón Paz, *The Unprepared Pacific Northwest Faces "Dangerous" Heat*, N.Y.Times, July 26, 2022, https://www.nytimes.com/live/2022/07/19/us/weather-forecast-news-summer.

Washington, opened cooling centers because few homes in the region have air conditioning.[16]

"According to the World Health Organization, in the 16 years from 2000 to 2016, an additional 216 million people have been exposed to heat waves, and it's getting worse."[17] Importantly, these increasing heatwaves are also deadly, both because of the heat itself and as a result of ancillary impacts, like melting snow and wildfires. In July 2022, both Portugal and Spain saw more than 1,000 people die in less than two weeks.[18] Adding June 2022 and Germany and Britain, the European death toll was already more than 4600 people by the end of the July.[19] Heat waves in the United States killed at least 19 people in just July and 29 people in the first seven months of 2022, reaching temperatures over 110°F in places like Arizona and Texas.[20]

The heatwaves of 2022 illustrate a profound reality of climate change: even if humanity manages to keep global average warming to no more than 2°C, people are going to die. Those deaths will increase exponentially if global average warming reaches 4°C or more—an event that could occur by the end of this century or shortly thereafter—or if, even with less warming, the consequences are more dire than expected.[21] Law and politics have to internalize these new deadly realities.

Somewhat perversely, enhanced "natural" disasters resulting from climate change—increasing numbers of stronger hurricanes, wildfire, flooding, winter freezes, heat waves—are among the easiest aspects of climate change for the law to handle, because they trigger "normal" disaster planning and preparedness. Disasters like the 2021 winter freeze in Texas[22] may continue to take us by surprise from time to time, but by and large the law already

---

16. *Id.*
17. Georges C. Benjamin, *Thousands of Heat-Related Deaths: Europe's Clarion Call for Climate Action*, The Hill, July 25, 2022, https://thehill.com/opinion/energy-environment/3573621-thousands-of-heat-related-deaths-europes-clarion-call-for-climate-action/.
18. Ivana Saric et al., *Heat Wave Kills More Than 2,000 People in Spain and Portugal*, Axios (updated July 21, 2022), https://www.axios.com/2022/07/18/heat-wave-europe-death-toll.
19. *See* Benjamin, *supra* note 17.
20. Adam Sabes, *Heat Wave Responsible for Multiple Deaths Across US*, FoxNews (July 23, 2022, 4:31 PM), https://www.foxnews.com/us/heat-wave-responsible-multiple-deaths-across-us.
21. J.B. Ruhl & Robin Kundis Craig, *4°C*, 106 Minn. L. Rev. 191, 214-17 (2021). Of course, debate over how warm the planet will become, and how quickly, continues. Notably, there are recent indications that the "post 2°C" future is less likely to reach an increase in global average temperatures of 4°C or more any time soon. Scott Dance, *A New Climate Reality: Less Warming, but Worse Impacts on the Planet*, Wash. Post, Jan. 6, 2023, https://www.washingtonpost.com/climate-environment/2023/01/06/climate-change-scenarios-extremes/. Nevertheless, those same studies indicate that the impacts from lesser warming will still be worse than expected. *Id.* For purposes of this chapter, the severity of the impacts is more important than how warm the planet actually becomes.
22. *Historic Winter Outbreak February 11-20, 2021*, National Weather Serv. (as viewed Oct. 22, 2022), https://www.weather.gov/hgx/2021ValentineStorm.

accepts that disasters happen and that people may die in them, even with the best preparation. Tort and criminal law can generally fill in the gaps if a government agency or private business really screws up, as Pacific Gas and Electric's (PG&E's) liability for California wildfires demonstrates.[23]

Even so, as many have already noted, climate-related disasters are not equitable in their impacts. For example, many factors affect who actually dies in a heatwave beyond the intensity and duration of the temperature. Factors that contribute to deaths caused by the heat itself include: age (the very young and the very old tend to be more vulnerable); pregnancy; preexisting health conditions like diabetes; medications that interfere with thermoregulation; work environment; availability of cooling, e.g., air conditioning, cooling centers; the urban heat island effect; lack of trees and green space; poverty; existing environmental injustice; and pollution.[24] Heat can also indirectly cause death by exacerbating wildfire, destabilizing ice and snowpack, and warping or destroying infrastructure, especially transportation infrastructure.[25]

In other words, whether a person dies in a heatwave is often a complex combination of individual health factors, where the person sits on several non-climate spectrums of inequality (including income, environmental conditions, and healthcare availability), where the person chooses to live, that location's capacity to prepare and respond, and sheer dumb luck (good or bad). How should the law respond?

This chapter takes four passes at answering that question. First, it explores the possible goal of achieving survival equity—that is, of using the law to adjust existing inequalities so that every human's chances of surviving despite climate change are roughly equal. Specifically, viewed from the now-hypothetical perspective of sometime prior to climate change impacts becoming serious, does climate change demand that the law seek to do something different from the normal pursuit of equity? This chapter posits that this question is both uncomfortable—because it might require governments to re-allocate scarce resources to *future* equity rather than to righting contemporary wrongs—and lacking empirical assessment, meaning that most countries are pursuing climate justice on the reasonable but blind assumption that improving equity today in the more pedestrian senses will also improve survival equity when climate change impacts become really bad.

23. Bloomberg, *PG&E Resolves Potential Criminal Liability from Dixie, Kinkade Fires*, Mercury News (as updated Apr. 11, 2022, 3:36 pm), https://www.mercurynews.com/2022/04/11/pge-resolves-potential-criminal-liability-from-dixie-kincade-fires/; Ivan Penn, *PG&E Says it Faces a Federal Inquiry and $1.15 Billion in Losses Over the Dixie Fire*, N.Y. Times, Nov. 1, 2021, https://www.nytimes.com/2021/11/01/business/energy-environment/pge-dixie-fire.html.

24. *See* Benjamin, *supra* note 17.

25. *Id.*

This chapter then turns for its second and third passes to the concept of triage as a potential legal modality for dealing with climate change equity as climate change unfolds on the ground. Triage is a method for literally deciding who lives and who dies when resources to save everyone do not exist. It starts at the smaller scale of climate disasters, suggesting that, in fact, the triage model could work quite well to promote equity in the face of relatively local climate disasters. At the global scale, however, true equity would require triaging across national borders—a fact that will likely undermine the usefulness of triage-based allocation of survival resources in the face of worsening climate change. The chapter concludes that instead of attempting to decide who will die, governments might better pursue survival equity through policies that reduce consumerism and equitably discourage the human population's continued growth.

A First Cut: The Goal of Survival Equity

Elsewhere I have explored the concept of survival equity in a climate-changed world.[26] As I noted in that previous discussion:

> Given that the risk of death for everyone increases dramatically as global average temperature rises, climate change survival equity . . . cannot be premised on reducing the absolute risk of dying for individuals in the world's most vulnerable populations. Instead, the problem is one of bringing the relative risks of dying into some sort of global parity.[27]

As with vulnerability to heat waves, however, the number of differences between places and among individuals makes the description of this global parity intrinsically difficult.[28] As a result, I posited a negative definition of survival equity, which

> should mean that any individual's chances of surviving and thriving are not statistically correlated with the person's race, ethnicity, class, religion, socially assigned gender-based status, or relationship to colonialism. Instead, the [warming] world will be a lot more equitable if a person's chances of survival are, on the whole, either (1) relatively random from a social policy perspective (e.g., the result of genetics or freak disasters); (2) based on characteristics that we all will share (e.g., vulnerabilities associated with aging or special protections accorded children); or (3) the result of individual choice (e.g., refusing to

26. Karrigan Börk et al., *Adapting to a 4°C World*, 52 Envtl. L. Rep. 10211, 10232 (Mar. 2022).
27. *Id.*
28. *Id.*

> move out of harm's way when all individuals have the means and opportunity to do so).[29]

In a perfect world, the next step would be to figure out the relationship between the pursuit of climate change survival equity and the improvement of non-climate change-related inequities, what I termed "day-to-day equity."[30] Three broad categories of relationships are possible. First, it might be "that the actions we should be taking now to promote survival equity . . . are not the same as the actions we want to take now to promote day-to-day social equity"[31]—that is, that the pursuit of day-to-day equity and the pursuit of survival equity require significantly different investments of resources. Of course, if resources and capacities were both unlimited, the world could still pursue both goals simultaneously, but that is unlikely to be the case in most places. As a result,

> if this scenario turns out to be generally true, then governments, politicians, and populations face trade offs between the two equity goals and hard choices regarding the resource allocations to each. In the hardest of all scenarios, compromises in resource allocation achieve neither goal, meaning that the world must prioritize between achieving day-to-day social equity in the near term and ensuring the highest amount of survival equity in the future.[32]

The second general relationship is the more intuitive possibility—that improving day-to-day equity now will also improve survival equity in the future.[33] Specifically, "this scenario incorporates a logical projection of causation: improved day-to-day equity now will also, over time, dramatically improve the adaptive capacity of marginalized and otherwise vulnerable groups and individuals to survive a 4°C warmer world."[34] While this scenario "feels right," however, governments should resist the temptation to assume its correctness merely as the most politically expedient approach to investing in equity improvements. Remaining oblivious to the possibility that "common sense" and the intuition that promoting day-to-day equity *must*, somehow, promote climate change survival are simply wrong, and the consequent effective refusal to confront any real trade offs that actually exist between contemporary and future equity, are themselves decisions. Moreover, they are decisions that privilege (temporary) social improvements in the present over survival equity in the future.

29. *Id.*
30. *Id.*
31. *Id.* at 10232.
32. *Id.*
33. *Id.* at 10232-33.
34. *Id.* at 10233.

The third possible scenario is one that J.B. Ruhl and I raised in *4°C*[35]—namely, "that a radically warmer world somewhat ironically creates exactly the disruptive opportunity needed to both radicalize the pursuit of social equity and make it possible for the world to shed the social and economic institutions and structures, such as institutionalized racism, that currently thwart attempts to increase social equity."[36] This scenario suggests that achieving day-to-day equity at either a U.S. or global scale requires real revolution, not incremental modification of existing conditions, allowing social equity—albeit, in a survival mode—to possibly become one of climate change's silver linings.[37] It remains, nevertheless, a silver lining that comes at great ecological, individual, and social cost if climate change involving average global warming of more than 2°C is necessary to finally shake loose the inequities that currently plague societies around the world, including in the United States.

A Second Cut: Triage in Response to Climate Disasters

Whichever relationship between day-to-day equity and survival equity turns out to be the most correct, law and governance must also continue to wrestle with the more granular allocation of resources when climate disasters actually occur, as during the summer 2022 heat waves. Triage is likely to provide an important and generalizable framework for actualizing this more localized and individualized form of survival equity.

The most difficult problems that climate change creates for law are issues of how and when to decide to cut off resource investment in lost causes. As such, "[c]limate change is creating a world of triage."[38] Triage can provide a model for prioritizing investment in natural resources, such as aquatic ecosystems, and their management as they transform under the impacts of climate change.[39] It also has important functions to serve in climate disasters, when—closer to how triage is used in emergency medicine—the decision-makers know that people will die (or die faster) as a result of how decisions to allocate aid and other resources are made.

Resource allocation to improve survival depends on scale. As scholars note, "Decisions about distributing scarce health care resources can arise at

35. Ruhl & Craig, *supra* note 21, at 267-69.
36. Börk et al., *supra* note 26, at 10233.
37. *Id.*
38. Robin Kundis Craig, *"Stationarity Is Dead"—Long Live Transformation: Five Principles for Climate Change Adaptation*, 34 Harv. Envtl. L. Rev. 9, 16 (2010).
39. Robin Kundis Craig, *Climate Change, Regulatory Fragmentation, and Water Triage*, 79 Univ. Colo. L. Rev. 825, 920-25 (2008).

all levels, from societal choices within a national health care system (macroallocation) to individuals allocating immediate emergency treatment and transport among the multiple severely injured survivors of a motor vehicle crash or industrial accident (microallocation)."[40] In medicine, triage generally applies in the microallocation settings.[41] "Triage" derives from the French word "trier," which means "to sort,"[42] and in all its applications this sorting function is critical. "Originally triage described the first aid treatment of battle casualties in collection stations at the front before their evacuation to hospitals located behind the lines."[43] Baron Dominique Jean Larre, a surgeon in Napoleon's army, regularized the modern conception of triage by dispatching wounded soldiers from the front lines to hospitals according to who needed care most urgently, rather than in order of military rank, as had been the common practice.[44] In that sense, therefore, triage allows for increased equity in an admittedly grim situation, allocating scarce medical resources on the basis of who will benefit from them most, not on the basis of rank or other privilege.

Nevertheless, emergency triage also encompasses difficult decisions of who lives and who dies. Thus, while one focus of early military triage systems was to increase the speed with which the seriously wounded received care, in 1846 in the United States, "John Wilson noted that lifesaving surgery could only be made available to those most in need if treatment was withheld," withholding this costly treatment from those likely to die "and defer[ing it] for those whose injuries were slight."[45] These are the classic three categories of military and disaster medical triage: (1) people who will likely live even without (immediate) medical care; (2) people who are likely to die regardless if they get access to the medical care available (which, importantly, is not usually the best medical care possible); and (3) people whose survival or death probably depend on whether they get priority access to the medical care available. This third category are the people who actually get immediate medical attention.

Critically, triage is a method of allocating scarce resources. When hospitals are plentiful and their capacity exceeds the number of victims being considered, there is no sustained need to triage victims or patients, except maybe

40. Kenneth V. Iserson & John C, Moskop, *Triage in Medicine, Part I: Concept, History, and Types*, 49 ANNALS EMERGENCY MED. 275, 275 (2007).
41. *Id.*
42. *Id.*; Katharyn Kennedy et al., *Triage: Techniques and Applications in Decisionmaking*, 28 ANNALS EMERGENCY MED. 136, 136 (1996).
43. *Id.*
44. *Id.* at 137.
45. *Id.*

with respect to who is loaded into the ambulances first—and in a world of plentiful ambulances, doctors, hospital beds, and operating theaters, first transportation goes to the near-dead who need Herculean interventions.[46] "At the other extreme, if there are no healthcare resources available, triage is pointless."[47] Instead, it is when medical care is available but limited, in supplies or treatment capacity or both, that triage has a role to perform. Moreover, if medical resources are severely constrained, the people sorted into the third category (those receiving immediate treatment) might be quite small. If done right, however, triage promotes survival equity: the people, whoever they are, who can most benefit from the limited medical treatment supplies and capacity available get treated.

There is no escaping the fact that allocation of limited resources requires difficult decisions based on the reality that the most severely wounded cannot be saved under battlefield or disaster conditions. Expending medical supplies and attention in the attempt to save the doomed might, however, result in the death of another, less wounded, soldier—two deaths instead of one.[48] By not "wasting" limited medical resources on those who do not need them to survive and those who will not survive even if all resources available are expended, triage saves lives; fewer people die overall than if allocation of resources were haphazard or prioritized on some (inequitable) basis other than medical need. For example, as a result of improved triage techniques—technology *and* rules—the time between injury and definitive care for U.S. soldiers dropped from 12 to 18 hours during World War II to 2 hours during the Vietnam War, with mortality rates dropping from 4.7% to 1%.[49]

Disaster situations, too, may necessitate triage because of "shortages of personnel, equipment, and transportation vehicles,"[50] making traditional triage techniques directly relevant to climate change adaptation. As on the battlefield, disaster "triage must be conducted with the purpose of doing the greatest good for the largest number of people," invoking a different approach to life-or-death decision making than the more familiar scenario of a doctor treating a single patient.[51] Thus, as on the battlefield, "it may be appropriate to use limited resources for those most likely to survive."[52] Moreover, care

46. *See* Iserson & Moskop, *supra* note 40, at 275.
47. *Id.*
48. In the same vein, when I went through lifeguard training, my instructor drilled into us: "Better one than two, better him than you."
49. Kennedy et al., *supra* note 42, at 137.
50. *Id.* at 139-40.
51. *Id.* at 137-38.
52. *Id.* at 140.

will often be more limited[53] and the triaging decisions less precise in the immediate response to a disaster, including climate disasters. Specifically:

> Triage of mass casualties in the civilian disaster setting has some differences from the military model. Initially there may not be time to set up field hospitals, necessitating the use of surviving facilities. Personnel are not usually at risk from military attack, but other dangers such as hazardous-materials exposure and building instability must be considered.[54]

Triage in a disaster situation, as on a battlefield, seeks as a first step to sort out the victims who need urgent or emergency care. Yet, given the additional complications, undertriage rates—failure to identify victims in this category—during disasters are deemed acceptable if they are less than 5%.[55]

Nevertheless, the key task of disaster triage remains sorting of the victims. Multiple triage categorization systems exist, but most place victims into three to five categories.[56] The most difficult category—indeed, so difficult that some systems do not formally acknowledge it—is the group of patients or victims who are dead or expected to die, often "described with the term 'expectant' or the color black."[57] In particular, while those people who have already died pose little ethical issue for the triaging official, writing off the dying to achieve the overall goal of saving as many as possible is unavoidably distressing.[58] "Traditional medical personnel have experienced difficulties in categorizing patients as 'expectant' because in normal circumstance the full resources of available medical technology would be brought to bear and whatever heroic measures deemed necessary would be taken."[59]

The ethics of triage thus require the decisionmakers to take a victim-wide perspective that focuses on maximizing the number of survivors. In this sense, "[c]orrect triage is crucial and has a profound effect on the management of disaster victims. It may be the most important medical task performed at the disaster site."[60] This need for good triage work will be equally true for climate disasters such as the 2022 heatwaves, increasingly severe storms, and wildfires, among others. Indeed, employing good triage planning in advance of climate disasters and then accurately deploying the triage

53. *Id.*
54. Kennedy et al., *supra* note 42, at 138.
55. *Id.* at 138. Because the main risk of overtriage—sending the minorly injured to critical care facilities—is overburdening those facilities, overtriage rates of up to 50% are deemed acceptable. *Id.* at 139.
56. *Id.* at 140.
57. *Id.*
58. *Id.*
59. *Id.* at 140
60. *Id.* at 141.

standards developed will likely increase *both* climate disaster survival *and* survival equity.

A Third Cut: Can There Be Equitable Triage at Larger Scales?

Introduction: Changing the Scale Complicates Triage

As noted, the concept of triage can be distressing, especially when the sorters consciously decide that the severely wounded must be deemed hopeless in light of the resources available. For this reason among others, triage planning—that is, establishing the criteria for sorting victims before any actual emergency—is generally considered a critical component of ethical medical triage.[61] Nevertheless, at the scale of individual victims in the immediate aftermath of a climate disaster or climate change-induced outbreak of violence,[62] triage based on triage planning will likely be generally accepted as a necessary approach to chaotic conditions that increases the chances that more people will survive.

A stickier question is whether the concept of triage can equitably "scale up." For this thought experiment, the key issue becomes: in a world of increasingly limited resources as global average temperatures increase 2 degrees Celsius (2°C) to 4°C or possibly more, can those people, communities, and nations who continue to have sufficient resources to survive ever equitably "write off" people or places that just cost too much to save?

As noted, allocation of survival-related goods and services can occur at larger societal scales than a local and immediate disaster or emergency. Indeed, "triage" itself "was originally used to describe the sorting of agricultural products."[63] Climate change will make rationing of scarce supplies and resources increasingly necessary.

Critically, moving from microallocation triage to macroallocation triage or rationing already changes the relevant decisionmaker, elevating triage from a healthcare process run by an individual "triage officer" to governance decisions made by legislatures and/or executive agencies and officials about how to allocate survival "resources to different population groups."[64] In medical triage, moreover, "[t]he triage officer uses an established system or plan, usually based on an algorithm or a set of criteria, to determine a specific

61. Iserson & Moskop, *supra* note 40, at 276.
62. *See* Andrew Guzman, Overheated: The Human Cost of Climate Change 132-171 (Oxford Univ. Press 2013) (describing how climate change, even at 2°C of warming, will likely increase violence and war around the world).
63. Iserson & Moskop, *supra* note 40, at 275.
64. *Id.* at 276.

treatment or treatment priority of each patient," and these relatively objective standards "distinguish[] triage from purely ad hoc or arbitrary decisions about distribution of health care resources."[65] In contrast, as a governance and usually governmental function, macroallocation of survival resources intrinsically admits politics into the rationing decisions, potentially complicating adherence to objective and equitable criteria.

In addition, macroallocation triage also changes the nature of the triage problem. In a medical triage situation following a climate disaster, resources (both supplies and medical personnel) are limited, and there is only one dimension to the decision: who gets those resources. Macroallocation, in contrast, also increases the political dimension of climate change triage simply because there is no hard limit on the appropriate response or the resources to allocate, as well as an increased timeline of decision making. Thus, in addition to changing the decisionmaker and decision-making process, the move to macroallocation triage increases: (1) the uncertainty surrounding the decision to allocate (or not allocate) resources to a specific community; (2) the range of allocation decisions that are possible; and (3) the complexity of the causal relationship between the allocation decision made and the effect on the target community. While it is substantially certain that the grievously wounded will die (because there are limits to what medicine can accomplish), it is not, perhaps, substantially certain (at least not to the same degree) that climate-vulnerable places and people will die—or that a proffer of aid will (or even can) guarantee their survival. As a result, the ethics of rationing and eventually triaging[66] at a larger scale will vary depending on the exact situational context.

Equitably Triaging Places

The redesign mode of climate change adaptation that J.B. Ruhl and I discuss in *4°C* is in fact a form of triage, focusing on who has to move and when and where they should go.[67] The context in which we present that discussion,

65. *Id.*

66. For purposes of this chapter, rationing and triage are best viewed as two stages in the distribution of increasingly scarce resources. Rationing "refers to resource distribution but implies that the available resources are not sufficient to satisfy all needs or wants. It also implies that some system or method is being used to guide this distribution, such as the card systems used to ration gasoline and food in the United States during World War II." Iserson & Moskop, *supra* note 40, at 275. "Triage," in contrast, indicates scarcity significant enough to warrant a protocol or plan for unequal distribution of the relevant resources on the basis of the recipients' status and those resources' likelihood of significantly increasing the recipients' chances of survival. *Id.* at 275-76.

67. Ruhl & Craig, *supra* note 21, at 227-31.

however, is about triaging *places*, allowing for several components that render redesign adaptation triage more ethical than not.

First, the people most affected by the triaging—that is, the Americans in the coastal and southern parts of the country that become unlivable—were in our scenario part of the body politic of the decision-making government, with an ability to participate in that decision making and (at least in our minds) the freedom to decide to "go it alone" if migrating was that unpalatable. In our best-case scenario, despite the fact that it is a form of macroallocation guided by governments, redesign adaptation plays out through democratic and participatory decision making, increasing both the legitimacy and ethics of the decisions themselves.[68]

Second, in *4°C* we focused on triaging *places*, not people.[69] Deciding that a place has become uninhabitable while simultaneously helping the people who used to live there migrate to a safer location feels inherently more ethical than writing off the people, too. As we note more generally in that article, various governments and nongovernmental organizations are already identifying places that climate change is rendering uninhabitable, from island nations like the Maldives to Arctic villages to Bangladesh. The discussion so far, however, has always framed the issue in terms of assisting migration—that is, in terms of triaging places, but not people. Again, for the most part, this approach to redesign adaptation triage appears both necessary and ethically acceptable.

As we acknowledged and feared, however, participatory decision making, and indeed democracy itself, may be luxuries that do not survive a 4°C-warmer world. Moreover, from a more global perspective, they are already luxuries that much of the world still does not enjoy. There is every possibility, therefore, that even decisions to triage places could lose democratic legitimacy. Moreover, if decoupled from active assistance to the displaced, triaging places quickly morphs into triaging people, a far more ethically fraught quagmire.

Far More Difficult: Equitably Triaging People

It would be pollyannish in the extreme to expect that no government or community would ever triage *people* in a 4°C world. Indeed, medical triage during a disaster or other emergency is in fact a triaging of people at the microallocation scale. Governments will, however, find it difficult, as an intrinsic, practical, political, and legal matter, to *equitably* scale up deci-

68. In Chapter 10 of this volume, Josh Galperin powerfully explains the value of decisions reached through a robust democratic process.
69. *Id.* at 239-47.

sions to abandon whole communities, and perhaps even whole nations, as too expensive to save, either in terms of actual economics or in terms of a greater number of lives that could be saved elsewhere. Triage-by-fiat may be ethical on an individual scale during a disaster or attack; it will likely feel a whole lot less so when it involves governmental decision making on a larger scale in a context of increasing chaos and considerable uncertainty—particularly if that governmental decision making simultaneously reifies preexisting inequities. In many contexts, the line between legitimate triage of people and genocide (or genocide by neglect) will be razor thin.

Shared water resources, for example, may well provide some of the first triage-by-fiat macroallocation decisions. In most such situations, the upstream nation has a considerable advantage, because it can both use and control (for example, through dams and reservoirs) the water first, effectively refusing to share it with downstream neighbors.[70] Recent controversies over Ethiopia building its $5 billion Grand Ethiopian Renaissance Dam at the headwaters of the Nile River illustrate these tensions.[71] The dam is "the largest hydropower project in Africa and would create a reservoir containing 74 billion cubic meters of water—more than twice the operational capacity of Lake Mead on the Colorado River."[72]

In some senses, the dam rectifies Ethiopia's exclusion from the Nile; "Egypt and Sudan have water rights to the Nile, while Ethiopia was not allocated a quantifiable share. But as water and energy demand grows in the Nile River Basin, Ethiopia is asserting its needs for hydropower and irrigated agriculture to promote development."[73] Nevertheless, the dam also changes the dynamics of who can physically control the Nile River's life-sustaining waters. If, hypothetically, the Nile's flow dropped to the point where it could not sustain all three countries (Egypt, Ethiopia, and Sudan), Ethiopia's decision to cut off its downstream neighbors arguably could qualify as equitable triage: better that Ethiopians survive than that the vast majority of people in all three nations die.

One suspects, however, that Ethiopia would not be commended for making that difficult but necessary decision; universal condemnation seems far

---

70. A similar phenomenon occurs among states in the United States, and several scholars have observed that the U.S. Supreme Court's implementation of interstate equitable apportionment law greatly favors the upstream state. *See, e.g.*, Caroline Jaschke, Comment, Florida v. Georgia *(2021) Leaves Equitable Apportionment a Dripping Faucet for Downstream States*, 46 Harv. Envtl. L. Rev. 293, 296, 303-12 (2022).
71. Gary Polakovic, *Water Dispute on the Nile River Could Destabilize the Region*, USC News, July 13, 2021, https://news.usc.edu/188414/nile-river-water-dispute-filling-dam-egypt-ethiopia-usc-study/.
72. *Id.*
73. *Id.*

more likely. Indeed, and notably, popular culture is already beginning to play with the global triage narrative—and the triager is the clear villain. For example, in "Avengers: Infinity War,"[74] Thanos uses the infinity stones to eliminate half of all life in the universe, allegedly to eliminate conflicts over resources. To be sure, there is no reasoned sorting involved in Thanos' execution of the plan, so he is not really engaged in triage. Nevertheless, the core assumption—some have to die if many are to survive, because there are not enough resources to support everyone—is the same macroallocation problem climate change is likely to create. And, most importantly, there is no question in *anyone's* mind that Thanos is both the villain and a murderer. Indeed (spoiler alert!), the hero Avengers bring everyone back in the sequel, "Avengers: Endgame."[75]

So, on top of everything else, triage as the legal model of macroallocation would require a shift in cultural narratives and internationally acceptable norms.

Nevertheless, it is not particularly difficult to imagine adaptation contexts, even if global average temperature increases only 2°C to 3°C, in which an attempt to save everyone in the face of shrinking resources will only, as a practical matter, double, triple, quadruple—pick whatever multiplier resonates—the total number of people who die. This is the cannibalism-in-the-lifeboat or cannibalism-among-castaways ethical dilemma[76] writ large: Can any level of decision making ethically let one group of people die so another group survives, if that decision prevents the deaths of all (or all but a handful)? What does the ratio between those living and those dying have to be before decision makers stop being squeamish? Does it matter whether those who are left to die are chosen by lot rather than by some common group characteristic—that is, somewhat perversely, that we ethically prefer *not* to execute informed decisions about which resource allocations are likely to save the most lives overall? Or, if we are willing to let decisionmakers allocate survival resources based on group characteristic, does it matter what that group characteristic is—say, old age versus ethnic or cultural identity—and how current domestic and international law would treat the classification? And what happens when the group left or chosen to die rejects and resists that decision?

---

74. AVENGERS: INFINITY WAR (Marvel Studios 2018).
75. AVENGERS: ENDGAME (Marvel Studios 2019).
76. *See, e.g.*, Regina v. Dudley & Stephens, 14 QBD 273, DC (1884) (charging two castaways who killed a comatose cabin boy for food with murder). For a compendium of such cases, see ALLAN C. HUTCHINSON, IS EATING PEOPLE WRONG? GREAT LEGAL CASES AND HOW THEY SHAPED THE WORLD 13-40 (Cambridge Univ. Press 2011).

At this point, it should become obvious that redesign-adaptation triage is a form of cost-benefit analysis—but a cost-benefit analysis where the lives will often be real and identifiable, rather than statistical. At its most ethically neutral, this analysis asks: "How many climate change survivors can a given decisionmaker buy with the resources available to that decisionmaker?" Of course, whether the decisionmaker can acquire more resources (for example, through global aid) or whether different decisionmakers will assist (for example, through mass transportation of displaced persons to distant nations, relieving pressure on local resources) will be relevant to the analysis, but the basic "how many survivors for how many resources" analysis remains the same.

While this may be an ethically neutral framing, however, implementing the goal of saving the most lives possible will necessarily begin to define who the survivors can be. On average, children require fewer resources than adults, and investing in children's survival is, fairly literally, an investment in the future. But children need caretakers and educators, and, if the immediate survival strategy works, they will grow into adults who need more resources than they did as children at the same time that the planet's resource base continues to shrink. Thus, the time dimension of climate change survival equity is also important.

At about this point, the profound difficulties inherent in trying to make triage the legal and political model for survival equity macroallocation become obvious. Nevertheless, one more real-world obstacle remains: if the world is going to equitably triage people in this way to ensure the survival of the largest number of human beings (or human beings and other species), that triage decision making would have to be done at a global scale. And it almost certainly will *not* be.

Indeed, part of the problem in equitably scaling up the triage of persons is the mismatch between the global scale of climate change and the national scale of effective decision making. A universal world government *might* be able to ethically and equitably decide when particular communities must be cut off from the distribution of increasingly scarce resources. That is not, however, the world we live in—nor is it likely to be the world of even more extreme climate change, when even the survival of *national* governments will likely come into question.[77]

77. For popular discussions of how societies have changed based on both resource and other problems, see generally Jared Diamond, Collapse: How Societies Choose to Fail or Succeed (Viking 2005) and Jared Diamond, Upheaval: Turning Points for Nations in Crisis (Little Brown & Co. 2019) [hereinafter Upheaval].

As a result, any macroallocation triage decision making that takes place will likely be occurring at the nation-state level—and it is *not* likely to be equitable. For example, given the many refugee crises that the world has already witnessed (some of which already have had a climate change component),[78] it doesn't take too much effort to imagine situations in which neighboring communities and nations proactively tell threatened communities and nations: "You're on your own." One must suspect that the chances are exceedingly slim that climate change triage based on national-scale decision making will remain ethically neutral—that is, getting the most survivors given the resources available, regardless of who holds the resources and who the survivors would be.

Long before we get to a 4°C-warmer world, *every* nation will be working with reduced resources, and many will have long since devolved into tribalism.[79] Even wealthier nations that somehow manage to retain a functional national government and avoid internal and/or external armed conflict over their resources will be struggling to keep their own residents watered, fed, housed, and disease-free. Even in these nations, therefore, the temptation to write off outsiders—however "outsider" is defined—will increasingly become simultaneously a physical necessity given limited resources and a politically expedient, if not politically unavoidable, decision: internal peace and cooperation with redesign adaption may have to be bought at the expense of abandoning the rest of the world.

In other words, it is easy to expect that triaging of people at scale (macroallocation) *will* be a feature of a world coping with serious climate change, but the motivating principle will likely be "us versus them" rather than equitably maximizing overall survival. As such, moreover, hoarding of resources is also likely to start long before true survival trade offs are at issue. To stay with the cross-jurisdictional water example, upstream nations may well cut off downstream nations to keep water not only to drink, bathe, and water crops, but potentially to run washing machines, fill pools, and grow lawns. Thus, triage of people at scale is unlikely to be a tool for overall climate

78. For example, the United Nations reports that, already, 21.5 million people per year on average " have been forcibly displaced by weather-related events–such as floods, storms, wildfires and extreme temperatures–since 2008." Sean McCallister, *There Could Be 1.2 Billion Climate Refugees by 2050. Here's What You Need to Know Now*, Zurich Mag., Jan. 13, 2023, https://www.zurich.com/en/media/magazine/2022/there-could-be-1-2-billion-climate-refugees-by-2050-here-s-what-you-need-to-know#:~:text=And%20as%20the%20threat%20of,and%20extreme%20temperatures%20%E2%80%93%20since%202008..

79. *See* Upheaval, *supra* note 77, at 391-422 (discussing climate change, resource consumption, population, and the fate of the world).

change survival equity but instead a process that reifies existing day-to-day inequities into survival inequities.

Conclusion

A question this chapter has not considered is whether survival equity is worth pursuing. It's a hard sell, because at heart it seeks to equalize the chances of dying, and there is every reason to suspect that the communities and countries that already have an advantage when it comes to critical resources—water, agricultural land, climates amenable to growing food, and resources for building—will be increasingly disinclined to share as those resources become critically short. As Jared Diamond has pointed out, "It's certain that, within the lifetimes of most of us, per-capita consumption rates in the First World will be lower than they are now. The only question is whether we shall reach that outcome by planned methods of our own choice, or by unpleasant methods not of our own choice."[80] Climate change beyond 1.5°C of warming is an unpleasant method not completely of our own choosing.

Regardless of climate change scenario, survival equity will require significant governmental and social effort, expenditure of resources, and use and expansion of capacities. It will probably also require inversions and adjustments to the status quo, changing power and wealth dynamics in ways that the currently wealthy and powerful of the world are likely to actively resist, in many places violently. Above all, the pursuit will require a sustained commitment to the rule of law and to social equality despite an increasingly chaotic world, if climate change continues to intensify on its current trajectory.

That's a lot to ask of 8 to 11 billion people who are also increasingly thirsty, hungry, broiled, flooded, frozen, infected, displaced, probably frightened and/or angry, and possibly subject to (or causing) increasing violence. It is one thing to commit to a more equitable planet when that pursuit means making the most vulnerable better off at relatively little cost to the privileged. Indeed, the global community apparently endorsed one such mechanism at the 27th Conference of the Parties (COP27) to the United Nations Framework Convention on Climate Change in November 2022, where the parties agreed to a "loss and damage fund" for vulnerable countries.[81] Survival equity will require a different level of commitment as climate change progresses to the point where reallocation of resources starts to look like a zero-sum game with

---

80. *Id.* at 416.
81. *COP27 Reaches Breakthrough Agreement on New "Loss and Damage" Fund for Vulnerable Countries*, U.N. Climate Change (Nov. 20, 2022), https://unfccc.int/news/cop27-reaches-breakthrough-agreement-on-new-loss-and-damage-fund-for-vulnerable-countries.

deadly stakes—where actively increasing one group's chances of survival (say, through a donation of food and water) only decreases the chances that the donating group will survive. To put it another way, survival equity in a world that exceeds 2°C of warming could mean that everyone has a 10% chance of surviving to age 30, or something similar.

Moreover, even a committed and sustained pursuit of survival equity will not allow the beneficiaries of that pursuit to escape all the local and regional deadly events that climate change is already bringing: survival equity, after all, simply means that any given person's chances of dying are generally unrelated to their race, gender, post-colonial status, and so forth. Roughly equalizing the risk of death does not, by itself, reduce the overall number of deaths that any climate change future will cause.[82] Indeed, *radical* equalization of the risk of death could well mean that the overall number of deaths actually will increase because the number of people at the brink of their resilience to thirst, hunger, disease, heat, or cold will increase. Given this potential reality, nations may well question whether the global pursuit of truly equalized survival equity at the level of the individual is really a goal worth pursuing, especially in light of the very real geophysical differences in community vulnerabilities. If so, again, nonequitable triage will be the likely result.

Two other factors of how human equity plays out through climate change are worth considering in this context. First, the global North consumes far more than its fair share of the earth's resources. The Global Footprint Network, for example, reports that the ecological footprint of the average U.S. citizen is 7.0 global hectares, 5.4 hectares of which go to "short-lived household consumption."[83] Even looking nationally, this is too much consumption: "The U.S., with its vast resources, has 3.7 global hectares available for each resident but this must accommodate millions of species."[84] Globally, this level of consumption is indefensible, because worldwide only 1.7 hectares were available per person in 2015[85]—and earth's human population has only increased since then.

Second, that increasing human population size will, inescapably, be a key factor in how climate change mortality plays out,[86] particularly with respect to non-disaster death—and, notably, for both humans and the other species with which they compete. For this and other reasons, population

82. *See* Ruhl & Craig, *supra* note 21, at 276 (noting that, under current climate change trajectories, "human suffering is likely to increase dramatically").
83. *Sustainable Lifestyles: A Brief Look at Lifestyle Impacts in the USA,* Global Footprint Network, 5 (2015), https://www.footprintnetwork.org/content/documents/WBCSD_SLWGUS15.pdf.
84. *Id.*
85. *Id.*
86. Diamond, Upheaval, *supra* note 77, at 392, 410-16.

control should be a far more significant component of both climate change mitigation and climate change adaptation policies than it currently is. Every aspect of this wicked problem would be far easier to deal with if the global human population were still under 3.3 billion, as it was the year the author was born (1964).

There are, of course, numerous inequities in most forms of population control that governments have implemented in the past. For example, the Cato Institute correctly concluded that forced sterilization and forced abortions, whether by governments or other individuals, are far too prone to abuse to be justifiable population control measures.[87] In contrast, changing cultural norms and nudges to signal approval of smaller families[88] and, most importantly, empowering women through education and access to jobs[89] are far preferable paths to reducing the global human population size.

Nevertheless, climate change—especially the path to a more-than-2°C warmer world—changes the stakes for population-control policies and that fact has potential implications for future social equity just as climate change itself does. Essentially, we can reduce the human population ourselves, or climate change will increasingly do it for us—equitably or not.

87. Chelsea Follett, *The Cruel Truth About Population Control*, Cato Inst. (June 13, 2019), https://www.cato.org/commentary/cruel-truth-about-population-control.

88. For example, Singapore used a "Stop at 2" campaign in the 1980s to encourage family planning, but in 2001 it introduced a "Baby Bonus" scheme to encourage more births in light of its declining birthrate and aging population. Sarah Keating, *The Nation that Thrived by "Nudging" Its Population*, BBC Future (Feb. 20, 2018), https://www.bbc.com/future/article/20180220-the-nation-that-thrived-by-nudging-its-population.

89. Ushma D. Upadhyay et al., *Women's Empowerment and Fertility: A Review of the Literature*, 115 Soc. Sci. Med. 111, 116-18 (2014).

Supplying Life Necessities in a Climate-Changed Future

Shi-Ling Hsu

Climate change poses an almost uncountable number of threats to human commerce and civilization. Climatic events such as tropical cyclones, extreme rainfall and flooding, drought, and extreme temperatures are dangerous by themselves, but in addition, they pose a longer term and more systemic threat by stressing natural and built systems[1] that supply life necessities such as food, water, and energy. Availability of these goods will become sporadic and uncertain, and at times quantities of these goods will be significantly lower than normal.[2] Unfortunately, demand for life necessities is very strong at low quantities—they are necessities, after all. Shortages will drive up prices sharply, posing hardships that will be especially severe for poor households.

Widespread, climate-driven shortages are not yet common headlines, in part because they are not occurring frequently in affluent countries. But some relatively short-lived crises, and some less serious but longer term crises, portend a darker future. After an historically brutal five-year drought ending in 2017, the state of California had slipped into another one only two years later.[3] Smaller towns and independent water districts in California are fretting about how to cope with longer and more severe droughts.[4] Texans suffered through a prolonged blackout in February 2021 when the state's electricity and natural gas systems were battered by a severe—but not unprecedented—

1. *See, e.g.*, R.L. Wilby, *A Review of Climate Change Impacts on the Built Environment*, 33 Built Env't 31 (2007).
2. For a review of the resource impacts of climate change, see The Intergovernmental Panel on Climate Change, Special Report: Global Warming of 1.5°C 175-311 (2018), https://www.ipcc.ch/sr15/.
3. Soumya Karlamangla, *What a Dry January Means for California's Drought*, N.Y. Times, Jan. 21, 2022, https://www.nytimes.com/2022/01/21/us/california-drought-rainfall.html.
4. For example, a predominantly Latino town of 700 in the Central Valley of California lacked tap water when its only pump broke in the middle of a June heat wave. Melissa Montalvo, *An Entire California Town Is Without Running Water—In a Heat Wave*, Cal. Matters, June 28, 2021, https://calmatters.org/california-divide/2021/06/california-water-drought-shortage-crisis-well-failure-teviston/.

winter storm.[5] Single-family homeowners in Texas found themselves saddled with monthly gas or electricity bills exceeding $10,000.[6] Energy prices rose so precipitously during the winter storm crisis because in times of shortage, energy suppliers may, if authorized by Texas regulators, demand exorbitant prices.[7] Since climatic events are projected to be more frequent and more severe in the future, it does not take much imagination to foresee both deeper and broader hardships.

It is also very plausible to imagine multiple, overlapping climatic events compounding harms. Texans could find themselves battered by winter storms as they are still seeking to rebuild from a coastal hurricane. Californians could find themselves short on power *and* water in the aftermath of a wildfire made widespread and catastrophic from prolonged drought. While these kinds of climate disasters impose harm and misery, a potentially more dangerous threat is the cumulation of these disasters knocking out supply systems not just for a few days, but weeks or months.

This chapter addresses the need for governments to ensure a supply of three specific life necessities: (1) energy; (2) water; and (3) food. Certainly, other things could be added to this list, such as housing, healthcare, education, and freedom from environmental harm. But there is nothing quite as delegitimizing for a government (and perhaps nothing quite as politically destabilizing) as its failure to be able to ensure these three things. While affluent societies usually undertake extensive measures to be able to guarantee availability of these three life necessities, access is still very far from universal and could become dangerously problematic in a climate-changed future.

This chapter suggests that governments may be able to avert this kind of suffering by proactively developing a capacity to be a supplier of last resort for these basic life necessities. It can do this by creating a trust instrument with the ability to produce or supply basic life necessities should shortages occur. Such an instrument, which I have dubbed a "Resources Trust,"[8] would

5. James Doss-Gollin et al., *How Unprecedented Was the February 2021 Texas Cold Snap?*, 16 Envtl. Res. Letters 064056, at 2-3 (2021), https://iopscience.iop.org/article/10.1088/1748-9326/ac0278/pdf.

6. *See, e.g.*, Giulia McDonnel Nieto del Rio et al., *His Lights Stayed on During Texas' Storm. Now He Owes $16,752*, N.Y. Times, Feb. 20, 2021, https://www.nytimes.com/2021/02/20/us/texas-storm-electric-bills.html; Konstantin Toropin, *A Texas Woman Sues an Electric Company After Her Bill Was Nearly $10,000*, CNN (Feb. 25, 2021), https://www.cnn.com/2021/02/25/us/texas-winter-storm-griddy-lawsuit-trnd/index.html (discussing a lawsuit initiated by a Houston resident against Griddy Energy after she was charged $9,546 for 19 days' worth of electricity).

7. Will Englund & Neena Satija, *As Texans Went Without Heat, Light, or Water, Some Companies Scored a Big Payday*, Wash. Post, Feb. 27, 2021, https://www.washingtonpost.com/business/2021/02/27/texas-power-winners-losers/ ("Comstock Resources, which is controlled by Jerry Jones, 'took advantage of the spike in natural gas,' obtaining it for 'super premium' prices") [hereinafter Englund & Satija].

8. Shi-Ling Hsu, *Climate Triage: A Resources Trust to Address Inequality in a Climate-Changed World*, 50 Envtl. L. 97 (2020).

be operated by a governmental entity with a charter to provide emergency standby capacity to produce and distribute life necessities should climatic changes interfere with the ability of existing markets and systems to ensure an adequate supply.

Importantly, a Resources Trust should not normally interfere with ongoing market or administrative processes that supply life necessities. Existing systems to supply and distribute life necessities are too vital and important and, in any case, are needed to provide the bulk of supply, even in times of crisis. A Resources Trust is a contingent supplier, activated only when certain signs of shortage appear, such as spiking prices or widespread shortages. Fortunately, the amount supplied by a Resources Trust need not be very large. A Resources Trust need only inject some supplemental supply, enough to relieve immediate crises of supply and bring prices down to more manageable levels. The demand for life necessities flattens out quickly once basic needs are met.

This chapter describes the nature of climatic threats to systems of supply for life necessities and how a Resources Trust instrument could address shortages that may occur in a climate-changed future.

The Threat Climate Change Poses to the Supply of Life Necessities

Climate change intensifies hydrological cycles, changing where, when, and how intensely precipitation occurs.[9] Some regions of the world will be drier over quite a long term.[10] For the southwestern United States, for example, the 22-year period from 2000-2021 was the driest in the past 1,200 years.[11] The Colorado River Compact (Compact), negotiated in 1922 by the seven states in the Colorado River Basin (and later Mexico),[12] originally apportioned 16.5 million acre-feet of water.[13] That allocation turns out to have been overly

9. *See id.* at 178; *see also* 2 U.S. Global Change Res. Prog., Fourth National Climate Assessment: Impacts, Risks, and Adaptation in the United States 37 (2018) [hereinafter USGCRP].

10. David R. Easterling et al., *Precipitation Change in the United States*, *in* 1 U.S. Global Change Res. Prog., Climate Science Special Report: Fourth National Climate Assessment 207, 218 (2017), https://science2017.globalchange.gov/downloads/CSSR_Ch7_Precipitation.pdf.

11. A. Park Williams et al., *Rapid Intensification of the Emerging Southwestern North American Megadrought 2020-2021,* 12 Nature Climate Change 232 (2022).

12. The Compact was negotiated between Arizona, California, Colorado, Nevada, New Mexico, Utah, and Wyoming. Colorado River Compact, ch. 189, 1923 Colo. Sess. Laws 684 (1923) (codified as amended at Colo. Rev. Stat. §§37-61-101 to -104 (2012)), https://www.usbr.gov/lc/region/pao/pdfiles/crcompct.pdf.

13. *Id.* art. III(a).

optimistic: from 2000 to 2020 the average flow in the Colorado River has been only 12.4 million acre-feet.[14]

Climate change bodes ill for water supply in the southwestern United States, most troublingly California. California grows about 14% (by value) of all agricultural goods in the United States.[15] The historic drought from 2012 to 2017[16] offered ominous warnings about a climate-changed future in California. The water restrictions imposed by the state and by the water districts were generally minor—lawn watering restrictions seem to make up the bulk of the questions and complaints from consumers[17]—but much of the shortfall in water supply was made up by increasing groundwater pumping.[18] Unsustainable even in the absence of a drought,[19] groundwater overdraft is a ticking time bomb. Groundwater is simply not being replenished at rates anywhere near the rates at which it is being depleted.[20] In a drier, climate-changed future with less precipitation,[21] California will have to move beyond prohibitions on lawn watering. Already, the smaller and less powerful water districts in California are scrambling to find future water rights.[22] Diminishing water supply is a climate crisis occurring in real time.

A water crisis is also, in some vital regions, a potential food crisis. California grows about 60% of all vegetables, fruit, and tree nuts produced in the

14. Charles V. Stern & Pervaze A. Sheikh, Cong. Res. Serv. R45546, Management of the Colorado River: Water Allocations, Drought, and the Federal Role 15 (2021), https://crsreports.congress.gov/product/pdf/R/R45546.

15. California Dep't Food & Agric., Agricultural Statistics Review 2019-2020, at 2 (2021) ("California remained the leading state in cash farm receipts in 2019 . . . "), https://www.cdfa.ca.gov/Statistics/PDFs/2020_Ag_Stats_Review.pdf.

16. Bettina Boxall, *Gov. Brown Declares California Drought Emergency Is Over*, L.A. Times, Apr. 7, 2019, at A1.

17. Sam Sanders & Matt Bloom, *Some Answers to Your Questions About California Water Use*, NPR.ORG (June 11, 2015), https://www.npr.org/sections/thetwo-way/2015/06/11/413742521/some-answers-to-your-questions-about-california-water-use; Adam Nagourney, *California Imposes First Mandatory Water Restrictions to Deal With Drought*, N.Y. Times, Apr. 1, 2015, https://www.nytimes.com/2015/04/02/us/california-imposes-first-ever-water-restrictions-to-deal-with-drought.html.

18. Charles V. Stern et al., Cong. Res. Serv., R44456, Central Valley Project (CVP) Operations: In Brief (Apr. 13, 2016) ("Groundwater provides about 45% of California's water supply in an average year; however, under drought conditions, such as in 2015, groundwater may supply as much as 65% of the state's water needs.").

19. Sarfaraz Alam et al., *Post-Drought Groundwater Storage Recovery in California's Central Valley*, 57 Water Resources Rsch. 1 (2021).

20. The Ogallala Aquifer has also historically experienced unsustainable groundwater withdrawals. Bruno Basso et al., *The Future of Agriculture Over the Ogallala Aquifer: Solutions to Grow Crops More Efficiently With Limited Water*, 1 Earth's Future 39, 39 (2013).

21. Williams et al., *supra* note 11, at 232.

22. *See, e.g.*, Mary Callahan, *Public Officials Scrambling for Solutions Amid Water Emergency on the Mendocino Coast*, Press Democrat, July 22, 2021, https://www.pressdemocrat.com/article/news/public-officials-scrambling-for-solutions-amid-water-emergency-on-the-mendo/.

United States[23] and 40% of all organic production in the United States.[24] Trouble for California agriculture is trouble for the American consumer. And yet, once groundwater depletion begins to constrain water supply, Californians' water-usage sacrifices must go beyond forbearance from lawn watering. California is also an economy that would be the fifth largest in the world if it were a country, ahead of the United Kingdom.[25] If water truly runs short, it will be a monumental challenge to allocate water between California agriculture and productive domestic and industrial uses.

Climate change also directly harms food supply through hotter temperatures.[26] Modern crop and livestock agriculture has become more intensive and more productive,[27] but the increased technical efficiency is constrained by a narrower set of climatic conditions.[28] More intensive production requires a more predictable supply of inputs: water shortages or high temperatures (or both) would not just be devastating to a large number of farms, but catastrophic to an entire system of food production.

Finally, climate change will affect energy supply in many ways, but perhaps most directly through the lack of water for hydropower. The historically wet Pacific northwestern United States and southwestern Canada are expected to be hotter and drier in a climate-changed future.[29] The Canadian province of British Columbia, as well as Oregon and Washington have relied on strong and steady annual rainfall and snowpack to fill reservoirs that supply water to hydroelectric dams that generate electricity[30]: British Colum-

---

23. *See supra* note 15, at 11-12 (authors calculations).
24. *Id.*
25. California's gross domestic product (GDP) in 2020 was $3.07 trillion. *Gross Domestic Product by State, 3rd Quarter 2021*, Bureau of Econ. Analysis (Dec. 23, 2021), https://www.bea.gov/sites/default/files/2021-12/qgdpstate1221_1.pdf. The fifth largest national economy, that of the United Kingdom, had a GDP in 2020 of $2.76 trillion. The World Bank, *GDP (Current US$)—United Kingdom,* https://data.worldbank.org/indicator/NY.GDP.MKTP.CD?locations=GB (last visited Feb. 25, 2022).
26. For example, wheat grain decreases significantly when exposed to 86 degrees Fahrenheit for just eight hours. Robert Henson, A Thinking Person's Guide to Climate Change 225-26 (2d ed. 2019).
27. *See, e.g.*, Shi-Ling Hsu, *Scale Economies, Scale Externalities: Hog Farming and the Changing American Agricultural Industry,* 94 Or. L. Rev. 23, 24-25 (2015) ("While agricultural production historically took place on a vast, sprawling potpourri of independent farms, the engine of modern production is a consolidated network of efficient, cost-conscious, and interrelated operations.").
28. Henson, *supra* note 26, at 219:

    In recent years, a variety of factors (no doubt including the influence of factory farming) has led to an enormous global reliance on a tiny number of staple crops. Out of some 50,000 edible plant species, a mere three—wheat, rice, and maize (corn)—make up more than half of the world's current food supply.
29. Benjamin I. Cook et al., *Climate Change and Drought: From Past to Future,* 4 Current Climate Change Reps. 164 (2018) ("Fingerprints of anthropogenic climate change consistent with long-term warming projections have been identified for droughts in California, the Pacific Northwest, Western North America, and the Mediterranean.").
30. *See* Kevin Lillis, *The Columbia River Basin Provides More Than 40% of Total U.S. Hydroelectric Generation,* U.S. Energy Info. Admin. (June 27, 2014), https://perma.cc/Q7KT-VKRN.

bia's provincial electricity utility is even called BC Hydro.[31] British Columbia relies on hydropower for over 90% of its electricity,[32] Oregon, 50%, and Washington, 66%.[33] Gradual changes in precipitation might induce gradual shifts in electricity generation and water supply, but multi-year droughts may cause severe disruption that could threaten electricity supply. Alternative sources of electricity cannot be built overnight, and it is impossible to escape the pessimistic thought that in a crisis, much of that lost capacity would be replaced by natural gas generation.

A Simplified Model of Climate Crisis in Life Necessities

This chapter uses a highly simplified economic model to illustrate the problem with supplying life necessities. That is not because this model accurately represents markets for these life necessities. Laws and regulations governing electricity and water rights and provision are bewilderingly heterogenous and complex, and are not governed, at least at the retail level, by normal markets. Supply and demand of life necessities are idiosyncratic, but even a simplified graphical representation shows how important and difficult it is to maintain stability of supply. This model also makes clear why the job of a Resources Trust should be modest, limited to injecting a supplementary supply of a life necessity and restoring some normalcy without taking over supply and fully restoring markets.

At levels varying with affluence, governments undertake measures to ensure the supply of vital life necessities such as food, water, and electricity. Water and electricity are usually provided by utility companies, often regulated (to varying extents) by governmental bodies or commissions. So there is not, as is with suppliers of less idiosyncratic, less regulated goods, price sensitivity to supply. Governments have constructed systems of supply for water and electricity that before the era of climate change, were reliable but inflexible.

Food is not provided by utilities and is, unlike water and electricity, governed by markets, albeit highly subsidized ones. In the United States, production of a handful of agricultural commodities is highly subsidized either

31. BCHydro, *About Us*, https://www.bchydro.com/toolbar/about.html (last visited July 28, 2022).
32. Canadian Energy Regulator, *Provincial and Territorial Energy Profiles—British Columbia*, Government of Can. (Aug. 14, 2018), https://perma.cc/EE59-JK74 ("About 90% of electricity in B.C. is produced from hydroelectric sources.").
33. U.S. Energy Info. Admin., *Electricity—Detailed State Data, Annual Data 1990-2020*, https://www.eia.gov/electricity/data/state/ (last visited July 28, 2022).

directly or indirectly,[34] and a nutrition assistance program for poor families represents the federal effort to ensure food security. The federal program, the Supplemental Nutritional Assistance Program,[35] is meant as a supplement to state programs, so much is left up to the individual states.

What is true of all three (energy, water, and food) is that against the backdrop of routine and abundant supply with which consumers in affluent countries have become accustomed, demand is elastic. That is, consumers are neither willing to pay very much at the margins, nor very interested in conservation for a modest amount of savings. By contrast, when these three commodities are scarce, or when their supply becomes uncertain, demand becomes intense; willingness to pay increases dramatically. By definition, necessities, in the range in which they become essential, are extremely valuable.

Figure 1 thus incorporates these features. In a normal state unaffected by climate change, the supply and demand of a life necessity can be depicted by S_0, steeply sloping to indicate that quantities are not easily changeable and insensitive to price, at least in the short and intermediate time frames

Figure 1. A Simplified Model of Demand for Life Necessities With Climate-affected Supply

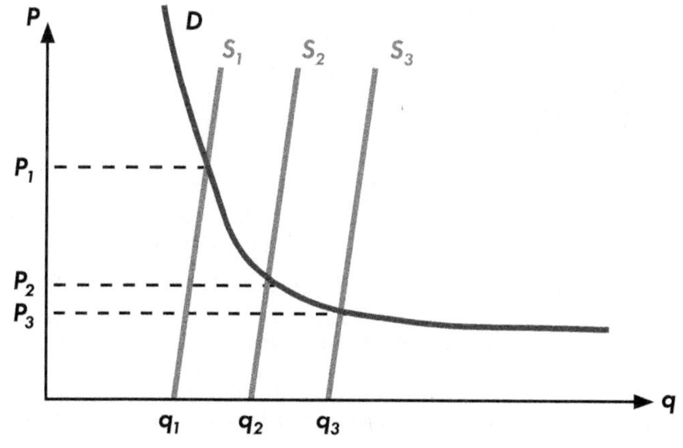

34. *See, e.g.*, Bruce A. Babcock, *The Concentration of U.S. Agricultural Subsidies*, 7 Iowa Ag. Rev. (Fall 2001), https://www.card.iastate.edu/iowa_ag_review/fall_01/concentration.aspx.
35. Randy Alison Aussenberg, Cong. Res. Serv. R42505, Supplemental Nutrition Assistance Program (SNAP): A Primer on Eligibility and Benefits 3 (Dec. 29, 2014), https://www.every-crsreport.com/files/20141229_R42505_f38ed440935e47efc9ee891d3a6e2ee8ab71a189.pdf.

considered in this chapter. In a climate-changed future, however, it is quite possible that the supplies of life necessities might shift leftward, indicating a contraction in supply. This could be a prolonged drought reducing the supply of water or electricity or a flood or extreme heat destroying large amounts of agricultural goods. A supply reduced by climate change is $\boldsymbol{S_1}$.

Demand for life necessities is, in a normal state, very elastic, so that the demand curve $\boldsymbol{D}$ is flat if supply is normal at $\boldsymbol{S_0}$, with quantity at $\boldsymbol{q_0}$ and market clearing price at $\boldsymbol{p_0}$. Water and electricity typically constitute a relatively small fraction of household budgets when supplies are robust,[36] and people are willing to pay only small amounts for more. But if supply shrinks and is represented by $\boldsymbol{S_1}$, then demand intensifies: the willingness to pay increases to $\boldsymbol{p_1}$, and quantity is much lower at $\boldsymbol{q_1}$. When tap water is irregular or when brownouts occur, people are willing to pay substantially more to ensure that their basic needs are met. Homeowners may easily eschew watering their lawn, but they will likely pay more to be able to continue to shower, prepare meals, and flush toilets. In states such as Florida and Texas that experience power losses following hurricanes, some homeowners install backup generators,[37] a household asset that may only be needed a few days a year (but probably more in a climate-changed future).[38] In this climate-changed world of scarcity, people would have to pay more for less, if they even can.

The job of a Resources Trust would be to inject some *supplemental* supply to ease demand down to levels at which the needs are not so pressing and market clearing prices not so high. It is *not* necessary for a Resources Trust to entirely restore supply (which could be very difficult), but just push supply back out to $\boldsymbol{S_2}$, at which point demand weakens just enough to ease pressure, with quantities lower at $\boldsymbol{q_2}$ and prices higher but more reasonable at $\boldsymbol{p_2}$.

As it happens, Figure 1 is a highly simplified, unusual, but reasonably accurate representation of the failures of the Texas electricity markets during the winter storm of 2021 that killed (conservatively estimated) 246 Texans.[39]

---

36. The fraction of expenditures of a household budget devoted to electricity ranges, from richest to poorest, from 1.6% to 3.7%, and for "water and other public services" from 0.8% to 1.4%. U.S. Bureau Lab. Stat., Table 1101. Quintiles of Income Before Taxes: Annual Expenditure Means, Shares, Standard Errors, and Coefficients of Variation, Consumer Expenditure Survey 2019 (Sept. 2020), https://www.bls.gov/cex/tables/calendar-year/mean-item-share-average-standard-error/cu-income-quintiles-before-taxes-2019.pdf.

37. Brendan Gibbons, *Facing Power Grid Anxiety, Texans Are Buying Generators and Bracing for Blackouts*, San Antonio Rep., July 4, 2021, https://sanantonioreport.org/facing-power-grid-anxiety-texans-are-buying-generators-and-bracing-for-blackouts/.

38. *See* USGCRP, *supra* note 9: "In the future, the total number of tropical storms is generally projected to remain steady . . . but the most intense storms are generally projected to become more frequent . . . ."

39. Patrick Svitek, *Texas Puts Final Estimate of Winter Storm Death Toll at 246*, Tex. Trib., Jan. 3, 2022, https://www.texastribune.org/2022/01/02/texas-winter-storm-final-death-toll-246/. *But see* Peter

Energy infrastructure is large and expensive and cannot be made to suddenly produce more, so supply is relatively fixed. In Texas, retail electricity prices (those paid by customers) are regulated by the state public utilities commission (PUC). The PUC authorizes electricity providers to raise prices, up to a statutory maximum of $9,000, per megawatt-hour in times of shortage, about 30 times normal spot prices,[40] hoping the added financial incentive to produce electricity in times of dire need is great and will keep up supply. In 2021, it did not. One-half of all Texans covered by the Electric Reliability Council of Texas lost power at some point during the storm.[41]

Texas had another energy market that failed during the storm: markets for natural gas that supply more than one-half of the state's power plants. For natural gas in Texas, there was and is no price or quantity regulation, and as cold weather caused many natural gas suppliers to shut down,[42] natural gas supplies contracted sharply and prices spiked. Some natural gas suppliers made enormous profits from the crisis.[43] An executive of a natural gas company that profited exorbitantly boasted that the winter storm was "like hitting the jackpot."[44]

Texas is an anomalous state in that it keeps its own electricity grid, avoiding interconnection with power plants and customers in other states in order to avoid federal regulation by the Federal Energy Regulatory Commission (FERC).[45] It is also atypical in that it does not impose "resource adequacy" requirements on electricity providers, which would pay electricity providers to provide standby capacity, power sources for when unexpected problems occur.[46] Texas relies heavily on high prices to make sure electricity and natural gas flow when it is most needed. Texas electricity provides a perfect

---

Aldhous & Zahra Hirji, *Texas Is Still Not Recognizing the Full Death Toll of Last Year's Devastating Winter Storm*, BUZZFEED NEWS, Jan. 5, 2022, https://www.buzzfeednews.com/article/peteraldhous/texas-winter-storm-death-toll ("An updated analysis [. . .] puts the number [of deaths] at more than 750.").

40. Joshua W. Busby et al., *Cascading Risks: Understanding the 2021 Winter Blackout in Texas*, 77 ENERGY RES. & SOC. SCI. 1, 6 (2021).

41. *Id.*

42. *Id.*

43. Kevin Crowley et al., *Gas Sellers Made $11 Billion While Millions of Texans Were Without Power in February*, FORTUNE, July 9, 2021, https://fortune.com/2021/07/09/gas-sellers-made-11-billion-texas-winter-blackout/.

44. *See* Englund & Satija, *supra* note 7.

45. FERC, *ERCOT*, FERC.GOV, https://www.ferc.gov/industries-data/electric/electric-power-markets/ercot (last updated July 13, 2020):

> The transmission grid that the ERCOT independent system operator administers is located solely within the state of Texas and is not synchronously interconnected to the rest of the United States. The transmission of electric energy occurring wholly within ERCOT is not subject to the Commission's jurisdiction under sections 203, 205, or 206 of the Federal Power Act.

46. James Bushnell et al., *Capacity Markets at a Crossroads* (Energy Inst. at Haas, Working Paper No. 278, 2017), https://haas.berkeley.edu/wp-content/uploads/WP278.pdf.

example of how things might go wrong when climatic changes disrupt supply systems.

For the supply of water and for the supply electricity in most states other than Texas, interpreting the model of supply and demand shown in Fig. 1 is less straightforward. Although markets for water exist, trading does not occur at nearly the volume or frequency that would render it susceptible to a simple model of supply and demand. Water and electricity are mostly supplied by utilities, often regulated by public commissions, so markets are intermediated by the rules imposed upon suppliers, which preclude the buying and selling of water or electricity. So it might not necessarily be the case that a climate crisis would literally cause a spike in prices. But drought or extreme weather would create hardship and difficulty of access that could be very costly in other ways. The insight gleaned from Fig. 1 for intermediated goods, such as water and electricity is that service will be uneven, and rationing and brownouts will become a fact of life. In times of shortage and supply interruption, scarcity will be costly; that may be reflected by high prices, or other hardships, such as queuing or rationing. And it is hard to escape the suspicion that in times of scarcity, those with the means to do so will find a way to pay a premium for vital life necessities such as electricity, water, and food.[47]

Finally, it is worth considering how climate change might constrict the supply of food enough to lead to large-scale food shortages. Unlike water and electricity outside of Texas, the supply and demand for food is dictated by markets. Agriculture in affluent countries is often subsidized,[48] so it might seem overly pessimistic to think that food might run short. Even if a major agricultural producer such as the State of California were to sharply curtail production, one might expect that global trade would always be there to pick up the slack. But that expectation runs up against a continuing litany of bad news for farmers in poor countries[49] and increasing global migrations suggesting that farming is failing all over the world.[50] While regional and

47. As an example of the measures that are taken to deal with scarcity, a Saudi water company has leased farmland in Arizona to grow alfalfa, which is then reportedly transported back to Saudi Arabia to feed its cows. *Saudi Water Deal Threatening Water Supply in Phoenix*, Ariz. PBS, June 23, 2022, https://azpbs.org/horizon/2022/06/saudi-water-deal-threatening-water-supply-in-phoenix/.

48. *See, e.g.*, Daniel A. Sumner, *Agricultural Subsidy Programs*, Encyclopedia Econ. & Hist., https://perma.cc/KYN8-8XYN (last visited Feb. 25, 2022).

49. Climate change has already been devastating to agriculture in Central America. *See, e.g.*, Timothy S. Thomas et al., Project Note, *Climate Change and Agriculture in Central America and the Andean Region*, Int'l Food Pol'y Res. Inst. (Dec. 2018) ("Existing risks to vulnerable natural and human systems, including agricultural and food systems, will be amplified by climate change . . . ."), https://ebrary.ifpri.org/utils/getfile/collection/p15738coll2/id/132953/filename/133157.pdf.

50. Sarah Bermeo, *Climate Migration and Climate Finance: Lessons From Central America*, Brookings Future Dev. Blog (Nov. 19, 2021), https://www.brookings.edu/blog/future-development/2021/11/19/

international trade can alleviate climate-induced shortfalls in food production, the global breadth and ubiquity of climate change suggest that it would be foolish to rely upon it as a backstop.

A Resources Trust

A Resources Trust would be charged with being able to inject some supply to prevent prices from spiking to levels that would render life necessities prohibitively expensive for poor households. A Resources Trust *should not* disturb extant markets or other institutions that would normally supply life necessities. Thus, the job of a Resources Trust is to stand by under normal circumstances and, only in a crisis situation, leap into action and inject some supplemental supply. Again, referring back to Figure 1, the job of a Resources Trust would be to restore enough supply so as to alleviate extreme pressures when scarcity drives consumption down to levels at which people are willing to pay exorbitantly high amounts for life necessities. Resources Trusts need not (and indeed should not) restore levels of supply and consumption back to preexisting levels; they need only supply enough to prevent extreme hardships due to a lack of life necessities.

In fact, by its purpose, a Resources Trust is maladaptive. By ensuring availability of life necessities and effectively placing an upper limit on prices, it may discourage conservation measures. It may forestall needed reforms to water allocation or dull the urgency of building out electricity storage. That would be ironic and certainly an undesirable side effect of constructing some safety net for life necessities. All climate policies, however, face trade offs. A Resources Trust trades away some incentives to conserve, in exchange for security of life necessities. The merits of such a trade off are contestable, but this chapter starts from the normative premise that it is one worth making.

That said, this trade off underscores the need for a Resources Trust to be limited in its charter to specific actions under specific circumstances and to otherwise avoid disturbing extant markets, institutions, and supply chains. Restricting the situations in which a Resources Trust might act, by limiting it to extreme scarcities and spiking prices, would minimize the built-in disincentives to conserve. Catastrophic situations are not ones that markets handle very effectively anyway.[51] But in the interests of avoiding solutions worse than the problem, modesty should be the rule for Resources Trusts.

---

climate-migration-and-climate-finance-lessons-from-central-america/.

51. *See, e.g.*, Jacob Mays et al., *Private Risk and Social Resilience in Liberalized Electricity Markets* 18-19 (USAEE Working Paper No. 21-526, 2021), https://papers.ssrn.com/sol3/papers.cfm?abstract_id=3936984.

Energy

In lieu of capacity markets or resource adequacy requirements, a Resources Trust in Texas might have been chartered to supply electricity when electricity loads are dangerously close to exceeding supply, necessitating brownouts or blackouts. How might it do that while avoiding disturbance of normal markets? One example might be energy storage batteries: a Resources Trust in Texas could hold large amounts of electricity in batteries. Electricity storage costs have declined drastically in recent years, and it is no longer cost-prohibitive to store large amounts of electricity.[52] In fact, a Texas Resources Trust holding electricity storage capacity could build up its reserve of electricity using its enormous wind capacity.[53] The intermittency of wind energy is a disadvantage in terms of supplying the "baseload" power needed to ensure a core supply of electricity for a large population, but the intermittency is no obstacle to doing the job of recharging an electricity storage battery. Outside of Texas, in which capacity markets are common, a Resources Trust might still act as an independent guarantor of supplemental supply.

Water

Although storing water would be more difficult, it is not unheard of. For example, Arizona law allows water users to receive transferable credits for injecting unused water into underground aquifers, with the advantage that water stored underground does not evaporate and recharges depleted groundwater supplies.[54] On a smaller scale, unused gravel pits are now sometimes used for water storage, providing some much-needed flexibility.[55] Given the extent to which groundwater supplies are depleted, it is quite possible that underground aquifers could act as storage spaces for Resources Trusts, though some accounting and water delivery means would be needed.

52. *See, e.g.*, U.S. Energy Info. Admin., Battery Storage in the United States: An Update on Market Trends 2 (2021), https://www.eia.gov/analysis/studies/electricity/batterystorage/pdf/battery_storage_2021.pdf.
53. U.S. Energy Info. Admin., *Texas: State Profile and Energy Estimates*, EIA.gov (Apr. 15, 2021), https://www.eia.gov/state/analysis.php?sid=TX.
54. Sharon Megdal et al., *Water Banks: Using Managed Aquifer Recharge to Meet Water Policy Objectives*, 6 Water 1500, 1504 (2014).
55. *See, e.g.*, Caitlin Coleman, *South Platte: Reclaiming Gravel Pits as Reservoirs*, Water Education Colorado (May 26, 2021), https://www.watereducationcolorado.org/publications-and-radio/headwaters-magazine/spring-2021-storage/south-platte-reclaiming-gravel-pits-as-reservoirs/.

Another possibility for obtaining water for a Resources Trust is to collect *options* for future water use.[56] There is no need, given the contingent job of a Resources Trust, to hold the entire usufructuary water right. Rather, a Resources Trust holding water options could, when the need arises, exercise the option to acquire, at some future time, a stated quantity of water for a stated price.[57]

Finally, a Resources Trust might acquire water by acquiring land with appurtenant water rights. Harvard University's investment instrument has acquired enough vineyard land in California to become one of the 20 largest vineyard owners in the state.[58] Harvard's interest is not primarily in growing grapes, but in the groundwater rights appurtenant to its properties.[59] The grape-growing and wine-making business, however, provides a cash flow to offset the capital costs of acquiring the land while preserving the option of using the groundwater for some other, more pressing purpose, should water shortages compel it. Acquisitions like Harvard's are particularly fitting for a Resources Trust: those land assets represent a secure option on water (provided that other groundwater users don't deplete the aquifer) and, as a bonus, minimize the taxpayer burden by generating what amounts to a side income.

A Resources Trust with a government charter may be legislatively granted certain privileges, such as exemption from use-it-or-lose-it rules that discourage conservation and efficiency.[60] Private nonprofit water trusts already acquire water rights for instream flows,[61] so the idea that a governmental Resources Trust could acquire water rights for dry years is not a radical departure from current water law. Indeed, state and federal governments often transact water for environmental purposes.[62] More controversially, a Resources Trust might even be granted the power of eminent

56. *See, e.g.*, Claire D. Tompkins & Thomas A. Weber, *Option Contracting in the California Water Market*, 37 J. Reg. Econ. 107 (2010).

57. An option is a financial contract that gives an investor the right, but not the obligation, to either buy or sell an asset at a pre-determined price by a specified date. Merriam-Webster (2019), https://www.merriam-webster.com/dictionary/option (accessed Feb. 8, 2019).

58. Russell Gold, *Harvard Amasses Vineyards—and Water,* Wall St. J., Dec. 11, 2018, at A1.

59. *Id.*

60. *See, e.g.*, Henry E. Smith, *Governing Water: The Semicommons of Fluid Property Rights*, 50 Ariz. L. Rev. 445, 469 (2008).

61. Peter W. Culp et al., Shopping for Water: How the Market Can Mitigate Water Shortages in the American West 23 (2014), https://tinyurl.com/y9rsq8n8.

62. Jedidiah Brewer et al., *Transferring Water in the American West: 1987-2005*, 40 J. L. Reform 1021, 1039 (2007):

> [Environmental] transactions generally are initiated by either the federal or state governments, and . . . aimed at wetlands restoration, fish and wildlife habitat preservation or protection, and augmenting stream flows. The most active parties are the U.S. Fish and Wildlife Service and state departments of fish and game.

domain over water, with a view toward closing out the most stubbornly wasteful water uses.

Food

If storing or holding water is challenging, storing food to prepare for a climate-induced food crisis is nearly impossible. In modest quantities, a Resources Trust could do what households routinely do: store canned foods for fairly long periods of time. This would be one piece of a portfolio for ensuring access to food in a climate emergency, but relying too much on this strategy would generate a large amount of food and container waste. Another food acquisition strategy could be, as is the case with water, to secure options for agricultural commodities. Commodities futures contracts are familiar, widely traded financial instruments,[63] and a Resources Trust could be just another trader in options for soybeans, wheat, oats, corn, rice, sugar, or livestock[64] at some series of future dates at which there might be a shortage.

Given the extensive needs that are likely to arise from climate-induced food crises, these two food acquisition strategies may fall short of the needs. An additional, different kind of strategy is needed.

One additional strategy for food acquisition is to be a marginal supplier of agricultural goods but retain a capacity to increase production when necessary to address a climate-induced food crisis. Being a marginal supplier of agricultural goods is important to minimize disturbance of extant markets. At the same time, a Resources Trust must have the capacity to step in and increase production when needed, that is, when markets are failing. It is a delicate task to be a reliable backup without disturbing ongoing production. A Resources Trust requires some capacity for cultivation, but not so much as to set up a parallel, competing system of production.

As an example, there is at least one way for a Resources Trust to walk this fine line: greenhouse agriculture. Intensive greenhouse agriculture can grow an astonishing amount of food with a small footprint, a fraction of the water, pesticides, and nutrient pollution of conventional farming in the United States. The Netherlands, a country of a little more than 13,000 square

63. A commodity futures contract is an agreement to buy or sell a particular commodity at a future date at a fixed price and quantity. U.S. Commodities Futures Trading Comm., *Futures Markets Basics*, https://www.cftc.gov/ConsumerProtection/EducationCenter/FuturesMarketBasics/index.htm (accessed Feb. 7, 2019).

64. For a list of commonly traded agricultural commodities, see Frank J. Fabozzi et al., *A Primer on Commodity Investing, in* The Handbook of Commodity Investing 2-37, 8 (F. Fabozzi et al. eds., 2008).

miles,[65] a little more than one-half the size of West Virginia,[66] grows enough to be the second largest food exporter in the world,[67] almost three-quarters that of the United States.[68] Per land area, Dutch greenhouses can produce 10 times as much lettuce as American growers and 15 times as many tomatoes[69]—and 13 times as many tomatoes per unit of water as conventional American agriculture.[70]

Producing with greenhouse agriculture is slightly more expensive than conventional agriculture, but that makes it ideal in terms of avoiding interference with extant markets. What greenhouses can produce is modest amounts of certain foods at higher prices, with the potential to grow much larger amounts of food if necessary. Greenhouses are more space-efficient and, unlike traditional crop farming, can be expanded vertically and constructed to accommodate multiple levels of crops.[71] Greenhouse agriculture would also reduce the greenhouse gas (GHG) emissions of food production, relative to conventional agriculture.[72]

A detailed exposition of the potential for greenhouse agriculture as a backstop for food provision is beyond the scope of this chapter. Suffice it to say, however, that increasing certainty of food production in a climate-changed future requires a migration of production away from conventional methods that are sensitive to climate and toward more industrialized methods. Unlike

65. U.S. Cent. Intelligence Agency, The World Factbook, Europe: Netherlands (2022), https://www.cia.gov/the-world-factbook/countries/netherlands/#geography.

66. West Virginia has 24,038 square miles of land. World Population Review, *United States by Area 2022* (2022), https://worldpopulationreview.com/state-rankings/states-by-area.

67. Government of the Neth., *Agric. and Horticulture*, https://www.government.nl/topics/agriculture/agriculture-and-horticulture (last visited Feb. 19, 2022).

68. The value of 2020 U.S. agricultural exports was $162 billion. U.S. Department of Agric. (USDA), Foreign Agric. Serv., *Global Agriculture System*, https://apps.fas.usda.gov/gats/ (last visited Feb. 19, 2022). In 2020, the Netherlands exported €95.6 billion, the equivalent of about $117 billion. Government of the Neth., *Record-High Dutch Export of Agricultural Goods in 2020* (Feb. 16, 2021), https://www.netherlandsandyou.nl/latest-news/weblog/blog-posts/2021/dutch-export-of-agricultural-goods-in-2020. Currency conversion was 1.222811 euros, which equals $1 U.S. on December 31, 2020.

69. *Dutch Greenhouses Have Revolutionized Modern Farming*, Civ. Eng'r (Feb. 6, 2018) (showing 10 times the yield for lettuce), https://tinyurl.com/y4bas39x; Dutch Greenhouses, Blog: *How on Earth Have the Dutch Done It?* (Mar. 16, 2018 (showing Dutch tomato yield at 144,352 tons per square mile). Average tomato yield in the United States was 28,600 pounds per acre in 2015. *See* USDA, Vegetable 2016 Summary 89 (2017), which translates into 9,152 tons per square mile.

70. Brad Plumer, *Can We Grow More Food on Less Land? We'll Have to, a New Study Finds*, N.Y. Times, Dec. 6, 2018, at A8, https://www.nytimes.com/2018/12/05/climate/agriculture-food-global-warming.html (surveying needs for efficiency in agriculture).

71. *See, e.g.*, HOVE Int'l Inc., *Multi-Level Growing*, https://www.hoveintl.com/multi-level-growing (last visited July 28, 2022).

72. Although crop cultivation generally fixes ambient carbon dioxide, the way agriculture is commonly practiced, by plowing and ripping apart soil, methane and nitrous oxide are emitted, and account for the majority of emissions of these two powerful GHGs. Mitigation is possible through different soil practices. *See, e.g.*, Pete Smith, et al., *Greenhouse Gas Mitigation in Agriculture*, 363 Phil. Trans. Royal Soc. B 789 (2008).

other industrializations, however, greenhouse agriculture, if done carefully, could be a substantial improvement in terms of the myriad environmental and social problems with conventional agriculture.

Implementation

A Resources Trust is not as radical as it sounds. For example, federal government provision of energy, even amidst predominantly private provision, is familiar: the Tennessee Valley Authority (TVA) is a federally chartered corporation that acts as an electricity and flood-control utility.[73] The Bonneville Power Administration (BPA) is a U.S. Department of Energy entity that serves the Pacific Northwest.[74] The Central Valley Project (CVP) is a complex, 400-mile network of dams, reservoirs, canals, and hydroelectric facilities that deliver water and power to California's agricultural powerhouse, the Central Valley.[75] All these entities have presented and created problems with their operations, not the least of them environmental. But at least in form, a Resources Trust is familiar.

Also familiar are government organizations and agencies that buffer against adversity, present and future. Sovereign wealth funds are state-owned investment vehicles that are meant to provide economic stabilization and diversification and a general rainy-day fund.[76] Oil-rich jurisdictions have a particular interest in economic stability given the volatility of oil revenues.[77] Worldwide, sovereign wealth funds hold about $8 trillion in assets.[78] For example, Norway's massive Government Pension Fund Global holds $1 trillion in assets.[79] Alaska, through its Permanent Fund Corporation, takes the added step of distributing some proceeds to its residents.[80]

A Resources Trust is different in scope, but not in concept, from sovereign wealth funds. Both are forward-looking entities with the goal of ameliorat-

73. TVA, *About Us*, https://www.tva.gov/About-TVA (accessed June 21, 2019).
74. BPA, *About Us*, https://www.bpa.gov/news/AboutUs/Pages/default.aspx (accessed June 21, 2019).
75. U.S. Bureau of Reclamation Mid-Pacific Region, *Central Valley Project (CVP)*, https://www.usbr.gov/mp/cvp/ (accessed June 21, 2019).
76. Sovereign Wealth Fund Inst., *What Is a Sovereign Wealth Fund?* (2018), https://www.swfinstitute.org/sovereign-wealth-fund/.
77. Mehmet Caner & Thomas Grennes, *Sovereign Wealth Funds: The Norwegian Experience*, 33 World Econ. 597, 599 (2010):

    The Norwegian government has acknowledged the transitory nature of oil revenue. Crude-oil production in the North Sea has been declining steadily since 2001, and oil prices have been extremely erratic. One purpose of the Fund is to allow Norwegians to smooth the pattern of their spending relative to the volatile pattern of the nation's oil revenue.

78. Sovereign Wealth Fund Inst., *Sovereign Wealth Fund Rankings* (2019), https://www.swfinstitute.org/sovereign-wealth-fund-rankings/ (accessed Feb. 18, 2019, pdf on file with author).
79. *Id.*
80. Alaska Stat. §43.23.005-43.34.035 (2017).

ing hardship. Both are government chartered, but largely independent from executive or legislative prerogative. And both are chartered to avoid interfering with normal markets.

A Resources Trust would differ from a sovereign wealth fund, however, in having a more complicated mandate. It is one thing to have a charter to safeguard investment returns, it is another to make sure a citizenry receives life necessities. Life necessities are difficult to produce, difficult to allocate, and difficult to distribute. A Resources Trust must additionally do all of this on a contingent basis, acting only when institutions and markets—those calibrated to ensure production of and access to life necessities—fail. A Resources Trust would require the acquisition of physical assets, many of them illiquid, and which would require a larger and more varied staff to manage it.

It is beyond the scope of this chapter to set forth a detailed blueprint for a Resources Trust. Rather, I raise three questions for implementing a Resources Trust to help identify critical planning hurdles. Resolution of these issues would depend greatly upon the chartering jurisdiction, and space precludes a comprehensive consideration of all the complicated implementation issues. Instead, this chapter identifies some considerations to illustrate the tractability of the implementation challenges for the purpose of making the idea of a Resources Trust seem more choate.

State or Federal

A Resources Trust could be chartered at several different levels of government. The realpolitik of climate change and, more prosaically, climate resilience, changes unpredictably,[81] making it difficult to predict where the idea of a Resources Trust might gain traction.

A *federal* Resources Trust would have the advantage of funding sources. A Resources Trust is costly, both as a start-up expenditure and as an ongoing expense. But the core purpose of a Resources Trust is security. The most worrying effect of climate change is civil unrest stemming from conflict over scarce resources. This possibility has already attracted attention from officials

81. It would have been difficult, for example, to even imagine a high-cost "Green New Deal" emerging in the U.S. House of Representatives before the 2018 elections. *See, e.g.*, Lisa Friedman, *Dianne Feinstein Lectures Children Who Want Green New Deal, Portraying It as Untenable*, N.Y. Times, Feb. 22, 2019, https://www.nytimes.com/2019/02/22/climate/feinstein-sunrise-green-new-deal.html?searchResultPosition=1 (noting 12 Democratic senators support the Green New Deal). Rep. Francis Rooney (R-FL), one of the most conservative members of the Republican party, has seen fit to cosponsor a carbon tax bill with his Democratic colleague Rep. Ted Deutsch (D-FL), one of the most liberal members of Congress. Nick Sobczyk, *Lawmakers Roll Out Landmark Bipartisan Carbon Bill*, E&E Daily, Nov. 28, 2018, https://www.eenews.net/stories/1060107547.

in the U.S. Department of Defense (DOD) and the U.S. Department of Homeland Security (DHS).[82] It does not seem fanciful that funding for a Resources Trust might be a fairly modest item in the Pentagon's $700 billion budget[83] or in DHS' $47.5 billion budget.[84] Also, the accounting challenges of identifying beneficiaries and the logistical challenges of distributing goods and tracking them are ones that have already been undertaken, respectively, by the Internal Revenue Service and the DOD. In particular, the distribution of humanitarian assistance by military units seems a good match for a Resources Trust.[85] Finally, constituting a Resources Trust at the federal level would take advantage of scale economies and of the diverse resources of the entire country, potentially shifting surplus resources in one part of the country to another in need.[86]

The downside of a federal Resources Trust is, of course, that it must be funded by Congress, and climate policy continues to face considerable political resistance at the federal level.[87] This downside would be much less pronounced at the state level. Certainly, the prospect of increasing taxes is more plausible at the state than the federal level.[88] Perhaps most relevant,

82. The DOD noted in 2010 that "climate change, energy security, and economic stability are inextricably linked." U.S. DOD, QUADRENNIAL DEFENSE REVIEW REPORT 84 (Feb. 2010). DHS noted in 2010 that "climate change is expected to increase the severity and frequency of weather related hazards, which could, in turn, result in social and political destabilization, international conflict, or mass migrations." DHS, HOMELAND SEC. REVIEW REPORT, QUADRENNIAL DEFENSE REVIEW REPORT (2020).

83. Christine Negroni, *Military Spending Is Up but Aerospace and Defense Workers Are Scarce*, N.Y. TIMES, July 16, 2018, at A1, https://www.nytimes.com/2018/07/16/us/military-aerospace-defense-workers.html.

84. Press Release, U.S. DHS, Department of Homeland Security Statement on the President's Fiscal Year 2019 Budget (2018), https://www.dhs.gov/news/2018/02/12/department-homeland-security-statement-president-s-fiscal-year-2019-budget.

85. [NAME REDACTED], CONG. RESEARCH SERV., RL34639, THE DEPARTMENT OF DEFENSE ROLE IN FOREIGN ASSISTANCE: BACKGROUND, MAJOR ISSUES, AND OPTIONS FOR CONGRESS 1 (2008):

> Since at least the 19th century, U.S. military forces have provided urgent assistance to foreign populations in time of disasters, such as earthquakes and floods. More recently, U.S. military forces have also provided aid in humanitarian crises such as famines and forced population movements. DOD aids foreign populations under authorities to conduct humanitarian assistance in a variety of other circumstances . . . . http://tinyurl.com/y2tradc4.

86. Inter-basin water transfers have often been proposed to move water from where it is abundant to where it is scarce. Not only, however, do these projects tend to be expensive, they also raise ecological concerns. *See, e.g.*, Bryan R. Davies et al., *An Assessment of the Ecological Impacts of Inter-Basin Water Transfers, and Their Threats to River Basin Integrity and Conservation*, 2 AQUATIC CONSERVATION: MARINE & FRESHWATER ECOSYSTEMS 325, 327 (1992) ("Any transfer of water within or between basins will have physical, chemical, hydrological and biological implications for both donor and recipient systems, as well as for their estuaries and local marine environments.").

87. Republican members of Congress were still trying to prohibit federal agencies from using the social cost of carbon for decision making. Nick Sobczyk, *Republicans Introduce Bill to Nix Social Cost of Carbon*, E&E DAILY, July 26, 2022.

88. Six states raised income or other taxes in 2018: Hawai'i, Illinois, Kansas, Oregon, South Carolina, and Tennessee. Sean Williams, *6 States Raising Taxes in 2018*, MOTLEY FOOL, Dec, 12 2017, https://www.fool.com/taxes/2017/12/12/6-states-raising-taxes-in-2018.aspx.

10 mineral-producing states have used severance taxes to fund state sovereign wealth funds, which have been managed mostly without controversy.[89] While a Resources Trust is a more complicated undertaking than an investment vehicle, at least for these states, the administrative infrastructure is in place. A Resources Trust could at least start with a simple rededication of severance tax revenues. The revenues can be sizeable: in Texas, 2017 oil and gas severance revenues were about $3 billion,[90] and Alaska's Permanent Fund Corporation manages an endowment of about $60 billion.[91]

Of course, chartering a Resources Trust at the state level would have drawbacks as well. The existence of a Resources Trust in some states but not others may spur one or both of two things: (1) migration into states with Resources Trusts; or (2) markets for life staples crossing state lines. If a Resources Trust is truly just another supplier in otherwise functional markets, then injecting supply into one state will inevitably result in some supply leaking to residents in other states. That would be the logical consequence of allowing beneficiaries to re-sell their allotted resources. But if the objective is to guarantee state residents with needed resources, then perhaps leakage, while inefficient, would at least not defeat the purposes of a Resources Trust.

Other jurisdictional scales are possible. One way to take advantage of economies of scale, avoid dysfunctional federal politics, and reduce leakage, is to establish a Resources Trust at a regional level. States contracting to pool resources and jointly operate a Resources Trust are effectively diversifying a resource base and pooling risk. The Regional Greenhouse Gas Initiative (RGGI) is an example of a regional arrangement, a common market of nine Mid-Atlantic and New England states designed to cap GHG emissions from their respective power sectors and allow the trading of emissions credits among electricity generators in those states.[92]

---

89. *See, e.g.*, Edwin M. Truman, *A Blueprint for Sovereign Wealth Fund Best Practices*, Peterson Inst. for Int'l Econ., Policy Brief PB08-2, at 3 (2008) (describing tensions raised by sovereign investing as "hypothetical"), http://tinyurl.com/y32kb9f5. The 10 states are: Alaska, Texas, New Mexico, Wyoming, North Dakota, Alabama, Utah, Idaho, Louisiana, and West Virginia. Sovereign Wealth Fund Inst., *supra* note 78. Alaska's Permanent Fund makes an annual distribution to Alaska residents, which is sometimes politically contested. Nathaniel Herz, *Alaska House Votes to More Than Double PFDs, Splintering Majority and Threatening Budget Progress*, Anchorage Daily News, Mar. 26, 2018, http://tinyurl.com/ybv8pdbk.

90. Alex Samuels, *Hey, Texplainer: How Does Texas' Budget Use Taxes from Oil and Natural Gas Production?* Tx. Trib. (Jan. 5, 2018), https://www.texastribune.org/2018/01/05/hey-texplainer-how-does-texas-budget-use-taxes-oil-and-natural-gas-pro/

91. Alaska Permanent Fund Corp., *Who We Are*, https://apfc.org/ (last visited July 28, 2022).

92. RGGI, *Elements of RGGI* (2019), https://www.rggi.org/program-overview-and-design/elements (accessed Feb. 20, 2019).

Sunrise, Sunset

A Resources Trust is a safety measure, not a pretext for a governmental effort to assume control of energy, water, and food provisions. State-owned enterprises can crowd out private investment, possibly even causing private provision to shrivel away.[93] That said, a supplier of last resort requires a working infrastructure, and it would be wasteful for a Resources Trust to remain completely idle while it awaits a climate-induced shortage. This delicate balance between being a marginal supplier while having the capacity to spring into action requires some rules for activation and deactivation.

When would a Resources Trust be authorized to spring into action? Fundamentally, intervention should be authorized when individuals have difficulty with access to life necessities. "Access" is challenging to define, but there are some ways to spot a *lack* of access. Rapid price increases is one example—but only *rapid* price increases. Prices normally change in response to changing long-term conditions, a normal and essential function of a market. Over time, climatic changes *should* alter prices, reflecting greater scarcity and new supply challenges, and over time, consumers and producers should adjust. Climate change will render certain commodities more scarce, so it would be not only unobjectionable, but also desirable that prices change over the long-term to reflect scarcity. But sudden, *rapid* price increases pose a threat to the stability of civil society.

Long queues are another possible indicator. A clear sign that the Texas electricity markets and water suppliers had failed was the existence of long lines of Texans waiting for hours in the sub-freezing temperatures for water. If time that might otherwise be spent productively is diverted to waiting in line for food, water, or gasoline, then a serious market failure has occurred.

Concomitantly, a Resources Trust should also be chartered to stand down and cease supply when supply pressures have eased, and normal institutions and markets are once again able to meet demand. Again, climatic changes will and should change the prices of goods; a return to normalcy need *not* be a return to pre-crisis price levels. But once lines disappear, once prices begin to fall, a Resources Trust should begin its withdrawal of supplemental supplies.

---

93. Finance firms have long complained about competing with government-backed mortgage finance companies Fannie Mae and Freddie Mac, which take advantage of lower interest rates available to the U.S. government. *See, e.g.*, Viral V. Acharya et al, Guaranteed to Fail: Fannie Mae, Freddie Mac, and the Debacle of Mortgage Finance 112 (2011).

Governance and Oversight

Organizational governance is the subject of a dense and sprawling literature in law and in other fields. But the core duty of being a standby provider of last resort requires the exercise of discretion in a wide variety of potentially fraught tasks: determining whether the emergency conditions exist that warrant intervention, as well as those warranting exit; deciding what assets to acquire—water options, land with surface water rights, or land with groundwater rights—and how such assets should be put to use in the event of a climate-induced shortage; management of those assets so as to preserve their value and avoid interfering with markets; and some ministerial but still tricky tasks, such as identifying beneficiaries and distributing life necessities in an orderly fashion. Some consideration of governance is important.

Again, several models exist, and sovereign wealth funds leap to mind. Norway's $1 trillion Government Pension Fund Global[94] is managed by Norway's central bank under the oversight of the Ministry of Finance.[95] Its charter requires that it "seek to achieve the highest possible return after costs measured in the investment portfolio's currency basket"[96] and adds that a "good long-term return is considered dependent on sustainable development in economic, environmental, and social terms, as well as well-functioning, legitimate and efficient markets."[97] Within this vague standard there are more detailed restrictions, such as benchmark indices,[98] but otherwise, the operational decisions of the fund are made within a familiar corporate structure of an executive board overseeing executives and a collection of committees and staff.[99] A Norwegian central bank was never going to be rife with corruption, but even by Scandinavian standards, the fund has been uncannily free of controversy.[100] Key to maintaining a reputation for cleanliness

94. *See, e.g.*, Gordon L. Clark & Ashby H.B. Monk, *The Norwegian Pension Fund: Ethics Over Efficiency*, 3 Rotman J. Int'l. Pension Mgmt. 14, 14 (2010) ("The fund . . . is widely recognized as transparent and well governed.").

95. The Act on the Government Petroleum Fund (Act of June 22, 1990, No. 36) (Nor.); *amended*, The Government Pension Fund Act (Act of Dec. 21, 2005, No. 123) (Nor.) [hereinafter Government Pension Fund Act].

96. *Id.* §1-3(1).

97. *Id.* §1-3(3).

98. Investments in European markets (including Norway) must be weighted 2.5 times that of investments in the United States and Canada. Government Pension Fund Act, *supra*, note 95, §3-3(2). The ratio of government bonds to private bonds be 70-30, *id.* §3-2(1). Equities must constitute 50-80% of the portfolio. *Id.* §3-4(1).

99. Norges Bank, Governance Model (2016), https://www.nbim.no/en/organisation/governance-model/ (accessed Feb. 21, 2019).

100. *See, e.g.*, Clark & Monk, *supra*, note 94, at 18 ("In the case of GPFG, it is apparent that public and political legitimacy currently trumps functional legitimacy. As such, the fund still enjoys widespread support."); Larry Cata Backer, *Sovereign Wealth Funds as Regulatory Chameleons: The Norwegian*

are its extensive requirements for transparency and accountability.[101] Reports are frequent and detailed, with explanations of changes in investment strategies[102] made to the Finance Minister.[103] The same plaudits of transparency and efficiency are also frequently given to the Alaska Permanent Fund, which also adopts a similar level of legislative oversight.[104]

Another model for Resources Trust governance is publicly chartered corporations. Federal government corporations (FGCs), have been chartered by the U.S. government for over 200 years.[105] FGCs have assumed a wide variety of forms with a wide variety of governance structures. Some are wholly owned by the federal government and are thus subject to most Administrative Procedure Act requirements.[106] Some are under private ownership, usually with publicly traded shares, but still generally permit federal officials to appoint some of the directors.[107] As noted above, the TVA, the BPA, and the CVP actually supply water and electricity. Incorporated FGCs can be effective suppliers if they serve a public good that requires a significant amount of private transacting, such as lending, borrowing, or insuring. Carrying out transactions that are considered routine in the private sector could be onerous if subject to federal or state administrative law. Operating a Resources Trust would require similar public-good orientation and dexterity in operations.

The critical decisions made by a Resources Trust—how to accumulate assets, when to enter and exit markets, and how to avoid market interference—are potentially contentious decisions that should be anticipated by words of limitation in their charter. Some deference for management of a Resources Trust is called for; management requires not just investment expertise, but expertise in the provision and distribution of water, food, and energy. But because of the potential for interference with markets for energy, water, and food, robust oversight and chartered limitations must be maintained.

Sovereign Wealth Funds and Public Global Governance Through Private Global Investment, 41 Geo. J. Int'l L. 425, 441 (2010) ("One of the most distinguishing, and lauded, features of the GPF is its transparency.").

101. Clark & Monk, *supra* note 94, at 17.
102. Backer, *supra* note 100, at 456.
103. Government Pension Fund Act, *supra* note 95, §2-2(3).
104. Landry Signé, *Africa's Natural Resource Revenue for All: The Alaska's Permanent Fund Dividend Model*, Brookings Inst. Africa in Focus (June 26, 2018), http://tinyurl.com/ycmbzzke.
105. A. Michael Froomkin, *Reinventing the Government Corporation*, 1995 U. Ill. L. Rev. 543, 547.
106. *Id.* at 554-55.
107. *Id.* at 555.

Conclusion

Like other proactive policies, a Resources Trust would face political headwinds in any jurisdiction. It requires spending money to prepare for future and uncertain hardship, never a political layup. And it would not address the most visceral effects of climate change, those spectacularly damaging events such as tropical cyclones, extreme rainfall and floods, and wildfires. The potential, however, for climate change to induce apocalyptic outcomes emanates from its potential to collapse governments, and there is nothing quite so delegitimizing as the inability of a large swath of a citizenry to obtain access to life necessities. It is also worth remembering that American taxpayers spend a fair amount of money on agricultural subsidies that stabilize prices for farmers.[108] It should not seem perverse to spend some money to stabilize prices for consumers.[109]

A Resources Trust should *not supplant* private markets or institutions and should minimize any disturbances; but it should *supplement* them, infusing additional supply when needed. That said, a commitment to ensure that every person within a chartering jurisdiction has access to energy, water, and food is a non-market allocation. As such, it conflicts with conventional economic wisdom, which generally frowns upon government intervention in the face of shortages.[110] Nevertheless, lack of access to life necessities is destabilizing; extant markets and institutions will have already failed.

---

108. *See, e.g.*, David M.G. Newbery & Joseph E. Stiglitz, *The Theory of Commodity Price Stabilization Rules: Welfare Impacts and Supply Responses*, 89 Econ. J. 799, 799 (1979).
109. The matter of food price stabilization has always been a more pressing matter in developing countries. Unlike rich consumers, consumers in developing countries cannot buffer against high food prices by cutting back on discretionary expenses. C. Peter Timmer, *The Macro Dimensions of Food Security: Economic Growth, Equitable Distribution, and Food Price Stability*, 25 Food Pol'y 283, 284 (2000) ("That rich countries have little to fear from hunger is a simple consequence of Engel's law; consumers have a substantial buffer of non-food expenditures to rely on, even if food prices rise sharply. In a market economy, the rich do not starve.").
110. *See, e.g.*, Milton Friedman, *Blaming the Obstetrician*, Newsweek, June 4, 1979, at 70 ("There is an energy crisis, there are gasoline lines, for one reason and one reason only. Because government has decreed that there shall be.").

climate change could result in a global catastrophe."[5] As we contemplate the all-too-real possibility of a worst-case climate world, a critical climate dominance lens allows us to see difference and expose both the peril and the promise it brings in the climate adaptation context. Here we begin this process by bringing a climate dominance perspective to bear in the contexts of climate migration, climate gentrification, and ecosystem management to explore how surfacing and decentering dominance now allows us to contemplate more equitable and effective adaptation planning before we find ourselves in a climate endgame world.[6]

Climate Migration and Dominance in a 4°C World

In its Sixth Assessment Report (AR6), the Intergovernmental Panel on Climate Change (IPCC) stated that "[i]t is unequivocal that human influence has warmed the atmosphere, ocean and land" and that human-induced climate change is "affecting many weather and climate extremes in every region across the globe" bringing about "changes in extremes such as heatwaves, heavy precipitation, droughts, and tropical cyclones."[7] Projected climatic changes create a series of intersecting risks that necessitate adaptation efforts, including: temperature increases, extreme weather events, sea-level changes, drought, food scarcity, fresh water shortages, extreme precipitation, changing patterns of disease, ocean acidification, and wildfires. Individually and cumulatively, these risks will undermine social stability across the globe, and the impacts will be unevenly distributed and differently experienced. Moreover, as described in the Fourth National U.S. Climate Assessment, "the impacts of climate change are already being felt in communities across the country," and "[f]uture climate change is expected to further disrupt many areas of life." As climate change progresses, differences will become increasingly acute:

> [I]mpacts within and across regions will not be distributed equally. People who are already vulnerable, including lower-income and other marginalized communities, have lower capacity to prepare for and cope with extreme weather and climate-related events and are expected to experience greater

---

5. Luke Kemp et al., Perspective, *Climate Endgame: Exploring Catastrophic Climate Scenarios*, 119 Proc. Nat'l Acad. Sci., no. 34, Aug. 1, 2022, at 1, https://www.pnas.org/doi/abs/10.1073/pnas.2108146119.
6. *See id.*
7. IPCC, Climate Change 2022: The Physical Science Basis, Headline Statements 1 (2022), https://www.ipcc.ch/report/ar6/wg1/downloads/report/IPCC_AR6_WGI_Headline_Statements.pdf.

impacts. Prioritizing adaptation actions for the most vulnerable populations would contribute to a more equitable future within and across communities.[8]

The effects of climate change already pose a complex set of risks for natural and human systems. In a worst-case climate world, these effects will intensify and, in turn, amplify differences in how individuals and communities experience climate change. Consider, for example, how patterns of migration and displacement in a "four degree Celsius- (4°C)-warmer world will expose and intensify differences."

It is projected that even mild climate change will increase patterns of migration and displacement of people both within and across national borders creating a myriad of social, economic, and legal challenges. For example, the most recent IPCC report confirmed that climate change "is contributing to humanitarian crises" and that "[c]limate and weather extremes are increasingly driving displacement,"[9] with displacement and involuntary migration likely to increase over time.[10] As Jane McAdam suggests, "migration can be a form of adaptation to environmental and climate change, and in many cases will be an extremely effective way to build long-term resilience," but it will also disrupt the stability and sense of place and well-being of millions of people.[11] The number and diversity of people affected will be vast and varied. It will include people who are displaced and communities into which displaced people migrate. Climate migration will reshape coastal communities, farming communities, urban communities and beyond. People affected by climate migration will come from rich and poor communities, from different racial, religious, and political backgrounds.[12]

Estimates vary for how many people will be displaced by climate-related impacts. Early assessments suggested that climate change might drive 200 million or more people to migrate by 2050.[13] More recent estimates range

8. U.S. Global Change Research Program, *Fourth National Climate Assessment: Volume II: Impacts, Risks, and Adaptation in the United States*, Summary Findings (2018), https://nca2018.globalchange.gov [hereinafter *Fourth National Climate Assessment*].
9. Hans-O. Pörtner et al., Intergovernmental Panel on Climate Change, Climate Change 2022: Impacts, Adaptation, and Vulnerability: Summary for Policymakers B.1.7 (2022), https://report.ipcc.ch/ar6wg2/pdf/IPCC_AR6_WGII_SummaryForPolicymakers.pdf.
10. *Id.* at B.4.7.
11. Jane McAdam, Climate Change-Related Displacement of Persons, in The Oxford Handbook of International Climate Change Law (Cinnamon P. Carlarne et al. eds., 2016).
12. Climate change is already affecting millions of people around the world and those numbers will grow exponentially over time leading to increased flows of internal and external migration. "Human migration is a natural response to these climate change pressures and is one of many adaptation measures that people will take in response to climate change." Caleb Robinson et al., *Modeling Migration Patterns in the USA Under Sea-Level Rise*, PLOS ONE 1-2 (2020), https://journals.plos.org/plosone/article?id=10.1371/journal.pone.0227436 [https://perma.cc/26S4-9JC4].
13. Katrina Miriam Wyman, *Responses to Climate Migration*, 37 Harv. Envtl. L. Rev. 167, 168 (2013).

from between 25 million to 1 billion by 2050,[14] with the World Bank estimating that absent rapid and concerted climate action upwards of 216 million people could be forced to migrate internally alone by 2050.[15] Of course, it is difficult to accurately predict future numbers of climate migrants due to uncertainty about the local impacts of climate change[16] and a lack of empirical studies exploring the links between climate change and human migration patterns.[17] Moreover, future flows of climate migration are difficult to estimate because climate impacts are often not the sole cause of displacement[18] and because climate-induced migration is unlikely to follow historic migration patterns. What is clear is that, even in a best-case climate world, climate-induced migration is inevitable. What is unknown is the degree of social disruption and displacement that we will experience in a 4°C world; it is likely to be extreme, leading to, as Robin Kundis Craig describes it, the inevitable need to triage both places and people.[19] This is true even in the United States.

In the United States, climate impacts including sea-level rise, droughts, and flooding will drive human migration,[20] leading to a "redistribution of population across the United States, as people choose to locate in regions less susceptible to extreme climate."[21] Recent weather-related disasters bear this out. When Hurricane Katrina hit Louisiana in 2005, it displaced more than a million people. An estimated 250,000 displaced residents never returned

---

14. *Climate Migrants Might Reach 1 Billion by 2050*, OCHA (Aug. 21, 2017), https://reliefweb.int/report/world/climate-migrants-might-reach-one-billion-2050.
15. *Groundswell: Acting on Internal Migration*, World Bank (2021), https://openknowledge.worldbank.org/handle/10986/36248 (reporting that 216 million people could move within their own countries due to slow-onset climate change impacts by 2050, that they will migrate from areas with lower water availability and crop productivity and from areas affected by sea-level rise and storm surges, and that hotspots of internal climate migration could emerge as early as 2030 and continue to spread and intensify by 2050).
16. Wyman, *supra* note 13, at 171.
17. *See* Robinson et al., *supra* note 12, at 20, discussing the few studies that have taken place and noting the need to improve understanding of "how climate change driven migration will differ from 'business as usual' forms and motivations humans have to migrate."
18. As McAdam sums up:

    [C]limate change will interact with a range of economic, social, and political drivers, which themselves affect migration. For this reason, it is conceptually sounder to view climate change-related movement as a part of global migration dynamics, rather than as a discrete, independent category. Climate change-related displacement is likely to take different forms, and will require a variety of responses at the local, national, regional, and international levels.

    McAdam, *supra* note 11, at 520
19. *See* Robin Kundis Craig, *Survival Equity and Climate Change Triage: How to Decide Who Lives and Who Dies*, *in* Facing the Worst Climate Case: The Role of Law (2023).
20. *Fourth National Climate Assessment*, *supra* note 8, at 335, 675.
21. Qin Fan et al., *Climate Change, Regional Impacts, and Migration in the United States*, 5 J. Ass'n Env't & Res. Economists 3 (2018).

to New Orleans.[22] More recently, in the wake of Hurricane Maria in 2017, almost one-quarter of a million people migrated from Puerto Rico to Connecticut, Florida, Illinois, Massachusetts, New Jersey, New York, Pennsylvania, with many migrants moving to Central Florida.[23]

If climate migration is bound to intensify in a 4°C world, as seems likely, viewing it through the critical lens of dominance allows us to better understand how existing hierarchies of power and categorical distinctions that manifest as differences will shape how people experience climate migration. Surfacing these hierarchies and differences now in a not-yet-worst-case climate world gives us the opportunity to develop more effective and equitable adaptation strategies and, at a minimum, to avoid building climate law on top of existing hierarchies in ways that imbed inequality. In particular, with respect to climate migration, a climate dominance framework provides a tool for identifying and undercutting existing dominant structures that may manifest as xenophobia,[24] nationalism, and parochialism in the face of climate-induced migration. Even for internal migrants, anti-migrant sentiment and stigmatization of "otherness" will pose profound challenges, particularly for at risk and historically excluded communities such as communities of color, low-income communities, and the elderly. Exploring the differential impacts of climate migration now can improve understanding of how climate-induced migration might exacerbate existing patterns of racial, environmental, and socioeconomic inequality in a 4°C world.[25]

To better understand how differences manifest and matter in the climate migration context, it is helpful to think about the different types of communities that will be affected by climate migration. Anna Marandi and Kelly Main offer a helpful typology for categorizing U.S. cities that will be affected by climate migration:

> (1) vulnerable cities—those that will suffer significant losses in population and tax revenue; (2) recipient cities—those that serve as unsuspecting or unwilling "receiving communities" from sudden onset disasters without preparation; and (3) climate destinations cities seeking to rebrand their communi-

22. *See* Allison Plyer, *Facts for Feature: Katrina Impact*, Data Center (Aug. 26, 2016), https://www.datacenterresearch.org/data-resources/katrina/facts-for-impact/.
23. Anna Marandi & Kelly Leilani Main, *Vulnerable City, Recipient City, or Climate Destination? Towards a Typology of Domestic Climate Migration Impacts in US Cities*, 11 J. Envtl. Stud. & Sci. 465 (2021), https://link.springer.com/article/10.1007/s13412-021-00712-2 [hereinafter *Vulnerable City, Recipient City, or Climate Destination?*].
24. E. Tendayi Achiume, *Governing Xenophobia*, 51 Vand. J. Transnat'l L. 333, 336 (2018).
25. *Vulnerable City, Recipient City, or Climate Destination?*, *supra* note 23.

ties as "climate havens" that welcome displaced residents through equitable planning and preparation.[26]

This is not an exhaustive picture of the range of communities that will be affected, but it is a helpful starting point for bringing a critical perspective to bear to explore the differential effects of climate migration.

Vulnerable locales are those that will not only be hit hard by climate change but also will likely lose population.[27] Examples of such areas include: Kivalina, Alaska; Isle de Jean Charles and New Orleans, Louisiana; Staten Island, New York; and Tyrell County, North Carolina. Many of these communities have already experienced outward migration because of past weather-related disasters.[28] Many of those that have and are likely to be displaced are low-income communities and communities of color.

Many of the people displaced from vulnerable places will end up in recipient cities. There are dozens of these potential recipient communities around the United States. Much learning is left to do about these communities—which communities fall into this category, how prepared they are for climate change migrants, how community values and norms regarding place might be mobilized to create opportunities or barriers to the ability of climate migrants to not only find spaces to survive, but also places to thrive. But what we do know is that many—if not most—are unprepared for vast inflows of migrants, and many are likely to adopt a nativist approach to the influx of climate-displaced peoples.[29]

As past examples of what this kind of flow might look like, when Hurricane Katrina hit New Orleans, more than 250,000 people fled to Houston, Texas. Of those immediate evacuees, an estimated 22,5000 households permanently settled in Harris County, Texas (home of Houston).[30] When

26. *Id.* (emphasis added).

27. Other hard-hit areas, e.g.: West Palm Beach, Florida; varies areas of New York; and Houston, Texas, might see continuing population growth, at least in the short term. Much of this depends on physical and economic infrastructure.

28. *Id.*

29. *See, e.g.*, Reeve Hamilton, *The Huddled Masses*, TEX. TRIB., https://www.texastribune.org/2010/08/30/five-years-houstonians-conflicted-about-katrina/. For a discussion of how nativist perspectives have infused U.S. immigration policy, see George J. Sánchez, *Face the Nation: Race, Immigration, and the Rise of Nativism in Late Twentieth Century America*, 31 INT'L MIGRATION REV. 1009, 1021 (1997); Stephen Lee, *The Economic Dimensions of Family Separation*, 71 DUKE L.J. 845, 906 (2022) ("The broad and inclusive nature of labor protections are negotiated and implemented within a political environment with streaks of nativism and nationalism. Those on the political right often invoke nativist sentiments to argue against increasing migration opportunities."); Demetrios G. Papademetriou et al., *In Search of a New Equilibrium: Immigration Policymaking in the Newest Era of Nativist Populism*, MIGRATION POL'Y INST. (Nov. 2018).

30. *Hurricane Katrina Migration: Where Did People Go? Where Are They Coming From Now?*, TIMES-PICAYUNE (Aug. 27, 2015; updated July 18, 2019), https://www.nola.com/news/article_b84a9b86-e0dc-511a-872d-09fef0012508.html.

Hurricane Maria devastated Puerto Rico in 2017, nearly one-quarter of a million Puerto Ricans fled. Many of those households permanently resettled in Central Florida, including many in and around Orlando.[31] Following the 2018 Camp Fire in Paradise, California, of the over 56,000 people who fled their homes, nearly 20,000 ended up in the nearby town of Chico, California. Within days of the Paradise Camp Fire, "20,000 evacuees and hundreds of emergency responders were staying at emergency shelters, hotels, rentals, or camped out in the Walmart and Target parking lots. Almost overnight, the college town saw growth not expected for an additional two decades."[32] In Chico, like in Houston, Orlando, and other cities experiencing dramatic inflows of evacuees and migrants, the city was ill-prepared to accommodate its new residents. Initial compassion for evacuees rapidly "devolved into resentment as rents rose and evictions increased."[33] Similar patterns of ill-preparedness for climate migrant—manifesting in place-based resentments and pushback that frame community values, norms, and needs as being threatened by migrants—can be seen all over the country.[34]

The last category of cities worth considering from a climate dominance perspective are the self-styled "climate havens." Cities such as Duluth, Min-

31. *Vulnerable City, Recipient City, or Climate Destination?*, *supra* note 23.
32. *Id.*
33. *Id.*
34. For an excellent discussion of anticipated levels of migration driven by sea level rise, alone, and the possible impact of the influx of migrants on recipient communities, *see* Mathew E. Hauer, *Migration Induced by Sea-Level Rise Could Reshape the U.S. Population Landscape*, 7 Nature Climate Change 321 (2017) (suggesting that cities "such as Austin Texas, Orlando Florida, Atlanta Georgia, and Houston Texas could see more than 250,000 previously unforeseen future [sea level rise] net migrants"and finding that and over the coming century could place undue burden in these places if accommodation strategies are left unplanned"[f]or many destinations, such as Riverside California, Phoenix Arizona, Las Vegas Nevada, and Atlanta Georgia, already experiencing water management and growth management challenges, the SLR migrants who wash across the landscape." *Id.* at 323-24). Inequality also manifests in the federal government's response to people displaced by climate-related disasters. *See, e.g.*, Hannah Perls, *U.S. Disaster Displacement in the Era of Climate Change: Discrimination and Consultation Under the Stafford Act*, 44 Harv. Envtl. L. Rev. 511, 538-39 (2020):

> Hurricane Katrina exposed major inequities in the federal government's disaster response, including disproportionate access to evacuation routes, housing, and shelters for racial and ethnic minorities. More recently, researchers found that HUD's CDBG-DR design and implementation rules for the 2017 Gulf Coast hurricanes diverted funding away from housing assistance for renters, privileging homeowners and thus reinforcing longstanding housing inequities. In Texas after Hurricane Harvey, 52% of surveyed white residents reported being able to access disaster aid, as compared to 46% of Hispanic residents and 32% of black residents. Other recent investigations found that at any given level of local damage, the more aid an area receives from FEMA, the more wealth inequality increases in that area along lines of race, education, and homeownership; that FEMA's cost-benefit calculations exacerbate wealth inequality; and that nationwide, white communities disproportionately receive more federal buyouts after a disaster than communities of color.

See also Abrahm Lustgarten, *How Climate Migration Will Reshape America. Millions Will Be Displaced. Where Will They Go?*, N.Y. Times, Sept. 15, 2020, https://www.nytimes.com/interactive/2020/09/15/magazine/climate-crisis-migration-america.html.

nesota; Buffalo, New York; and Cincinnati and Cleveland, Ohio, are branding themselves as good places to live in a climate-changed world— cities that both seek to be "climate-proof" and are eager to welcome new folks in.

The idea of climate havens is still a new one and is unexplored in the scholarly literature, but there is growing interest in the role that climate havens might play as climate impacts intensify and climate displacement increases.[35] In contrast to recipient cities that adopt nativist outlooks,[36] climate havens represent an inclusionary mindset. But what will this inclusion look like in practice, especially in a 4°C world? Who will these cities welcome—both in the near term and in the worst-case climate scenario? How equipped are they to accommodate different kinds of climate migrants? Will the emphasis be on attracting voluntary migrants whose privilege allows them the opportunity to move to a safe environment—for example, those "100 million young adults who aren't sure where their next job will be or which places will be ecologically stable"[37]—or will it be on providing inclusive and welcoming environments for those people who are displaced by climate-related disasters and "may have limited resources to relocate or rebuild"?[38]

Mobility is power and power is dominance. As Doreen Massey suggests, "mobility, and control over mobility, both reflects and reinforces power. It is not simply a question of unequal distribution, that some people move more than others, and that some have more control than others. It is that the mobility and control of some groups can actively weaken other people."[39] Thus, even as we consider the promise and possibility of climate havens, a climate dominance approach encourages us to think about how existing structures of power shape the ability of these cities to appreciate and respond to the risks and impacts of climate change for different communities of residents, both present and future.

35. *Vulnerable City, Recipient City, or Climate Destination?*, *supra* note 23:

> The term "climate haven" first made headlines in a New York Times article that featured Professor Jesse Keenan, entitled "Want to Escape Global Warming? These Cities Promise Cool Relief." Since then, a significant amount of media attention has been given to the potential of legacy cities like Duluth, MN; Buffalo, NY; and Cincinnati, OH, to absorb climate migrants from less hospitable places of the country in the coming decades.

36. Here recognizing that the categories of recipient cities and climate havens are not mutually exclusive. That is, recipient cities will vary in how they respond to climate migrants and while there may be recipient cities that adopt nativist and exclusionary approaches to climate migrants, there may also be recipient cities that adopt more inclusionary climate haven-oriented mindsets.

37. Parag Khanna & Susan Joy Hassol, *America's Next Great Migrations Are Driven by Climate Change*, Sci. Am., Oct. 14, 2021, https://www.scientificamerican.com/article/americas-next-great-migrations-are-driven-by-climate-change/.

38. Dan Kraker, *Climate-Proof Duluth? Why the City Is Attracting "Climate Migrants,"* MPR News, Oct. 4, 2021, https://www.mprnews.org/story/2021/10/04/climateproof-duluth-why-the-city-is-attracting-climate-migrants.

39. Doreen Massey, *A Global Sense of Place*, *in* Space, Place, & Gender 146-56 (1994).

When we view the realities of extreme climate migration through a dominance lens, for example, we might recognize that communities that center nativism values or parochialist practices tend to cast their community values as being in competition with migrants. Nativism tends to result in increased tension and bigotry, aggravating existing concerns over stresses on limited resources and the perceived challenges to co-existence. As a result, both communities rendered uninhabitable by climate change—that is, vulnerable cities—and communities that become climate-recipient cities or climate havens will be affected.

In vulnerable cities, sense of place may transition from one of living and thriving to one of surviving. The displaced will face the well-chronicled physical, mental, and economic challenges of migrants. At every stage, from encountering climate extremes at one's home, through the difficult decision to abandon one's home, to the arduous process of finding a new place to live, climate-displaced people will experience extreme stress and trauma.[40] Dominant voices tend to drown out place-based perspectives of the marginalized and disadvantaged communities, a problem that will be exacerbated by extreme climate change.

Communities that become climate recipient spaces and climate havens will face different challenges. Certain climate recipient cities might be wary of an influx of migrants. But while nativist climate recipient communities try to erect barriers to migrants, inclusionary-minded climate havens will find ways to open their arms to climate-displaced peoples, seeing the influx of new people as a way to revitalize declining cities and an opportunity to deepen sense of community in a climate-stressed world.[41] In both contexts,

40. *See, e.g.*, Jeffrey R. Baker & Allyson McKinney Timm, *Zero-Tolerance: The Trump Administration's Human Rights Violations Against Migrants on the Southern Border*, 13 Drexel L. Rev. 581, 614 (2021) (citing a 2019 American Medical Association letter to the U.S. Department of Homeland Security calling for humanitarian response to migration at the southern border and highlighting the lifelong trauma migrant children and families experience:

> Families seeking refuge in the U.S. already endure emotional and physical stress, which is only exacerbated when they are separated from one another or held in family detention facilities during the pendency of their immigration proceedings. It is well known that childhood trauma and adverse childhood experiences created by inhumane treatment often create negative health impacts that can last an individual's entire lifespan.

See also Becky L. Jacobs, *Perpetuating Persecution: Mental Health and Psychosocial Barriers to U.S. Immigration*, 27 Tex. J. C.L. & C.R. 1 (2021):

> Many of these individuals suffer common mental disorders, some of which are associated with the trauma that they experienced during the violence or other circumstances that resulted in their displacement, including post-traumatic stress disorder (PTSD), hypervigilance, depression, anxiety, panic attacks, and somatization. See also Stephen Paskey, *Telling Refugee Stories: Trauma, Credibility, and the Adversarial Adjudication of Claims for Asylum*, 56 Santa Clara L. Rev. 457 (2016).

41. There are interesting intersections to consider between the impacts of climate change and other disasters, such as the COVID-19 pandemic, which cumulatively might drive demographic changes.

the idea of place and the self-assessment that comes with it could allow communities to decenter nativist concerns and recognize that migration is not a cultural distinction, but a human situation.

Exploring current and projected migration trends now—in a not-yet-worst-case climate world—is critical to understanding existing hierarchies of power and the differences they manifest so that we can begin the process of decentering dominant ideas and better accounting for how differences manifest and matter when it comes to understanding the impacts of climate change and climate migration while we still have time to create equitable adaptation strategies for all.[42] Centering these different senses of community and place is central to climate resilience and climate equity in a 4°C world. We still have time to avoid the human triage that Craig warns of in her chapter, "Survival Equity and Climate Change Triage: How to Decide Who Lives and Who Dies."[43] This is the work of a critical climate dominance approach.

Climate migration, of course, will not occur in isolation. It will take place against a preexisting backdrop of systemic inequality and racial dominance.

Racial Dominance and Risks of Climate Gentrification

Racial dominance of space is a current reality. Judge Carlton W. Reeves of the U.S. District Court of the Southern District of Mississippi illustrated the problem of racial domination in his decision *Jamison v. McClendon*.[44] In 2013, Clarence Jamison was driving to his home in South Carolina in his recently purchased 2001 convertible Mercedes. As he drove through Mississippi, Mr. Jamison passed a police officer who was parked on the side of the road. The officer stopped Mr. Jamison on grounds that the temporary tag on the car was "folded over."[45] The officer flashed lights and Mr. Jamison pulled to the side of the road.

At trial, there was some controversy as to whether the temporary tag was in fact folded or if it was (as testified to by Jamison) properly secured

For example, there is evidence that COVID-19 has driven shifts in where people choose to live, with particular declines in the number of people who want to live in urban centers *See, e.g.*, Thomas B. Edsall, *How a "Golden Era" for Large Cities Might Be Turning Into an "Urban Doom Loop,"* N.Y. Times, Nov. 30, 2022, https://www.nytimes.com/2022/11/30/opinion/covid-pandemic-cities-future.html.

42. For an in-depth discussion of the different strategies cities are (and are not) using to disrupt dominance in climate action planning and climate adaptation planning, see Cinnamon P. Carlarne & Keith H. Hirokawa, *Disrupting Dominance* (work-in-progress on file with authors). In relevant part, the authors argue that climate adaptation planning should center human vulnerability as a necessary precondition to developing more equitable and effective adaptation planning.
43. Craig, *supra* note 19.
44. 476 F. Supp. 3d 386 (S.D. Miss. 2020).
45. *Id.* at 392.

and readable in plain sight.[46] Nevertheless, that issue was irrelevant, as the police officer insisted on searching the car based on his representation that he had been given information that the car was being used to transport cocaine.[47] The officer knew that this was a blatant lie, but repeated the lie as he attempted to secure (and ultimately succeeded in securing) consent to the search.[48] The officer dismantled parts of the car and brought in his canine, yet found nothing suspicious or illegal in the vehicle. The officer promptly drove away, but only after Mr. Jamison sat, waiting, for two hours on the side of the road.[49]

The circumstance is not shocking merely because it happened. Judge Reeves explained with ironical undertones that Mr. Jamieson was *not* engaged in the types of dangerous activities that other African Americans had committed to garner the attention and brute force of police officers.[50] In his opinion, Judge Reeves noted:

> Clarence Jamison wasn't jaywalking.
>
> He wasn't outside playing with a toy gun.
>
> He didn't look like a suspicious person.
>
> He wasn't suspected of selling loose, untaxed cigarettes.
>
> He wasn't suspected of passing a counterfeit $20 bill.
>
> He didn't look like anyone suspected of a crime.
>
> He wasn't mentally ill and in need of help.
>
> He wasn't assisting an autistic patient who had wandered away from a group home.
>
> He wasn't walking home after an afterschool job.
>
> He wasn't walking back from a restaurant.
>
> He wasn't hanging out on a college campus.
>
> He wasn't standing outside his apartment.
>
> He wasn't inside his apartment eating ice cream.
>
> He wasn't sleeping in his bed.

46. *Id.* at 394.
47. *Id.* at 393.
48. *Id.* at 393-94.
49. *Id.* at 395.
50. *Id.* at 390-94.

He wasn't sleeping in his car.

He didn't make an improper lane change.

He didn't have a broken tail light.

He wasn't driving over the speed limit.

He wasn't driving under the speed limit.[51]

The court pointed out that Mr Jamison's offense—an offense committed in white space[52]—was driving while Black. In Mitchell Jackson's words: "Check the books—slave passes, vagrancy laws, Harvard's Skip Gates arrested outside his own crib—Blacks ain't never owned the same freedom of movement as whites."[53]

The court found it relevant to give thanks that Mr. Jamison left the incident alive.[54] Judge Reeves also made a more subtle point: there is no place Mr Jamison could go, no activity he could engage in, that would have produced a different result.[55] Mr. Jamison will always be Black to those who see Blackness as an element of crime or, more accurately, to those who see that Blackness transforms a non-criminal act into a criminal one.[56] To Judge Reeves' dismay in the *Jamison* case,[57] the justice system illustrates neither understanding nor any incentive to ask what violence and trauma was done to Mr. Jamison. Having been denied a remedy in court, Mr. Jamison was without any remedy at all.

The contemporary tools of racial domination—including redlining, racial profiling, exclusion, and explicit and implicit bigotry—are regularly employed to maintain the white space. In this way, racism produces spaces

51. *Id.* at 390-91. Although I have omitted the judge's internal citations for purposes of brevity, each of the distinguished circumstances describes an event in which a Black person was subjected to the brutal use of force by police officers.

52. Elijah Anderson, *The White Space*, 1 Socio. Race & Ethnicity 10, 10 (2015).

53. Mitchell S. Jackson, *Twelve Minutes and a Life: Ahmaud Arbery Went Out for a Jog and Was Gunned Down in the Street. How Running Fails Black America*, Runner's World, June 18, 2020, https://www.runnersworld.com/runners-stories/a32883923/ahmaud-arbery-death-running-and-racism/.

54. *Jamison*, 476 F. Supp. 3d at 391.

55. We might add to Judge Reeves' list many things, but for purposes of this article, we should add the recent arrest of Marc Peeples, who was arrested for gardening while Black. Katelyn Kavel, *This Michigan Man Was Arrested for Gardening While Black. Gov. Whitmer Would Make That 911 Call a Hate Crime*, Gander, July 9, 2020, https://gandernewsroom.com/2020/07/09/gardening-black-911-hate-crime/.

56. For an insightful analysis of distinct differences of policing across racialized geographies, see Elaine Sharpe, *Politics, Economics, and Urban Policing: The Postindustrial City Thesis and Rival Explanations of Heightened Order Maintenance Policing*, 50 Urb. Aff. Rev. 340 (2014).

57. Judge Reeves noted that the court was bound by precedent that extends the shield of qualified immunity to even brutal law enforcement actions. "This has to stop." 476 F. Supp. 3d at 392 (quoting the U.S.Court of Appeals for the Fourth Circuit in *Estate of Jones v. City of Martinsburg, W. Va.*, 961 F.3d 661, 673 (4th Cir. 2020), *as amended* (June 10, 2020)).

marked with power disparities and structural inequities. Such tools do and will continue to appear prominently as we employ adaptive policies to meet climate change. Racial dominance is an inevitable background shaping climate risk and climate difference. In the adaptation context, racial domination of space results in an unequal distribution of adaptive capacity: white privilege in this context will come to mean the availability of opportunities—generally exclusively held—to prepare for the economic, social, and environmental changes that accompany climatic shifts. The ongoing, dramatic examples seen in our early climatic struggles, including flooding in eastern Kentucky,[58] wildfires in California,[59] and the mega drought of the West,[60] illustrate that times of shortage and scarcity are not likely to be addressed through principles of collective well-being and sharing.[61] Instead, the impacts of such disasters will be amplified for some as a result of the dominance of existing hierarchies of power and aggressive individualism that inheres in our political economy.

Of course, it is not a novel observation that race is a significant factor in identifying disadvantaged communities, including a community's vulnerability to climate change impacts, and it is similarly accepted that adaptive capacity is unevenly enjoyed in racialized communities.[62] There is now extensive scholarly work examining how climate change deepens inequality by disproportionately affecting members of society who already face higher

58. *See, e.g.*, Julia Jacob & Melissa Griffin, *Scientists Explain How the Deadly Flooding in Kentucky Got So Bad: "It Was Bound to Be Catastrophic,"* ABC News, Aug. 3, 2022, https://abcnews.go.com/US/scientists-explain-deadly-flooding-kentucky-bad-bound-catastrophic/story?id=87832020.

59. *See, e.g.*, Winston Choi-Shagrin & Elena Shao, *Why Does the American West Have So Many Wildfires?*, N.Y. Times, Aug. 1, 2022, https://www.nytimes.com/2022/08/01/climate/wildfire-risk-california-west.html.

60. A. Park Williams et al., *Large Contribution From Anthropogenic Warming to an Emerging North American Megadrought*, 368 Science 314, 314 (2020). *See also* Scientific Visualization Studio, *SVS: Megadrought in U.S. West Projected to Be Worst of the Millennium*, Nat'l Air & Space Ass'n (Feb. 12, 2015), https://svs.gsfc.nasa.gov/cgi-bin/details.cgi?aid=4270 [https://perma.cc/FV72-96Z6].

61. At least in the case of the megadrought in the West, the western water law doctrine of prior appropriation "is every man for himself, and is indivudalism in the highest degree." Samuel Wiel, *Theories of Water Law*, 27 Harv. L. Rev. 530, 542 (1914).

62. *See* Anthony Oliver Smith, *Disasters and Forced Migration in the 21st Century*, Items Insights From Soc. Sci. (June 11, 2006), https://items.ssrc.org/understanding-katrina/disasters-and-forced-migration-in-the-21st-century/ (discussing "how social systems generate the conditions that place different kinds of people, often differentiated along axes of class, race, ethnicity, gender, or age, at different levels of risk from the same hazard."); Adger et al., *supra* note 2, at 1593. For further work exploring the relationship between race and systemic exclusion that influences planning, including adaptation planning, see Keith H. Hirokawa, *Race, Space, and Place: Interrogating Whiteness Through a Critical Approach to Place*, 29 Wm. & Mary J. Race, Gender, & Soc. Just. 279 (2023), https://scholarship.law.wm.edu/wmjowl/vol29/iss2/2 and K-Sue Park, *This Land Is Not Our Land*, 87 U. Chi. L. Rev. 1977, 2023 (2020).

levels of vulnerability.[63] Indeed, we are already witnessing the frustrations of the politically powerless that find themselves vulnerable to climate gentrification.[64] Climate gentrification refers to the

> general circumstances in which one of the forces that cause the displacement of people from a neighborhood is climate change. . . . Briefly, the empirical observation of climate gentrification through this research is established when real estate values of property under threat of sea-level rise (low-lying areas) appreciate at a lower rate than values of property at higher ground. At the same time, Keenan has observed that coastal properties' values have fallen.[65]

Climate gentrification is already displacing racialized and low-income communities where the topography or other locationally dependent advantages of such communities offer adaptive capacity. In Miami, Florida, for example, coastal property owners are retreating to inland, higher elevation neighborhoods, a situation which unsurprisingly targets affordable neighborhoods and accompanies infrastructure and other investments, all of which drives higher and unaffordable rents and displaces current residents.[66] Robynne Boyd explains:

> Much of the city sits just six feet above sea level, and many neighborhoods are vulnerable to the expected sea-level rise of 14 to 34 inches by 2060. Former [Sen.] Bill Nelson [D-Fla.] has called the city "ground zero" for climate change. Meanwhile, at higher elevations, many of the residents of Liberty City and other underserved Black and Latino communities say they feel pressure from real estate developers to sell their homes.[67]

---

63. *See generally* Alice Kaswan, *Climate Adaptation and Theories of Justice*, *in* Philosophy, Law, and Environmental Crisis 97 (Alain Papaux & Simone Zurbuchen eds., 2016).

64. As noted by Jesse Keenan and colleagues climate gentrification analysis is premised on

> the need to promulgate a broader awareness of the processes shaping socioeconomic vulnerabilities and not just physical environmental exposure. Likewise, it highlights the dynamic and dependent relationships of elements of the built environment (e.g., housing, transportation, public facilities) that may either exacerbate vulnerabilities associated with climate change impacts or are themselves exacerbated by such impacts.

Jesse M. Keenan et al., *Climate Gentrification: From Theory to Empiricism in Miami-Dade County, Florida*, 13 Env't Res. Letters 054001 (2018).

65. Sue Trone & Ryan Shedd, *The City of Miami in the Context of Climate Change, Population Growth, and Development Pressure: Policy and Strategy Recommendations*, City of Miami (Nov. 2019), https://southeastfloridaclimatecompact.org/wp-content/uploads/2020/03/Climate-Gentrification-in-Miami_FINAL-1.pdf.

66. *See* Keenan et al., *supra* note 64. Climate gentrification "is based on a simple proposition: climate change impacts arguably make some property more or less valuable by virtue of its capacity to accommodate a certain density of human settlement and its associated infrastructure." *Id.*

67. Robynne Boyd, *Has Climate Gentrification Hit Miami? The City Plans to Find Out*, NRDC (Mar. 11, 2019), *available at* https://www.nrdc.org/stories/has-climate-gentrification-hit-miami-city-plans-find-out.

Climate gentrification is a contemporary reality that amplifies existing patterns of racial dominance of space.[68] With little (if any) political attention being paid to climate gentrification and little existing political will to account for the impacts of climate gentrification, communities will be displaced as a worst-case climate scenario influences which properties are deemed valuable and habitable. More often than not, those that are displaced will be racialized and low-income communities. Displacement from climate gentrification is the space counterpart to the dilemma of climate migration, where established communities are seen as obstacles to adaptation of those with the most means and the most power. Like climate migration, exploring ongoing patterns of climate gentrification now—in a not-yet-worst-case climate world—is critical to understanding how existing systems of racial and economic dominance enable climate gentrification. Again, this is the work of a climate dominance approach.

Topographical Advantage Creating Climate Vulnerabilities

Viewing climate migration and climate gentrification through the lens of climate dominance exposes how hierarchies of power create differences that shape how and where people are able to live, thrive, and survive in a climate-changed world. Topographical advantage similarly shapes climate difference. In fact, it shapes the daily lived experiences of communities across the country. Topography and geography intersect with cultural differences to shape how and by whom resources are controlled, who they are available to, and how individual and community risks are determined in a climate-changed world. Bringing a climate dominance framework to bear in the context of topographical advantage allows us to see how power can be relational to space and to detect and surface different forms of dominion

68. Forms of racial dominance, including climate gentrification, intersect with other forms of dominance, including topographical dominance, which is described in the following section. The lenses we bring to bear to surface and interrogate systems of dominance in the climate context are not exclusive and often intersect and overlap in interesting and important ways. For a fuller discussion of the different but related lenses that can be brought to bear to explore difference and dominance in the climate change context, see Hirokawa & Carlarne, *supra* note 3 (exploring differences through three related but distinct lenses: space, which illustrates the ways that location may determine one's needs and advantages; place, which recognizes that the historical development of a community, together with a shared sense of place, brings with it a certain dependency on beliefs, predispositions, and prejudices; and time, through which we acknowledge that present actions have a real and measurable impact on future generations, particularly when we limit our priorities to values that serve our present needs).

over space, e.g., white spaces,[69] redlining,[70] zoning,[71] control of ecosystem services,[72] property rights.[73]

Here, we look at topographical advantage in the context of a single watershed—the Poesten Kill—to interrogate and unravel how existing hierarchies of power shape profound differences in who has access to vital ecosystem services and to imagine how these power differences will be compounded in a 4°C world, if left unaddressed in the present.

The Poesten Kill in eastern New York provides an illustrative example of topographical dominance throughout most of its 26-mile route as it flows from the rural, forested lands on the Rensselaer Plateau, into and through agricultural areas and the suburban towns of Poestenkill and Brunswick, and finally into the urbanized areas of South Troy.[74] Throughout the reach of the creek, the Poesten Kill serves a variety of human needs (such as land use types and lifestyles) and ecosystem functions (such as biodiversity). It also presents ecosystem disservices[75] to communities situated in vulnerable locations in the watershed during significant storm events. Paying attention to ecosystem services derived from the Poesten Kill now can help identify which stakeholders are in positions of dominance as they control the delivery

69. *See* Anderson, *supra* note 52, at 11.

70. *See* KEEANGA-YAMAHTTA TAYLOR, RACE FOR PROFIT: HOW BANKS AND THE REAL ESTATE INDUSTRY UNDERMINED BLACK HOMEOWNERSHIP 18-19 (UNC Press 2019).

71. *See, e.g.*, Daniel R. Mandelker, *Racial Discrimination and Exclusionary Zoning: A Perspective on Arlington Heights*, 55 TEX. L. REV. 1217, 1218-19 (1977) (exploring the U.S. Supreme Court's decision in *Village of Arlington Heights v. Metropolitan Hous. Dev. Corp.*, finding "that exclusionary zoning does not constitute state-imposed racial discrimination unless it is shown that a municipality initiated the zoning exclusion with a racially discriminatory motive or intent" and arguing that "this interpretation is inconsistent with a fair reading of the fourteenth amendment's prohibition of racial discrimination). *See also* Christopher Silver, *The Racial Origins of Zoning: Southern Cities From 1910-40*, 6 PLAN. PERSP. 189 (2007).

72. *See* Keith H. Hirokawa et al., *Mapping Ecosystem Benefit Flows to Normalize Equity*, 54 ARIZ. ST. L.J. 819 (2023).

73. *See generally* Keith H. Hirokawa, *Three Stories About Nature: Property, the Environment, and Ecosystem Services*, 62 MERCER L. REV. 541 (2011).

74. Analyzing flood control benefit flows from rural, forested, and agroecosystems into urbanized areas is a common study unit, in large part because flood control services are directional, and flooding damages in urbanized areas are more pronounced. *See, e.g.*, Victor Martínez-García et al., *The Economic Value of Flood Risk Regulation by Agroecosystems at Semiarid Areas*, 266 AGRIC. WATER MGMT. 1 (2022); Stoyan Nedkov & Benjamin Burkhard, *Flood Regulating Ecosystem Services—Mapping Supply and Demand, in the Etropole Municipality, Bulgaria*, 21 ECOLOGICAL INDICATORS 67, 67-68 (2012).

75. In hazard risk planning, ecosystem services focus on severe storm events and other natural risks, such as landslides, earthquakes, drought, forest fires, flooding, and so on. Whereas ecosystem services provide humans with the benefits of functioning ecosystems, severe storm events challenge human life and well-being and have been referred to as "ecosystem disservices." Julien Blanco et al., *Ecosystem Disservices Matter: Towards Their Systematic Integration Within Ecosystem Service Research and Policy*, 36 ECOSYSTEM SERVS. 100913 (2019); Jari Lyytimäki et al., *Nature as a Nuisance? Ecosystem Services and Disservices to Urban Lifestyle*, 5 ENVTL. SCI. 161 (2008). In other instances, ecosystem services analysis focuses on basic human needs for clean water, agricultural needs for pollinators, or structural support needs for home construction.

of ecosystem services to other stakeholders, including water availability, flood management, and water quality benefits of the creek. Such an analysis illustrates the inequitable distribution of power over those ecosystem services, a situation that will be apparent and problematic in local and regional adaptation policies now and will be further amplified in a worst-case climate world.

The Poesten Kill has served various functions in the region for hundreds, if not thousands of years. The area was inhabited by the Mohicans until the sale of lands in the region to the Dutch merchant Kiliaen van Rensselaer in 1624.[76] It is thought the flow of the Poesten Kill (and that of its tributaries) has been controlled by several dams over the years, but little evidence is left of most such structures. Today, the creek begins at Dyken Pond, a man-made waterbody on the Rensselaer Plateau that was constructed in 1902 for flood control purposes.[77] As the Poesten Kill flows toward the Hudson River Estuary, it is fed by springs, Bonesteel Creek, Newfoundland Creek, Sweet Milk Creek, and the Quacken Kill, as well as a number of unnamed tributaries.[78] The creek discharges into the Hudson River in the highly urbanized city of Troy. Along the way, the Poesten Kill serves local populations as a source of drinking water, irrigation of agricultural lands, power generation, and sawmills. The creek, which has been designated as a trout-bearing stream,[79] also draws crowds who appreciate the aesthetics and recreational opportunities of the Poesten Kill Gorge and Barberville Falls.[80]

For purposes of this section, we address climate vulnerability as a calculation of ecosystem services loss and benefit. Ecosystem services represent the notion that humans derive benefits from functioning ecosystems, where access to ecosystem services comprises a form of wealth. "Ecosystem services," which refers to "the ecological characteristics, functions, or processes that directly or indirectly contribute to human well-being: that is, the benefits that people derive from functioning ecosystems,"[81] are critical to human well-being. Humans rely on ecosystems to deliver essential services, such as the production of goods, the regulation of climatic conditions, support for

---

76. John Warren, The Poesten Kill: Waterfalls to Waterworks in the Capital District 2 (Charleston, South Carolina: The History Press 2009).
77. *Id.* at 18.
78. Town of Poestenkill, *Natural Resources Inventory* (2019) at 43.
79. *See, e.g.*, New York Dep't of Env't Conserv., *Public Fishing Rights Maps: Poesten Kill and Quaken Kill*, https://www.dec.ny.gov/docs/fish_marine_pdf/pfrPoestenk.pdf.
80. Town of Poestenkill, *supra*, note 78.
81. Robert Costanza et al., *Twenty Years of Ecosystem Services: How Far Have We Come and How Far Do We Still Need to Go?*, 28 Ecosystem Servs. 1, 2 (2017). The term has also been defined as the "wide range of conditions and processes through which natural ecosystems, and the species that are part of them, help sustain and fulfill human life." Gretchen C. Daily et al., *Ecosystem Services: Benefits Supplied to Human Societies by Natural Ecosystems*, 2 Issues Ecology 1, 2 (1977).

ecosystem processes, and services that provide cultural value (including spiritual, educational, and recreational needs).[82] Adopting an ecosystem services perspective helps us understand the risks that some face when they lose access to certain ecosystem processes that provide services, and it also illustrates how such losses might be driven by those in control of land on which ecosystem processes take place—those with power or dominance over the ecosystem services.[83]

An inventory of ecosystem services from the Poesten Kill helps to recognize where land use changes cause ecosystem benefit disruption,[84] including how land use choices undermine needed ecosystem benefits and increase vulnerabilities.[85] This analysis involves an interdisciplinary examination that considers human thriving (or survival) in geographical and climatic conditions based on a variety of socioeconomic and ecological factors, including wealth, location, and needs.[86] From an ecosystem services perspective, attention to ecosystem service dependencies and vulnerabilities "can give valuable insight into social needs and reliance on the service (for example, for safety or subsistence) capturing both socioeconomic and environmental conditions."[87]

Riparian areas provide many services. A detailed inventory of riparian services will be location-dependent due to variation of local topography and geology, wildlife and biodiversity needs, land uses, and hydrology (among others). In general, however, riparian areas regulate base flow, recharge aquifers, support aquatic and terrestrial life, influence water quality, and prevent downstream flooding. In the Poesten Kill watershed, several services appear most prominent. First, the rural riparian areas of the Poesten Kill have a lot of work to do. The thousands of acres of forested lands and wetlands on the plateau, which are occasionally managed to produce forest products, also regulate water flows and water quality, stabilize the landscape and capture

82. James Salzman et al., *Protecting Ecosystem Services: Science, Economics, and Law*, 20 Stan. Envtl L.J. 309, 311 (2001).

83. Robert Costanza et al., *The Value of the World's Ecosystem Services and Natural Capital*, 387 Nature 253, 253 (1997).

84. Kenneth J. Bagstad et al., *From Theoretical to Actual Ecosystem Services: Mapping Beneficiaries and Spatial Flows in Ecosystem Service Assessments*, 19 Ecology & Soc'y 64, 73 (2014) ("Incorporating ecosystem services into decision-making can change the way a problem is perceived and the way solutions are formulated because decision makers consider not only changes to ecological conditions but also how these changes can affect people.").

85. Lydia P. Olander et al., *Benefit Relevant Indicators: Ecosystem Services Measures That Link Ecological and Social Outcomes*, 85 Ecological Indicators 1262, 1271 (2018).

86. Chundi Chen et al., *Ecosystem Services Mapping in Practice: A Pasteur's Quadrant Perspective*, 40 Ecosystem Servs. 101042 (December 2019), https://doi.org/10.1016/j.ecoser.2019.101042 (emphasizing the importance of using mapping indicators that "will be directly relevant to people's values, needs and demands, instead of purely ecological biophysical measures or general socio-economic data").

87. S. Wolff et al., *Mapping Ecosystem Services Demand: A Review of Current Research and Future Perspectives*, 55 Ecological Indicators 159, 163 (2015).

carbon.[88] Riparian-associated wetlands also make substantial contributions to human well-being. Wetlands filter contaminants from fresh water while facilitating nutrient cycling and provision of habitat and biomass production. Wetlands also are responsible for producing goods that humans use as food, fuel, and building materials.[89] In the meantime, wetland processes recharge aquifers, absorb storm surges, and generally influence the hydrological cycle. Soils along the Poesten Kill, which facilitate most, if not all other ecosystem processes,[90] vary from highly drained gravel and sandy loam, to less permeable types, such as clay.[91] The mix of soils along the Poesten Kill play a vital role in regulating water flows and providing a shallow aquifer for domestic uses. The forested lands, wetlands, and soils of the Poesten Kill, thus provide innumerable essential ecosystem services for communities throughout the watershed.

The Poesten Kill is also the source of ecosystem disservices, in large part due to development and landscape changes that have degraded the ability of the watershed to provide ecosystem services. People in the Poesten Kill watershed have suffered significant flood damages from recent storm events.[92] Moreover, flooding events, which can lead to death, property loss,

88. Norman Myers, *The World's Forests and Their Ecosystem Services in Ecosystem Services Supplied by Soil, in* Nature's Services: Societal Dependence on Natural Ecosystems 215-16 (Gretchen C. Daily et al. eds., 1997):

> They stabilize landscapes. They protect soils and help them to retain their moisture and to store and cycle nutrients. They serve as buffers against the spread of pests and diseases. By preserving watershed functions, they regulate water flows in terms of both quantity and quality, thereby helping to prevent flood-and-drought regimes in downstream territories. They are critical to the energy balance of the earth. They modulate climates at local and regional levels to regulation of rainfall regimes and the albedo effect; and at planet-wide level, they help to contain global warming by virtue of the carbon stocks in their plants (especially trees) and soils.

89. *See generally* S. Farber et al., *Linking Ecology and Economics for Ecosystem Management*, 56 Bioscience 121 (2002).

90. Gretchen C. Daily et al., *Ecosystem Services Supplied by Soil, in* Nature's Services: Societal Dependence on Natural Ecosystems 113, 113 (Gretchen C. Daily et al. eds., 1997); Steven Banwart et al., *Soil Processes and Functions Across an International Network of Critical Zone Observatories: Introduction to Experimental Methods and Initial Results*, 344 C.R. GeoScience 758, 759-60 (2012):

> [S]oils provide . . . important functions including supporting and sustaining our terrestrial ecosystems, regulating the atmosphere through carbon storage, filtering water, recycling waste, preserving heritage, acting as an aesthetic and cultural resource, whilst maintaining a vital gene pool and biological resource from which many of our antibiotics have been derived.

91. Although not addressed herein, Poestenkill also benefits from the productive agroecosystems between the Rensselaer Plateau and the city of Troy. Jose A. Zabala et al., *A Comprehensive Approach for Agroecosystem Services and Disservices Valuation*, 768 Sci. Total Env't 144859 (2020). Agroecosystems in the Poestenkill watershed reduce flooding damage and "influence[] social welfare by regulating floods through water retention capacity of the vegetation and soil during a flood." *See* Martinez-Garcia et al., *supra* note 74.

92. *See* Martinez-Garcia et al., *supra* note 74: ("In 2019 alone, floods accounted for 49% of all natural disasters and 68% of the population affected by natural disasters worldwide."); Lelys Bravo de Guenni

infectious diseases, and other impacts related to the loss of food and shelter[93] have resulted in disproportionate impacts in low-income communities due to disparities in infrastructure investments and community capacity to respond to storm events.[94]

In this context, topographical domination can be a function of location and control. Property ownership results in a significant amount of control being exercised in upstream riparian areas; these upstream decisions affect whether downstream stakeholders will continue to receive ecosystem benefits. Logging and vegetation clearing in upland areas, such as forested areas on the plateau, as well as conversion of areas to agriculture, reduce the ability of the ecosystem to absorb storm surges and water flows, causing downstream flooding in the city of Troy.[95] Dam construction and stream channelization affect water flows and impair the stream's ability to regulate water quality and quantity. Land use development—particularly the construction of impermeable surfaces such as roads, parking lots and rooftops—affects the functionality of soils and degrades habitat productivity. Moreover, development and the exercise of the right to exclude curtails recreational opportunities throughout the entire length of the Poesten Kill. Property ownership is the single most significant factor influencing the continuing receipt of ecosystem benefits by downstream users. Combined with the likelihood that property ownership within the watershed occurs outside of the jurisdiction where ecosystem services are needed (such as flood control), downstream users of the Poesten Kill are especially vulnerable to the preferences and privileges of the upstream property owners.

The Poesten Kill is a fairly standard watershed in terms of the services it offers and the communities it serves. Looking at topographical dominance in this context thus helps us understand the complex hierarchies of power that shape human well-being along watersheds. What we can see by looking at the systems of power in the Poesten Kill is how upstream users and, in particular, upstream property owners have significant power over how riparian

---

et al., *Regulation of Natural Hazards: Floods and Fires*, *in* 1 Ecosystems and Human Well-Being: Current State and Trends Assessment 441, 447 (Richard Norgaard ed., 2005).

93. Bravo de Guenni et al., *supra* note 92, at 452.

94. *See id.*

95. *See, e.g.*, Onondaga Env't Inst., *An Assessment of Water Quality in the Poesten Kill Watershed*, N. Y. State Dep't Envtl. Conservation Hudson River Estuary Program ii-iii (2019), https://oei2.org/wp-content/uploads/2020/05/POESTWatershedPlan_MERGE.pdf. *See generally* Hirokawa et al., *supra* note 72 (discussing how upstream ecosystem management decisions impact downstream users and exploring these patters of decision making to show how mapping benefit flows from ecosystem service can advance understanding of the power relationships among ecosystem stakeholders, focusing on the different levels of power between those with the opportunity to control the flow of ecosystem services, e.g., upstream users, and those whose well-being depends on them, e.g., Troy residents).

ecosystems will operate. These upstream decisions shape the benefits—for example, clean water, recreation, flood protection—and costs—for example, contaminated water, lack of access to recreation activities, flooding—that downstream users will experience. These differences already matter. In a 4°C world where access to water and flood control becomes of utmost importance, these differences will have profound impacts on human well-being.

Topographical dominance exists in virtually every ecosystem across the United States. These patterns of dominance are sometimes subtle and sometimes obvious but almost always politically fraught to engage. Yet surfacing and engaging existing patterns of dominance is essential to understanding how climate adaptation strategies will amplify or ease difference in ways that will shape the future lives of communities across the country. Exposing these patterns of topographical power now is the work of a critical climate dominance approach.

Conclusion

Climate change is our reality. And climate dominance is the context within which we experience climate change. Climate dominance is a circumstance of the past and present that will have certain and significant impacts on the adaptive capacity of communities as we confront climate change. Ignoring dominance now will result in policies that further entrench inequities and exacerbate disparities throughout our social, economic, and ecological systems. By identifying and centering dominance now in a not-yet-worse-case climate world, we can appreciate topographical, racial, cultural, and economic differences that help us understand where adaptive advantages lie in any particular community. In this chapter, we begin this process of identifying and undermining climate dominance in the contexts of climate migration, climate gentrification, and ecosystem management to contemplate more equitable adaptation planning.

Conclusion

Challenges of Law, Governance, and Equity in Implementing Climate Policies

Shannon M. Roesler

As the authors of this volume were writing about the challenges of adapting to high levels of global warming, Congress passed landmark climate legislation designed to accelerate the transition to a low-carbon economy. In August 2022, after Senate Democrats used the reconciliation process to bypass the need for Republican votes, President Joe Biden signed the Inflation Reduction Act (IRA), legislation that contains $369 billion in clean energy subsidies.[1]

Although many climate advocates had hoped for much more, IRA is a rare victory in an era of political polarization and gridlock. Its tax credits and rebates are likely to bolster the markets for renewable energy (both utility scale and distributed), residential electrification, electric vehicles, and more. Moreover, IRA attaches some subsidies to prevailing wage standards and sourcing requirements for batteries and renewable energy technologies designed to support domestic manufacturing. It also provides incentives for investment in communities disproportionately burdened by fossil-fuel pollution. In short, it incorporates principles of a Green New Deal that support a transition away from fossil fuels that addresses social inequities and create economic opportunity. Paired with the billions of dollars dedicated to energy infrastructure in the Bipartisan Infrastructure Law of 2021,[2] IRA has the potential to create a new clean energy economy and more resilient electric grid.

Months later, the U.S. Environmental Protection Agency (EPA) reinforced these subsidies with proposed regulations targeting greenhouse gas (GHG) emissions from new vehicles and gas- and coal-fired power plants.[3] By setting limits with electrification as the goal, the proposed emissions

1. Inflation Reduction Act, Pub. L. No. 117-169, 136 Stat 1818 (Aug. 16, 2022).
2. Infrastructure Investment and Jobs Acts, Pub. L. No. 117-58, 135 Stat. 429 (2021).
3. New Source Performance Standards for Greenhouse Gas Emissions From New, Modified, and Reconstructed Fossil Fuel-Fired Electric Generating Units; Emission Guidelines for Greenhouse Gas Emissions From Existing Fossil Fuel-Fired Electric Generating Units; and Repeal of the Affordable Clean Energy Rule, 88 Fed. Reg. 33240 (May 23, 2023) (proposed rule).

standards for new light- and medium-duty vehicles could cut the emissions of two-thirds of new vehicles to zero by 2032.[4] The proposed power plant rules seek to cut emissions by phasing in requirements for carbon capture and storage or (in the case of natural gas units) co-firing with low-GHG hydrogen.[5] These rules are part of the Biden Administration's efforts to slash emissions by 50% by 2030 and achieve net-zero emissions by 2050.[6]

Federal agencies have been scrambling to ensure the subsidies have pathways for implementation and rules are finalized as quickly as possible. In addition to the EPA, the U.S. Departments of Energy, the Interior, and Treasury have been tasked with new mandates to create and oversee the implementation of federal funds not only toward grid and vehicle electrification, but also toward improved drinking water infrastructure, cleanup of contaminated lands, and investment in environmental justice communities.[7] State and local governments have roles to play as well in implementing federal programs. For example, states will be responsible for administering rebates to property owners who make upgrades to appliances (with a preference for electrification) and improve their properties' energy efficiency.

Of course, all of this is happening in the shadow of deep uncertainty about how much mitigation IRA will achieve and the fate of mitigation efforts in the rest of the world. Everyone working to implement and take advantage of these steps toward decarbonization is reminded regularly of how tenuous they are. Although EPA finalized modified versions of its GHG emissions rules (as this book was going to press), they will now face litigation.[8] Subsidies are typically more difficult to undo because they create

4. Multi-Pollutant Emissions Standards for Model Years 2027 and Later Light- Duty and Medium-Duty Vehicles, 88 Fed. Reg. 29184 (May 5, 2023) (proposed rule).
5. *See* U.S. EPA, Fact Sheet, Greenhouse Gas Standards for Fossil Fuel-Fired Power Plants Proposed Rule (Apr. 2023), https://www.epa.gov/system/files/documents/2023-05/FS-OVERVIEW-GHG-for%20Power%20Plants%20FINAL%20CLEAN.pdf.
6. *See* White House, Fact Sheet: President Biden to Catalyze Global Climate Action Through the Major Economies Forum on Energy and Climate (Apr. 20, 2023), https://www.whitehouse.gov/briefing-room/statements-releases/2023/04/20/fact-sheet-president-biden-to-catalyze-global-climate-action-through-the-major-economies-forum-on-energy-and-climate/#:~:text=Putting%20the%20Power%20Sector%20on%20a%20Path%20to%20Net%20Zero%20Emissions&text=President%20Biden%20has%20set%20an,by%20no%20later%20than%202050.
7. *See* U.S. EPA, Inflation Reduction Act (IRA) Overview (2022), and U.S. EPA, Fact Sheet: EPA and the Bipartisan Infrastructure Law (2022), https://www.epa.gov/infrastructure/fact-sheet-epa-bipartisan-infrastructure-law.
8. Multi-Pollutant Emissions Standards for Model Years 2027 and Later Light- Duty and Medium-Duty Vehicles, 89 Fed. Reg. 27842 (Apr. 18, 2024); New Source Performance Standards for Greenhouse Gas Emissions from New, Modified, and Reconstructed Fossil Fuel-Fired Electric Generating Units, 89 Fed. Reg. 39798 (May 9, 2024).

new markets and constituencies. But the latest fight over the debt ceiling demonstrated that many lawmakers would be willing to roll them back.[9]

Progress on climate mitigation remains halting and uncertain. So, while we should celebrate climate-mitigation victories, we must also plan for a world where these victories do not materialize or are simply not enough, that is, a world with high levels of warming. And as the chapters in this volume demonstrate, planning for the possibility of high-level warming requires critically evaluating the role of law, governance, and equity in constructing our future.

Effective laws and governance as well as economic mobility are essential if we wish to pursue the most desirable path. The climate models considered in the latest International Panel on Climate Change (IPCC) assessment, use a set of five narratives about the future of global socioeconomic development to forecast different warming scenarios.[10] These five "shared socioeconomic pathways" offer different visions of the future based on the influence of various socioeconomic factors.[11] The worst-case narrative with the steepest challenges to *both* mitigation and adaptation forecasts a world defined by rising nationalism, decreasing global cooperation, and increasing inequality. It is a world unable to adapt because democratic institutions fail, and cooperation is impossible.

Similarly, the authors in this volume highlight how our laws, governance structures, and approaches to equity often falter or fail in the face of climate adaptation. They also share the urgency to act now in planning for the climate disruptions we know are coming. Without better planning at all scales of government, we ensure a cycle in which climate impacts such as wildfires and sea-level rise devastate communities, making the most vulnerable even more vulnerable to the next disruption.

IRA and the current administration's Justice 40 initiative[12] both recognize the pressing need for climate adaptation in communities that have been disproportionately burdened by environmental harms. But these commitments face implementation challenges as they navigate established legal and governance structures that are often deployed to undermine environmental protections and pursue political agendas.

---

9. Manuel Quinones, *What's In and What's Out of the Debt Ceiling Compromise*, E&E News (May 30, 2023).
10. IPCC, Climate Change 2021: The Physical Science Basis (2021), https://www.ipcc.ch/report/ar6/wg1/.
11. *See* Brian C. O'Neill, *The Roads Ahead: Narratives for Shared Socioeconomic Pathways Describing World Futures in the 21st Century*, 42 Global Env't Change 169 (2017).
12. White House, Justice 40 (2022).

A few examples may illustrate the problem. In May 2023, some in Congress attempted to undo climate subsidies and mitigation measures by using them as bargaining chips in a battle over whether the United States would default on its debt. Fortunately, the negotiated debt ceiling agreement did not undermine these measures, but it did greenlight the completion of the Mountain Valley pipeline, which will transport natural gas from West Virginia to southern Virginia.[13] The pipeline has long been opposed by the communities through which it passes, including low-income and minority communities who will likely experience disproportionate health impacts from the project.[14]

Environmental justice advocates have also expressed disappointment in the stringency of the EPA's proposed emissions standards for heavy-duty trucks and buses.[15] The proposed GHG emissions standards for these large vehicles are less stringent than EPA's proposed standards for light- and medium-duty cars, and they do not include further limitations on conventional pollutants such as particulate matter and nitrogen oxides that have negative health impacts on the environmental justice communities that often border major highways.[16]

Decisions made by state agencies and elected officials also undermine federal climate measures designed to assist low-income individuals and communities. For example, a handful of states recently refused federal money to help staff and create the administrative structures necessary to implement the IRA rebates for residential electrification and energy efficiency.[17] These rebates would help make clean energy investments affordable for low- and moderate-income households. Notably, many of these upgrades lower energy bills and improve indoor air quality. Sadly, some politicians seem categorially opposed to any federal funding (whether it is for food assistance, healthcare, or clean energy) that goes only to those who fall below designated levels of income and wealth—in other words, those who most need assistance.[18]

Furthermore, opposition to clean energy is not limited to state governments. Because local governments still largely control the siting of renewable

13. Emma Dumain, *Debt Limit Deal Would Complete Mountain Valley Pipeline*, E&E News (May 28, 2023).
14. Niina H. Farah, *How Va. Pipeline Ruling May Reshape Environmental Justice*, E&E News (July 20, 2021).
15. Greenhouse Gas Emissions Standards for Heavy-Duty Vehicles, 88 Fed. Reg. 25926 (Apr. 27, 2023).
16. *See* Jean Chemnick, *"Cleaner Is Not Clean": Truck Rule Deflates EJ Groups*, E&E News (Apr. 25, 2023).
17. *See* Erin Jordan, *Iowa Shuns $3M Federal Grant for Climate Change Plans*, The Gazette, Apr. 6, 2023.
18. *See* Kyle Swenson, *Iowa to Spend Millions Kicking Families Off Food Stamps. More States May Follow*, Wash. Post, Apr. 18, 2023; Caleb McCullough, *Iowa Lags in Postpartum Medicaid Coverage for New Moms*, The Gazette, Apr. 9, 2023.

energy generation and transmission lines, one community (or a subset of that community) can exercise veto power over a project that would advance clean energy regionally. For example, a wind transmission "superhighway" across Oklahoma designed to carry energy to Tennessee gained the support of communities in Oklahoma, but drew opposition from communities in Arkansas.[19] Moreover, even in blue states like New York and Vermont, communities have used local zoning laws to veto renewable energy projects based on aesthetic considerations.[20]

Property owners in these communities likely feel entitled to preserve the view from the spaces they occupy. Indeed, their beliefs regarding the entitlements that come from owning property are bolstered by a contemporary political movement that understands individual property rights as absolute and beyond regulations that protect human welfare. This view prevailed, for example, in the U.S. Supreme Court's recent five-four decision on the scope of the Clean Water Act's protection of wetlands on private lands. In *Sackett v. U.S. Environmental Protection Agency*, the Court rejected a decades-long approach by the U.S. Army Corps of Engineers and EPA to regulate wetlands "adjacent" to traditionally covered waters.[21] Its interpretation of "adjacent" will likely result in lost federal jurisdiction over 50% or more of previously covered wetlands, which jeopardizes the ecosystem services, such as flood control, that wetlands provide.[22] In reaching its conclusion, the majority emphasized the role of property rights in narrowing its interpretation of the statute.[23] As Justice Elena Kagan aptly observed, the majority placed "a thumb on the scale for property owners—no matter that the Act . . . is all about stopping property owners from polluting."[24]

This approach to property rights and governmental authority will undermine efforts to mitigate and adapt to climate change. If our laws and institutions do not reject this myopic frame—one that seeks first to safeguard the entitlements of those lucky to have them—we are more likely to face a future of inequality, instability, and conflict that makes it harder to adapt and virtually impossible to mitigate climate change. And this in turn will further increase inequality and burden the most vulnerable. As several

19. *See* Russell Gold, Superpower: One Man's Quest to Transform American Energy (2019).
20. *See, e.g.*, Ecogen Ltd. Liab. Corp. v. Town of Italy, 438 F. Supp. 2d 149, 158 (W.D.N.Y. 2006) (noting, in deciding a challenge to a moratorium on wind turbines, that "aesthetic character" is a valid governmental interest); April McCullum, *No Large Wind Projects Are Under Consideration in Vermont for the First Time in Years*, Burlington Free Press, Jan. 27, 2020 (noting the absence of proposed wind projects and the "passionate debate over wind turbine siting" in Vermont).
21. No. 21-454, slip op. at 27 (S. Ct. May 25, 2023).
22. E.A. Crunden, *Post-Sackett, Chaos Erupts for Wetlands Oversight*, E&E News (June 6, 2023).
23. *Sackett*, No. 21-454, at 23.
24. *Id.* at 4 (Kagan, J., concurring in the judgment).

authors in this volume have argued, we can avert this future only by tending to our democracy at all levels of government and demanding effective implementation of our commitments to equality and justice.

Index

Notes